Houghton Mifflin Mathematics

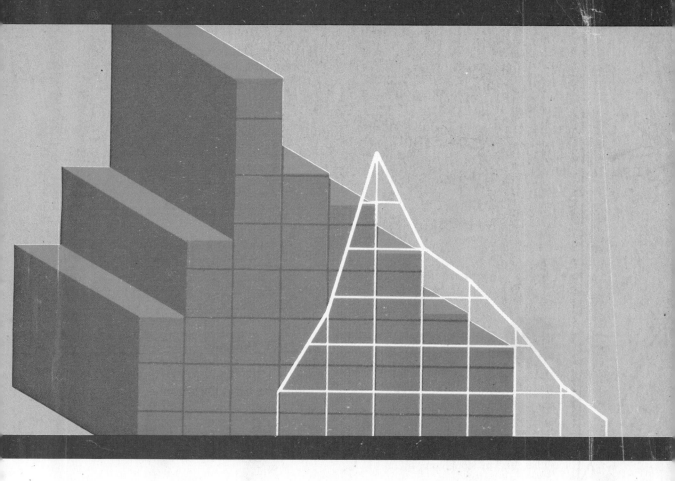

Authors

W.G. Quast   William L. Cole   Thelma Sparks

Mary Ann Haubner   Charles E. Allen

Coordinating Author

Ernest R. Duncan

Houghton Mifflin Company   BOSTON

Atlanta   Dallas   Geneva, Ill.   Lawrenceville, N.J.   Palo Alto   Toronto

Authors

W.G. Quast
Slippery Rock University
Slippery Rock, Pennsylvania

Thelma M. Sparks
Anne Arundel County Schools
Annapolis, Maryland

Charles E. Allen
Los Angeles Center for Enriched Studies
Los Angeles Unified School District
Los Angeles, California

William L. Cole
Michigan State University
East Lansing, Michigan

Mary Ann Haubner
Mount Saint Joseph College
Cincinnati, Ohio

Coordinating Author

Ernest R. Duncan
Professor Emeritus
Rutgers University
New Brunswick, New Jersey

Consultants

Gloria J. Edwards
Teacher
Claremont Middle School
Oakland, California

Margaret Thomas
Mathematics Coordinator
Putnam City School District
Oklahoma City, Oklahoma

Printed in U.S.A.

ISBN: 0-395-46217-7

ABCDEFGHIJ-D-9876543210-898

CONTENTS

1 NUMERATION AND UNITS OF MEASUREMENT 1

Place Value and Whole Numbers 2
Expanded Form of Decimals 4
Graphing on the Number Line 6
Comparing and Ordering Numbers 8
Rounding Numbers 10
Problem Solving *Strategy: The Four-Step Plan* 12
CHECKPOINT 1
Metric Units of Length 14
Metric Units of Capacity 16
Metric Units of Mass 18

Precision in Measurement 20
Problem Solving *Strategy: Reading Information from a Diagram* 22
U. S. Customary Units 24
CHECKPOINT 2
CHAPTER 1 TEST 26
MATHEMATICS AND SOCIAL STUDIES 27
ENRICHMENT *Egyptian and Roman Numeration* 28
CUMULATIVE REVIEW 30
COMPUTER LITERACY 32

2 ADDITION AND SUBTRACTION OF WHOLE NUMBERS AND DECIMALS 33

Variables and Equations 34
Properties of Addition 36
Addition of Whole Numbers 38
Addition of Decimals 40
Problem Solving *Strategy: Too Much or Too Little Information* 42
CHECKPOINT 1
Subtraction of Whole Numbers 44
Subtraction of Decimals 46
Working with Units of Measure 48

Working with Time 50
Problem Solving *Strategy: Using Graphs and Tables* 52
CHECKPOINT 2
CHAPTER 2 TEST 54
MATHEMATICS AND LIBRARY 55
ENRICHMENT *Clock Arithmetic* 56
CUMULATIVE REVIEW 58
COMPUTER LITERACY 60

3 MULTIPLICATION AND DIVISION OF WHOLE NUMBERS AND DECIMALS 61

Equations: Multiplication
   and Division **62**
Properties of Multiplication **64**
Order of Operations **66**
Multiplication of Whole Numbers **68**
Multiplication of Decimals **70**
Exponents and Place Value **72**
   CHECKPOINT 1
Problem Solving *Strategy:*
   Multi-Step Problems **74**
Division of Whole Numbers **76**
Division of Decimals by
   Whole Numbers **78**

Multiplication and Division
   by Powers of Ten **80**
Division by Decimals **82**
Estimating Quotients **84**
Problem Solving *Strategy:*
   Using Estimation **86**
   CHECKPOINT 2
   CHAPTER 3 TEST **88**
      MATHEMATICS AND SCIENCE **89**
      ENRICHMENT *Scientific Notation* **90**
      CUMULATIVE REVIEW **92**
      COMPUTER LITERACY **94**

4 GEOMETRY, PERIMETER, AREA 95

Points, Lines, Planes **96**
Angle Measure and Congruence **98**
Special Angles **100**
Polygons **102**
Problem Solving *Strategy: Using*
   Patterns **104**
Triangles **106**
Quadrilaterals **108**
   CHECKPOINT 1
Perimeter **110**
Circumference **112**
Areas of Rectangles and Squares **114**

Areas of Parallelograms,
   Triangles, and Trapezoids **116**
Area of a Circle **118**
Problem Solving *Strategy:*
   Using Formulas **120**
   CHECKPOINT 2
   CHAPTER 4 TEST **122**
      MATHEMATICS AND ART **123**
      ENRICHMENT *Square Roots* **124**
      CUMULATIVE REVIEW **126**
      COMPUTER LITERACY **128**

5 NUMBER THEORY AND DEVELOPING FRACTIONS 129

Divisibility **130**
Factors and Greatest Common
   Factors **132**
Primes and Composites **134**
Problem Solving *Strategy:*
   Open-ended Problems **136**
Fractions **138**
Equivalent Fractions **140**
Lowest Terms **142**
Multiples and Least Common
   Multiples **144**
Comparing and Ordering
   Fractions **146**
   CHECKPOINT 1

Mixed Numbers **148**
Fractions and Decimals **150**
Decimals and Fractions **152**
Problem Solving *Strategy:*
   Estimation with Fractions **154**
   CHECKPOINT 2
   CHAPTER 5 TEST **156**
    MATHEMATICS AND
    SOCIAL STUDIES **157**
    ENRICHMENT *Using Prime Factors*
    to Find the GCF and the LCM **158**
    CUMULATIVE REVIEW **160**
    COMPUTER LITERACY **162**

6 ADDITION AND SUBTRACTION OF FRACTIONS 163

Addition and Subtraction
   of Fractions **164**
Addition of Fractions With
   Different Denominators **166**
Subtraction of Fractions With
   Different Denominators **168**
Problem Solving *Stategy:*
   Reasonable Answers **170**
   CHECKPOINT 1

Addition of Mixed Numbers **172**
Subtraction of Mixed Numbers
   Without Renaming **174**

Subtraction of Mixed Numbers
   From Whole Numbers **176**
Subtraction of Mixed Numbers
   With Renaming **178**
Problem Solving *Strategy:*
   Interpreting Answers **180**
   CHECKPOINT 2
   CHAPTER 6 TEST **182**
    MATHEMATICS AND SHOP **183**
    ENRICHMENT *Functions* **184**
    CUMULATIVE REVIEW **186**
    COMPUTER LITERACY **188**

7 MULTIPLICATION AND DIVISION OF FRACTIONS   189

Multiplication of Fractions and
   Whole Numbers   **190**
Multiplication of Fractions   **192**
Multiplication of Mixed Numbers   **194**
Problem Solving   *Strategy:*
   Working Backwards   **196**
   CHECKPOINT 1
Reciprocals   **198**
Division of Fractions and
   Whole Numbers   **200**
Division of Fractions   **202**

Division of Mixed Numbers   **204**
Problem Solving   *Strategy:*
   Choosing the Operation   **206**
   CHECKPOINT 2
   CHAPTER 7 TEST   **208**
    MATHEMATICS AND HISTORY   **209**
    ENRICHMENT   *Base Two and*
    Base Eight Numeration   **210**
    CUMULATIVE REVIEW   **212**
    COMPUTER LITERACY   **214**

8 PRE-ALGEBRA EQUATIONS   215

Mathematical Expressions   **216**
Evaluating Mathematical
   Expressions   **218**
Equations   **220**
Inverse Operations: Addition
   and Subtraction   **222**
Inverse Operations:
   Multiplication and Division   **224**
Writing and Solving Equations   **226**
Problem Solving   *Strategy:*
   Trial and Error   **228**
   CHECKPOINT 1
Inequalities   **230**

Solving Inequalities   **232**
Equations in Two Variables   **234**
Graphing Coordinates   **236**
Problem Solving   *Strategy:*
   Using Equations   **238**
   CHECKPOINT 2
   CHAPTER 8 TEST   **240**
    MATHEMATICS AND
    GEOGRAPHY   **241**
    ENRICHMENT   *Repeating*
    Decimals as Fractions   **242**
    CUMULATIVE REVIEW   **244**
    COMPUTER LITERACY   **246**

9 RATIOS AND PROPORTIONS 247

Ratio **248**
Rate **250**
Proportions **252**
Problem Solving *Strategy:*
    Consumer Applications
    and Charts **254**
Proportions and Equivalent
    Fractions **256**
Proportions and Cross
    Multiplication **258**
    CHECKPOINT 1
Scale Drawing **260**

Reading Maps **262**
Problem Solving *Strategy:*
    Using Proportions **264**
Similar Triangles **266**
Using Similar Triangles **268**
    CHECKPOINT 2
    CHAPTER 9 TEST **270**
        MATHEMATICS AND MUSIC **271**
        ENRICHMENT *Scale Factor* **272**
        CUMULATIVE REVIEW **274**
        COMPUTER LITERACY **276**

10 PERCENTS 277

Percents **278**
Decimals and Percents **280**
Percents and Fractions **282**
Fractions and Percents **284**
Problem Solving *Strategy:*
    Consumer Applications and
    Tables and Graphs **286**
    CHECKPOINT 1
Finding a Percent **288**
Finding a Percent of a Number **290**
Finding the Original Number **292**

Problem Solving *Strategy:*
    Simplifying Problems **294**
    CHECKPOINT 2
    CHAPTER 10 TEST **296**
        MATHEMATICS AND SCIENCE **297**
        ENRICHMENT *Percents*
        and Proportions **298**
        CUMULATIVE REVIEW **300**
        COMPUTER LITERACY **302**

11 PERCENTS AND CONSUMER APPLICATIONS 303

Percent Equations **304**
Interest **306**
Problem Solving *Strategy:*
   Organizing Information
   into a Chart **308**
Percent of Change **310**
Tax Rates **312**
Problem Solving *Strategy:*
   Consumer Applications
   and Graphs **314**
   CHECKPOINT 1
Discounts and Markups **316**

Commission **318**
Problem Solving *Strategy:*
   Using Logic **320**
Circle Graphs **322**
Budgets **324**
   CHECKPOINT 2
   CHAPTER 11 TEST **326**
   MATHEMATICS AND SOCIAL
   STUDIES **327**
   ENRICHMENT *Compound Interest* **328**
   CUMULATIVE REVIEW **330**
   COMPUTER LITERACY **332**

12 PRE-ALGEBRA INTEGERS 333

Integers and Absolute Value **334**
Comparing and Ordering Integers **336**
Addition of Integers **338**
Subtraction of Integers **340**
Multiplication of Integers **342**
Division of Integers **344**
Problem Solving *Strategy:*
   Consumer Applications
   and Tables **346**
   CHECKPOINT 1
Solving Equations with Integers **348**
Graphing on a Coordinate Plane **350**

Graphing Equations with
   Two Variables **352**
Graphing Systems of Equations **354**
Geometric Transformations **356**
Problem Solving *Strategy:*
   Logical Thinking **358**
   CHECKPOINT 2
   CHAPTER 12 TEST **360**
   MATHEMATICS AND SCIENCE **361**
   ENRICHMENT *Rational Numbers* **362**
   CUMULATIVE REVIEW **364**
   COMPUTER LITERACY **366**

13 GEOMETRY, SURFACE AREA, VOLUME 367

Identifying Congruent Figures **368**
Constructing Geometric Figures **370**
Constructing Congruent Angles **372**
Constructing Bisectors **374**
Symmetry **376**
Problem Solving *Strategy:*
  Sort and Classify **378**
  CHECKPOINT 1
Classifying Geometric Shapes **380**
Surface Area: Prisms
  and Pyramids **382**
Surface Area: Cylinders **384**

Volume: Prisms **386**
Volume: Cylinders **388**
Problem Solving *Strategy:*
  Drawing a Diagram **390**
  CHECKPOINT 2
  CHAPTER 13 TEST **392**
    MATHEMATICS AND SHOP **393**
    ENRICHMENT *The*
    Pythagorean Theorem **394**
    CUMULATIVE REVIEW **396**
    COMPUTER LITERACY **398**

14 PROBABILITY AND STATISTICS 399

Probabilities and Outcomes **400**
Counting Possible Outcomes **402**
Tree Diagrams **404**
Independent Probabilities **406**
Dependent Probabilities **408**
Range and Mean **410**
Median and Mode **412**
Problem Solving *Strategy:*
  Sampling and Estimating **414**
  CHECKPOINT 1
Double-Bar Graphs **416**

Double-Line Graphs **418**
Frequency Tables **420**
Problem Solving *Strategy: Surveys
  and Estimating* **422**
  CHECKPOINT 2
  CHAPTER 14 TEST **424**
    MATHEMATICS AND HEALTH **425**
    ENRICHMENT *Histograms* **426**
    CUMULATIVE REVIEW **428**
    COMPUTER LITERACY **430**

TABLE OF MEASURES   431
EXTRA PRACTICE   432
USING MENTAL MATH, ESTIMATION,
  AND A CALCULATOR   460
PROBLEM SOLVING ACTIVITIES   471
GLOSSARY   477
INDEX   484
CREDITS   494

About 100,000 spectators attended the opening ceremonies of the 1984 Summer Olympics. For each spectator that day, about 57 more attended the games. Did more than 5 million attend?

NUMERATION AND UNITS OF MEASUREMENT

PLACE VALUE AND WHOLE NUMBERS

How many people do you estimate watched the 1984 Summer Olympics? The actual number is shown in the place value chart below.

Billions			Millions			Thousands			Ones		
hundreds	tens	ones	hundreds	tens	ones	hundreds	tens	ones	hundreds	tens	ones
		1	5	0	6	0	9	0	9	2	3

We read the number shown above as *one billion, five hundred six million, ninety thousand, nine hundred twenty-three.* This is the **word form** for the number.

The **standard form** is 1,506,090,923. The digit 6 is in the millions' place. Its value is 6 × 1,000,000, or 6,000,000.

The **expanded forms** show the value of each digit.

long form: (1 × 1,000,000,000) + (5 × 100,000,000) + (6 × 1,000,000) + (9 × 10,000) + (9 × 100) + (2 × 10) + (3 × 1)

short form: 1,000,000,000 + 500,000,000 + 6,000,000 + 90,000 + 900 + 20 + 3

Think: Most calculators display only eight digits. What is the greatest place value in an eight-digit number?

CLASS EXERCISES

What is the word form for the number?

1. 4832   **2.** 2400   **3.** 15,605   **4.** 1,030,009

What is the value of the digit 2 in the number?

5. 25,637   **6.** 410,219   **7.** 8,261,014   **8.** 201,038,653

PRACTICE

Write the standard form.

9. 2 thousand 6 hundred 9

10. 40 thousand, 3 hundred 96

11. 5 million, 42 thousand

12. 16 billion, 2 hundred

13. 300,000 + 4000 + 80 + 6

14. 800,000,000 + 70,000 + 500 + 3

Write the value of the underlined digit.

15. 18<u>5</u>6

16. 21,48<u>7</u>

17. 50<u>9</u>,688

18. 1,4<u>0</u>9,022

19. 21,008,<u>5</u>92

20. 742,9<u>5</u>1,300

21. 1,4<u>8</u>7,659,281

22. <u>6</u>,427,302,900

Write the short expanded form.

23. 756

24. 1290

25. 3092

26. 42,986

27. 500,030

28. 708,000

29. 1,000,200

30. 2,000,080

★ **31. Think:** How many four-digit numbers can be written using all the digits 6, 7, 8, and 9?

What value of the digit 5 would you subtract from the calculator display to get the given number?

CALCULATOR

32. 5,555,055

33. 5,505,555

34. 5,555,505

PROBLEM SOLVING APPLICATIONS
Reading Information from a Table

Use the table to complete the report. Write the amounts in standard form.

The total spending for personal recreation in one year was $ __(35.)__ . Consumers spent $ __(36.)__ on admission to movies and $ __(37.)__ on admission to sports. Notice that consumers spent $ __(38.)__ on toys and sports equipment and only $ __(39.)__ on books.

Spending for Personal Recreation in One Year (Millions of Dollars)	
Books	6,975
Toys and sports equipment	30,630
Admission to movies	4,339
Seeds and plants	5,329
Admission to sports	2,059
Other	51,714
Total	$101,046

EXPANDED FORM OF DECIMALS

If you split a whole into 10 equal parts, each part is a tenth of the whole. If you split a whole into 100 equal parts, each part is a hundredth.

Our number system is based on tens. The decimal point is placed between the ones and the tenths. The word *and* marks the position of the decimal point when you read the number.

To read the number in the chart, notice that the last digit, 2, is in the *millionths'* place. The **word form** for the number is *six and one hundred seventy-two millionths*. It is also read as *six point zero zero zero one seven two*. The **standard form** is 6.000172.

a unit — 10 pieces — 100 pieces

one — a tenth — a hundredth

ones	.	tenths	hundredths	thousandths	ten-thousandths	hundred-thousandths	millionths
6	.	0	0	0	1	7	2

In the **expanded forms** the value of each digit is shown.

long form: $(6 \times 1) + (1 \times 0.0001) + (7 \times 0.00001) + (2 \times 0.000001)$
short form: $6 + 0.0001 + 0.00007 + 0.000002$

Writing extra zeros after the last digit in the decimal does not change the value of the number. The decimals 0.6, 0.60, and 0.600 are called **equivalent decimals.**

CLASS EXERCISES

Name the place value of the underlined digit.

1. 0.7
2. 4.36
3. 35.8
4. 7.008
5. 10.004
6. 0.0005
7. 0.5341
8. 8.0217
9. 0.99998
10. 2.05766
11. 3.98432
12. 6.04842
13. 0.002974
14. 2.148639
15. 9.021044

16. Think: Refer to the diagrams on page 4 to explain why $0.2 = 0.20$.

PRACTICE

Complete.

17. $0.68 = 0.6 + $ ▓

18. $3.14 = 3 + $ ▓ $+ 0.04$

19. $0.55 = $ ▓ $+ 0.05$

20. $5.103 = 5 + 0.1 + 0.00 + $ ▓

21. $4.017 = $ ▓ $+ 0.0 + 0.01 + 0.007$

Write the standard form.

22. 263 thousandths

23. 8 millionths

24. 60 hundredths

25. $0.01 + 0.009$

26. $4 + 0.08 + 0.005$

27. $0.6 + 0.03 + 0.001$

Name the two equivalent decimals.

28. 27; 2.70; 27.0

29. 0.15; 0.150; 0.015

30. 3.5; 3.500; 3.050

31. 0.00684; 0.06840; 0.006840

32. 0.0209; 0.02900; 0.02090

Write the answer.

33. 7×10

34. 15×100

35. 32×1000

36. $412 \div 10$

37. $600 \div 100$

38. $9411 \div 1000$

MIXED REVIEW

PROBLEM SOLVING APPLICATIONS
Open-Ended Problems

The time it takes a computer to do a calculation may be measured in milliseconds (ms), microseconds (mus), or nanoseconds (ns).

0.001 s = 1 millisecond
0.000001 s = 1 microsecond
0.000000001 s = 1 nanosecond

Use the information in the table to give another name for the given time. There may be more than one correct answer.

39. 0.008 s

40. 0.000007 s

41. 0.000000005 s

★ **42.** 3.005 s

★ **43.** 0.486752 s

★ **44.** 0.000003295 s

GRAPHING ON THE NUMBER LINE

When one number is greater than or less than a second number, we may use inequality symbols to express the relationship in two ways.

$$19 \text{ is greater than } 14 \qquad 14 \text{ is less than } 19$$
$$19 > 14 \qquad\qquad 14 < 19$$

A way to picture this relationship is on a **number line.** To draw a number line, first mark off equally spaced points along a straight line. Then label the points in increasing order from left to right, one number for each point. The point paired with a number is called the **graph** of that number. The graph of 17 is between the graphs of 14 and 19.

```
   |     |     |     •     |     |     •     |     •
  11    12    13    14    15    16    17    18    19
```

$$14 < 17 < 19 \quad \text{or} \quad 19 > 17 > 14$$

We can read the inequality $14 < 17 < 19$ as *17 is between 14 and 19.*

Decimals can also be pictured on a number line. The number line below is marked off in tenths, from 2.5 to 3.2.

```
   |     |     |     |     |     |     |     |
  2.5   2.6   2.7   2.8   2.9   3.0   3.1   3.2
```

Think: Extend the number line mentally. What is the next whole number after 3.2?

CLASS EXERCISES

Express in words.

1. $34 < 57$　　　**2.** $180 > 96$　　　**3.** $1.8 < 2.9$　　　**4.** $2.941 < 40.35$

5. $11 < 23 < 40$　　　**6.** $0.017 < 0.22 < 0.31$　　　**7.** $5.66 > 5.64 > 5.6$

Write another inequality that expresses the same relationship.

8. $28 > 15$　　　**9.** $107 < 234$　　　**10.** $4.17 < 6.03$　　　**11.** $51.6 > 6.15$

12. $0.4 < 0.7 < 0.9$　　　**13.** $567 > 549 > 521$　　　**14.** $257.5 > 184 > 92.5$

Draw a number line and graph the numbers.

15. 9, 12, 15, 17   **16.** 38, 41, 42, 44   **17.** 0.3, 0.4, 0.7, 0.9

18. 7.8, 8, 8.6, 8.9, 9   **19.** 46.7, 46.8, 46.9, 47.3   **20.** 99.8, 100, 100.3, 100.7

Write using > or < to express the relationship.

21. 71 is less than 85

22. 9.18 is greater than 6.07

23. 31 is between 30 and 32

24. 0.43 is between 0.42 and 0.44

★**25.** 15.6 is greater than 15.2 and less than 15.9

★**26.** 244 is less than 510 and greater than 185

27. What is the greatest whole number between 500,000 and 600,000?

28. Name the whole numbers between 19.01 and 21.99.

MENTAL MATH

PROBLEM SOLVING APPLICATIONS
Using a Time Line

Use the time line below to answer.

29. What event took place between 1525 and 1550?

30. What event occurred after 1650 but before 1675?

31. Which happened first, the founding of Quebec or the settling of Jamestown?

★**32.** Could Balboa have met Drake during his travels?

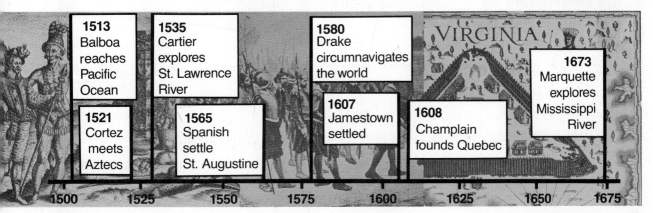

1513 Balboa reaches Pacific Ocean

1521 Cortez meets Aztecs

1535 Cartier explores St. Lawrence River

1565 Spanish settle St. Augustine

1580 Drake circumnavigates the world

1607 Jamestown settled

1608 Champlain founds Quebec

1673 Marquette explores Mississippi River

VIRGINIA

1500   1525   1550   1575   1600   1625   1650   1675

COMPARING AND
ORDERING NUMBERS

The first Concorde flight from Paris to Washington, D.C., flew at a rate of 1023 mi/h. Two years later, the same flight flew at a rate of 1037 mi/h. Which flight had a faster rate?

Starting from the left, compare the digits in 1023 and 1037 by place value. Find the first place where the digits differ.

$$1 \quad 0 \quad 2 \quad 3$$
$$1 \quad 0 \quad 3 \quad 7$$

The same digits. ⎯⎯⎯⎯⎯⎯ 3 is greater than 2.

$$1037 > 1023$$

The second flight had a faster rate.

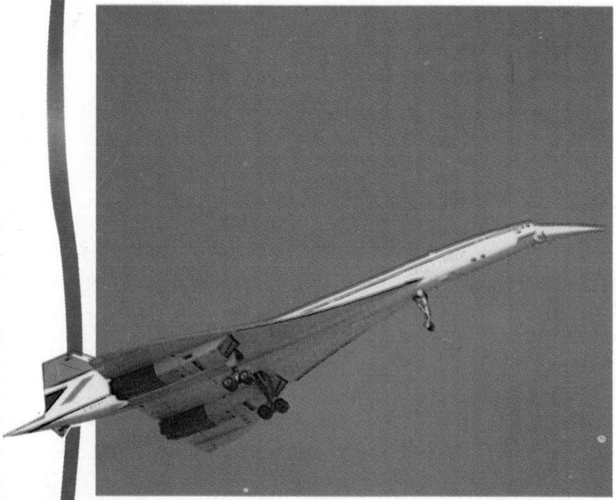

A quick way to compare whole numbers that have a different number of digits is to count the digits. The whole number with the most digits is greatest.

To compare decimals, first line up the decimal points. Then compare the digits just as with whole numbers starting with the left-most place value.

$$0.4618 > 0.4609$$

Think: Can we also say that the decimal with the most digits is always the greatest? | 3.87 | | 0.38652 |

CLASS EXERCISES

Starting from the left, at which place value do the digits first differ?

1. 615; 613

2. 2717; 2317

3. 3284; 3789

4. 0.0325; 0.0327

5. 12.089; 12.725

6. 40.03; 40.003

PRACTICE

Use >, <, or = to complete.

7. 0.371 ■ 0.378

8. 1746 ■ 1764

9. 12,729 ■ 12,725

10. 0.024 ■ 0.24

11. 20.05 ■ 20.050

12. 56.31 ■ 56.311

Write *true* or *false*.

13. 210 > 201

14. 3098 > 3908

15. 9006 < 9060

16. 75,367 = 7536

17. 7.79 = 7.709

18. 17.83 < 7.831

Order from least to greatest.

19. 6007, 6070, 6700

20. 19.84, 1.894, 14.98, 1.849

★**21.** 0.099, 0.909, 0.1, 0.109, 0.901, 0.09, 0.199

Name the whole numbers that will make the sentence true.

★**22.** 599 < ■ < 602

★**23.** 137.89 < ■ < 139.19

Name the smaller number shown on the calculator.

24. | 2.89 | | 2.843 |

25. | 65.061 | | 6.5061 |

26. | 125.01346 | | 125.01364 |

27. | 80.615 | | 80.654 |

CALCULATOR

PROBLEM SOLVING APPLICATIONS
Comparing Data

Solve.

28. Florida has an area of 58,560 square miles. Georgia has an area of 58,876 square miles. Which state has a greater area?

29. In 1980, Baltimore had a population of 875,504. Phoenix had a population of 764,911, and San Antonio had 785,410. Which city had the smallest population?

★**30.** In a race, Lee had a time of 2 min 36.01 s. Jane had a time of 2 min 35.07 s. Who won the race?

ROUNDING NUMBERS

Soo-ling estimated that the distance to the ocean was *about* 50 mi. The actual distance was 54.6 mi. The number line below shows that 54.6 is closer to 50 than to 60. We say that 54.6 *rounded to the nearest ten is* 50.

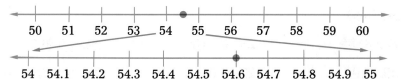

The number line marked off in tenths shows that 54.6 is closer to 55 than to 54. We say that 54.6 *rounded to the nearest whole number is* 55.

NUMBER	ROUNDED TO THE NEAREST	DIGIT TO THE RIGHT	IS IT 5 OR MORE?	ROUND
14,854	thousand	8	yes	up to 15,000
14,854	ten	4	no	down to 14,850
6.9621	tenth	6	yes	up to 7.0
6.9621	hundredth	2	no	down to 6.96

CLASS EXERCISES

Is the number closer to 20 or to 30 on the number line?

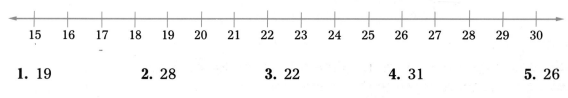

1. 19   **2.** 28   **3.** 22   **4.** 31   **5.** 26

Is the number closer to 7 or to 8 on the number line?

6.5 6.6 6.7 6.8 6.9 7 7.1 7.2 7.3 7.4 7.5 7.6 7.7 7.8 7.9 8 8.1 8.2 8.3 8.4 8.5

6. 7.6   **7.** 7.3   **8.** 6.8   **9.** 8.1   **10.** 7.9

PRACTICE

Round to the greatest place value.

11. 486   **12.** 6783   **13.** 2,451,904   **14.** 36.23   **15.** 5.0065

16. 79,546   **17.** 3.96   **18.** 33,567,119   **19.** 548   **20.** 419.2

Round to the place underlined.

21. 8̲62   **22.** 3̲150   **23.** 6̲4,139   **24.** 9̲9,999

25. 355̲,629   **26.** 0.9̲6   **27.** 0.018̲4   **28.** 0.86̲35

29. 0.769̲6   **30.** 5̲.7   **31.** 8.473̲6   **32.** 563,999̲.5

Is the estimate reasonable?
Write *yes* or *no*.

33. Pluto is about 6000 million kilometers from the sun.

34. Mars is about 2300 million kilometers from the sun.

35. Neptune is between 4000 million kilometers and 5000 million kilometers from the sun.

36. Venus and Earth are both about 100 million kilometers from the sun.

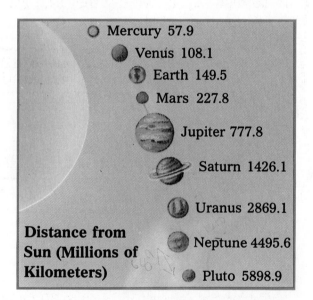

Mercury 57.9
Venus 108.1
Earth 149.5
Mars 227.8
Jupiter 777.8
Saturn 1426.1
Uranus 2869.1
Neptune 4495.6
Pluto 5898.9

Distance from Sun (Millions of Kilometers)

PROBLEM SOLVING APPLICATIONS
Estimation

Suppose you are a reporter. Write a headline for each fact, using numbers rounded to the nearest million.

37. An estimated 25,678,415 people went to the polls.

38. An estimated 4,587,182 copies of the novel have been sold.

39. In one year the U.S. spent an estimated $210,715,349,000 on phone calls.

40. In one year the U.S. spent an estimated $579,011,294,000 on advertising.

PROBLEM SOLVING
Strategy: The Four-Step Plan

Which swimmer is faster?

To solve problems, it is necessary to plan and to ask questions that will help you organize your thinking.

Brooks: 3 min 58.23 s

Ross: 3 min 58.17 s

1. Understand the problem.

2. Make a plan.

3. Use the plan to do the work.

4. Answer and check for reasonableness.

What are the facts? What do you need to know?	Brooks: 3 min 58.23 s Ross: 3 min 58.17 s Which swimmer is faster?
What do you do to solve the problem?	Compare the times.
Show the work.	3 min 58.17 s < 3 min 58.23 s
Is the answer reasonable? Does it answer the question?	Ross is faster. Yes. Ross's time is less, so Ross is faster.

CLASS EXERCISES

How would you solve the problem? Write C for compare, O for order, or R for round. Then answer the question.

1. A swimmer averaged 4.86 mi/h in a race. What is the swimmer's speed to the nearest mile per hour?

2. Lewis finished the 200 m butterfly in 3 min 5.96 s. Green finished in 3 min 4.97 s. Davis finished in 3 min 5.09 s. In what order did they finish?

3. A total of 312 divers entered the diving competition. To the nearest hundred, about how many divers were there?

PRACTICE

Use the fact and a plan to write and answer a question.

4. *Fact:* There were 13,614 spectators at the swim meet.

5. *Fact:* The U.S. team finished the relay in 3 min 19.26 s. The Japanese team finished in 3 min 20.01 s. The Greek team finished in 3 min 19.36 s.

6. *Fact:* The finishing time for Phillips was 2 min 2.9 s. The finishing time for Hernandez was 2 min 3.3 s.

> *Plan:*
>
> Round
> Order
> Compare

Solve.

7. The heights of the swimmers are 5 ft 11 in., 6 ft 2 in., 5 ft 10 in., and 6 ft 3 in. How would you order them from shortest to tallest?

8. Diver 134 had a score of 9.9. Diver 267 had a score of 10.0. Which diver had the higher score?

★ 9. Matthew Webb was the first swimmer to swim the English Channel. It took him 21 h 45 min. To the nearest hour how long did it take him to swim the channel?

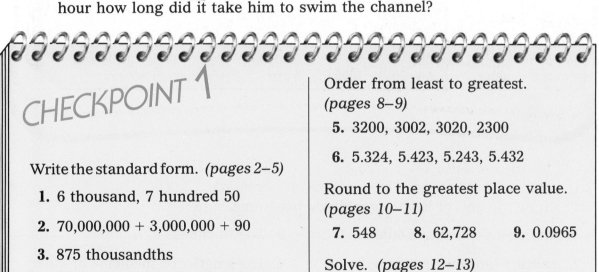

CHECKPOINT 1

Write the standard form. *(pages 2–5)*

1. 6 thousand, 7 hundred 50

2. 70,000,000 + 3,000,000 + 90

3. 875 thousandths

Draw a number line and graph the numbers. *(pages 6–7)*

4. 42.3, 42.5, 43, 43.1

Order from least to greatest. *(pages 8–9)*

5. 3200, 3002, 3020, 2300

6. 5.324, 5.423, 5.243, 5.432

Round to the greatest place value. *(pages 10–11)*

7. 548   8. 62,728   9. 0.0965

Solve. *(pages 12–13)*

10. What is $5674 rounded to the nearest thousand?

Extra Practice on page 432

METRIC UNITS OF LENGTH

The basic unit of length in the metric system is the **meter (m).** You can estimate that a meter is about the distance from a doorknob to the floor.

To measure shorter lengths we use **centimeters (cm)** and **millimeters (mm).** A centimeter is about the distance across the head of a thumbtack. A millimeter is about the thickness of the point of a thumbtack.

A **kilometer (km)** is used to measure long distances. At normal walking speed, it takes about 10 min to walk one kilometer.

RELATIONSHIP		EXAMPLES
A millimeter is a tenth of a centimeter.	1 mm = 0.1 cm 10 mm = 1 cm	7 mm = 0.7 cm 30 mm = 3 cm
A centimeter is a hundredth of a meter.	1 cm = 0.01 m 100 cm = 1 m	5 cm = 0.05 m 600 cm = 6 m
A millimeter is a thousandth of a meter.	1 mm = 0.001 m 1000 mm = 1 m	4 mm = 0.004 m 2000 mm = 2 m
A meter is a thousandth of a kilometer.	1 m = 0.001 km 1000 m = 1 km	6 m = 0.006 km 8000 m = 8 km

CLASS EXERCISES

Which metric unit of length would you use to measure?

1. The distance across Oklahoma

2. The thickness of a dime

3. Fabric to make curtains

4. The length of a medicine dropper

Complete.

5. In 8 m there are ▮ cm.
   To change meters to centimeters, you _?_ by 100.

6. In 300 cm there are ▓ m.

To change centimeters to meters, you __?__ by 100.

PRACTICE

Complete.

7. 1 km = 1000 m
4 km = ▓ m
36 km = ▓ m

8. 1 m = 100 cm
3 m = ▓ cm
12 m = ▓ cm

9. 1 m = 1000 mm
6 m = ▓ mm
58 m = ▓ mm

10. 1 mm = 0.001 m
5 mm = ▓ m
670 mm = ▓ m

11. 1 m = 0.001 km
7 m = ▓ km
4300 m = ▓ km

12. 1 cm = 0.01 m
8 cm = ▓ m
250 cm = ▓ m

13. 600 cm = ▓ m

14. 8000 cm = ▓ m

15. 5 m = ▓ cm

16. 7 m = ▓ cm

17. 3 km = ▓ m

18. 90 mm = ▓ cm

Choose the best estimate. Write *a*, *b*, or *c*.

19. The length of a camera
  a. 14 mm   **b.** 14 cm   **c.** 14 m

ESTIMATE

20. The depth of an ocean trench
  a. 9 m   **b.** 9 km   **c.** 9 cm

21. The width of a pencil point
  a. 5 mm   **b.** 5 cm   **c.** 5 m

PROBLEM SOLVING APPLICATIONS
Using Information from a Chart

Complete.

22. 10 dm = ▓ m

23. 1 hm = ▓ dam

24. 300 m = ▓ dam = 3 ▓

hectometer	dekameter	meter	decimeter
hm	dam	m	dm
100 m	10 m	1 m	0.1 m

Which is the greater length?

25. 15 m or 1 dam

26. 4 hm or 300 m

27. 0.8 m or 7 dm

★**28.** The length of a soccer field is 110 m. Is this 1.1 hm or 11 hm?

★**29.** The length of a basketball court is 260 dm. Is this about 30 m long?

METRIC UNITS OF CAPACITY

The amount of fluid a container will hold is called its **capacity.** In the metric system the **liter (L)** may be used to measure capacity. You can estimate that a liter of orange juice will fill about 4 glasses.

Smaller capacities are measured in **milliliters (mL).** An eyedropper will hold about 1 mL of liquid.

The amount of space contained in a cube with all edges 1 cm long is a **cubic centimeter.** Such a cube has a fluid capacity of 1 mL.

The chart below shows how these units are related.

RELATIONSHIP		EXAMPLES
A milliliter is a thousandth of a liter.	1 mL = 0.001 L 1000 mL = 1 L	8 mL = 0.008 L 3000 mL = 3 L
A liter is a thousand milliliters.	1 L = 1000 mL 0.001 L = 1 mL	9 L = 9000 mL 0.006 L = 6 mL

CLASS EXERCISES

Which metric unit of capacity would you use to measure?

1. A drop of rain

2. Water in a bathtub

3. A large can of paint

4. Milk in a small carton

Complete.

5. In 26 L there are ■ mL.
To change liters to milliliters, you _?_ by 1000.

6. In 8000 mL there are ■ L.
To change milliliters to liters, you _?_ by 1000.

PRACTICE

Complete.

7. 1 L = 1000 mL
9 L = ▓ mL
16 L = ▓ mL

8. 1 mL = 0.001 L
6 mL = ▓ L
7000 mL = ▓ L

9. 1 L = 1000 mL
25 L = ▓ mL
2.5 L = ▓ mL

10. 3.1 L = ▓ mL

11. 4.6 L = ▓ mL

12. 500 mL = ▓ L

13. 72 mL = ▓ L

14. 700 mL = ▓ L

15. 0.1 mL = ▓ L

Choose the best estimate. Write *a*, *b*, or *c*.

16. The capacity of a mug
a. 20 mL **b.** 200 mL **c.** 2 L

ESTIMATE

17. The capacity of a large pool
a. 1.2 L   **b.** 120 L   **c.** 12,000 L

18. The capacity of a car's fuel tank
a. 6 L   **b.** 60 L   **c.** 600 mL

19. The capacity of a spoon
a. 25 mL **b.** 250 mL **c.** 25 L

20. The capacity of a glass of juice
a. 250 mL **b.** 2500 mL **c.** 25,000 mL

PROBLEM SOLVING APPLICATIONS
Using Information from a Chart

kiloliter	hectoliter	dekaliter	liter	deciliter	centiliter	milliliter
kL	hL	daL	L	dL	cL	mL
1000 L	100 L	10 L	1 L	0.1 L	0.01 L	0.001 L

Complete.

21. 1 kL = ▓ hL

22. 1 L = ▓ dL

23. 1000 mL = ▓ cL = ▓ dL = 1 ▓

24. 7000 L = ▓ daL = ▓ hL = ▓ kL

Which is the greater capacity?

25. 3 L or 200 cL

26. 4000 L or 36 kL

27. 1000 L or 10 daL

★**28.** A bottle contains 126 L. Is this 0.126 kL or 1.26 kL?

★**29.** A medicine dropper contains 0.009 L. Is this less than 1 cL?

METRIC UNITS OF MASS

The amount of matter in an object is its **mass.** In the metric system large masses are measured in **kilograms (kg).** You can estimate that the mass of an electric iron is about 1 kg. Smaller masses are measured in **grams (g)** and **milligrams (mg).** You can estimate that the mass of a paper clip is about 1 g and the mass of a grain of sand is about 1 mg.

A milliliter of water has a mass of about 1 g. A liter of water has a mass of about 1 kg. **Think:** Could you lift a two-liter container filled with water?

The chart below shows how these units of mass are related.

	RELATIONSHIP	EXAMPLES
A milligram is a thousandth of a gram.	1 mg = 0.001 g 1000 mg = 1 g	250 mg = 0.250 g 4000 mg = 4 g
A kilogram is a thousand grams.	1 kg = 1000 g 0.001 kg = 1 g	2 kg = 2000 g 0.005 kg = 5 g

CLASS EXERCISES

Which metric unit of mass would you use to measure?

1. An apple
2. A butterfly
3. A seventh grader
4. A toaster

Complete.

5. In 9 kg there are ■ g.
   To change kilograms to grams, you _?_ by 1000.

6. In 3000 mg there are ■ g.
   To change milligrams to grams, you divide by ■.

PRACTICE

Complete.

7. 1 kg = 1000 g
  5 kg = ■ g
  60 kg = ■ g

8. 1 g = 1000 mg
  7 g = ■ mg
  420 g = ■ mg

9. 1 mg = 0.001 g
  3 mg = ■ g
  1600 mg = ■ g

10. 5 kg = ■ g

11. 17,000 g = ■ kg

12. 74 kg = ■ g

13. 2000 g = ■ kg

14. 9 kg = ■ g

15. 2000 mg = ■ g

Choose the best estimate. Write *a*, *b*, or *c*.

16. The mass of a bowling ball
  a. 700 mg   **b.** 7 kg   **c.** 70 g

17. The mass of a blade of grass
  a. 1 kg   **b.** 1 g   **c.** 1 mg

18. The mass of a melon
  a. 2.5 g   **b.** 2.5 kg   **c.** 250 kg

19. The mass of a fish hook
  a. 2 g   **b.** 20 g   **c.** 2 mg

20. The mass of a safety pin
  a. 1 g   **b.** 100 g   **c.** 1000 g

PROBLEM SOLVING APPLICATIONS
Using Information from a Chart

hectogram	dekagram	gram	decigram	centigram
hg	dag	g	dg	cg
100 g	10 g	1 g	0.1 g	0.01 g

Complete.

21. 1 hg = ■ dag

22. 10 g = ■ dg

23. 1500 cg = ■ dg = 15 ■

24. 9 hg = ■ dag = ■ g

Which is the greater mass?

25. 15 dg or 10 g

26. 8 dag or 71 g

27. 42 hg or 100 g

★ **28.** The mass of a cubic centimeter of oak is 0.7 g. Is the mass of a cubic centimeter of oak greater than or less than the mass of a cubic centimeter of water?

PRECISION IN MEASUREMENT

All measurements are approximations. The **precision** of a measurement depends on the unit of measure you use. A smaller unit results in a more precise measurement.

Look at the ruler and calculator. You can measure the height of the calculator to the nearest centimeter. For greater precision measure the height to the nearest millimeter.

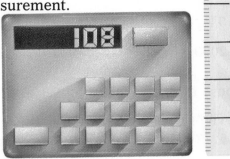

To the nearest centimeter: 4 cm
To the nearest millimeter: 38 mm

To the nearest centimeter, both paper clips are 2 cm long. The actual length of each paper clip is within 0.5 cm of 2 cm. This allowance of half a unit either way is called the **greatest possible error (GPE)** of the measurement. Since the GPE is 0.5 cm, we may record the length of both paper clips as

$$2 \pm 0.5 \text{ cm}$$

which is read as *2 plus or minus 0.5 centimeters.*

CLASS EXERCISES

Which unit of measure gives the more precise measurement?

1. meter, centimeter

2. liter, milliliter

3. millimeter, meter

4. decimeter, millimeter

5. kilometer, meter

6. gram, kilogram

The capacity of a jar is recorded as 673 ± 0.5 mL.

7. What is the capacity of the jar to the nearest milliliter?

8. What is the greatest possible error (GPE) of the measurement?

9. What is the greatest actual capacity of the jar?

10. What is the least actual capacity of the jar?

PRACTICE

Measure to the nearest centimeter and millimeter.

11. _____   12. _____

13. _____

Name the more precise measurement.

14. 6 cm or 58 mm   15. 2 kg or 1780 g

16. 431 mL or 0.5 L   17. 35 mm or 0.04 m

A measurement is given to the nearest unit. What is the GPE
of the measurement?

18. 402 mL   19. 936 g   20. 524 m   21. 181 mm

22. 35 kg   23. 15 L   24. 371 cm   25. 967 mg

★ 26. The mass of a chicken is 3.15 kg to the nearest hundredth
      of a kilogram. What is the GPE?

Write the answer.

| 27. $16 + 3$ | 28. $8 + 5$ | 29. 16×2 | 30. $72 \div 9$ |
| 31. 3×12 | 32. $39 - 36$ | 33. $24 \div 3$ | 34. $80 - 13$ |

**MIXED
REVIEW**

PROBLEM SOLVING APPLICATIONS
Reasonable Answers

Solve.

35. The capacity of a bottle is be-
    tween 355 mL and 365 mL. What
    is its capacity to the nearest ten
    milliliters?

36. Two towns are between 31.5 km
    and 32.5 km apart. What is the
    distance between them to the
    nearest kilometer?

★ 37. A ribbon is 12 m long to the near-
      est meter. What are its maximum
      and minimum lengths?

★ 38. The mass of a hummingbird is 2 g
      to the nearest gram. What are its
      maximum and minimum masses?

PROBLEM SOLVING

Strategy: Reading Information
from a Diagram

1. Understand
2. Plan
3. Work
4. Answer/Check

Data are not always given in the words of the problem. Sometimes you need to read the information from a drawing, a chart, or a table in order to solve the problem.

In the metric system, temperature is measured in **degrees Celsius (°C).** You can think of the scale on a thermometer as a vertical number line. Each mark on the scale represents a change of 10°.

You can see on the thermometer at the right that the temperature in a freezer may be −20°, read *20 degrees below zero.*

You can use the scale on a thermometer to find the difference between temperatures. For example, look at the scale and count the groups of ten degrees to find the difference between −20° and 20°. The difference is 40°.

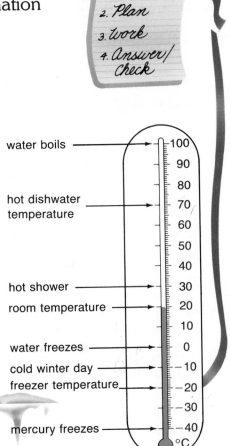

- water boils — 100
- 90
- 80
- hot dishwater temperature — 70
- 60
- 50
- 40
- hot shower — 30
- room temperature — 20
- 10
- water freezes — 0
- cold winter day — −10
- freezer temperature — −20
- −30
- mercury freezes — −40
- °C

CLASS EXERCISES

Use the thermometer above to read the temperature.

1. Cold winter day

2. Room temperature

3. Water boiling temperature

4. Mercury freezing temperature

Choose the more likely temperature for the activity. Write *a* or *b.*

5. Planting bulbs
   a. 20°C   b. 0°C

6. Bicycling
   a. 75°C   b. 25°C

7. Downhill skiing
   a. 19°C   b. −5°C

8. Swimming in a lake
   a. 30°C   b. 10°C

PRACTICE

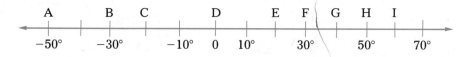

A   B   C   D   E   F   G   H   I

−50°   −30°   −10°   0   10°   30°   50°   70°

Choose the letter that shows the Celsius temperature on the thermometer scale above that is closest to the temperature given.

9. Butter melts at 30.6°

10. Body temperature of sparrow, 41°

11. Body temperature of a spiny anteater, 23.5°

12. Arctic water temperature, −1.1°

Find the difference between the two Celsius temperatures.

13. between 10° and −10°

14. between 20° and 60°

15. between −30° and 20°

16. between −40° and 40°

For Exercises 17–22 refer to the chart.

17. Which city had the highest record temperature?

18. Which city had the lowest record temperature?

19. Which two cities had low temperatures exactly 15° apart?

★**20.** What is the difference between the record low and the record high temperatures in San Francisco?

★**21.** What is the difference between the record low and the record high temperatures in Moscow?

★**22.** In which city is the difference between the record high and record low temperatures the least?

RECORD CELSIUS TEMPERATURES OF SELECTED CITIES

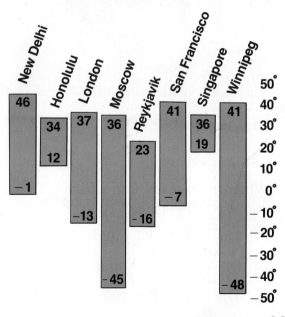

U.S. CUSTOMARY UNITS

The tables below summarize the relationships among the U.S. Customary Units of measure for length, capacity, and weight.

LENGTH
12 inches (in.) = 1 foot (ft)
3 feet = 1 yard (yd)
36 inches = 1 yard
1760 yards = 1 mile (mi)
5280 feet = 1 mile

CAPACITY (LIQUID)
8 fluid ounces (fl oz) = 1 cup (c)
2 cups = 1 pint (pt)
2 pints = 1 quart (qt)
4 quarts = 1 gallon (gal)

WEIGHT
16 ounces (oz) = 1 pound (lb)
2000 pounds = 1 ton (t)

When working with the customary units use the equivalents shown to change from one unit to another. For example:

Length
    12 in. = 1 ft
    15 in. = 1 ft 3 in.

Capacity
    4 qt = 1 gal
    9 qt = 2 gal 1 qt

Weight
    16 oz = 1 lb
    25 oz = 1 lb 9 oz

CLASS EXERCISES

Which customary unit of length, capacity, or weight would you use to measure?

1. The length of a milk carton

2. A small can of paint

3. Oil in a storage tank

4. A load of steel

5. The weight of a hairpin

6. The length of the Colorado River

PRACTICE

Complete.

7. 16 in. = 1 ft ⬛ in.   **8.** 5 c = ⬛ pt 1 c   **9.** 20 oz = 1 lb ⬛ oz

10. 40 in. = ⬛ yd 4 in.   **11.** 2 ft 14 in. = 3 ft ⬛ in.   **12.** 3 lb 19 oz = ⬛ lb 3 oz

13. 4 qt 3 pt = 5 qt ⬛ pt   **14.** 5 gal 7 qt = ⬛ gal 3 qt

PROBLEM SOLVING APPLICATIONS
Multi-Step Problems

Solve.

15. A recipe for hotcakes calls for 3 c of milk. Should you buy a pint or a quart of milk?

16. Laurie needs curtains for the window in her room. Each panel needs 4 yd of material. Is 26 ft of material enough?

★ **17.** You can buy nails in one-pound boxes for 89¢ each, or in a package of 8 two-ounce boxes for 99¢. Which is a better buy?

CHECKPOINT 2

Complete. *(pages 14–19)*

1. 3 m = ⬛ cm   **2.** 2 km = ⬛ m

3. 2 L = ⬛ mL   **4.** 6 kg = ⬛ g

Name the more precise measurement. *(pages 20–21)*

5. 0.7 kg or 693 g

6. 310 mL or 0.3 L

Refer to the chart. *(pages 22–23)*

AVERAGE HITS PER GAME			
Cooper	1.94	Marjan	0.93
Knell	1.68	Torez	1.34

7. Which player had the highest average? the lowest?

Complete. *(pages 24–25)*

8. 18 in. = ⬛ ft 6 in.

9. 22 oz = 1 lb ⬛ oz

Extra Practice on page 432

CHAPTER 1 TEST

Write using ■ > ■ > ■. *(pages 2–9)*

1. 8009, 8900, 8090   **2.** 3.7, 3.007, 3.07   **3.** 0.142, 0.214, 0.14

Round to the place underlined. *(pages 10–11)*

4. 9,987,654   **5.** 67.1399   **6.** 5.25   **7.** 0.219

Solve. *(pages 12–13)*

8. The top hitters had batting averages of 0.3273, 0.3450, 0.3237, and 0.3331. From greatest to least, what is the order of the averages?

Complete. *(pages 14–21)*

9. 15 km = ■ m   **10.** 25 mL = ■ L   **11.** 12 kg = ■ g

Choose the best estimate. Write *a*, *b*, or *c*. *(pages 14–21)*

12. The mass of an egg
     a. 66 g   **b.** 66 kg   **c.** 66 mg

13. The length of an index card
     a. 13 cm   **b.** 13 m   **c.** 13 dm

Use facts from the chart to solve. *(pages 22–23)*

14. Which substance has the highest boiling point?

15. What is the boiling point of iron?

16. Which two substances have boiling points of about 2000°C?

SUBSTANCE	BOILING POINT
Gold	2807°C
Iron	2570°C
Lead	1740°C
Tin	2270°C

Choose the best estimate. Write *a*, *b*, or *c*. *(pages 24–25)*

17. The capacity of a kettle
     a. 4 oz   **b.** 4 pt   **c.** 4 gal

18. The width of a door
     a. 32 yd   **b.** 32 ft   **c.** 32 in.

Extra Practice on page 433

MATHEMATICS and SOCIAL STUDIES

COUNTRY	POPULATION	AREA (SQUARE MILES)
Bangladesh	96,540,000	55,598
Canada	24,882,000	3,851,809
China	1,022,000,000	3,691,521
India	730,572,000	1,229,737
Singapore	2,500,000	239
U.S.A.	234,249,000	3,540,939
USSR	272,500,000	8,649,489

WHO'S KEEPING SCORE?

1. Name the country with the greatest population.

2. Which two countries have populations closest to 250 million?

3. Does the country with the greatest population also have the greatest area?

4. Which country's population has been rounded to the nearest 10 thousand?

5. Round the population of the U.S.A. to the nearest 10 million.

6. From least to greatest list the countries with populations greater than 100 million.

★ 7. Facts about countries are constantly changing. Name two references you can use to look up current information such as that listed above.

Enrichment

The ancient Egyptians had a system for writing numbers that did not use the idea of place value. They used the symbols in the chart below.

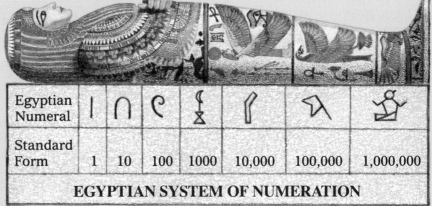

Egyptian Numeral							
Standard Form	1	10	100	1000	10,000	100,000	1,000,000

EGYPTIAN SYSTEM OF NUMERATION

The Egyptians wrote numbers by using combinations of these symbols. Usually the symbols needed were written in order from the greatest to the least value.

Standard Form   **Egyptian Numeral**

457   → (4 × 100) + (5 × 10) + (7 × 1) →

The Egyptian system of numeration was an *additive system* because the values of the symbols were added.

Write the standard form.

1.   2.   3.   4.

EGYPTIAN AND ROMAN NUMERATION

Write the Egyptian numeral.

5. 37   6. 528   7. 2374

8. 40,361   9. 1,201,405

The ancient Romans invented another additive system that did not use place value.

ROMAN NUMERAL	STANDARD FORM	ROMAN NUMERAL	STANDARD FORM
I	1		
V	5	$\overline{V}$	5000
X	10	$\overline{X}$	10,000
L	50	$\overline{L}$	50,000
C	100	$\overline{C}$	100,000
D	500	$\overline{D}$	500,000
M	1000	$\overline{M}$	1,000,000

ROMAN SYSTEM OF NUMERATION

Each symbol was used as often as needed. For example:

III = 3   XXX = 30   MMM = 3000

For numbers that were 1000 times the value of the symbols, a bar was placed over each symbol. For example:

V = 5 $\overline{V}$ = 5000   M = 1000 $\overline{M}$ = 1,000,000

The earliest Romans wrote 4 as IIII. A *subtractive* feature was added to the system at a later time. A lesser symbol to the left of a greater symbol was subtracted. A lesser symbol to the right of a greater symbol was added. For example:

IV = 5 − 1 = 4 $\overline{CM}$ = 1,000,000 − 100,000 = 900,000
VI = 5 + 1 = 6 $\overline{MC}$ = 1,000,000 + 100,000 = 1,100,000

Write the standard form.

10. LXXVIII   **11.** LXIV   **12.** $\overline{X}$CDXXII   **13.** $\overline{MCLCCCI}$

Write the Roman numeral.

14. 88   **15.** 1492   **16.** 3955   **17.** 20,916

CUMULATIVE REVIEW

Choose the correct answer. Write *a*, *b*, *c*, or *d*.

What is the value of the underlined digit?

1. 60<u>7</u>,833,059

   a. 7 millionths
   b. 7 millions
   c. 7 ten millions
   d. None of these

2. 6.01<u>4</u>275

   a. 2 thousandths
   b. 2 ten-thousandths
   c. 2 thousands
   d. None of these

3. 0.<u>0</u>538

   a. 0 ones
   b. 0 tenths
   c. 0 tens
   d. None of these

What is the standard form?

4. 23 billion, 7 thousand

   a. 23,700,000
   b. 23,007,000,000
   c. 23,000,007,000
   d. None of these

5. 9 millionths

   a. 0.00009
   b. 9,000,000
   c. 0.000009
   d. None of these

6. 0.6 + 0.0009

   a. 6.0009
   b. 0.60009
   c. 0.6009
   d. None of these

Complete using the correct signs.

7. 83.4 ▮ 83.3 ▮ 83

   a. > >
   b. < <
   c. > <
   d. None of these

8. 2.5 ▮ 2.50 ▮ 2.500

   a. < <
   b. > >
   c. = =
   d. None of these

9. 1.0 ▮ 0.9 ▮ 0.09

   a. > >
   b. = =
   c. < <
   d. None of these

Round.

10. 43,511 to the nearest thousand

   a. 40,000
   b. 4,000
   c. 44,000
   d. None of these

11. 0.9327 to the nearest hundredth

   a. 0.94
   b. 0.93
   c. 0.9427
   d. None of these

12. 69.5 to the nearest ten

   a. 70
   b. 69
   c. 60
   d. None of these

Which is the best estimate?

13. The capacity of a soup bowl

    a. 300 mL

    b. 3 mL

    c. 3 L

    d. 30 L

14. The length of a bath tub

    a. 2 km

    b. 2 kg

    c. 20 m

    d. 2 m

15. The height of a person

    a. 1.7 m

    b. 17 m

    c. 17 cm

    d. 170 m

16. The height of a giraffe

    a. 18 ft

    b. 18 in.

    c. 18 yd

    d. 18 mi

17. The weight of a seventh grader

    a. 100 oz

    b. 100 lb

    c. 100 t

    d. 10 lb

18. The capacity of an eye dropper

    a. 1 fl oz

    b. 1 c

    c. 10 fl oz

    d. 10 c

LANGUAGE and VOCABULARY REVIEW

Match each term with its description.

1. Equivalent decimals

2. Kilometer

3. Tenth

4. Graph of a number

5. Expanded form

6. Cubic centimeter

A. Point on a number line paired with a number

B. Amount of space in a cube with all edges 1 cm long

C. Metric unit used to measure long distances

D. One of 10 equal parts of a unit

E. Notation that shows the value of each digit

F. Decimals that name the same number

HISTORY OF THE COMPUTER

COMPUTER LITERACY

1642 Arithmetic Machine was the first mechanical adding machine.

These machines had moving parts called *gears*.

1830 Analytical Engine was designed to store numbers and do all four operations.

1890 Tabulating Machine could sort, count, and do all four operations.

1940's ENIAC was the first electronic digital computer. It could do 5000 additions in one second.

This machine had no moving parts. It had vacuum tubes.

1950's. Transistors were developed. Smaller, faster computers could do over 3,000,000 operations per second.

These machines had transistors instead of vacuum tubes.

1960's to Present. Computers developed that can do over 30,000,000 operations per second.

These machines have silicon chips instead of transistors.

Use the facts to answer the questions.

1. About how many centuries did it take for the modern computer to develop?

2. What could the Tabulating Machine do?

3. When were transistors used in computers?

4. How many additions could the ENIAC do in 1 min?

2

The Great Pyramid is built of stone blocks. After using 2 million blocks, the builders still needed 300,000 more to complete the job. Write in standard form the total number of blocks used.

ADDITION AND SUBTRACTION OF WHOLE NUMBERS AND DECIMALS

VARIABLES AND EQUATIONS

An **equation** is a mathematical sentence with an equals sign. An equation tells us that two quantities are equal. Since $4 + 2$ and 6 name the same number, we can write the equation $4 + 2 = 6$.

Sometimes a letter is used to represent a number. A letter used in this way is called a **variable.** For example, to **solve** $n + 3 = 9$, replace n with a number that will make $n + 3 = 9$ a true statement. Test different values for n.

$$n + 3 = 9$$

Replace n with 5: $5 + 3 = 9$ False
Replace n with 6: $6 + 3 = 9$ True

When we replace n with the number 6, we form a true statement. We call 6 the **solution** of the equation $n + 3 = 9$.

Ⓜ You can solve simple addition and subtraction equations mentally by thinking of number facts.

| **Think:** 7 plus what number is 11? | $7 + b = 11$ $7 + 4 = 11$ | **Think:** What number minus 2 is 6? | $y - 2 = 6$ $8 - 2 = 6$ |

So, $b = 4$.   So, $y = 8$.
The solution is 4.   The solution is 8.

CLASS EXERCISES

Write *true* or *false*.

1. $9 - 5 = 4$

2. $10 - 3 = 9$

3. $6 + 7 = 12$

4. $5 + 8 = 15$

5. $12 - 4 = 8$

6. $9 + 8 = 18$

Is the underlined number the solution of the equation?
Write *yes* or *no*.

7. $a + 3 = 6$
$\underline{9} + 3 = 6$

8. $5 + b = 15$
$5 + \underline{7} = 15$

9. $11 + m = 13$
$11 + \underline{2} = 13$

PRACTICE

Is 3 a solution of the equation? Write *yes* or *no*.

10. $14 - p = 11$ **11.** $y + 17 = 20$ **12.** $8 - x = 3$

13. $h + 5 = 8$ **14.** $9 - r = 12$ **15.** $z + 4 = 14$

Answer the question. Write *yes* or *no*.

16. $k - 3 = 12$ Is 9 a solution?   **17.** $7 + n = 12$ Is 5 a solution?

★ **18.** $25 - m = 14$ Is 19 a solution?   ★ **19.** $39 + b = 47$ Is 8 a solution?

Use mental math to solve the equation.

20. $5 + 3 = t$ **21.** $11 - 4 = k$

22. $4 + 6 = m$ **23.** $8 - 2 = n$

★ **24.** $30 - y = 20$ ★ **25.** $d + 14 = 50$

MENTAL MATH

PROBLEM SOLVING APPLICATIONS
Equations

Choose the equation that best describes the problem.
Write *a*, *b*, or *c*.

26. I am thinking of a number 6 less than 23.
     a. $p - 23 = 6$ **b.** $23 - 6 = p$ **c.** $23 - p = 6$

27. If I add 9 to my number, the sum is 17.
     a. $x + 9 = 17$ **b.** $17 + x = 9$ **c.** $9 + 17 = x$

Choose the equation that does not describe the problem.
Write *a*, *b*, or *c*.

★ **28.** Joshua has 18 bottles. How many more does he need to total 31?
     a. $31 - 18 = y$ **b.** $18 + 31 = y$ **c.** $18 + y = 31$

★ **29.** Elka and George Clinton invited 47 guests to the performance. Elka invited 28 guests. How many did George invite?
     a. $28 + t = 47$ **b.** $47 - 28 = t$ **c.** $47 + 28 = t$

PROPERTIES OF ADDITION

Here are some properties of addition. When parentheses are used, the addition inside the parentheses is done first.

Commutative Property
Changing the order of the addends does not change the sum.

$4 + 3 = 7 \qquad 3 + 4 = 7$
so, $4 + 3 = 3 + 4$

In general: $a + b = b + a$

Associative Property
Changing the grouping of the addends does not change the sum.

$(6 + 4) + 5 = 15 \qquad 6 + (4 + 5) = 15$
so, $(6 + 4) + 5 = 6 + (4 + 5)$

In general: $(a + b) + c = a + (b + c)$

Zero Property
The sum of *zero* and any other number is that number.

$0 + 4 = 4 \qquad 4 + 0 = 4$

In general: $0 + a = a$ and $a + 0 = a$

Ⓜ Because of the commutative and associative properties of addition, you can add the numbers in a column or in a chain of addends in any order. To help you add mentally, look for addends whose sum is 10. For example,

To add: $6 + 8 + 4 + 2$
Think: $6 + 8 + 4 + 2$
$= 10 + 10 = 20$

To add: $17 + 23 + 31 + 19$
Think: $17 + 23 + 31 + 19$
$= 40 \quad + \quad 50 \quad = 90$

CLASS EXERCISES

Complete. Then name the property illustrated.

1. $8 + 2 = \blacksquare$
  $2 + 8 = \blacksquare$

2. $5 + 0 = \blacksquare$
  $0 + 5 = \blacksquare$

3. $6 + (2 + 7) = 6 + \blacksquare = \blacksquare$
  $(6 + 2) + 7 = \blacksquare + 7 = \blacksquare$

4. $6 + \blacksquare = 6$

5. $8 + 4 = \blacksquare + 8$

6. $\blacksquare + 9 = 9 + 3$

7. $0 + 2 = \blacksquare$

8. $(5 + \blacksquare) + 1 = 5 + (2 + 1)$

9. $4 + (8 + 2) = (\blacksquare + 8) + 2$

PRACTICE

Use the properties to solve.

10. $3 + 2 = 2 + n$ **11.** $12 + 5 = b + 12$ **12.** $1 + 5 = 5 + s$

13. $0 + 3 = m$ **14.** $f + 0 = 8$ **15.** $5 + d = 5$

16. $4 + (1 + 2) = (4 + 1) + t$ **17.** $7 + (8 + 2) = (7 + c) + 2$

Name the property illustrated.

18. $182 + 0 = 182$ **19.** $321 + 16 = 16 + 321$ **20.** $27 + (13 + 8) = (27 + 13) + 8$

★**21.** $x + y = y + x$ ★**22.** $0 + k = k$ ★**23.** $(t + m) + n = t + (m + n)$

Use mental math to find the sum.

24. $5 + 8 + 3 + 12$ **25.** $16 + 15 + 13 + 4$ **26.** $6 + 11 + 14 + 9$

27. $15¢ + 30¢ + 5¢ + 18¢$ **28.** $75¢ + 18¢ + 25¢ + 22¢$

29. $80¢ + 30¢ + 21¢ + 20¢$ **30.** $14 + 8 + 16 + 22$

31. $9 + 20 + 11 + 6$ ★**32.** $15 + 28 + 12 + 15$

★**33.** $75¢ + 90¢ + 35¢ + 10¢$ ★**34.** $150 + 260 + 140 + 350$

Round to the greatest place value.

35. 9002   **36.** 21,940   **37.** 38,604

38. 0.654   **39.** 5.398   **40.** 7.007

MIXED REVIEW

PROBLEM SOLVING APPLICATIONS
Choosing the Operation

Solve.

41. There are 13 cans of tomato soup, 26 cans of chicken noodle soup, 7 cans of beef stew, and 9 cans of vegetable soup left. How many cans are there?

42. The odometer on Julio's car shows 31,496 mi. Miriam's car has 31,946 mi and Wilson's car has 31,694 mi. Which car has the greatest mileage?

ADDITION OF WHOLE NUMBERS

In a recent survey 357 people said they were against Proposition A, 132 people were in favor of it, and 84 people were undecided. How many people were surveyed?

Before adding the numbers, do a quick mental estimate of the sum. Round each addend to its greatest place value, and then add.

$$\begin{array}{r} 357 \\ 132 \\ + \ 84 \end{array} \Rightarrow \begin{array}{r} 400 \\ 100 \\ + \ 80 \\ \hline 580 \end{array}$$

The estimate is 580.

Next, find the actual sum. Add the ones, then the tens, and then the hundreds. Use your estimate to check the reasonableness of this sum.

$$\begin{array}{r} \overset{1}{3}57 \\ 132 \\ + \ 84 \\ \hline 3 \end{array} \qquad \begin{array}{r} \overset{1}{3}\overset{1}{5}7 \\ 132 \\ + \ 84 \\ \hline 73 \end{array} \qquad \begin{array}{r} \overset{1}{3}\overset{1}{5}7 \\ 132 \\ + \ 84 \\ \hline 573 \end{array}$$

A total of 573 people were surveyed.

CLASS EXERCISES

Add.

1. $\begin{array}{r} 2 \\ +6 \end{array} \Rightarrow \begin{array}{r} 22 \\ + \ 6 \end{array}$

2. $\begin{array}{r} 6 \\ +3 \end{array} \Rightarrow \begin{array}{r} 66 \\ + \ 3 \end{array}$

3. $\begin{array}{r} 5 \\ +7 \end{array} \Rightarrow \begin{array}{r} 25 \\ + \ 7 \end{array}$

4. $\begin{array}{r} 7 \\ +9 \end{array} \Rightarrow \begin{array}{r} 37 \\ + \ 9 \end{array}$

5. $\begin{array}{r} 40 \\ +27 \end{array} \Rightarrow \begin{array}{r} 140 \\ + \ 27 \end{array}$

6. $\begin{array}{r} 25 \\ +16 \end{array} \Rightarrow \begin{array}{r} 325 \\ + \ 16 \end{array}$

7. $\begin{array}{r} 46 \\ +20 \end{array} \Rightarrow \begin{array}{r} 546 \\ +320 \end{array}$

8. $\begin{array}{r} 17 \\ +54 \end{array} \Rightarrow \begin{array}{r} 417 \\ +254 \end{array}$

PRACTICE

Estimate. Then add. Use the estimate to check your answer.

9. $\begin{array}{r} 54 \\ +38 \end{array}$

10. $\begin{array}{r} 72 \\ +28 \end{array}$

11. $\begin{array}{r} 364 \\ + \ 59 \end{array}$

12. $\begin{array}{r} 738 \\ + \ 75 \end{array}$

13. $\begin{array}{r} 365 \\ + \ 35 \end{array}$

14. 7607	15. 6372	16. 8640	17. 2645	18. 9276
+3958	+1209	+2827	+7688	+9716

19. 72 + 83 + 94 + 45

20. 3 + 25 + 8 + 23

21. 141 + 74 + 288 + 366

22. 307 + 123 + 86 + 92

23. 2091 + 895 + 98 + 1498

24. 4790 + 74 + 9062 + 3829

25. 38,421	26. 584,612	27. 82,602	28. 86,859
7,646	39,837	178,257	572,770
+10,871	+ 94,601	+684,141	+674,952

Compare the estimate and the sum. Explain the error.

ESTIMATE

29. 167 + 294
   estimate: 500
   sum: 361

30. 986 + 78
   estimate: 1080
   sum: 1766

PROBLEM SOLVING APPLICATIONS
Working with Patterns

You may want to use pencil and paper or a calculator to answer the questions about the square array of numbers at the right.

31. Find the sum of the numbers in each row.

32. Find the sum of the numbers in each column.

33. Find the sum of the numbers in each diagonal.

34. In a magic square the sum of the numbers in each row, column, and diagonal is the same. Is this a magic square?

52	61	4	13	20	29	36	45
14	3	62	51	46	35	30	19
53	60	5	12	21	28	37	44
11	6	59	54	43	38	27	22
55	58	7	10	23	26	39	42
9	8	57	56	41	40	25	24
50	63	2	15	18	31	34	47
16	1	64	49	48	33	32	17

★ **35.** Find the sum of the four numbers in the green square. Try other squares like this. Do you get the same sum?

★ **36.** Find the sum of the numbers in the eight blue squares. Can you find other V-shaped patterns of numbers that have the same sum?

ADDITION OF DECIMALS

Since you know how to add whole numbers, you can easily add decimals. To find a decimal sum write the numbers in a column with the decimal points lined up.

Sometimes it helps to annex, or add, zeros so all the addends have the same number of decimal places. Here's an example.

$$9.98 + 35.8 + 64 = ?$$

$$\begin{array}{r} 9.98 \\ 35.80 \\ +64.00 \\ \hline 109.78 \end{array}$$

Remember to write the decimal point in the sum. When adding decimals with pencil and paper or with a calculator, it is important to estimate the sum to check your answer. To estimate decimals, round each addend to its greatest place value.

$$9.7 + 0.28 + 8.4 \quad \Rightarrow \quad 10 + 0.3 + 8 = 18.3.$$

Think: Is the calculator sum, 18.38, a reasonable answer?

CLASS EXERCISES

Estimate the sum.

1. $7.1 + 0.4 + 3.5$ **2.** $5.6 + 2.43 + 3.3$ **3.** $3.9 + 2.04 + 5.2$

4. $\$9.50 + \$3.25 + \$4.75$ **5.** $\$.82 + \$.42 + \$2.30$ **6.** $\$6.71 + \$3.04 + \$.70$

Is the estimate reasonable? Write *yes* or *no*.

7.	**8.**	**9.**	**10.**	**11.**
$\begin{array}{r} 4.21 \\ +0.83 \\ \hline 4.8 \end{array}$	$\begin{array}{r} \$2.65 \\ +\ 3.44 \\ \hline \$6 \end{array}$	$\begin{array}{r} 7.4132 \\ +13.009 \\ \hline 20 \end{array}$	$\begin{array}{r} 20.872 \\ +19.026 \\ \hline 49 \end{array}$	$\begin{array}{r} 43.301 \\ +\ 7.098 \\ \hline 53 \end{array}$

12. Think: What are two things you would tell someone to keep in mind when adding decimals?

PRACTICE

Estimate. Then add. Use the estimate to check your answer.

13.   2.6
    1.29
 +3.8

14.   1.045
    0.96
 +1.73

15.   8.02
  31.15
 +53.447

16.   21.24
  13.79
 + 6.8

17.   36.35
  74.182
 +12.3

18. $6.35
   .72
 + 3.40

19. $9.27
   .86
 + 5.60

20. $12.73
  4.07
 + 10.50

21. $8.95
  9.20
 + .95

22. $ .75
  18.04
 + .60

23. $38.2 + 7.5 + 4.83 + 5.08$

24. $25.96 + \$42.29 + \$4.75$

25. $\$21.45 + \$15.29 + \$7.15 + \$19.65$

26. $12.093 + 3.07 + 0.8216 + 5.9$

Answer the question.

27. $27.1 + a = 28$ Is 9 a solution?

28. $375.45 + b = 376$ Is 0.55 a solution?

★ **29.** $39.5 + c = 39.55$ What is the solution?

★ **30.** $124.3 + t = 126$ What is the solution?

Use a calculator to add. Then estimate to check.

31. $35.622 + 189.01$

32. $9.484 + 22.3067$

33. $4.156 + 0.8237 + 6.23$

34. $92.3001 + 41.2047 + 38.07$

CALCULATOR

PROBLEM SOLVING APPLICATIONS
Using Mental Math or a Calculator

Solve.

35. Tania bought items that cost $1.25, $3.30, $4.75, $2.20, and $5.60. How much did she spend in all?

36. Roger bought a cassette for $7.35. Joan bought two for $3.50 each. Who spent more money?

★ **37.** Lianne used a calculator to add $6.88, $4.19, $.79, and $11.05. The calculator showed 12.91. She estimated the sum should be about $22. Explain the mistake she made.

PROBLEM SOLVING
Strategy: Too Much or Too Little Information

1. Understand
2. Plan
3. Work
4. Answer/Check

Some problems cannot be solved because of missing information. Other problems supply more information than you need, so you must choose the needed data.

The pictograph below shows the number of albums sold at Sounds Swell in December. Each symbol, ⊙, represents 20 albums while each half symbol, ◖, represents 10 albums.

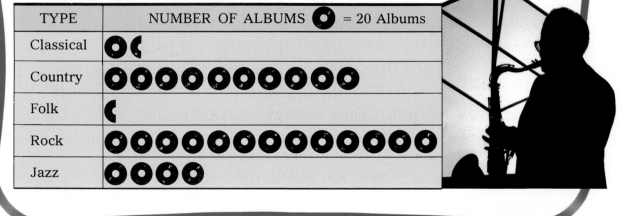

ALBUMS SOLD AT SOUNDS SWELL IN DECEMBER

TYPE	NUMBER OF ALBUMS ⊙ = 20 Albums
Classical	⊙◖
Country	⊙⊙⊙⊙⊙⊙⊙⊙⊙⊙
Folk	◖
Rock	⊙⊙⊙⊙⊙⊙⊙⊙⊙⊙⊙⊙⊙
Jazz	⊙⊙⊙⊙

CLASS EXERCISES

Refer to the pictograph to answer. If there is not enough information to answer the question, write *missing data*. If there is more information than you need, describe the extra data and then answer the question.

1. What type of album had the greatest sales?

2. How many classical albums were sold?

3. How many jazz albums were sold at a reduced price?

4. In December, rock albums were on sale for about $6 each and country for about $4 each. How many more rock albums did they sell than country albums?

PRACTICE

Solve if the problem has enough information. If there is not enough information, describe the missing data. Exercises 5 and 6 refer to the pictograph.

5. How much money did the shop make from the sale of the Barney 200?

6. How many Acton SLR cameras were sold?

7. Tania is 14 years old. Her sister is 9 years old. Their mother's age is 10 years more than twice Tania's age. How old is their mother?

★ **8.** An elevator has a maximum capacity of 1125 kg. Two men who are about 90 kg each, one woman, and three children are on the elevator. Would it be safe to put a container that is 384 kg on the elevator with the people?

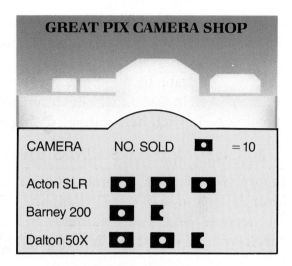

GREAT PIX CAMERA SHOP

CAMERA	NO. SOLD	◖ = 10
Acton SLR	◖ ◖ ◖	
Barney 200	◖ ◖	
Dalton 50X	◖ ◖ ◖	

CHECKPOINT 1

Answer the question. Write *yes* or *no*. *(pages 34–37)*

1. $x + 12 = 16$
   Is 8 a solution?

2. $11 - y = 7$
   Is 5 a solution?

3. $8 + 13 = w + 8$
   Is 7 a solution?

Estimate. Then add. *(pages 38–41)*

4. $326 + 73$ **5.** $58.1 + 2.95$

Solve. If there is not enough information, write *missing data*. *(pages 42–43)*

6. Ten boxes of pencils were used for a computer-scored test. Each box had 20 pencils. How many boxes are left?

Extra Practice on page 434

SUBTRACTION OF WHOLE NUMBERS

Last year Village Nursery ordered 694 packs of seeds. This year they ordered 1003 packs. How many more packs did they order this year?

First make a quick estimate of the difference. Round each number to its greatest place value, then subtract.

$$\begin{array}{r} 1003 \\ -\ 694 \end{array} \Rightarrow \begin{array}{r} 1000 \\ -\ 700 \\ \hline 300 \end{array}$$

The estimate is 300.

Now find the exact difference. Before you subtract, rename 1003 to form 99 tens and 13 ones. Compare the answer and your estimate to check your answer. You can also add to check your answer.

$$\begin{array}{r} \overset{9\ 9\ 13}{\cancel{1003}} \\ -\ 694 \\ \hline 9 \end{array} \qquad \begin{array}{r} \overset{9\ 9\ 13}{\cancel{1003}} \\ -\ 694 \\ \hline 09 \end{array} \qquad \begin{array}{r} \overset{9\ 9\ 13}{\cancel{1003}} \\ -\ 694 \\ \hline 309 \end{array}$$

Village Nursery ordered 309 more packs of seeds this year.

Think: What number can you add to 309 to check your answer?

CLASS EXERCISES

Complete the renaming.

1. 20 = 1 ten ▓ ones   **2.** 70 = ▓ tens 10 ones   **3.** 81 = 7 tens ▓ ones

4. 54 = ▓ tens 14 ones **5.** 800 = ▓ tens 10 ones **6.** 901 = ▓ tens 11 ones

7. 386 = ▓ tens 16 ones **8.** 2063 = 205 tens ▓ ones **9.** 1007 = ▓ tens 17 ones

Tell whether or not you need to rename to subtract.
Write *yes* or *no*.

10. 64	**11.** 35	**12.** 27	**13.** 86	**14.** 106
−23	−10	−19	−57	− 92

15. Think: Is it ever necessary to rename more than 10 in any place?

PRACTICE

Estimate. Then subtract.

16.   58
    − 9

17.   83
    − 7

18.   46
    −38

19.   71
    −56

20.   81
    −29

21.   637
    − 85

22.   866
    − 98

23.   400
    −285

24.   620
    −109

25.   805
    − 78

26.   9084
    − 187

27.   3000
    − 497

28.   6307
    −2085

29.   3560
    −1508

30.   4268
    −1079

Solve for n.

31. $529 - 368 = n$

32. $844 - 378 = n$

33. $5041 - 103 = n$

34. $8700 - 5067 = n$

35. $7284 - 5176 = n$

36. $9008 - 3859 = n$

★ **37.** $183 - n = 103$

★ **38.** $n - 199 = 1$

★ **39.** $5888 - n = 4800$

The subtraction was done on a calculator. Write the number you can add to the displayed answer to check it.

40. $7963 - 4681$ `3282`

41. $4098 - 359$ `3739`

42. $3199 - 2476$ `723`

43. $1912 - 746$ `1166`

CALCULATOR

PROBLEM SOLVING APPLICATIONS
Choosing the Operation

Solve.

44. The Adelphi Theater has seating for 6850 people. At a recent charity performance, only 184 seats were empty. How many seats were occupied?

45. Andy took 2 rolls of pictures during vacation. Each roll contained 24 shots. Of the photos taken, 9 didn't turn out in one roll and 7 in the other. How many pictures turned out from the 2 rolls?

SUBTRACTION OF DECIMALS

Cross-country skis are on sale for $79.85. Their regular price is $105. How much can you save by buying them on sale?

A quick estimate, $100 − $80, shows that you can save about $20. To find the exact difference, write $105 as $105.00 to get the same number of decimal places in both numbers. Then line up the decimal points, rename, and subtract as with whole numbers. You can save $25.15 during the sale.

$$\begin{array}{r} {}^{9\ 14\ \ 9\ 10} \\ \$\ \not{1}\,\not{0}\,\not{5}\,.\,\not{0}\,\not{0} \\ -\ \ \ \ 7\ 9\,\raisebox{0.3ex}{.}\,8\ 5 \\ \hline \$\ \ \ 2\ 5\,.\,1\ 5 \end{array}$$

 To find the exact difference mentally, use the *adding-on method*. Take the sale price of $79.85 and add on $.15 to get $80.00. Then add on $25.00 to get $105.00. The total added on is $25.15, the exact difference.

$$\begin{array}{r} \$79.85 \\ +\quad .15 \\ \hline \$80.00 \\ +\ 25.00 \\ \hline \$105.00 \end{array}\ \Big] \$25.15$$

CLASS EXERCISES

Subtract.

1.
$$\begin{array}{r} 9 \\ -4 \\ \hline \end{array} \qquad \begin{array}{r} 0.9 \\ -0.4 \\ \hline \end{array} \qquad \begin{array}{r} 0.09 \\ -0.04 \\ \hline \end{array}$$

2.
$$\begin{array}{r} 52 \\ -28 \\ \hline \end{array} \qquad \begin{array}{r} 5.2 \\ -2.8 \\ \hline \end{array} \qquad \begin{array}{r} 5.20 \\ -2.80 \\ \hline \end{array}$$

3.
$$\begin{array}{r} 0.837 \\ -0.612 \\ \hline \end{array} \qquad \begin{array}{r} 8.37 \\ -6.12 \\ \hline \end{array} \qquad \begin{array}{r} 0.0837 \\ -0.0612 \\ \hline \end{array}$$

4.
$$\begin{array}{r} 457 \\ -420 \\ \hline \end{array} \qquad \begin{array}{r} 4.57 \\ -4.20 \\ \hline \end{array} \qquad \begin{array}{r} 0.0457 \\ -0.0420 \\ \hline \end{array}$$

5.
$$\begin{array}{r} 0.734 \\ -0.134 \\ \hline \end{array} \qquad \begin{array}{r} 7.34 \\ -1.34 \\ \hline \end{array} \qquad \begin{array}{r} 73.4 \\ -13.4 \\ \hline \end{array}$$

How would you rewrite one of the numbers to get the same number of decimal places in both?

6. $8.05 - 6$

7. $3.781 - 2.4$

8. $10.1 - 7.0335$

9. $48.0193 - 9.6$

10. $197 - 76.808$

11. $59.1 - 20.0067$

PRACTICE

Estimate. Then subtract.

12.   2.046
     −0.53

13.   8.923
     −3.83

14.   6.27
     −5.4416

15.   9.8
     −7.01

16.   35.6
     −17.0764

17.   0.03
     −0.0076

18.   0.7
     −0.2385

19.   8
     −6.184

20. 10
     −9.302

21.   2600
     − 751.35

22. $6.25 − $4.80

23. $8.96 − $5.99

24. $8.04 − $2.17

25. 1.08 − 0.9

26. 0.4 − 0.0015

27. 1000.6 − 84

28. 200.75 − 4

29. 40.63 − 9.5211

30. 5.7 − 2.3006

Use the adding-on method to find the difference mentally.

31. $20 − $12.25

32. $10 − $4.50

33. $7 − $3.29

34. $7.03 − $4.63

★**35.** $39.01 − $38.56

★**36.** $100.17 − $89.90

MENTAL MATH

PROBLEM SOLVING APPLICATIONS
Using Mental Math

Solve.

37. Arthur has a list of the supplies he bought: calculator, $10.99; tape dispenser, $5.30; notebook, $2.85; mechanical pencil, $8.50; three-ring binder, $3.85. Which was the least expensive item?

38. Yolanda has a twenty-dollar bill and nine pennies. She bought $15.04 worth of groceries. How much money should Yolanda hand to the cashier if she wants a five-dollar bill back in change?

★**39.** On Monday the Japanese Yen (¥) to U.S. Dollar ($) exchange rate was 242 ¥ to $1.00. On Wednesday it was 238 ¥ to $1.00. On Friday it was 240 ¥ to $1.00. How many Yen did the Towne National Bank get in exchange for $10,000 on Wednesday?

WORKING WITH UNITS OF MEASURE

Sometimes in order to subtract units of measure you need to rename first. In the example below you need to rename 7 ft 2 in. before you can subtract the measures. Recall that 12 in. = 1 ft.

$$
\begin{array}{r}
7 \text{ ft } 2 \text{ in.} \\
-3 \text{ ft } 9 \text{ in.} \\
\end{array}
\Rightarrow
\begin{array}{r}
6 \text{ ft } 14 \text{ in.} \\
-3 \text{ ft } 9 \text{ in.} \\
\hline
3 \text{ ft } 5 \text{ in.}
\end{array}
$$

In the following example, you need to rename the sum so that the answer is in simplest form. Recall that 16 oz = 1 lb.

$$
\begin{array}{r}
2 \text{ lb } 8 \text{ oz} \\
+5 \text{ lb } 11 \text{ oz} \\
\hline
7 \text{ lb } 19 \text{ oz}
\end{array}
\Rightarrow 8 \text{ lb } 3 \text{ oz}
$$

E You can make quick estimates of sums and differences when working with units of measure. Round up if the measure of the smaller unit is more than half the larger unit. Round down if it is less than half the larger unit. In the example below, recall that 8 fl oz = 1 c.

Think: Is 6 fl oz more than half a cup?	Estimate	Actual Sum
2 c 6 fl oz	3 c	2 c 6 fl oz
+3 c 3 fl oz	+3 c	+3 c 3 fl oz
	6 c	5 c 9 fl oz $\Rightarrow$ 6 c 1 fl oz

CLASS EXERCISES

Complete the renaming.

1. 3 ft 28 in. = ▇ ft 4 in.

2. 9 yd 8 ft = 11 yd ▇ ft

3. 6 lb 20 oz = 7 lb ▇ oz

4. 16 pt 1 c = 15 pt ▇ c

5. 3 lb 10 oz = ▇ lb 26 oz

6. 7 t 1300 lb = ▇ t 3300 lb

PRACTICE

Estimate. Then add or subtract. Write in simplest form.

7.   4 ft 9 in.
      +2 ft 4 in.

8.   5 qt 1 pt
      +3 qt 1 pt

9.   7 yd 1 ft
      −5 yd 2 ft

10.   6 c 2 fl oz
      −1 c 7 fl oz

11.   5 c 5 fl oz
      −4 c 1 fl oz

12.   31 lb 12 oz
      + 9 lb 11 oz

13.   30 yd 26 in.
      −24 yd 35 in.

14.   9 yd 2 in.
      −6 yd 10 in.

15.   15 t 1800 lb
      + 2 t 500 lb

16.   13 qt 1 pt
      + 1 qt 1 pt

17.   26 yd 1 ft
      +14 yd 2 ft

18.   18 lb 15 oz
      + 3 lb 14 oz

19.   3 mi 1360 ft
      −2 mi 1495 ft

20.   6 t 300 lb
      +   1700 lb

★ **21.**   9 qt
      −1 gal 2 qt

★ **22.**   6000 ft
      −1 mi 500 ft

★ **23.** 5 ft 9 in. + 2 ft 10 in. + 8 in.

★ **24.** 2 c 4 fl oz + 4 c 7 fl oz + 9 c

★ **25.** 6 qt 1 pt − 3 pt

★ **26.** 13 c 2 fl oz − 19 fl oz

Write the answer.

27. 42 + 60

28. 39 + 60

29. 14 + 59

30. (7 + 12) − 8

31. (36 + 60) − 47

32. (85 + 19) − 7

MIXED REVIEW

PROBLEM SOLVING APPLICATIONS
Multi-Step Problems

Solve.

33. A bag of potatoes weighs 30 oz. Is this about 2 lb?

34. A sign by the drawbridge reads "No trucks over 10 tons allowed." Can a truck carrying 25,000 lb of grain cross the bridge?

35. John's bulletin board is 4 ft 2 in. wide. Yukio's bulletin board is 1 yd 1 ft wide. Who has the wider bulletin board?

★ **36.** When Flight 312 left Seattle, there were 9 gal of juice on board. The flight attendants served 16 qt on the way to Dallas. How much juice was left for the return flight?

WORKING WITH TIME

The time that passes between the start and end of an event is the **elapsed time.**

60 seconds (s) = 1 minute (min)
60 minutes = 1 hour (h)
24 hours = 1 day (d)

Joyce read from 9:35 A.M. until 11:15 A.M. How long did she read?

Think: How can you rename 11 h 15 min in order to subtract?

$$\begin{array}{r} 11\text{ h }15\text{ min} \\ -\ 9\text{ h }35\text{ min} \end{array} \Rightarrow \begin{array}{r} 10\text{ h }75\text{ min} \\ -\ 9\text{ h }35\text{ min} \\ \hline 1\text{ h }40\text{ min} \end{array}$$

Joyce read for 1 h 40 min.

M You can also find the answer mentally.

Think: From 9:35 to 10:35 is 1 h.
From 10:35 to 11:15 is 40 min.
So, from 9:35 to 11:15 is 1 h 40 min.

To find the elapsed time that passes noon or midnight, add 12 h to the ending time before you subtract. For example, what is the elapsed time from 10:25 P.M. until 6:40 A.M.?

This is a multiple-exposure photograph of the Arctic sun between 11 P.M. and 1 A.M.

$$\overset{\text{add 12}}{\begin{array}{r} 6\text{ h }40\text{ min} \\ -10\text{ h }25\text{ min} \end{array}} \Rightarrow \begin{array}{r} 18\text{ h }40\text{ min} \\ -10\text{ h }25\text{ min} \\ \hline 8\text{ h }15\text{ min} \end{array}$$

The elapsed time is 8 h 15 min.

CLASS EXERCISES

Does the elapsed time pass noon or midnight? Write *yes* or *no*.

	1.	2.	3.	4.	5.
STARTING TIME	8:45 A.M.	4:06 P.M.	9:30 P.M.	10:52 P.M.	1:46 P.M.
ENDING TIME	2:30 P.M.	11:17 P.M.	5:29 A.M.	6:18 A.M.	7:00 P.M.

PRACTICE

Add or subtract. Write the answer in simplest form.

6. 6 h 42 min
−2 h 30 min

7. 10 h 57 min
− 9 h 41 min

8. 12 min 36 s
+ 8 min 20 s

9. 5 h 48 min
+9 h 12 min

10. 7 h 26 min
+5 h 34 min

11. 23 min 8 s
−   50 s

12. 10 h
− 4 h 16 min

13. 2 h
−1 h 47 min

★ **14.** 5 h 20 min 6 s
−3 h 47 min 13 s

★ **15.** 3 h 42 min 35 s
+   18 min 47 s

★ **16.** 11 d 20 h 40 min
+ 9 d 7 h 34 min

Find the elapsed time.

17. 1:21 P.M. to 4:56 A.M.

18. 6:12 A.M. to 10:00 P.M.

19. 11:51 A.M. to 3:25 P.M.

20. 12:11 P.M. to 9:48 A.M.

Use mental math to find the elapsed time. Write *a* or *b*.

21. 3:20 A.M. to 11:57 A.M.
  a. 3 h 23 min
  b. 8 h 37 min

22. 1:06 P.M. to 8:32 P.M.
  a. 7 h 26 min
  b. 4 h 34 min

MENTAL MATH

PROBLEM SOLVING APPLICATIONS
Choosing a Strategy

Solve.

23. Walter has three assignments for tonight. He estimates it will take about 1 h 15 min to work on the science project, 40 min to write a composition, and 35 min to finish the math. If Walter wants to finish everything by 10:00 P.M. what is the latest time he can begin?

★ **24.** How many hours did Josie work this week?

DATE	9/16	9/17	9/18	9/19
TIME IN	1:35 P.M.	11:20 A.M.	8:50 A.M.	11:15 A.M.
TIME OUT	4:15 P.M.	2:40 P.M.	10:10 A.M.	6:20 P.M.

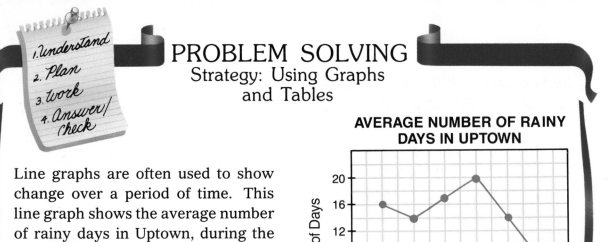

PROBLEM SOLVING
Strategy: Using Graphs and Tables

1. Understand
2. Plan
3. Work
4. Answer/Check

Line graphs are often used to show change over a period of time. This line graph shows the average number of rainy days in Uptown, during the six months listed.

You can see that in March the average number of rainy days is 17.

Sometimes it is easier to solve a problem by organizing the data in a table.

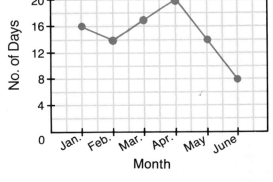

AVERAGE NUMBER OF RAINY DAYS IN UPTOWN

NUMBER OF RAINY DAYS IN UPTOWN						
MONTH	January	February	March	April	May	June
NO. OF DAYS	16	14	17	20	14	8

CLASS EXERCISES

Refer to the line graph or the table to answer. What was the number of rainy days for the month?

1. January   **2.** May   **3.** June   **4.** February   **5.** April

6. From January to June which month had the greatest number of rainy days?

7. Which months had the same number of rainy days?

8. From January to June which month had the fewest rainy days?

9. Did the number of rainy days increase or decrease from April to June?

PRACTICE

Carla is using a line graph to record the changes in weight of her puppy Waldo.

WALDO'S WEIGHT

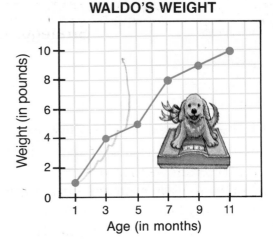

10. How many pounds did Waldo weigh at 9 months old?

11. By how many pounds did Waldo's weight increase over the 10-month period?

12. Organize the data into a table.

Below is a record of the temperature from 5 A.M. until noon.

TIME	5 A.M.	6 A.M.	7 A.M.	8 A.M.	9 A.M.	10 A.M.	11 A.M.	Noon
TEMPERATURE (°C)	0°	0.5°	1°	1°	1.5°	1°	2°	2°

13. What was the temperature at noon?

14. What was the temperature increase from 5 A.M. to 10 A.M.?

★ 15. Use the data in the table to draw a line graph.

CHECKPOINT 2

Estimate. Then subtract.
(pages 44–47)

1. 815
   −142

2. $67.55
   − 49.99

3. 5
   −0.879

Write the answer. *(pages 48–51)*

4. 10 ft 11 in. + 8 ft. 5 in.

Organize the data into a table.
(pages 52–53)

5. Lee's lowest math score was a 45 on the second test. She got 60 points on the first test. On the third and fifth tests, she scored 80. On the fourth test she scored 100.

Extra Practice on page 434

CHAPTER 2 TEST

Answer the question. Write *yes* or *no*. *(pages 34–37)*

1. $t + 6 = 11$ Is 5 a solution?   **2.** $12 - r = 8$ Is 6 a solution?

3. $m + 0 = 9$ Is 9 a solution?   **4.** $34 + 15 = y + 34$ Is 34 a solution?

Estimate. Then write the exact answer. *(pages 38–41)*

5. $253 + 86$ **6.** $3106 + 4911 + 207$ **7.** $\$5.49 + \$43.94 + \$6.57$

Solve. *(pages 42–43)*

8. Lee bought a kite on sale for $28.50. This was a saving of $5.00. How much was the original price?

Estimate. Then write the exact answer. *(pages 44–47)*

9. $1060 - 245$ **10.** $3.06 - 0.217$ **11.** $\$99.48 - \$56.79$

Estimate. Then write the exact answer. *(pages 48–51)*

12.   27 lb 13 oz
        $+$12 lb 10 oz

13.   2 ft 8 in.
        $-$1 ft 10 in.

14.   8 h 42 min
        $+$9 h 17 min

Refer to the line graph. *(pages 52–53)*

15. The school librarian keeps a record of the fines collected. Which month had the highest fine? the lowest?

16. During how many months did the librarian collect $20 or more in fines?

17. Did the librarian ever collect more than $40 during the months shown?

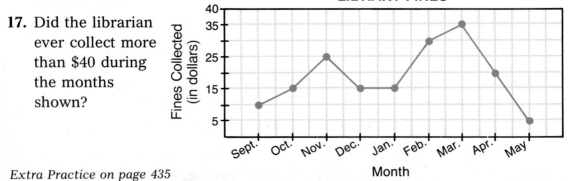

LIBRARY FINES

Extra Practice on page 435

MATHEMATICS and THE LIBRARY

A librarian named Melvil Dewey created the Dewey Decimal System as a way to classify library books. This system uses both whole numbers and decimals.

The chart at right lists the ten subject areas in Dewey's system.

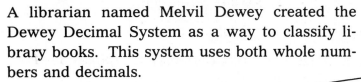

000–099	General Works (references)
100–199	Philosophy-Psychology
200–299	Religion-Mythology
300–399	Social Science
400–499	Philology (words)
500–599	Science
600–699	Useful Arts
700–799	Fine Arts
800–899	Literature
900–999	History

IS THIS CLASSIFIED INFORMATION?

To be more exact within each subject, Dewey used decimals. For example, the classification for cameras is 771.3.

Under which classification numbers would you look to find the books on each of the following subjects?

1. The American Revolution

2. A dictionary of medical terms

3. 18th Century English poetry

4. Early American painters

5. American literature is divided into five categories: Colonial, Post Revolutionary, Mid-1900's, Late 1900's, and 20th Century. Find out how Dewey classified each category.

Enrichment

You are familiar with the 12-hour clock. Did you know that the numbers on the 12-hour clock form a system of numbers used in a special kind of arithmetic?

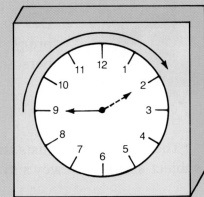

To find the sum of two clock numbers, think of the hour hand moving in a *clockwise* direction. For example, 5 h after 9 o'clock is 2 o'clock. We can express this sum using an equation.

$$9 + 5 \overset{12}{=} 2$$

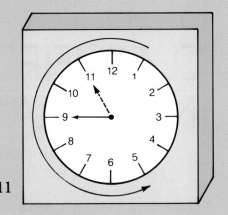

We show that this is a sum of clock numbers on a 12-hour clock by writing 12 over the equals sign.

To find the difference between two clock numbers, think of the hour hand moving in a *counterclockwise* direction. For example, 10 h before 9 o'clock is 11 o'clock. You can write an equation to show the difference.

$$9 - 10 \overset{12}{=} 11$$

Complete.

CLOCK ARITHMETIC

1. 6 h after 2 o'clock is ■ o'clock. $2 + 6 \overset{12}{=} ■$

2. 7 h before 10 o'clock is ■ o'clock. $10 - 7 \overset{12}{=} ■$

3. 8 h before 2 o'clock is ■ o'clock. $2 - 8 \overset{12}{=} ■$

4. 12 h after 5 o'clock is ■ o'clock. $5 + 12 \overset{12}{=} ■$

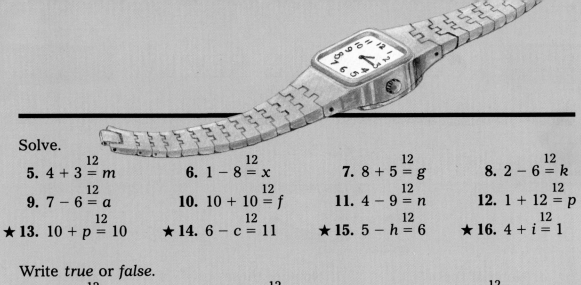

Solve.

5. $4 + 3 \overset{12}{=} m$ 6. $1 - 8 \overset{12}{=} x$ 7. $8 + 5 \overset{12}{=} g$ 8. $2 - 6 \overset{12}{=} k$

9. $7 - 6 \overset{12}{=} a$ 10. $10 + 10 \overset{12}{=} f$ 11. $4 - 9 \overset{12}{=} n$ 12. $1 + 12 \overset{12}{=} p$

★13. $10 + p \overset{12}{=} 10$ ★14. $6 - c \overset{12}{=} 11$ ★15. $5 - h \overset{12}{=} 6$ ★16. $4 + i \overset{12}{=} 1$

Write *true* or *false*.

17. $4 + 8 \overset{12}{=} 8 + 4$ 18. $(2 + 3) + 4 \overset{12}{=} 2 + (3 + 4)$ 19. $(3 + 4) - 5 \overset{12}{=} 3 + (4 - 5)$

On the clocks below sums and differences are found in the same way as on the 12-hour clock, but the arithmetic facts may be different.

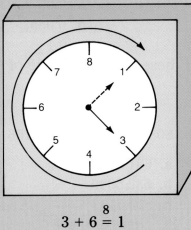

$3 + 6 \overset{8}{=} 1$

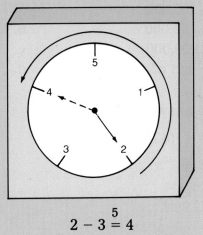

$2 - 3 \overset{5}{=} 4$

Add or subtract.

20. $4 + 5 \overset{8}{=} m$ 21. $6 + 7 \overset{8}{=} p$ 22. $3 - 3 \overset{8}{=} s$ 23. $1 - 6 \overset{8}{=} e$

24. $3 + 8 \overset{8}{=} w$ 25. $5 - 8 \overset{8}{=} b$ 26. $2 + 4 \overset{8}{=} b$ 27. $4 - 1 \overset{8}{=} d$

28. $3 + 4 \overset{5}{=} h$ 29. $4 + 2 \overset{5}{=} r$ 30. $2 - 4 \overset{5}{=} r$ 31. $1 - 3 \overset{5}{=} c$

32. $2 + 5 \overset{5}{=} k$ 33. $2 - 5 \overset{5}{=} b$ 34. $2 + 2 \overset{5}{=} b$ 35. $5 - 1 \overset{5}{=} d$

★36. $4 + t \overset{8}{=} 2$ ★37. $6 + k \overset{8}{=} 3$ ★38. $v + 3 \overset{5}{=} 1$ ★39. $g + 3 \overset{5}{=} 4$

57

CUMULATIVE REVIEW

Choose the correct answer. Write *a*, *b*, *c*, or *d*.

Complete using the correct sign.

1. 65.32 ▮ 65.320

    a. >
    b. <
    c. =
    d. None of these

2. 2.034 ▮ 2.0344

    a. >
    b. <
    c. =
    d. None of these

3. 531.289 ▮ 531.298

    a. >
    b. <
    c. =
    d. None of these

Round.

4. 3,462,058 to the nearest ten-thousand

    a. 3,400,000
    b. 3,462,000
    c. 3,000,000
    d. None of these

5. 2.359 to the nearest tenth

    a. 2.459
    b. 2.4
    c. 2.3
    d. None of these

6. 0.0548 to the nearest hundredth

    a. 0.05
    b. 0.055
    c. 0.1
    d. None of these

Find the answer.

7. 2487 + 1435 + 6982

    a. 9794
    b. 10,904
    c. 12,904
    d. None of these

8. 608.7 + 23.6589 + 0.156

    a. 631.5149
    b. 632.5049
    c. 622.5149
    d. None of these

Which is the best estimate?

9. 7942
  +4167

    a. 1000
    b. 1100
    c. 1200
    d. 12,000

10. 37,561
  +58,021

    a. 9000
    b. 100,000
    c. 900,000
    d. 10,000

11. 32.896
  + 9.633

    a. 30
    b. 40
    c. 50
    d. 60

12. 2.065
  +4.589

    a. 7
    b. 8
    c. 10
    d. 11

Answer the question.

13. Sue left the aquarium at 5:15 P.M. and traveled 20 mi. Which information is needed to figure out when she arrived home?

a. Her time of departure   **b.** The gas mileage   **c.** Her working hours   **d.** None of these

Find the answer.

14. $45,001 - 38,657$

    a. 6354
    b. 7354
    c. 6344
    d. None of these

15. $700.12 - 35.64$

    a. 664.48
    b. 644.58
    c. 764.48
    d. None of these

16. $6.140 - 0.377$

    a. 5.773
    b. 6.763
    c. 6.773
    d. None of these

Which is the best estimate?

17. $\begin{array}{r} 6504 \\ -3389 \\ \hline \end{array}$

    a. 4000
    b. 10,000
    c. 9000
    d. 6000

18. $\begin{array}{r} \$350.20 \\ -109.75 \\ \hline \end{array}$

    a. $400
    b. $300
    c. $100
    d. $500

19. $\begin{array}{r} 68.1 \\ -31.8 \\ \hline \end{array}$

    a. 100
    b. 50
    c. 40
    d. 90

20. $\begin{array}{r} 8.81 \\ -1.009 \\ \hline \end{array}$

    a. 0
    b. 7
    c. 8
    d. 1

LANGUAGE and VOCABULARY REVIEW

Write *true* or *false*. If *false*, write the correct statement by replacing the underlined word.

1. In $r + 17 = 23$, r is a <u>variable</u>.

2. The <u>associative</u> property states that changing the grouping of the addends does not change the sum.

3. In $y - 3 = 11$, 14 is a <u>variable</u>.

4. An <u>elapsed</u> time is the amount of time that passes between the start and the end of an event.

5. The <u>zero</u> property states that the sum of zero and any other number is that number.

COMPUTER SYSTEMS AND MEMORY

COMPUTER LITERACY

A computer system is made up of software and hardware.
Software consists of programs (instructions) that make the computer do a process. **Hardware** consists of the machine parts of the computer. They include input, process, output, and memory devices.

Memory devices are used to store data. There are two types:

Primary

Programs are stored internally on chips. This storage is both temporary (RAM) and permanent (ROM).

Secondary

Programs can be stored externally on disks and tapes. This storage can be permanent.

Memory is measured by the number of characters that can be stored. You use K or M to show the size of memory.

K = 1024 characters
8K = 8192 characters

M = 1,048,576 characters
3M = 3,145,728 characters

1. Characters are letters, numbers, symbols, and spaces. How many characters are in the first line of this page?

2. What kind of memory can be stored in a drawer or a school bag?

Estimate to compare memory sizes. Write < or > to complete.

3. M ▨ K   4. 32K ▨ 16M

5. 64M ▨ 238K

60

3

If you keep removing and bagging 50 oranges at a time from a pile of 200 oranges, how many bags will you fill? Will you have any oranges left over?

MULTIPLICATION AND DIVISION OF WHOLE NUMBERS AND DECIMALS

EQUATIONS: MULTIPLICATION AND DIVISION

To solve the equation, $5 \times y = 35$, find a value for y that will make a true statement. You can test different values for y.

$$5 \times y = 35$$

Replace y with 6:	$5 \times 6 = 35$	False
Replace y with 7:	$5 \times 7 = 35$	True

The solution of the equation $5 \times y = 35$ is 7.

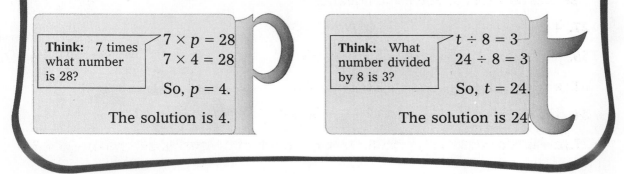 You can solve simple multiplication and division equations mentally by thinking of number facts.

Think: 7 times what number is 28?

$7 \times p = 28$
$7 \times 4 = 28$

So, $p = 4$.

The solution is 4.

Think: What number divided by 8 is 3?

$t \div 8 = 3$
$24 \div 8 = 3$

So, $t = 24$.

The solution is 24.

CLASS EXERCISES

Write *true* or *false*.

1. $7 \times 3 = 21$

2. $32 \div 4 = 8$

3. $7 \times 9 = 72$

4. $45 \div 5 = 8$

5. $36 \div 3 = 12$

6. $6 \times 5 = 30$

Is the underlined number a solution of the given equation? Write *yes* or *no*.

7. $n \times 3 = 18$
$\underline{6} \times 3 = 18$

8. $2 \times n = 12$
$2 \times \underline{7} = 12$

9. $10 \div k = 5$
$10 \div \underline{5} = 5$

10. $w \div 5 = 3$
$\underline{20} \div 5 = 3$

11. $c \times 6 = 48$
$\underline{7} \times 6 = 48$

12. $56 \div n = 7$
$56 \div \underline{8} = 7$

PRACTICE

Is 3 a solution of the equation? Write *yes* or *no*.

13. $5 \times a = 15$

14. $b \times 6 = 21$

15. $9 \times c = 27$

16. $30 \div d = 10$

17. $e \div 3 = 0$

18. $21 \div f = 7$

Answer the question. Write *yes* or *no*.

19. $7 \times q = 63$ Is 9 a solution?

20. $a \times 3 = 24$ Is 9 a solution?

21. $b \div 2 = 6$ Is 3 a solution?

22. $15 \div e = 3$ Is 5 a solution?

23. $16 \div f = 4$ Is 4 a solution?

24. $4 \times c = 0$ Is 1 a solution?

★**25.** $13 \times m = 52$ Is 4 a solution?

★**26.** $51 \div k = 17$ Is 3 a solution?

Use mental math to solve the equation.

27. $4 \times 5 = h$

28. $9 \times k = 36$

29. $j \div 2 = 2$

30. $25 \div r = 5$

31. $z \times 4 = 32$

32. $t \div 1 = 3$

33. $6 \times m = 42$

★**34.** $8 \times p = 80$

★**35.** $r \times 4 = 100$

★**36.** $45 \div x = 15$

★**37.** $a + a + a = 12$

★**38.** $18 - c - c = 0$

★**39.** $b + b + b + b = 8$

MENTAL MATH

PROBLEM SOLVING APPLICATIONS
Writing Equations

Choose the equation that best describes the problem.
Write *a*, *b*, or *c*.

40. A number divided by 7 equals 7.
   a. $7 \div n = 7$
   b. $n \div 7 = 7$
   c. $n = 7 \div 7$

41. A number less 6 is 9.
   a. $n = 9 - 6$
   b. $9 - n = 6$
   c. $n - 6 = 9$

42. A number multiplied by 2 gives a product of 18.
   a. $2 \times 18 = n$
   b. $2 \times n = 18$
   c. $n \times 2 = 18 \times 2$

★**43.** At $3 an hour for a number of hours, you earned $12.
   a. $n \times 3 = 12$
   b. $n = 36$
   c. $n + 3 = 12$

PROPERTIES OF MULTIPLICATION

Here are some properties of multiplication. Remember that we do operations in parentheses first.

Commutative Property	**Associative Property**
Changing the order of the factors does not change the product. $7 \times 2 = 14 \qquad 2 \times 7 = 14$ so, $7 \times 2 = 2 \times 7$ In general: $a \times b = b \times a$	Changing the grouping of the factors does not change the product. $(3 \times 2) \times 4 = 24 \qquad 3 \times (2 \times 4) = 24$ so, $(3 \times 2) \times 4 = 3 \times (2 \times 4)$ In general: $(a \times b) \times c = a \times (b \times c)$
Identity Property	**Zero Property**
The product of *one* and any other number is that number. $1 \times 9 = 9 \qquad 9 \times 1 = 9$ In general: $a \times 1 = a$ and $1 \times a = a$	The product of *zero* and any other number is zero. $0 \times 8 = 0 \qquad 8 \times 0 = 0$ In general: $a \times 0 = 0$ and $0 \times a = 0$

Distributive Property
The product of a factor and a sum is equal to the sum of the products. $3 \times (1 + 5) = 3 \times 6 = 18 \qquad (3 \times 1) + (3 \times 5) = 3 + 15 = 18$ so, $3 \times (1 + 5) = (3 \times 1) + (3 \times 5)$ In general: $a \times (b + c) = (a \times b) + (a \times c)$

M The properties can help you multiply mentally.

To multiply: $2 \times 7 \times 5$ To multiply: 5×28
Think: $10 \times 7 = 70$ **Think:** $5 \times (20 + 8) = (5 \times 20) + (5 \times 8)$
$= 100 + 40 = 140$

CLASS EXERCISES

Complete. Then name the property illustrated.

1. $6 \times 2 = \blacksquare$
    $2 \times 6 = \blacksquare$

2. $(8 \times 4) \times 3 = \blacksquare \times 3 = \blacksquare$
    $8 \times (4 \times 3) = 8 \times \blacksquare = \blacksquare$

3. $0 \times 4 = \blacksquare$
    $4 \times 0 = \blacksquare$

4. $2 \times (4 + 3) = 2 \times \blacksquare = \blacksquare$
    $(2 \times 4) + (2 \times 3) = \blacksquare + \blacksquare = \blacksquare$

PRACTICE

Use a property to solve. Name the property.

5. $b \times 1 = 7$

6. $n \times 8 = 0$

7. $k \times 4 = 4 \times 8$

8. $4 \times (5 + 3) = (4 \times d) + (4 \times 3)$

9. $(5 \times 3) + (5 \times 1) = 5 \times (3 + g)$

10. $9 \times h = 6 \times 9$

11. $(4 \times 2) \times 3 = p \times (2 \times 3)$

12. $683 \times f = 0$

13. $17 \times m = 2 \times 17$

14. $(2 \times 1) \times 4 = c \times (1 \times 4)$

★ **15.** $8 \times (d + 5) = 32 + 40$

★ **16.** $g \times (4 \times 5) = 12 \times 5$

Use mental math to find the product.

17. $5 \times 9 \times 2$

18. $4 \times 7 \times 5$

19. $25 \times 4 \times 2$

20. 5×46

21. 8×54

22. 6×13

★ **23.** $8 \times 3 \times 5$

★ **24.** 6×72

★ **25.** 8×35

MENTAL MATH

PROBLEM SOLVING APPLICATIONS
Using Properties

Solve.

26. The Country Pottery makes 2 shipments of 12 boxes each of pots every week. Each box contains 50 pots. What is the total?

27. Roberto Carmona drives 8 mi to the train station and then rides 13 mi to work. How many miles does he travel in a round trip?

★ **28.** Write a real-life situation that illustrates the fact $100 \times 0 = 0$.

ORDER OF OPERATIONS

Linda and Keo are using two different calculators to find the answer for $7 + 3 \times 10$. Linda's calculator shows $\exists \sqcap$. Keo's shows $|\square\square$. Which answer is correct?

To agree on answers, we must all follow the same rules for the order of operations:

---

1. When there are parentheses, or other grouping symbols, do all operations within them first.
2. Then do all multiplications and divisions in order from left to right.
3. Then do all additions and subtractions in order from left to right.

Following the rules above:

$$7 + 3 \times 10 = 7 + 30 = 37$$

7 plus the product of 3 and 10 is 37.

Linda's calculator follows the rules for the order of operations. To get the correct answer to $7 + 3 \times 10$ on Keo's calculator, he can find 3×10 first, then add 7.

Some calculators have parentheses keys to help you tell the calculator which operations to do first. **Think:** How can you place parentheses in $7 + 3 \times 10$ so that the answer is 100?

CLASS EXERCISES

Follow the order of operations. Name the operation you would do first to get the correct answer.

1. $6 + 2 \times 5$ **2.** $(6 + 2) \times 5$ **3.** $(12 - 6) \div 3$

4. $4 \times 3 + 8$ **5.** $36 - 12 \div 6$ **6.** $7 \times (8 + 5)$

7. $24 \div 3 + 5 \times 2$ **8.** $24 \div (3 + 5) \times 2$ **9.** $24 \div 3 + (5 \times 2)$

PRACTICE

Write the answer in simplest form.

10. $2 + 1 \times 3$ **11.** $(5 - 1) \div 2$ **12.** $3 \times 3 + 4 - 2$

13. $5 + 2 + 2 \times 3$ **14.** $6 + 2 \times 1 + 4$ **15.** $(8 - 1) \times (7 + 1)$

16. $3 + 2 \times 8 - 4 \times 2$ **17.** $8 \div (2 + 2) - 1$ **18.** $3 \times (4 + 2) - 2 \times 5$

19. $9 \times (2 + 6 - 4) \div 2$ **20.** $(24 + 18) \div 6$ **21.** $9 \times 4 \div 4 + 2$

22. $(3 \times 7 + 3) \div 3$ **23.** $40 \div 5 + 3 - 11$ **24.** $9 \times 2 + 3 + 4 - 21$

25. $12 + 3 \times 5$ **26.** $2 \times (4 + 1) - 1$ **27.** $7 \times 1 \times 5 - 4 \div 2$

28. $3 \times 2 + 3 \times 4$ **29.** $8 \times (5 - 3) + 27$ **30.** $3 + 4 \times (2 + 4) \div 8$

31. $(7 - 4) \times 6 + 2$ **32.** $15 \div 5 + 3 \times 6$ **33.** $17 - 3 \times 2 + (8 \div 2)$

★**34.** $(19 + 84 \div 4 \times 8 - 11) \div 4$ ★**35.** $38 - 25 \div (43 - 18) + 25$

Suppose your calculator does not follow our rules for the order of operations. Match the exercise with the correct way to enter it into the calculator. Write the correct letter.

CALCULATOR

36. $4 + 3 \times 2$ **A.** 2 ⊞ 4 ⊠ 3

37. $(3 + 2) \times 4$ **B.** 3 ⊠ 2 ⊞ 4

38. $3 \times (2 + 4)$ **C.** 3 ⊞ 2 ⊠ 4

PROBLEM SOLVING APPLICATIONS
Open-Ended Problems

Match the mathematical example with the words that describe it. Write the correct letter(s). There may be more than one answer.

39. $3 \times 9 + 2$ **A.** The sum when 9×2 is added to 3.

40. $3 \times (9 + 2)$ **B.** The product when $9 + 2$ is multiplied by 3.
     C. Three times nine, plus two.

41. $3 + 9 \times 2$ **D.** The sum of 9 and 2, multiplied by 3.

★**42.** Which of the mathematical examples in Exercises 39–41 is a way to write the cost of three $9 tickets and three $2 tickets?

MULTIPLICATION OF WHOLE NUMBERS

The decorating committee used 236 bunches of flowers for a parade float. If they put 18 flowers in each bunch, how many flowers did they use in all?

First do a quick mental estimate of the product. Round each factor to its greatest place value and multiply. An estimate helps you check the reasonableness of your answer.

$$
\begin{array}{c}
236 \\
\times 18
\end{array}
\Rightarrow
\begin{array}{c}
200 \\
\times 20 \\
\hline
4000
\end{array}
$$

The estimate is 4000.

To find the exact product, first multiply 236 by 8. Next multiply 236 by 10. Then add the two products. Compare the exact product with the estimate. The product is close to the estimate.

$$
\begin{array}{c}
236 \\
\times\,18 \\
\hline
1888
\end{array}
\Rightarrow
\begin{array}{c}
236 \\
\times 18 \\
\hline
1888 \\
2360
\end{array}
\Rightarrow
\begin{array}{c}
236 \\
\times 18 \\
\hline
1888 \\
2360 \\
\hline
4248
\end{array}
$$

They used a total of 4248 flowers.

When you use a calculator to multiply, check the reasonableness of your answer.

879 ⊠ 28 ▤

Think: $900 \times 30 = 27,000$
Will the exact product be greater or less than 27,000?

CLASS EXERCISES

Multiply.

1.
$$
\begin{array}{c} 64 \\ \times 3 \end{array}
\Rightarrow
\begin{array}{c} 64 \\ \times 20 \end{array}
$$

2.
$$
\begin{array}{c} 178 \\ \times 6 \end{array}
\Rightarrow
\begin{array}{c} 178 \\ \times 50 \end{array}
$$

3.
$$
\begin{array}{c} 256 \\ \times 2 \end{array}
\Rightarrow
\begin{array}{c} 256 \\ \times 40 \end{array}
\Rightarrow
\begin{array}{c} 256 \\ \times 300 \end{array}
$$

Will the exact product be more than 2400? Write *yes* or *no*.

4. 33×82 **5.** 80×27 **6.** 79×29 **7.** 43×64

8. Think: What digit will always be in the ones' place in the final product when you multiply by tens?

PRACTICE

Estimate. Then choose the most reasonable answer. Write *a*, *b*, or *c*.

9. 323×51 **a.** 1615   **b.** 16,473   **c.** 1632

10. 2582×38 **a.** 9804   **b.** 2620   **c.** 98,116

11. 1887×409 **a.** 771,783   **b.** 76,483   **c.** 9246.3

Estimate. Then multiply.

12.	13.	14.	15.	16.
34	172	237	724	827
$\times 2$	$\times 9$	$\times 7$	$\times 46$	$\times 91$

17.	18.	19.	20.	21.
2792	54,072	87,568	2537	96,884
$\times 59$	$\times 28$	$\times 37$	$\times 126$	$\times 306$

The final product is wrong. Locate where each error was made. A calculator may be helpful.

22.	23.	24.	★ 25.
358	702	917	394
$\times 16$	$\times 34$	$\times 27$	$\times 157$
2158	2808	6429	2138
3580	2160	18240	15700
5738	4968	14,669	39400
			57,238

CALCULATOR

PROBLEM SOLVING APPLICATIONS
Choosing the Operation

Solve.

26. Last year 50,998 flowers were bought for the parade. This year 63,872 flowers were bought. How many more were bought this year?

27. A stadium has 235 seats in each section. There are 15 sections. How many seats are there in all?

★ 28. The florist's helper makes one dozen corsages in 1 h 20 min. If he starts working at 9:30 A.M. on an order for 2 dozen corsages, at about what time will the order be finished?

MULTIPLICATION OF DECIMALS

To multiply 2.31 by 1.4, multiply as you do with whole numbers. Then place the decimal point in the final product according to this rule:

The number of decimal places in the final product is the sum of the number of decimal places in the factors.

$$
\begin{array}{r}
2.31 \longleftarrow \text{2 decimal places} \\
\times 1.4 \longleftarrow \text{1 decimal place} \\
\hline
924 \\
2310 \\
\hline
3.234 \longleftarrow \text{3 decimal places}
\end{array}
$$

A quick estimate shows you that the product is about 1×2, or 2. So the placement of the decimal point is correct.

Sometimes it is necessary to write zeros in the product in order to place the decimal point correctly.

$$
\begin{array}{r}
0.004 \longleftarrow \text{3 decimal places} \\
\times 0.02 \longleftarrow \text{2 decimal places} \\
\hline
0.00008 \longleftarrow \text{5 decimal places}
\end{array}
\qquad
\begin{array}{r}
0.0013 \longleftarrow \text{4 decimal places} \\
\times 0.07 \longleftarrow \text{2 decimal places} \\
\hline
0.000091 \longleftarrow \text{6 decimal places}
\end{array}
$$

CLASS EXERCISES

Write the product with the decimal point in the correct place.

1.	**2.**	**3.**	**4.**	**5.**	**6.**
3.6	0.36	0.036	5.3	0.53	0.053
$\times 4$	$\times 4$	$\times 4$	$\times 2.7$	$\times 2.7$	$\times 2.7$
144	144	144	1431	1431	1431

Choose the best estimate. Write a, b, or c.

7. 2.62×20.416
    a. 0.00006   **b.** 60,000   **c.** 60

8. 22.95×4.1
    a. 80   **b.** 0.08   **c.** 8000

9. 575×3.782
    a. 24   **b.** 0.024   **c.** 2400

10. 99.56×8.735
    a. 9   **b.** 900   **c.** 9000

11. 429×0.62
    a. 24,000   **b.** 240   **c.** 2400

12. 78.3×11.4
    a. 800   **b.** 8000   **c.** 80,000

PRACTICE

Multiply. Estimate to check.

13. 0.04
×8

14. 1.36
×4

15. 2.08
×7

16. 0.007
×2

17. 0.043
×5

18. $12.30
× 0.6

19. 6.208
×4.2

20. 1.64
×1.20

21. 9.81
×0.4

22. 20.123
×0.45

23. 0.04
×0.2

24. $1.20
×0.7

25. 0.0042
×0.061

26. 0.39
×0.008

27. 0.086
×3.9

28. 38.6 × 1.5

29. 0.6 × 2.4

30. 1.34 × 8.5

31. 48 × 0.098

32. 55.07 × 6.3

33. 6.45 × 4.97

★ **34.** 3.2 × 0.8 × 1.6

★ **35.** 2.51 × 1.8 × 6

Complete.

36. 750,083 = (7 × ▮) + (5 × ▮) + (8 × ▮) + (3 × 1)

37. 309,470 = (3 × ▮) + (9 × ▮) + (4 × ▮) + (7 × ▮)

PROBLEM SOLVING APPLICATIONS
Mental Math or Calculator

Tell whether you would choose mental math or a calculator to solve. Then solve.

38. A jet flew at 820.3 km/h for 6.5 h. How far did the jet travel during that time?

★ **39.** A nickel is 0.2 cm thick. How high will a stack of nickels worth $2 be?

★ **40.** The cost of electricity (kW·h) in John's town is computed at the following rate:

　　$2.25 for the first 20 kW·h
　　6.913¢ per kW·h for the next 50 kW·h
　　5.821¢ per kW·h for the next 100 kW·h

To the nearest cent, what is the cost if John uses a total of 165 kW·h?

EXPONENTS AND PLACE VALUE

You can express $2 \times 2 \times 2$ as 2^3. The raised numeral, 3, shows the number of times 2 is used as a factor. The number 2 is the **base.** The numeral 3 is the **exponent.**

We read 2^3 as *2 to the third power,* or *2 cubed.* We read 5^2 as *5 to the second power,* or *5 squared.*

A number with an exponent of 1 is the number itself.

$5^1 = 5$
$976^1 = 976$

Any number, except 0, with an exponent of 0 is 1.

$7^0 = 1$
$123^0 = 1$

Our place value system is based on powers of 10. The chart at the right lists the first five powers of 10. Notice that the exponent is equal to the number of zeros in the product.

$$
\begin{aligned}
10^0 &= & 1 \\
10^1 &= 10 & = 10 \\
10^2 &= 10 \times 10 & = 100 \\
10^3 &= 10 \times 10 \times 10 & = 1000 \\
10^4 &= 10 \times 10 \times 10 \times 10 & = 10{,}000
\end{aligned}
$$

Exponents can be used to write numbers in expanded form.

$$849 = 800 + 40 + 9$$
$$\text{or } (8 \times 100) + (4 \times 10) + (9 \times 1)$$
$$\text{or } (8 \times 10^2) + (4 \times 10^1) + (9 \times 10^0)$$

Some scientific calculators have an exponent key. Other calculators have a constant feature. For example, to find 9^5 press 9, ⊠, then the ⊟ key four times.

9 ⊠ ⊟ ⊟ ⊟ ⊟ 59049

CLASS EXERCISES

Complete.

1. $3 \times 3 = 3^{\blacksquare}$

2. $7 \times 7 \times 7 = 7^{\blacksquare}$

3. $2 \times 2 \times 2 \times 2 \times 2 = 2^{\blacksquare}$

4. $5 \times 5 \times 5 = 5^{\blacksquare}$

5. $12 \times 12 \times 12 = 12^{\blacksquare}$

6. $8 \times 8 \times 8 \times 8 \times 8 \times 8 \times 8 = 8^{\blacksquare}$

7. $81 = 9 \times 9 = 9^{\blacksquare}$

8. $64 = 4 \times 4 \times 4 = 4^{\blacksquare}$

9. $625 = 5 \times 5 \times 5 \times 5 = 5^{\blacksquare}$

Write the number using exponents.

10. 6×6 **11.** $2 \times 2 \times 2$ **12.** $4 \times 4 \times 4 \times 4$

13. $10 \times 10 \times 10 \times 10$ **14.** $20 \times 20 \times 20$ **15.** $3 \times 3 \times 3 \times 3$

Write the product.

16. 2^2 **17.** 4^2 **18.** 2^4 **19.** 1^3 **20.** 9^1 **21.** 2^5

22. 4^3 **23.** 3^4 **24.** 5^3 **25.** 6^3 **26.** 8^2 **27.** 7^3

28. 68^1 **29.** 78^0 **30.** 10^0 **31.** 10^5 **32.** 10^6 **33.** 10^7

Write in expanded form using exponents.

34. 748 **35.** 8315 **36.** 37,218 **37.** 465,297

38. 40,020 **39.** 80,070 **40.** 5,000,800 **41.** 86,000,000

Complete.

42. $\blacksquare^2 = 144$ **43.** $5^3 = \blacksquare$ **44.** $\blacksquare^3 = 1000$

★ **45.** $13^2 = \blacksquare$ ★ **46.** $\blacksquare^5 = 243$ ★ **47.** $30^3 = \blacksquare$

CALCULATOR

CHECKPOINT 1

Solve the equation. *(pages 62–65)*

1. $7 \times a = 49$ **2.** $24 \div b = 8$

3. $c \times 16 = 16$ **4.** $39 \times 0 = d$

5. $9 \times (6 + 2) = (9 \times 6) + (n \times 2)$

Write the answer in simplest form.
(pages 66–67)

6. $7 + 2 \times 3$ **7.** $(8 + 7) \times 2$

Multiply. *(pages 68–71)*

8. 305
   $\times 8$

9. 2754
   $\times 43$

10. 2360
   $\times 106$

11. 5.27
   $\times 600$

12. 0.891
   $\times 4.3$

13. 2.782
   $\times 0.031$

Write the product. *(pages 72–73)*

14. 2^4 **15.** 7^2 **16.** 10^4

Extra Practice on page 436

PROBLEM SOLVING
Strategy: Multi-Step Problems

1. Understand
2. Plan
3. Work
4. Answer / Check

Maria worked 45 h at the racquetball club this week. She earned $3.90 an hour for the first 40 h and double her hourly rate for overtime. How much money did she earn this week?

To solve this problem, you need to solve several simpler problems.

Monday
9 hours

Tuesday
7 hours

Wednesday
8 hours

How much does Maria earn in the first 40 h?	How many hours of overtime did Maria work?	What is Maria's overtime rate?
$3.90 × 40 $156.00	45 −40 5	$3.90 ×2 $7.80

How much does Maria earn in 5 h of overtime?

$7.80
× 5
$39.00

How much is the total amount earned?

$156.00 ⟵ first 40 h
+39.00 ⟵ 5 h of overtime
$195.00 ⟵ total earned

Maria earned $195.00 this week.

CLASS EXERCISES

Use the facts to answer the questions.

FACTS: You earn $4 an hour Mondays through Fridays, and double on Sundays. You worked 25 h from Monday through Friday. You worked 9 h on Sunday.

1. How much do you earn the first 25 h?

2. How much are you paid for each hour on Sunday?

3. How much do you earn in 9 h on Sunday?

4. How much do you earn in all for the week?

PRACTICE

Solve.

5. Ina worked 6.25 h on Monday, 5.5 h on Wednesday, and 4.75 h on Friday. She earns $4.20 an hour. How much did she earn in all?

6. At the Flower Shoppe, you can buy tulip bulbs in packages of three for $4.98, or packages of six for $8.94. Which is the greater price per bulb? How much greater?

7. Tina and a friend had lunch at Food Time. They had a tuna sandwich for $1.65, a chicken sandwich for $1.85, and two glasses of milk at $.60 each. The tax and tip was $1.00. If Tina paid with a $10 bill, how much change did she have after paying the bill?

8. Michael's bank statement showed: deposit $60, withdrawal $24, deposit $50, withdrawal $98, deposit $25, withdrawal $35, deposit $57. How much more money did Michael deposit than he withdrew?

9. It takes 2 h of labor at $5.65 per hour and $15.80 in materials to make a doghouse. What should you charge in order to make a $9 profit?

10. Jeff works at a music store after school. He works 2.5 h on Mondays, 3 h on Wednesdays, 4.5 h on Fridays, and 5 h on Saturdays. He earns $4.20 per hour. If he begins to save his earnings this week, how many weeks will he have to save in order to buy a $252 violin?

11. Section C tickets to a baseball game cost $5.75. Section B tickets cost $6.35. A total of 5200 section C tickets and 2450 section B tickets were sold. If $12,000 of the ticket money was donated to charity how much money was left?

★ 12. The daily rental is $24 for a sailboat, $12 for a rowboat, and $18 for a canoe. The rental receipts for today showed $456 for sailboats, $156 for rowboats, and $414 for canoes. How many boats were rented?

WHOLE NUMBER DIVISION

Each stage of a division has the same four steps. You repeat these steps as often as necessary to complete the division. The remainder at each stage should be less than the divisor. If it's not, increase your estimate. Let's divide 2750 by 182.

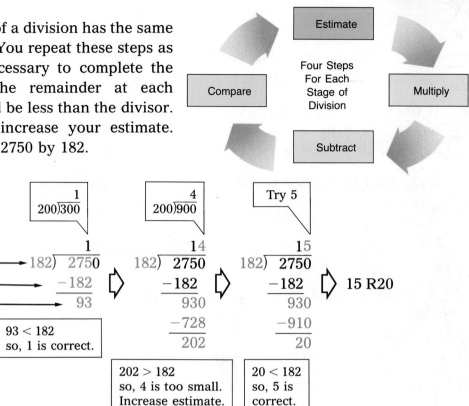

Estimate.

$$\begin{array}{r}1\\200\overline{)300}\end{array}$$

$$\begin{array}{r}4\\200\overline{)900}\end{array}$$

Try 5

Multiply. ⟶

$$\begin{array}{r}1\\182\overline{)\ 2750}\\-182\\\hline 93\end{array}$$

Subtract. ⟶

Compare. ⟶

93 < 182
so, 1 is correct.

$$\begin{array}{r}14\\182\overline{)\ 2750}\\-182\\\hline 930\\-728\\\hline 202\end{array}$$

202 > 182
so, 4 is too small.
Increase estimate.

$$\begin{array}{r}15\\182\overline{)\ 2750}\\-182\\\hline 930\\-910\\\hline 20\end{array}$$

⟹ 15 R20

20 < 182
so, 5 is correct.

To check the division, multiply the quotient 15 by the divisor 182. Then add the remainder. The answer should equal the dividend, 2750.

$$182 \times 15 + 20 = 2750$$

M Dividing by a number less than 10 is easy to do mentally. In the example at the right, the little numbers show the remainders that you have after each mental subtraction.

$$\begin{array}{r}1\ 2\ 3\ \text{R3}\\7\overline{)8_16_24}\end{array}$$

CLASS EXERCISES

Divide.

1. $6\overline{)54}$ $6\overline{)540}$ $6\overline{)542}$

2. $9\overline{)89}$ $9\overline{)890}$ $9\overline{)8943}$

3. $50\overline{)512}$ $48\overline{)512}$ $48\overline{)5120}$

4. $20\overline{)2237}$ $23\overline{)2237}$ $23\overline{)2337}$

PRACTICE

Divide and check.

5. $29\overline{)362}$ 6. $28\overline{)947}$ 7. $57\overline{)738}$ 8. $38\overline{)809}$

9. $27\overline{)1503}$ 10. $48\overline{)3576}$ 11. $24\overline{)7826}$ 12. $45\overline{)3481}$

13. $278\overline{)658}$ 14. $278\overline{)910}$ 15. $342\overline{)4723}$ 16. $518\overline{)7645}$

Use mental math to divide.

MENTAL MATH

17. $7\overline{)649}$ 18. $9\overline{)395}$ 19. $4\overline{)383}$

20. $8\overline{)933}$ 21. $5\overline{)436}$ 22. $3\overline{)278}$

What is $a \div b$? Tell whether it is easier to use mental math or
a calculator to divide. Then divide.

23. $a = 30{,}225$
    $b = 5$

24. $a = 80{,}668$
    $b = 172$

25. $a = 97{,}632$
    $b = 452$

PROBLEM SOLVING APPLICATIONS
Mental Math or Calculator

Tell whether you would choose mental math or a calculator to
solve. Then solve.

26. Grades 7–9 sold magazine subscriptions for a school fund-
raiser. The total profit was $588.
If the grades divide the profit
evenly, how much will each
grade receive?

27. In a city school, there are 9856
students and 352 teachers. The
students are to be divided equally
among the teachers for homeroom. How many students will be
assigned to each homeroom?

28. A total of 5637 vehicles cross the
intersection in front of Jefferson
High School in a seven-day period. At this rate, about how
many vehicles will cross the
intersection in one year?

★ 29. Pencils are packaged 12 to a box.
A carton holds 9 boxes. How
many cartons are needed to pack
1944 pencils?

DIVISION OF DECIMALS BY WHOLE NUMBERS

For a 12.5 km race, drivers complete 5 laps around an automobile track. How long is one lap?

To divide a decimal by a whole number, first place the decimal point in the quotient directly above the decimal point in the dividend. Then divide as you do with whole numbers. One lap is 2.5 km.

$$\begin{array}{r} 2.5 \\ 5\overline{)12.5} \\ -10 \\ \hline 25 \\ -25 \\ \hline 0 \end{array}$$

Sometimes you need to write zeros in a quotient.

$$\begin{array}{r} 0.073 \\ 6\overline{)0.438} \\ -42 \\ \hline 18 \\ -18 \\ \hline 0 \end{array} \qquad \begin{array}{r} 0.003 \\ 52\overline{)0.156} \\ -156 \\ \hline 0 \end{array}$$

In a division with a remainder, you may round the quotient. To round the quotient, divide to one decimal place to the right of the place to which you are rounding. In the example below, we divide to the thousandths' place by annexing zeros in the dividend. To the nearest hundredth, the quotient is 0.83.

$$7.5 \div 9 \longrightarrow \begin{array}{r} 0.833 \\ 9\overline{)7.500} \end{array}$$

CLASS EXERCISES

Write the quotient.

1. $3\overline{)27}$ $3\overline{)2.7}$ $3\overline{)0.27}$

2. $61\overline{)244}$ $61\overline{)24.4}$ $61\overline{)2.44}$

3. $24\overline{)312}$ $24\overline{)31.2}$ $24\overline{)0.312}$

4. $57\overline{)456}$ $57\overline{)4.56}$ $57\overline{)0.456}$

Place the decimal point and any zeros needed in the quotient.

5. $\begin{array}{r} 8 \\ 2\overline{)1.6} \end{array}$
6. $\begin{array}{r} 12 \\ 7\overline{)0.084} \end{array}$
7. $\begin{array}{r} 7 \\ 7\overline{)0.049} \end{array}$
8. $\begin{array}{r} 1 \\ 9\overline{)0.009} \end{array}$

PRACTICE

Divide and check.

9. $3\overline{)1.5}$ **10.** $6\overline{)0.72}$ **11.** $5\overline{)2.55}$ **12.** $2\overline{)0.632}$ **13.** $5\overline{)0.665}$

14. $7\overline{)6.216}$ **15.** $4\overline{)9.132}$ **16.** $9\overline{)81.54}$ **17.** $5\overline{)23.645}$ **18.** $8\overline{)8.48}$

19. $29\overline{)31.03}$ **20.** $75\overline{)45.75}$ **21.** $52\overline{)4.68}$ **22.** $21\overline{)48.3}$ **23.** $37\overline{)0.962}$

24. $56\overline{)1.176}$ **25.** $47\overline{)1.457}$ **26.** $49\overline{)11.27}$ **27.** $65\overline{)162.5}$ **28.** $63\overline{)0.441}$

29. $344\overline{)364.64}$ **30.** $5216\overline{)41.728}$ **31.** $109\overline{)1528.18}$ **32.** $238\overline{)285.6}$

Divide. Round to the hundredths' place.

33. $23.6 \div 3$ **34.** $85.26 \div 8$ **35.** $1.3 \div 6$ **36.** $17.7 \div 9$

Divide. Round to the thousandths' place.

37. $24.1 \div 7$ **38.** $32.7 \div 7$ **39.** $69.31 \div 4$ **40.** $40 \div 7$

41. $5 \div 7$ **42.** $51.4 \div 12$ **43.** $45 \div 32$ **44.** $187.3 \div 24$

45. Think: When the quotient is rounded, will the product of the quotient and the divisor equal the dividend? Explain.

PROBLEM SOLVING APPLICATIONS
Consumer Topics

Solve.

46. Daphne buys 4 new radial tires. The total cost is $207.60. How much does each tire cost?

47. Jack drove 1295.6 mi last month on 41 gal of gasoline. How many miles to the gallon did he get?

48. At an average rate of 55 km/h, how long, to the nearest tenth of an hour, will it take to drive 115 km?

49. A job is advertised at a yearly salary of $17,983. If there are 245 working days in a year and 7 h in a working day, what is the hourly pay to the nearest cent?

4 for
$207.60

MULTIPLICATION AND DIVISION BY POWERS OF TEN

Multiplication and division by powers of 10 follow a pattern.

$$7.23 \times 10 = 72.3 \qquad 42.7 \div 10 = 4.27$$

$$7.23 \times 100 = 723 \qquad 42.7 \div 100 = 0.427$$

When You Multiply by	The Decimal Point Moves	Example
10	one place to the right	$7.23 \times 10 = 72.3$
100	two places to the right	$7.23 \times 100 = 723$
1000	three places to the right	$7.23 \times 1000 = 7230$

When You Divide By	The Decimal Point Moves	Example
10	one place to the left	$42.7 \div 10 = 4.27$
100	two places to the left	$42.7 \div 100 = 0.427$
1000	three places to the left	$42.7 \div 1000 = 0.0427$

The decimal point is moved to the right when you multiply, and to the left when you divide. Insert zeros as needed.

To convert from one metric unit to another, you multiply or divide by a power of 10. It's easy if you just move the decimal point.

$$1 \text{ cm} = 10 \text{ mm} \qquad 1000 \text{ g} = 1 \text{ kg}$$
$$2.9 \text{ cm} = 29 \text{ mm} \qquad 500 \text{ g} = 0.5 \text{ kg}$$

CLASS EXERCISES

Write the answer with the decimal point in the correct place.

1. $3.7 \times 10 = 370$
$0.37 \times 10 = 370$

2. $7.6 \times 100 = 7600$
$7.63 \times 100 = 76300$

3. $8.3 \times 1000 = 83000$
$8.314 \times 1000 = 8314000$

4. $26 \div 10 = 26$
$2.6 \div 10 = 26$

5. $458 \div 100 = 458$
$4587 \div 100 = 4587$

6. $8351 \div 1000 = 8351$
$835.1 \div 1000 = 8351$

7. $3.5 \text{ cm} = 35 \text{ mm}$

8. $246 \text{ cm} = 246 \text{ m}$

9. $8400 \text{ m} = 8400 \text{ km}$

PRACTICE

Multiply or divide.

10. 7.4×10 **11.** 5.31×100 **12.** 3.91×10 **13.** 3.54×100

14. 7.2×100 **15.** 804×1000 **16.** 0.04×10 **17.** 0.76×100

18. $0.6 \div 10$ **19.** $1351 \div 1000$ **20.** $86.2 \div 100$ **21.** $84.6 \div 1000$

22. $381.4 \div 100$ **23.** $83.3 \div 10$ **24.** $1021 \div 100$ **25.** $68.32 \div 1000$

★ **26.** 8.7×10^3 ★ **27.** 34×10^2 ★ **28.** 25.1×10^2 ★ **29.** 9.52×10^3

★ **30.** $487 \div 10^2$ ★ **31.** $62.7 \div 10^3$ ★ **32.** $8.7 \div 10^2$ ★ **33.** $18.7 \div 10^2$

Complete the first 3 products. Then guess the next one and check your guess. A calculator may be helpful.

CALCULATOR

34. $5.2 \times 11 \quad = \blacksquare 7.2$
$5.2 \times 111 \quad = \blacksquare 77.2$
$5.2 \times 1111 = \blacksquare 777.2$
$5.2 \times \blacksquare \quad = 57777777.2$

35. $909 \times 2.2 = \blacksquare 999.8$
$909 \times 3.3 = \blacksquare 999.7$
$909 \times 4.4 = \blacksquare 999.6$
$909 \times \blacksquare = 7999.2$

PROBLEM SOLVING APPLICATIONS
Choosing the Operation

Solve.

36. How many meters are in 286 cm?

37. A sheet of cardboard is 0.48 cm thick. How high is a stack of 1000 sheets?

38. A business directory is to contain the names of 8279 businesses. If 100 names are listed on a page, will 80 pages be enough for each directory?

39. A box for mailing costs 19¢. How much will 1000 boxes cost?

★ **40.** Envelopes cost $40.95 per 1000 if you buy 1000, and $38.95 per 1000 if you buy 2000. What is the saving per envelope if you buy the larger quantity?

DIVISION BY DECIMALS

In a division, if you multiply both the divisor and the dividend by 10, the quotient remains the same. This is also true if you multiply both numbers by 100, or 1000, or any power of 10.

$$9\overline{)27} \quad 90\overline{)270} \quad 900\overline{)2700} \quad 9000\overline{)27{,}000}$$

each with quotient 3

You may use this idea to write a decimal divisor as a whole number before you divide. You multiply both numbers by a power of 10 that will result in a whole number divisor.

$8.2\overline{)43.46}$	$0.25\overline{)4.275}$	$0.094\overline{)20.68}$
Multiply by 10.	Multiply by 100.	Multiply by 1000.

$$
\begin{array}{r}
5.3 \\
82\overline{)434.6} \\
-410 \\
\hline
24\ 6 \\
-24\ 6 \\
\hline
0
\end{array}
\qquad
\begin{array}{r}
17.1 \\
25\overline{)427.5} \\
-25 \\
\hline
177 \\
-175 \\
\hline
2\ 5 \\
-2\ 5 \\
\hline
0
\end{array}
\qquad
\begin{array}{r}
220 \\
94\overline{)20{,}680} \\
-18\ 8 \\
\hline
1\ 88 \\
-1\ 88 \\
\hline
0
\end{array}
$$

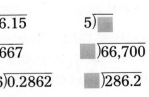

To plan this bridge in Natchez, Missouri, engineers needed to apply division with decimals.

CLASS EXERCISES

Complete.

1. $0.3\overline{)4.8}$ $\blacksquare\overline{)48}$ **2.** $0.5\overline{)26.15}$ $5\overline{)\blacksquare}$

3. $0.32\overline{)8.96}$ $32\overline{)\blacksquare}$ **4.** $0.29\overline{)667}$ $\blacksquare\overline{)66{,}700}$

5. $0.035\overline{)0.14}$ $35\overline{)\blacksquare}$ **6.** $0.106\overline{)0.2862}$ $\blacksquare\overline{)286.2}$

PRACTICE

Divide.

7. $0.6\overline{)8.4}$

8. $0.7\overline{)4.354}$

9. $0.6\overline{)38.49}$

10. $1.6\overline{)4.48}$

11. $7.5\overline{)26.25}$

12. $0.09\overline{)3.6}$

13. $0.38\overline{)0.95}$

14. $0.073\overline{)0.365}$

15. $0.12\overline{)0.156}$

16. $0.31\overline{)207.7}$

17. $0.12\overline{)2.508}$

18. $8.9\overline{)514.42}$

19. $0.109\overline{)0.1526}$

20. $6.3\overline{)279.09}$

21. $0.074\overline{)2.22}$

22. $0.26\overline{)8.164}$

23. $0.09\overline{)1.53}$

24. $0.012\overline{)5.52}$

25. $9.3\overline{)722.61}$

26. $0.123\overline{)0.1722}$

Write in order from least to greatest.

27. 380, 357, 350, 360, 340

28. 20, 10.9, 16, 11, 15.8

29. 5.19, 5, 3, 5.1, 5.02

30. 16.8, 20, 16, 10, 17

31. 17.63, 17.221, 17.06, 17.403

32. 1208, 846, 376, 700

MIXED REVIEW

PROBLEM SOLVING APPLICATIONS
Drawing a Picture

Solve. Drawing a picture may help.

33. Guard rails are put along a section of a highway 192.5 m long. The posts are 3.5 m apart. After the work crew installs the first post at the beginning of the section, how many more must they install?

34. On the highway, a car used 31.8 L of gasoline to travel 445.2 km. About how far did the car travel on each liter of gasoline?

35. A total of 41 emergency call boxes are put along a highway at intervals of 4.5 km. A call box is at each end of the highway. How long is the highway?

★ 36. A bridge is 493 m long. At every 4.25 m there is an expansion joint. Not counting the beginning and end of the bridge, how many joints are there?

ESTIMATING QUOTIENTS

A total of $1894.50 was collected at the gate to the annual school fair. The admission tickets cost $2.25 each. About how many people went to the fair?

To estimate quotients, think of **compatible numbers** that are easy to divide and are close to the actual numbers. Then divide.

Think: $2.25 is close to $2, and $1894.50 is close to $1800.

$$2.25\overline{)1894.50} \Rightarrow 2\overline{)1800}^{\,900}$$

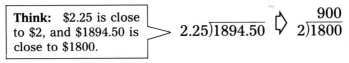

About 900 people went to the fair.

Here are some other examples:

Estimate: 547 ÷ 78   Estimate: 258.6 ÷ 1.8
     Think: 560 ÷ 80   **Think:** 300 ÷ 2
       about 7   about 150

CLASS EXERCISES

What two numbers will you use to estimate the quotient?

1. 846 ÷ 24

2. 26,535 ÷ 35

3. 73,584 ÷ 159

4. 23.69 ÷ 3.81

5. 37.12 ÷ 5.8

6. 449.8 ÷ 8.9

7. 625 ÷ 4.87

8. 832.4 ÷ 144

9. 2187 ÷ 0.65

PRACTICE

Estimate the quotient.

10. $95\overline{)7201}$ **11.** $18\overline{)2693}$ **12.** $286\overline{)61,483}$

13. $3.8\overline{)85.7}$ **14.** $72.5\overline{)210.64}$ **15.** $3.26\overline{)6.037}$

16. $2.05\overline{)673}$ **17.** $59\overline{)308.36}$ **18.** $429\overline{)1145.89}$

19. $552 \div 18$ **20.** $674 \div 23$ **21.** $268.7 \div 63$

22. $358.6 \div 1.8$ **23.** $278 \div 6.02$ **24.** $72.38 \div 0.059$

25. $90.07 \div 4.6$ **26.** $56.8 \div 0.009$ **27.** $3789 \div 4.32$

PROBLEM SOLVING APPLICATIONS
Using Estimation

Solve.

28. The civic auditorium has a seating capacity of 8784. If the auditorium is divided into 16 sections, about how many seats are in each section?

29. A cottage at the Mountain Retreats costs $460.60 for a 5-night stay. About how much is it per night?

30. Earl got a $156.60 paycheck this week. He earns $4.35 an hour. About how many hours did he work?

31. Jamie biked 214 mi in the last 17 days. About how many miles did he bike each day?

32. About how many silk flowers at $3.60 each can you buy with $48?

★ **33.** Roger drove 1460 mi to California. His car averaged 42 mi/gal. The price of gasoline was about $1.20 per gallon. About how much was the total cost of gasoline for the trip?

PROBLEM SOLVING
Strategy: Using Estimation

1. Understand
2. Plan
3. Work
4. Answer/ Check

You do not always need exact answers. Often you use an estimated answer to make a decision or to solve a problem.

Marco read in the paper that cassette tapes are on sale. He would like to buy two for $12.49 each and a third for $13.09. Are his $40 savings enough?

He can estimate the cost using the **front-end** digits for a first approximation and then adjust it for a closer estimate.

Think: $(2 \times \$10) + \$10$ is $30.

Adjust: About $2.50 more for each of the two and about $3 more for the third.

Estimate: $\$30 + \$5 + \$3 = \$38$

His savings of $40 will be enough.

Amanda has a 267-page reading assignment this semester. If she reads 17 pages a day, about how many days will it take to finish the assignment?

To find an estimate, she divides 300 by 20. It will take about 15 days.

CLASS EXERCISES

Tell what numbers you will use to estimate. Then answer the question.

1. The Glee Club has $300 collected from club dues. Does the club have enough money to take all 56 members to the concert if tickets cost $4.60 each?

2. Sergei has 18 math problems to finish 25 min before class. If it takes him about 2.5 min to do each problem, will he finish in time for class?

3. Vern earns $37.50 each week. He wants to buy a guitar that costs $316.65. If he saves his weekly paychecks, will he have enough money to buy the guitar in 5 weeks' time?

PRACTICE

Estimate the answer.

4. To train for the junior marathon, each student must run 11 mi a day for 29 days. About how many miles is this?

5. An amusement park plans to build three new rides at a cost of $285,732, $72,561, and $181,972. Is the final cost more than $500.000?

6. Arlene has budgeted $5 for a long distance call to her grandmother. If the rate is $1.95 for the first three minutes, and $.40 for each additional minute, can she talk for 15 min?

★ **7.** Mia is planning a bus excursion for 378 people. Each bus seats 48 passengers. At least how many buses should she reserve?

★ **8.** The Arctic tern is a bird that migrates about 19,500 km each year from the Arctic to the Antarctic. If the tern flies 8 h a day at an average speed of 25 km/h, about how many days does it take to complete the trip?

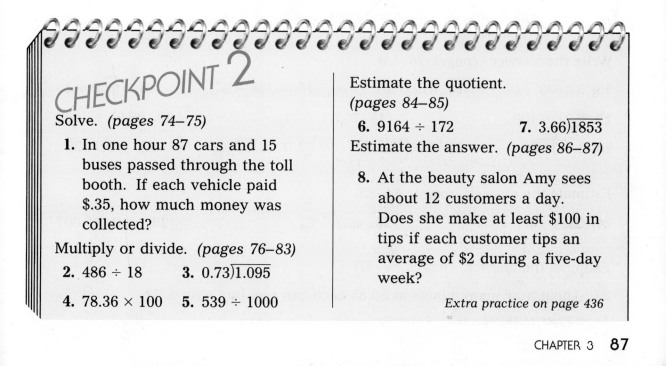

CHECKPOINT 2

Solve. *(pages 74–75)*

1. In one hour 87 cars and 15 buses passed through the toll booth. If each vehicle paid $.35, how much money was collected?

Multiply or divide. *(pages 76–83)*

2. $486 \div 18$

3. $0.73\overline{)1.095}$

4. 78.36×100

5. $539 \div 1000$

Estimate the quotient. *(pages 84–85)*

6. $9164 \div 172$

7. $3.66\overline{)1853}$

Estimate the answer. *(pages 86–87)*

8. At the beauty salon Amy sees about 12 customers a day. Does she make at least $100 in tips if each customer tips an average of $2 during a five-day week?

Extra practice on page 436

Answer the question. Write *yes* or *no*. *(pages 62–65)*

1. $n \times 6 = 48$ Is 7 a solution?   **2.** $36 \div r = 9$ Is 4 a solution?

3. $(8 \times 11) \times 6 = m \times (11 \times 6)$ Is 8 a solution?

4. $9 \times (g + 24) = (9 \times 17) + (9 \times 24)$ Is 9 a solution?

Estimate. Then write the exact answer. *(pages 66–71)*

5. 207×38 **6.** 0.071×3 **7.** 21.6×3.2 **8.** 36.7×0.08

Write the number using exponents. *(pages 72–73)*

9. 5×5 **10.** $8 \times 8 \times 8 \times 8$ **11.** $12 \times 12 \times 12$

Solve. *(pages 74–75)*

12. A roll of wallpaper costs $14.95 and a can of wallpaper paste costs $3.49. How much will a total of 8 rolls of wallpaper and 2 cans of wallpaper paste cost?

Write the answer. *(pages 76–83)*

13. $32\overline{)693}$ **14.** $412\overline{)9501}$ **15.** $4.248 \div 8$ **16.** $1.806 \div 43$

17. 6.71×100 **18.** 927.3×10 **19.** $86.01 \div 1000$

20. $8.3\overline{)34.86}$ **21.** $0.06\overline{)5.4}$ **22.** $0.42\overline{)9.702}$ **23.** $0.07\overline{)1.26}$

Estimate the answer. *(pages 84–85)*

24. $3194 \div 83$ **25.** $49.3 \div 61$ **26.** $64.9 \div 0.007$

Estimate the answer. *(pages 86–87)*

27. About how many plants at $5.85 each can you buy with $74?

Extra Practice on page 437

MATHEMATICS and SCIENCE

Every magnet has two ends, commonly called the north pole and the south pole. Magnets are pulled together or pushed apart by the force of magnetism. When nearby, a north pole will attract a south pole, while two identical poles will repel each other.

The force between two magnets weakens as the distance between them increases. If the distance between two magnets is doubled, the force is divided by 4. If the distance is multiplied by 3, the force is divided by 9. In each case, we divide the force by the square of the number by which we multiply the distance.

The force between two magnets is 900 units when they are 1 cm apart. What is the force at the new distance?

1. 2 cm apart   **2.** 5 cm apart

3. 10 cm apart   **4.** 0.5 cm apart

5. 1.2 cm apart   **6.** 0.3 cm apart

IS IT NATURALLY SQUARE?

The brightness of the light from a flashlight on an object depends on the distance between the object and the light. If the distance is multiplied by a number, the brightness is divided by the square of that number. For example, if the distance is doubled, the brightness is divided by 4.

The brightness of a flashlight on a screen is 3600 units at 1 ft apart. What is the brightness of the light at the new distance?

7. 2 ft apart   **8.** 6 ft apart

★ **9.** How far is the flashlight from the screen if the brightness between them is 400 units?

Enrichment

The width of the Milky Way galaxy from edge to edge is about

946,000,000,000,000,000 km.

Another way to write this number is in **scientific notation** as a product of two factors. One factor is a number between 1 and 10. The second factor is a power of 10.

For the first factor, move the decimal point to the left as many places as it takes to get a number between 1 and 10. 946,000,000,000,000,000 17 places	Next, use the number of places moved as the power of 10 for the second factor. 9.46×10^{17}

Is the number written in scientific notation? Write *yes* or *no*.

1. 24×10^7 **2.** 7×10^4 **3.** 6.9×5^2 **4.** 0.3×10^6

Complete.

5. $36,000,000 = 3.6 \times 10^{\blacksquare}$ **6.** $980,000,000,000 = 9.8 \times 10^{\blacksquare}$

7. $50,000,000,000,000 = 5 \times 10^{\blacksquare}$ **8.** $27,400,000,000 = 2.74 \times 10^{\blacksquare}$

Write in scientific notation.

9. 92,000   **10.** 136,000   **11.** 500,000

12. 7,000,000   **13.** 40,600,000

14. 650,000,000   **15.** 8,040,000,000

16. 3,400,000,000   **17.** 31,408,000,000

SCIENTIFIC NOTATION

The Earth's maximum distance from the sun is about 1.52×10^8 km. Any number in scientific notation can be written in standard form.

$$1.52 \times 10^8 = 1.52 \times 100,000,000$$
$$= 152,000,000$$

A quick way to find the standard form is to think of the decimal point moving to the right. The power of 10 tells you how many places to move it.

$$1.52 \times 10^8 = 152,000,000$$

8 places

The Earth is about 152,000,000 km from the sun.

Write the number in standard form.

18. 9×10^5 **19.** 2×10^8 **20.** 8.2×10^3 **21.** 5.1×10^7

22. Voyager II flew an indirect course of about 2.3×10^9 km to reach Saturn.

23. The diameter of Saturn's largest ring is about 4.8×10^5 km.

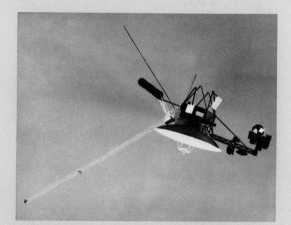

Write the number in scientific notation.

24. Saturn is about 1,600,000,000 km from the Earth.

25. Large distances are also measured in *light years*. One light year is about 9,460,000,000,000 km.

★ **26.** The estimated temperature of the sun's core is 25 million degrees Fahrenheit.

CUMULATIVE REVIEW

Choose the correct answer. Write *a*, *b*, *c*, or *d*.

Which is the best estimate?

1. The distance from New York to San Francisco
   a. 480 mm
   b. 4800 km
   c. 480 m
   d. 48,000 km

2. The thickness of a straight pin
   a. 1 mm
   b. 1 km
   c. 1 m
   d. 10 m

3. The capacity of a mug
   a. 24 L
   b. 240 L
   c. 240 mL
   d. 2400 L

4. The mass of a radio
   a. 400 kg
   b. 40 g
   c. 4 mg
   d. 4 kg

The capacity of a pitcher is recorded at $3 L \pm 0.5 L$.

5. What is the least actual capacity of the pitcher?
   a. 3 L
   b. 3.5 L
   c. 2.5 L
   d. None of these

6. What is the GPE of the measurement?
   a. 0.5 mL
   b. 0.5 L
   c. 3.5 L
   d. None of these

Which is the best estimate?

7. The height of a bookcase
   a. 6 in.
   b. 6 ft
   c. 6 yd
   d. 60 ft

8. The weight of a can of beans
   a. 10 oz
   b. 100 oz
   c. 10 lb
   d. 100 lb

9. The capacity of a flower vase
   a. 20 gal
   b. 2 qt
   c. 200 pt
   d. 200 gal

10. The width of a house
    a. 50 in.
    b. 50 mi
    c. 50 ft
    d. 5 ft

Find the answer.

11. 6.1 + 22.85 + 76.3 + 5.9
    a. 112.15
    b. 111.15
    c. 121.15
    d. None of these

12. 4.2 − 3.101
    a. 1.699
    b. 1.689
    c. 1.589
    d. None of these

Village Theatre kept a record of the tickets sold for the 7:20 P.M. movie Sunday through Thursday.

SUN.	MON.	TUES.	WED.	THURS.
143	56	47	49	55

13. Which night had the lowest attendance?

    a. Sunday
    b. Monday
    c. Tuesday
    d. None of these

14. On which two nights did the attendance drop below 50?

    a. Monday and Tuesday
    b. Tuesday and Wednesday
    c. Wednesday and Thursday
    d. None of these

LANGUAGE and VOCABULARY REVIEW

Choose the correct word to complete.

estimate   base   exponent
variable   commutative   associative

1. The equation $a \times b = b \times a$ illustrates the ___?___ property of multiplication.

2. In the equation $24 \div n = 6$, the letter n is a ___?___.

3. A(n) ___?___ helps you check the reasonableness of an answer.

4. The number 4 in 4^2 is the ___?___, while the number 2 is the ___?___.

CPU: ARITHMETIC-LOGIC UNIT

The most important part of the computer is the **Central Processing Unit** (CPU). It is where the computer follows instructions to change input to output.

One part of the CPU is the **Arithmetic-Logic Unit** (ALU). The ALU performs arithmetic operations and makes logical decisions based on the results of comparing data.

Operations	Comparisons
The ALU can only add. Multiplication is repeated addition. Subtraction is reversed addition. Division is repeated subtraction.	The ALU compares two numbers three ways. It tests whether $4 > 3$, $4 < 3$, or $4 = 3$. A test answer can only be true or false.

Based on the result of a comparison, a computer will do one of two things. It will do an instruction or it will go to another program line.

1. What two jobs does the Arithmetic-Logic Unit do?

Write *true* or *false*.

2. $50 > 4 \times (12 + 1)$

3. $0.3641 < 0.3589$

4. $9 \times (4 + 6) = 2 \times (39 + 6)$

5. $56{,}478{,}871 > 56{,}477{,}599$

6. $5 \times (10 - 4) + 6 = 4^2 \times (41 - 39)$

7. $2.75 = 2 + 0.05 + 0.7$

Describe the similarities and differences you see among the sails of this windjammer.

4

GEOMETRY, PERIMETER, AREA

POINTS, LINES, PLANES

A **point** shows an exact location. A **line** is a set of points that extends without end in two opposite directions. **Collinear** points are in the same line.

A **ray** is part of a line. It has one endpoint. The endpoint is named first.

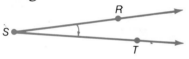

Ray *XY*, written $\overrightarrow{XY}$

An **angle** is formed by two rays that have the same endpoint. The endpoint is called the **vertex** of the angle. The rays are called the **sides** of the angle.

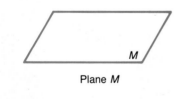

Angle *RST*, written ∠*RST*, ∠*TSR*, or ∠*S*

A **plane** is a set of points on a flat surface that extends without end.

Plane *M*

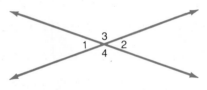

Line *AB*, written $\overleftrightarrow{AB}$
Points *A* and *B* are collinear.

A **line segment** is also part of a line. It has two endpoints.

Line segment *MG*, written $\overline{MG}$
The length of $\overline{MG}$ is written MG.

Lines that cross each other are called **intersecting lines**. **Vertical angles** are formed by two intersecting lines. Sometimes we use numbers to name the vertical angles.

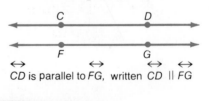

∠1 and ∠2 are vertical angles, so are ∠3 and ∠4.

Lines in a plane that do not intersect are called **parallel lines**.

$\overleftrightarrow{CD}$ is parallel to $\overleftrightarrow{FG}$, written $\overleftrightarrow{CD} \parallel \overleftrightarrow{FG}$

CLASS EXERCISES

Name the figure using the letters shown.

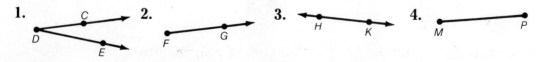

1.

2.

3.

4.

PRACTICE

Write *true* or *false*.

5. A line has an endpoint.

6. A line segment has two endpoints.

7. A ray has no endpoints.

8. A line is part of a line segment.

9. Parallel lines intersect.

10. Parallel lines form vertical angles.

Find the number that names the angle in the diagram below.

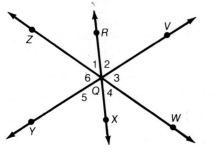

11. $\angle RQV$

12. $\angle VQW$

13. $\angle WQX$

14. $\angle XQY$

15. Name 3 pairs of vertical angles.

★**16.** Two other names for $\angle 5$ are $\angle XQY$ and $\angle YQX$. Why would $\angle Q$ not be a good name for $\angle 5$?

Exercises 17–21 refer to the diagram at the right.

17. Name a pair of parallel lines.

18. Name two pairs of intersecting lines.

19. Name two parallel line segments.

20. Name two angles that share vertex A.

21. Name the point where $\overleftrightarrow{SY}$ and $\overleftrightarrow{AB}$ intersect.

Draw a diagram of the figure.

22. $\overline{OT}$ **23.** $\angle MGH$ **24.** $\overrightarrow{EW}$ **25.** $\overleftrightarrow{AB} \parallel \overleftrightarrow{CD}$ **26.** $\overleftrightarrow{RS}$

PROBLEM SOLVING APPLICATIONS
Drawing a Diagram

What geometric figure does the example suggest?

27. The ceiling

28. The edge of a ruler

29. Railroad tracks

30. Spokes in a wheel

31. The tip of a pen

32. Antenna on a television set

33. The corners of a book

34. A balance beam

ANGLE MEASURE
AND CONGRUENCE

To measure an angle, you use a protractor. The unit of measure is called a **degree.** With most protractors you can measure up to 180 degrees (180°). Here's how to measure ∠ACB using the outer scale.

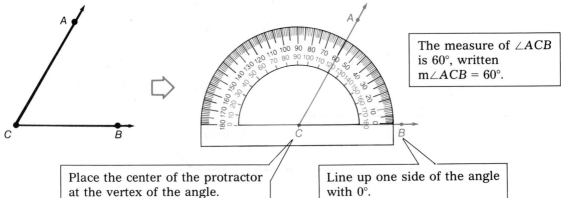

The measure of ∠ACB is 60°, written m∠ACB = 60°.

Place the center of the protractor at the vertex of the angle.

Line up one side of the angle with 0°.

Here's how to draw ∠XYZ with a measure of 60° using the inner scale of the protractor.

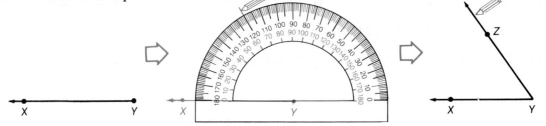

Angles with equal measures are called **congruent angles.** The symbol ≅ means *is congruent to.* Since m∠XYZ = m∠ACB, we can write ∠XYZ ≅ ∠ACB.

CLASS EXERCISES

What is the measure of the angle?

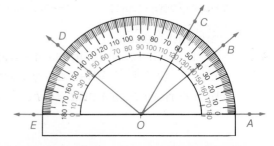

1. ∠AOB

2. ∠EOD

3. ∠AOC

4. ∠EOC

Use a protractor. What is the measure of the angle?

5.   **6.**   **7.**

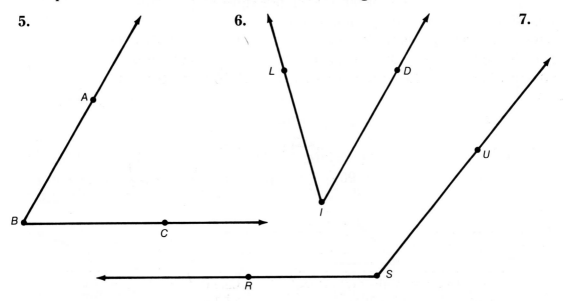

Use a protractor to draw the angle.

8. m∠DEF = 90°   **9.** m∠COB = 35°   **10.** m∠FAT = 120°

11. m∠LMN = 155°   **12.** m∠RUN = 15°   **13.** m∠TAB = 72°

14. Draw an angle congruent to ∠ACB on page 98.

★ **15.** Draw two congruent angles whose measures have the sum 90°.

PROBLEM SOLVING APPLICATIONS
Making Generalizations

Copy the diagram large enough to use with a protractor.

16. Use a protractor to measure the angles labeled 1 and 3, then 2 and 4. What do you notice about the measures of pairs of vertical angles?

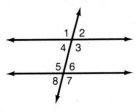

★ **17.** Use a protractor to measure the angles labeled 5 and 6, then 7 and 8. What do you notice about the sum of m∠5 + m∠6? the sum of m∠7 + m∠8?

SPECIAL ANGLES

An angle with a measure of 90° is called a **right angle.** The sides of a right angle are **perpendicular.**

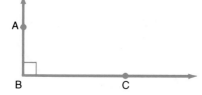

$\overrightarrow{BA}$ is perpendicular to $\overrightarrow{BC}$ $\overrightarrow{BA} \perp \overrightarrow{BC}$

The symbol ⌐ in the diagram shows that $m\angle ABC = 90°$.

An **acute angle** has a measure greater than 0° and less than 90°.

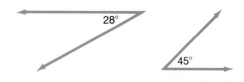

An **obtuse angle** has a measure greater than 90° and less than 180°.

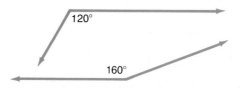

If the sum of the measures of two angles is 90°, the angles are **complementary.**

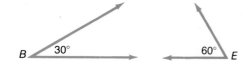

$m\angle B + m\angle E = 30° + 60° = 90°$
$\angle B$ and $\angle E$ are complementary.

If the sum of the measures of two angles is 180°, the angles are **supplementary.**

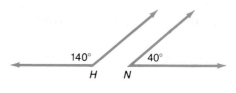

$m\angle H + m\angle N = 140° + 40° = 180°$
$\angle H$ and $\angle N$ are supplementary.

CLASS EXERCISES

Write *right, acute,* or *obtuse* to tell which kind of angle is shown.

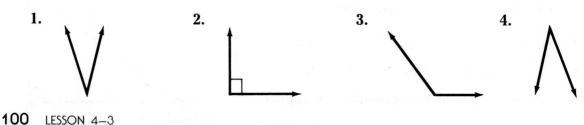

1.   2.   3.   4.

PRACTICE

Tell whether the angles are *complementary, supplementary,*
or *neither.*

5. 42°, 48°   **6.** 80°, 90°   **7.** 10°, 80°   **8.** 100°, 28°

9. 125°, 55°   **10.** 1°, 89°   **11.** 45°, 45°   **12.** 90°, 90°

Write the measure of the complementary angle.

13. 30°   **14.** 20°   **15.** 80°   **16.** 89°   **17.** 15°

Write the measure of the supplementary angle.

18. 100°   **19.** 120°   **20.** 40°   **21.** 4°   **22.** 90°

In the diagram at the right $\overleftrightarrow{AD} \parallel \overleftrightarrow{EH}$.

23. Name the acute angles.

24. Name the obtuse angles.

25. Name 4 pairs of supplementary angles.

★**26.** Name 4 pairs of congruent angles.

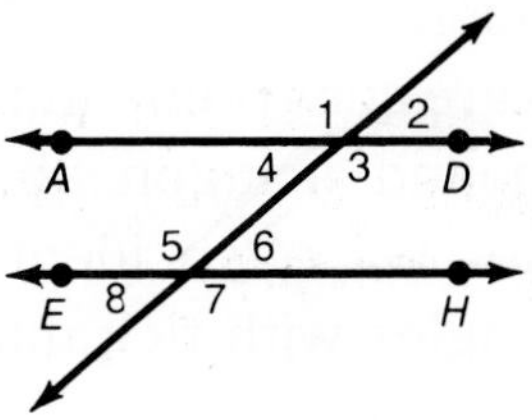

Estimate. Do you think the lines are perpendicular?
Write *yes* or *no.*

27.   **28.** 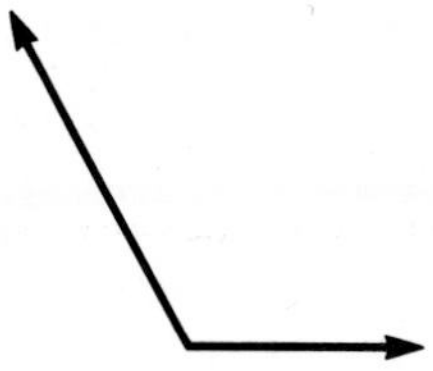   **29.**

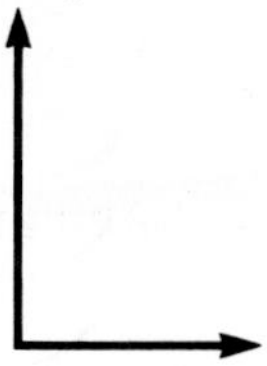

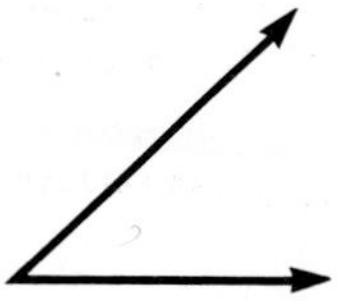

PROBLEM SOLVING APPLICATIONS
Interpreting a Diagram

Exercises 30–33 refer to the diagram at the right.

30. Name three acute angles.

31. Name a pair of perpendicular segments.

32. Name a pair of supplementary angles.

★**33.** Name a pair of complementary angles.

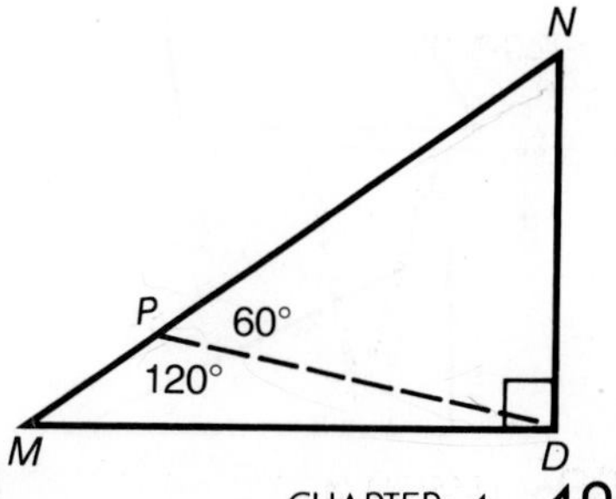

POLYGONS

A **polygon** is a plane figure formed by joining three or more line segments at their endpoints. Some polygons have special names according to the number of sides.

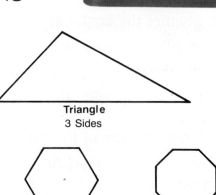

Triangle
3 Sides

Quadrilateral
4 Sides

Pentagon
5 Sides

Hexagon
6 Sides

Octagon
8 Sides

Line segments with the same length are **congruent line segments.** A **regular polygon** is a polygon in which all sides are congruent and all angles are congruent. The hexagon and octagon above are examples of regular polygons. We often identify congruent sides and congruent angles with tick marks and arcs as shown at the right.

A line segment that joins two vertexes of a polygon and is not a side of the polygon is called a **diagonal.** For example, $\overline{CA}$ and $\overline{CE}$ are diagonals, while $\overline{CD}$ is not.

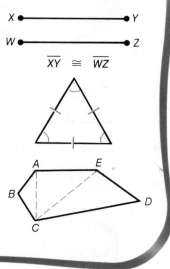

$$\overline{XY} \cong \overline{WZ}$$

CLASS EXERCISES

Count the number of sides in the polygon. Then name the polygon.

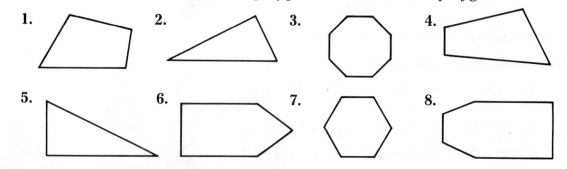

1.

2.

3.

4.

5.

6.

7.

8.

PRACTICE

The polygon is a regular polygon. Write the measures of all its sides, and all its angles.

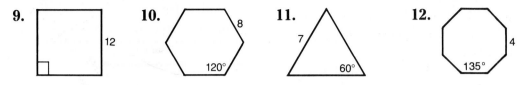

9. 12

10. 8 120°

11. 7 60°

12. 4 135°

Draw the polygon and all the diagonals from one vertex. Complete the chart.

	Polygon	Number of sides	Number of diagonals from one vertex
13.	Triangle	?	?
14.	Quadrilateral	?	?
15.	?	5	?
16.	?	6	?

★ **17.** How many diagonals from one vertex will there be in a polygon with 100 sides?

Complete.

18. $90 + 30 + 60 =$ ▧

19. $143 + 27 +$ ▧ $= 180$

20. $180 - 118 - 12 =$ ▧

21. $180 - 45 -$ ▧ $= 90$

MIXED REVIEW

PROBLEM SOLVING APPLICATIONS
Nonroutine Problems

Solve.

22. Use a protractor and ruler to draw a quadrilateral that is not regular but has all its angles congruent.

★ **23.** What is the measure of the angle made by the hands of a clock at 2 o'clock?

PROBLEM SOLVING
Strategy: Using Patterns

Sometimes a problem may seem very long or difficult to solve. In that case, it often helps to organize your information. You may then see a pattern. Use the pattern to answer the question.

Line segment XY is divided into two equal segments by point A.

How many points are needed to divide a line segment into 56 equal segments?

Organize your data to see if a pattern exists in the first few cases.

NO. OF SEGMENTS	2	3	4	5	6
NO. OF DIVIDING POINTS	1	2	3	4	5

From the information above you can see that the number of points is one less than the number of segments. So, 55 points will divide a line segment into 56 equal segments.

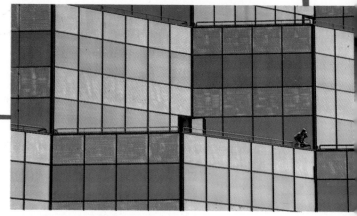

CLASS EXERCISES

Look for the pattern. Then name the next three numbers in the sequence.

1. 2, 4, 6, 8, . . .

2. 4, 7, 10, 13, . . .

3. 81, 72, 63, 54, . . .

4. 0, 3, 7, 12, 18, . . .

5. 1, 4, 9, 16, 25, . . .

6. 0.2, 0.7, 1.2, 1.7, 2.2, . . .

7. 4000, 400, 40, 4, . . .

8. 2, 6, 24, 120, . . .

PRACTICE

Solve.

9. a. A diagonal from one vertex divides a quadrilateral into 2 triangles. Diagonals from one vertex divide a pentagon into 3 triangles. Complete the chart.

NO. OF SIDES	4	5	6	7	8
NO. OF DIAGONALS FROM ONE VERTEX	1	2	?	?	?
NO. OF TRIANGLES	2	3	?	?	?

    b. What pattern do you see in the relationship between the number of diagonals and the number of triangles?

    c. What pattern do you see in the relationship between the number of sides and the number of triangles?

10. The numbers in the sequence 1, 3, 6, 10, . . . are called *triangular numbers* because you can stack them up in the shape of a triangle. For example:

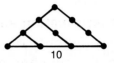

    a. Describe the pattern you see in the triangular numbers.

    b. What is the fifth triangular number?

    c. What is the 15th triangular number?

11. The numbers in the sequence 1, 4, 9, 16, . . . are called *square numbers*. For example:

    a. Describe the pattern you see in the square numbers.

    b. What is the fifth square number?

    c. What is the 10th square number?

★ **12.** Use the diagrams in Exercises 10 and 11 to help you find the first three *pentagonal numbers*.
(*Hint:* Use a regular pentagon.)

TRIANGLES

...e often used in construction because they form
...res. There are two ways to name a triangle.

...ay be described in terms of their sides.

 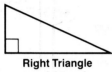

Equilateral Triangle
3 congruent sides
3 congruent angles

Isosceles Triangle
2 congruent sides
2 congruent angles

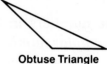

Scalene Triangle
no congruent sides
no congruent angles

Triangles may also be described in terms of their angles.

Right Triangle
one right angle

Acute Triangle
all angles acute

Obtuse Triangle
one obtuse angle

The angles of a triangle have a special
property. The sum of their measures is 180°.

M **Think:** If the measures of two angles are 45°
and 50°, how can you use mental math to find
the measure of the third angle?

90°

54°   36°

$90° + 54° + 36° = 180°$

CLASS EXERCISES

List all the terms that describe the triangle. Write *a*, *b*, *c*, *d*, *e*, or *f*.

a. acute   **b.** obtuse   **c.** right   **d.** scalene   **e.** isosceles   **f.** equilateral

1.   **2.**   **3.**   **4.**

PRACTICE

Tell whether the triangle is *acute*, *right*, or *obtuse*.

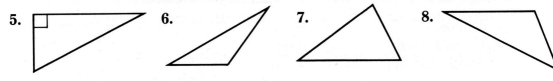

5.   6.   7.   8.

Tell whether the triangle is *scalene*, *isosceles*, or *equilateral*.

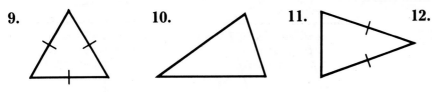

9.   10.   11.   12.

Use mental math to find the measure of the third angle of the triangle.

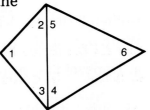

MENTAL MATH

13. 85°, 30°   14. 45°, 30°   15. 90°, 45°

16. 60°, 60°   17. 96°, 34°   18. 72°, 38°

Sketch a triangle to fit the description. Mark equal parts alike.

19. scalene   20. obtuse isosceles   21. right isosceles

22. acute   23. equilateral   24. isosceles, but not equilateral

PROBLEM SOLVING APPLICATIONS
Finding Patterns

Drawing all the diagonals from one vertex of a polygon divides the polygon into triangles. Use this fact to answer the question.

25. What is the sum of m∠1 + m∠2 + m∠3?

26. What is the sum of m∠4 + m∠5 + m∠6?

27. What is the sum of the measures of all six angles?

What is the sum of the measures of the angles of the polygon?

★ 28. a pentagon   ★ 29. a hexagon   ★ 30. an octagon

QUADRILATERALS

A **parallelogram** is a quadrilateral with the following properties:

1. Opposite sides are parallel.
2. Opposite sides are congruent.
3. Opposite angles are congruent.

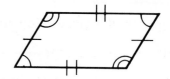

Some parallelograms have special names.

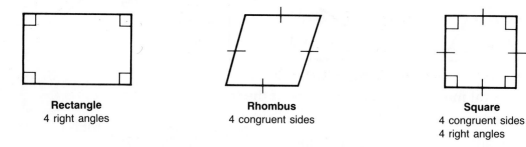

Rectangle
4 right angles

Rhombus
4 congruent sides

Square
4 congruent sides
4 right angles

Think: Can you also describe a square as a regular quadrilateral?

A **trapezoid** is a quadrilateral with only one pair of parallel sides. In the trapezoid at the right $\overline{PQ} \parallel \overline{SR}$, but $\overline{PS}$ is not parallel to $\overline{QR}$.

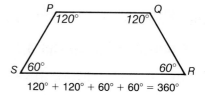

$120° + 120° + 60° + 60° = 360°$

The angles of a quadrilateral have a special property. The sum of their measures is always 360°.

CLASS EXERCISES

Name all the quadrilaterals that have the property.
Write *a*, *b*, *c*, *d*, or *e*.

a. trapezoid   **b.** parallelogram   **c.** rectangle   **d.** rhombus   **e.** square

1. Opposite sides are parallel.
2. Opposite sides are congruent.
3. Opposite angles are congruent.
4. All sides are congruent.
5. There are four right angles.
6. Only two sides are parallel.

PRACTICE

Is the statement *always true*, *sometimes true*, or *never true*?
Write *A*, *S*, or *N*.

7. A square is a parallelogram. **8.** A parallelogram is a trapezoid.

9. A rectangle is a square. **10.** A rhombus is a quadrilateral.

Complete. *MABC* is a rhombus. *MOPN* is a parallelogram.

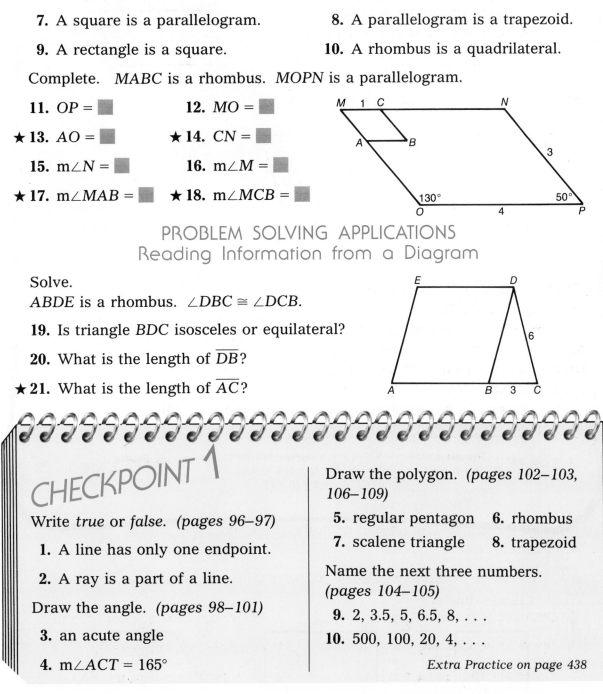

11. $OP = $ ▓

12. $MO = $ ▓

★ **13.** $AO = $ ▓

★ **14.** $CN = $ ▓

15. $m\angle N = $ ▓

16. $m\angle M = $ ▓

★ **17.** $m\angle MAB = $ ▓

★ **18.** $m\angle MCB = $ ▓

PROBLEM SOLVING APPLICATIONS
Reading Information from a Diagram

Solve.
ABDE is a rhombus. $\angle DBC \cong \angle DCB$.

19. Is triangle *BDC* isosceles or equilateral?

20. What is the length of $\overline{DB}$?

★ **21.** What is the length of $\overline{AC}$?

CHECKPOINT 1

Write *true* or *false*. *(pages 96–97)*

1. A line has only one endpoint.

2. A ray is a part of a line.

Draw the angle. *(pages 98–101)*

3. an acute angle

4. $m\angle ACT = 165°$

Draw the polygon. *(pages 102–103, 106–109)*

5. regular pentagon **6.** rhombus

7. scalene triangle **8.** trapezoid

Name the next three numbers.
(pages 104–105)

9. 2, 3.5, 5, 6.5, 8, . . .

10. 500, 100, 20, 4, . . .

Extra Practice on page 438

PERIMETER

You have a piece of molding 310 cm long. Do you have enough to make a rectangular frame 87 cm long by 32 cm wide?

The distance around a polygon is called the **perimeter.** To find the perimeter of a polygon, you add the lengths of all the sides.

First do a quick mental estimate of the sum.

$$(2 \times 90) + (2 \times 30) = 180 + 60 = 240$$

Then find the actual sum: $(2 \times 87) + (2 \times 32) = 174 + 64 = 238$

Compared to the estimate, your actual sum is reasonable. You have enough molding to make the frame.

A **formula** is a short way of stating a rule. We can write formulas for the perimeter of the polygons below. The length and width of a rectangle are often called the *base* and *height*.

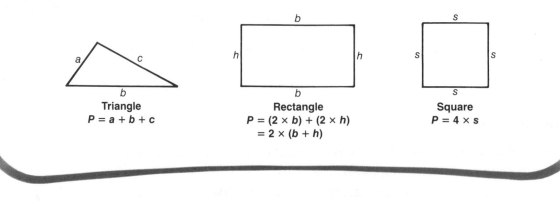

Triangle
$P = a + b + c$

Rectangle
$P = (2 \times b) + (2 \times h)$
$= 2 \times (b + h)$

Square
$P = 4 \times s$

CLASS EXERCISES

What is the perimeter?

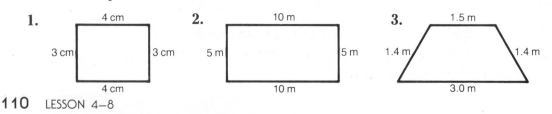

1. 4 cm · 3 cm · 3 cm · 4 cm

2. 10 m · 5 m · 5 m · 10 m

3. 1.5 m · 1.4 m · 1.4 m · 3.0 m

PRACTICE

What is the perimeter?

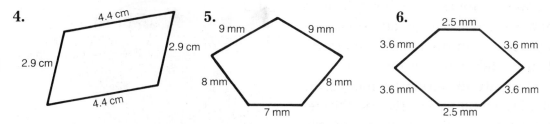

4. 4.4 cm, 2.9 cm, 2.9 cm, 4.4 cm

5. 9 mm, 9 mm, 8 mm, 8 mm, 7 mm

6. 2.5 mm, 3.6 mm, 3.6 mm, 3.6 mm, 3.6 mm, 2.5 mm

What is the perimeter of the rectangle? Use the formula.

7. $b = 6$ cm; $h = 8$ cm

8. $b = 70$ m; $h = 52$ m

9. $b = 82.1$ mm; $h = 90$ mm

10. $b = 8.5$ m; $h = 0.2$ m

Find the perimeter of the regular polygon.

11. hexagon
$s = 43$ cm

12. pentagon
$s = 16.9$ m

13. triangle
$s = 7$ ft

14. quadrilateral
$s = 15$ in.

Estimate the perimeter. The object has a rectangular shape.

15. Rug, 3.4 m by 2.1 m

16. Picture, 25 cm by 15 cm

17. Board, 82 cm by 40 cm

18. Mirror, 38 in. by 51 in.

19. Wall, 2.6 m by 1.3 m

20. Chair seat, 35 cm by 46 cm

ESTIMATE

PROBLEM SOLVING APPLICATIONS
Using Formulas

Use a formula to solve.

21. Melissa is building a fence around her rectangular-shaped backyard. The yard measures 17 ft by 23 ft. How much fencing material should she buy?

★ **22.** Alan used the formula $P = (2 \times b) + (2 \times h)$ for the perimeter of a rectangle. Mindy used the formula $P = 2 \times (b + h)$. Explain why they will get the same answer.

★ **23.** Frank has a 3 ft by 4 ft rectangular rug with a green border 6 in. from the edge of the rug. What is the inside perimeter of the green border?

CIRCUMFERENCE

A **circle** is the set of all points in a plane that are at the same distance from a point in the plane. The point is called the **center** of the circle.

A **radius** is a line segment that joins the center and a point on the circle. A segment that joins two points on a circle is called a **chord.** A chord that passes through the center of the circle is a **diameter** of the circle. The diameter of a circle is twice as long as its radius.

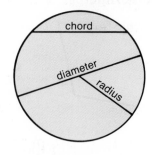

The distance around a circle is called the **circumference.** The quotient *circumference* ÷ *diameter* is the same number for all circles. We use the Greek letter π (pi) to stand for this number. A close approximation is 3.14. The symbol $\approx$ means *is approximately equal to.* Thus, we can write:

$$C \div d = \pi \qquad \text{or} \qquad C \div d \approx 3.14$$
$$C = \pi \times d \qquad \text{or} \qquad C \approx 3.14 \times d$$
$$C = 2 \times \pi \times r \qquad \text{or} \qquad C \approx 2 \times 3.14 \times r$$

You can use the formula to find the circumference of a bicycle tire 70 cm in diameter. $C \approx 3.14 \times 70 = 219.8$ (cm)

If you measure the circumference of a circle to be about 28.3 cm and the diameter about 9 cm, how can you use a calculator to verify the approximate value of π?

CLASS EXERCISES

Describe the part of the circle named.

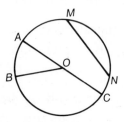

1. $\overline{AC}$ **2.** $\overline{OC}$ **3.** $\overline{MN}$ **4.** point O

Complete.

5. If $AO = 5$ cm, then $AC = $ ▢ cm.   **6.** If $AC = 12$ mm, then $OB = $ ▢ mm.

PRACTICE

For Exercises 7–24 use $\pi \approx 3.14$.

Find the circumference.

   7. $d = 35$ cm   **8.** $d = 50$ cm   **9.** $d = 24$ mm   **10.** $r = 15$ cm

11. $r = 18$ cm   **12.** $r = 17$ m   **13.** $d = 3.3$ cm   **14.** $d = 1.5$ mm

15. $d = 0.6$ km   **16.** $r = 10.8$ cm   **17.** $r = 1.4$ m   **18.** $r = 6.5$ mm

The diagrams below are parts of circles, and the angles are right angles. Find the perimeter.

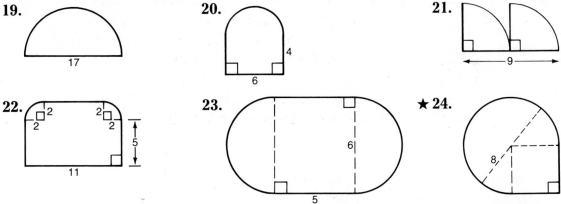

19.   17

20.   4   6

21.   9

22.   2   2   2   2   5   11

23.   6   5

★ **24.**   8

Computers have approximated π to over 1,000,000 decimal places. Many ancient peoples have also approximated π. Use your calculator to give the value each group used.

CALCULATOR

25. Romans:
    $\pi \approx 25 \div 8$

26. Egyptians:
    $\pi \approx 256 \div 81$

27. Chinese:
    $\pi \approx 355 \div 113$

PROBLEM SOLVING APPLICATIONS
Choosing a Strategy

Solve.

28. Can a circle with a radius of 7 cm fit inside a square with a perimeter of 36 cm?

★ **29.** A jogger runs daily at a steady pace of 6 mi/h for 5 h. The radius of Earth at the equator is about 4000 mi. About how many days would it take the jogger to complete a distance equal to the circumference at the equator?

AREAS OF RECTANGLES AND SQUARES

Andrea sewed squares of fabric together to make a quilt. To find the **area** of the quilt, she counts the number of squares used. She counts 24 squares.

Another way to find the area of the quilt is to use the formula for the area of a rectangle:

$$\text{Area} = \text{base} \times \text{height}$$
$$A = b \times h$$
$$= 6 \times 4 = 24$$

The area of the quilt is 24 square units.

Since a square is a special rectangle with the length equal to the width, you can use the letter s to identify the length of a side and write the formula for the area of a square as

$$A = s \times s, \text{ or } A = s^2.$$

Some metric units for measuring area are the square millimeter (mm^2), the square centimeter (cm^2), the square meter (m^2), and the square kilometer (km^2).

1 cm

1 mm²

$$1 \text{ cm}^2 = 10 \text{ mm} \times 10 \text{ mm}$$
$$= 100 \text{ mm}^2$$

E You can estimate that the area of a postage stamp is about 4 cm^2. How many square millimeters is that?

CLASS EXERCISES

What is the area?

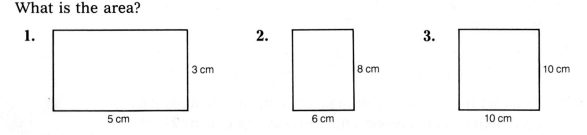

1.

3 cm

5 cm

2.

8 cm

6 cm

3.

10 cm

10 cm

PRACTICE

Complete.

4. $3 \text{ cm}^2 = \blacksquare \text{ mm}^2$ **5.** $8 \text{ cm}^2 = \blacksquare \text{ mm}^2$ **6.** $\blacksquare \text{ cm}^2 = 900 \text{ mm}^2$

What is the area of the rectangle?

	7.	8.	9.	10.	11.
BASE	20 cm	14 km	13 mm	7.5 m	16.41 cm
HEIGHT	8 cm	10 km	3 mm	8.3 m	4.9 cm

What is the area of the square?

12. $s = 9.8$ cm **13.** $s = 12$ in. **14.** $s = 30$ m **15.** $s = 13.4$ km

What is the area of the shaded region?

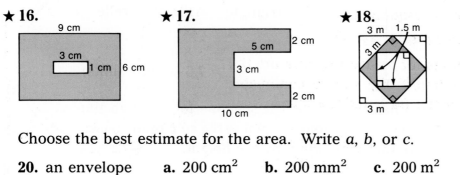

★ **16.**

★ **17.**

★ **18.**

★ **19.**

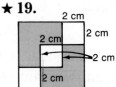

Choose the best estimate for the area. Write a, b, or c.

20. an envelope **a.** 200 cm^2 **b.** 200 mm^2 **c.** 200 m^2

21. a library card **a.** 40 cm^2 **b.** 40 mm^2 **c.** 40 m^2

22. an open field **a.** 5000 cm^2 **b.** 5000 mm^2 **c.** 5000 m^2

ESTIMATE

PROBLEM SOLVING APPLICATIONS
Choosing a Strategy

Solve.

23. How many square feet of wallpaper will you need to cover a wall 9 ft high by 16 ft wide?

24. Compare the areas of a square 15 cm on each side and a rectangle 11 cm by 8 cm. Which has the greater area?

★ **25.** Vinyl floor covering costs $4.50 per square foot. How much will it cost to cover a floor measuring 16 ft by 24 ft?

AREAS OF PARALLELOGRAMS, TRIANGLES, AND TRAPEZOIDS

The height of a parallelogram is the length of a perpendicular line segment that joins two opposite sides. The area of a parallelogram is the same as the area of a rectangle with the same base and height.

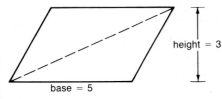

Area = base × height
$$A = b \times h$$
$$= 5 \times 3$$
$$= 15 \text{ (square units)}$$

A diagonal of a parallelogram divides the parallelogram into two triangles with equal areas. The area of one triangle is equal to the area of the parallelogram divided by 2.

Area of Triangle = Area of Parallelogram ÷ 2
$$A = b \times h \div 2$$
$$= 5 \times 3 \div 2$$
$$= 7.5 \text{ (square units)}$$

A trapezoid has two parallel bases, one longer than the other. The area of a trapezoid is equal to the sum of the bases divided by two, then multiplied by the height.

Area of Trapezoid = (sum of the bases ÷ 2) × height
$$A = (b_1 + b_2) \div 2 \times h$$
$$= (8 + 6) \div 2 \times 4$$
$$= 14 \div 2 \times 4$$
$$= 7 \times 4 = 28 \text{ (square units)}$$

CLASS EXERCISES

What is the area?

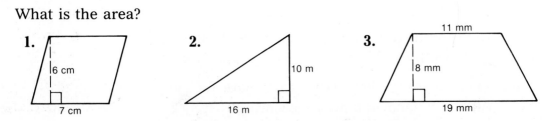

1. 6 cm, 7 cm

2. 10 m, 16 m

3. 11 mm, 8 mm, 19 mm

PRACTICE

What is the area of the parallelogram?

	4.	5.	6.	7.	8.	9.
BASE	30 cm	12 m	60 mm	33 cm	300 cm	12.3 cm
HEIGHT	4 cm	6 m	12 mm	10 cm	25 cm	12.3 cm

What is the area of the triangle?

	10.	11.	12.	13.	14.	15.
BASE	13 cm	20 mm	6 m	28 cm	12.3 m	24 mm
HEIGHT	6 cm	25 mm	6 m	4 cm	25 m	28.5 mm

What is the area of the trapezoid?

	16.	17.	18.	19.
BASES	6 cm, 4 cm	3 m, 9 m	10 mm, 16 mm	15 in., 18 in.
HEIGHT	3 cm	12 m	8 mm	7 in.

Write the answer.

20. 18^2 **21.** $8.2 \div 2$ **22.** 2.5^2

23. 3.14×2^2 **24.** $1.3^2 \times 7$ **25.** 3.14×5^2

MIXED REVIEW

PROBLEM SOLVING APPLICATIONS
Using Information from a Diagram

Solve. Use the diagram of the garden to answer.

26. What is the total area of all the flower beds?

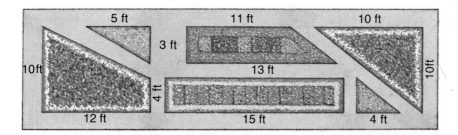

AREA OF A CIRCLE

The surface enclosed by a circle is the area of the circle. The area of the circle is equal to π times the radius squared.

$$A = \pi \times r^2$$

To find the approximate area of a circle, use $\pi \approx 3.14$. For example, what is the approximate area of a circle 6 m in diameter?

$$A = \pi \times r^2$$
$$\approx 3.14 \times 3^2$$
$$\approx 3.14 \times 9$$
$$\approx 28.26$$

The area is about 28.26 m^2.

If your calculator has a key labeled $\boxed{\pi}$, press it and it may show 3.1415927. If you use that key instead of 3.14 to figure area on a calculator, your answers will differ from those of this book. The calculator answers will be more precise.

CLASS EXERCISES

Complete.

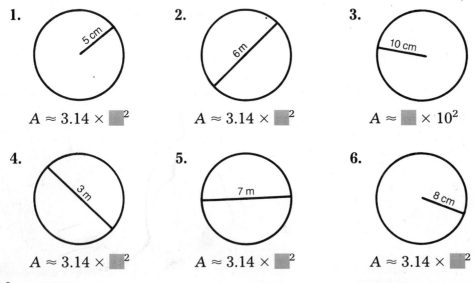

1.
5 cm

$A \approx 3.14 \times \blacksquare^2$

2.
6 m

$A \approx 3.14 \times \blacksquare^2$

3.
10 cm

$A \approx \blacksquare \times 10^2$

4.
3 m

$A \approx 3.14 \times \blacksquare^2$

5.
7 m

$A \approx 3.14 \times \blacksquare^2$

6.
8 cm

$A \approx 3.14 \times \blacksquare^2$

PRACTICE

What is the area of the circular-shaped item?

7. Cushion, radius 20 cm

8. Clock, radius 12 cm

9. Table top, radius 40 cm

10. Dart board, radius 60 cm

11. Lamp base, diameter 16 cm

12. Rug, diameter 80 cm

What is the area of the shaded region?

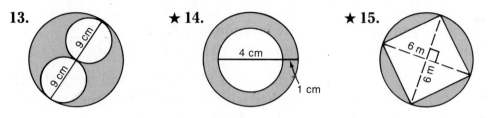

13. 9 cm 9 cm 9 cm

★ 14. 4 cm 1 cm

★ 15. 6 m 6 m

What is the area of the circle? Use $\pi \approx 3.14$.

16. $r = 6$ m   **17.** $r = 18$ cm   **18.** $r = 20$ mm

19. $d = 40$ cm   **20.** $d = 160$ mm   **21.** $d = 8.2$ m

CALCULATOR

PROBLEM SOLVING APPLICATIONS
Using Formulas

You are designing a circular fireplace with a radius of 3 ft. You want to put fireproof flooring 2 ft wide around the fireplace.

Solve. Round answers to the nearest whole number.

22. What is the area of the fireplace?

23. What is the outer circumference of the fireproof flooring?

★ 24. What is the area of the fireproof flooring needed to go around the fireplace?

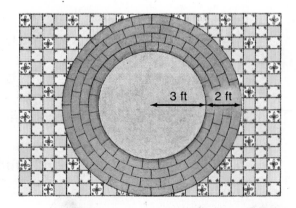

3 ft   2 ft

PROBLEM SOLVING
Strategy: Using Formulas

1. Understand
2. Plan
3. Work
4. Answer/Check

Formulas are often helpful in problem solving. A formula uses symbols instead of words to state a rule.

The City Club wants to line the edge of their swimming pool with blue tiles. Each tile is square and measures 1 ft in length. At each of the four corners they will use a white tile. How many tiles will they need in all?

To solve the problem, first choose the correct formula. To find the distance around the pool, use the formula for perimeter of a rectangle. The pool's dimensions are 10 ft by 30 ft.

$P = 2 \times (b + h)$
$ = 2 \times (10 + 30)$
$ = 2 \times 40 = 80$

The perimeter is 80 ft. They will need 80 blue tiles. Together with the white tiles, they will need a total of 84 tiles.

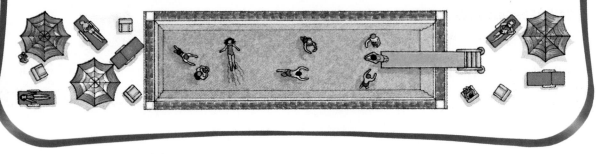

CLASS EXERCISES

Which formula would you use to solve?

1. Circumference of a drum

2. Area of a triangular sail

3. Perimeter of a stop sign

4. Perimeter of a baseball diamond

5. Area of a square floor

6. Area of a rectangular trampoline

PRACTICE

Use a formula to solve the problem.

7. What is the perimeter of a rectangular window that is 5 ft wide and 11 ft high?

8. What is the area of a triangular pennant 18 in. high and 6 in. at its widest?

9. What is the circumference of a jar with a 9 in. diameter?

10. A square field has sides of 245 m each. A rectangular field is 200 m long by 300 m wide.
    a. Which field has the greater perimeter?
    b. Which field has the greater area?
    c. What is the total area of both fields?

11. The floor space directly beneath the rotunda in the U.S. Capitol building is round with a diameter of about 30 m. About how many square meters of carpeting is needed to cover that area?

12. A bicycle tire has a diameter of 17 in. What distance does the tire cover in one complete revolution?

★ 13. The boom of a revolving sprinkler is 150 m long. What is the area of land covered by each revolution of the sprinkler?

★ 14. A lighthouse beacon can be seen 23 mi in all directions. Over how many square miles can the beacon be seen?

CHECKPOINT 2

Name the formula for the perimeter. (pages 110–113)

1. rectangle   2. triangle

3. square   4. circle

What is the area? (pages 114–117)

5. square: $s = 9$ cm

6. triangle: $b = 15$ in.; $h = 21$ in.

7. rectangle: $b = 14$ mm; $h = 7$ mm

8. trapezoid: $b_1 = 7$ m, $b_2 = 10$ m; $h = 8$ m

What is the area of the circle? (pages 118–119)

9. $r = 55$ cm   10. $d = 28$ mm

Use a formula to solve. (pages 120–121)

11. Which has the greater area, a circle with a radius of 4 m or a square measuring 8 m on each side?

12. What is the circumference of a wheel with a diameter of 2 m?

Extra Practice on page 438

CHAPTER 4 TEST

Use a protractor to draw the angle. *(pages 98–101)*

1. an obtuse angle

2. an angle complementary to a 30° angle

Draw the polygon. *(pages 102–103)*

3. quadrilateral   **4.** triangle   **5.** pentagon   **6.** hexagon

Look for the pattern to continue the sequence. *(pages 104–105)*

7.

NO. OF SIDES	3	4	5	6	7	8	9
SUM OF ANGLE MEASURES	180°	360°	540°	720°	?	?	?

Name the polygons that have the property. Write *a*, *b*, or *c*.
There may be more than one correct answer. *(pages 106–109)*

8. At least one pair of sides is parallel.

9. All sides are congruent.

10. All angles are acute.

A. rhombus

B. trapezoid

C. equilateral triangle

Find the perimeter or circumference. *(pages 110–113)*

11. regular hexagon: $s = 12.6$ cm

12. circle: $d = 14$ in.

Find the area. Use $\pi \approx 3.14$. *(pages 114–119)*

13. triangle: $b = 8$ mm, $h = 15$ mm

14. circle: $r = 3.5$ m

Use a formula to solve. *(pages 120–121)*

15. What is the area of a triangular flag 12 in. high and 4 in. at its widest?

16. Which has the smaller area, a square measuring 6 m on each side or a circle with a radius of 5 m?

Extra Practice on page 439

MATHEMATICS and ART

Artists have often used geometric shapes and figures to play tricks on our eyes to create an optical illusion.

Look at *Figure 1* at the right. Is $\overline{AB}$ congruent to $\overline{CD}$? Now use a ruler and measure the length of each segment.

Look at *Figure 2* at the right. Is $\overline{MN}$ congruent to $\overline{OP}$? Again, use a ruler to measure the length of each segment.

Figure 1

Figure 2

IS IT OR ISN'T IT?

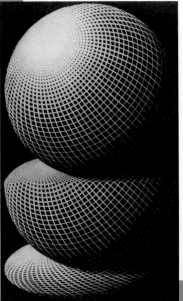

1. Which line looks longer? Measure. Were you right?

2. Which point is collinear with X and Y?

3. Is base 1 the same length as base 2?

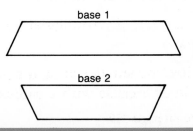

base 1

base 2

Enrichment

You find the area of a square by multiplying the length of a side by itself. The area of the square at the right is

$$4 \times 4 = 4^2.$$

For this reason, the expression 4^2 is read as *the square of four* or *four squared*.

Because $16 = 4^2$, we say that a **square root** of 16 is 4. The symbol for square root is $\sqrt{}$. You can write,

$$\sqrt{16} = 4.$$

We read $\sqrt{16}$ as *the square root of 16*.

Many calculators have a special key that can be used to find the square root of a number. On many calculators it looks like this $\boxed{\sqrt{}}$.

Write the square root. Use a calculator if you wish.

1. $\sqrt{36}$	**2.** $\sqrt{49}$	**3.** $\sqrt{81}$	**4.** $\sqrt{100}$	**5.** $\sqrt{1}$
6. $\sqrt{121}$	**7.** $\sqrt{169}$	**8.** $\sqrt{256}$	**9.** $\sqrt{625}$	**10.** $\sqrt{900}$

What is the length of the side of a square with the given area?

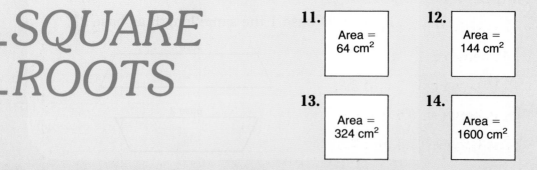

SQUARE ROOTS

11.
Area =
64 cm²

12.
Area =
144 cm²

13.
Area =
324 cm²

14.
Area =
1600 cm²

Often the square root of a number is not a whole number.
For example:

Think: Do you know two square numbers between which 18 lies?

$\sqrt{18} = ?$ 18 is between 16 and 25.
$\sqrt{18}$ is between $\sqrt{16}$ and $\sqrt{25}$.
$\sqrt{18}$ is between 4 and 5.

A square root table like the one at the right can be used to find a more exact value for $\sqrt{18}$. In this table, each square root is rounded to the nearest thousandth.

To use the table, find 18 in the *Number* column. Read the square root of 18 in the column to its right. The square root of 18 is *approximately* 4.243.

Use the table to find an approximate square root.

15. $\sqrt{2}$ **16.** $\sqrt{5}$ **17.** $\sqrt{9}$

18. $\sqrt{11}$ **19.** $\sqrt{15}$ **20.** $\sqrt{16}$

21. $\sqrt{17}$ **22.** $\sqrt{20}$

Write *true* or *false*.

23. $\sqrt{8}$ is between $\sqrt{4}$ and $\sqrt{9}$.

24. $\sqrt{21}$ is between $\sqrt{25}$ and $\sqrt{36}$.

25. $\sqrt{3}$ is between 1 and 2.

26. $\sqrt{41}$ is between 6 and 7.

27. $\sqrt{3}$ is between 1.7 and 1.8.

28. $\sqrt{15}$ is between 3.7 and 3.8.

29. $\sqrt{44}$ is between 6.5 and 6.6.

30. $\sqrt{57}$ is between 7.5 and 7.6.

NUMBER	SQUARE ROOT
1	1
2	1.414
3	1.732
4	2
5	2.236
6	2.449
7	2.646
8	2.828
9	3
10	3.162
11	3.317
12	3.464
13	3.606
14	3.742
15	3.873
16	4
17	4.123
18	4.243
19	4.359
20	4.472

CUMULATIVE REVIEW

Choose the correct answer. Write *a*, *b*, *c*, or *d*.

What is the value of the underlined digit?

1. 32,58<u>6</u>
  a. 60
  b. 600
  c. 6
  d. None of these

2. 7<u>88</u>,631,419
  a. 8,000
  b. 80,000,000
  c. 80,000
  d. None of these

3. 0.765<u>4</u>5
  a. 40
  b. 0.004
  c. 0.0004
  d. None of these

What is the order from least to greatest?

4. 4800, 4080, 4008, 4480
  a. 4008, 4080, 4480, 4800
  b. 4080, 4008, 4480, 4800
  c. 4800, 4480, 4080, 4008
  d. None of these

5. 0.485, 0.845, 0.85, 0.8
  a. 0.8, 0.85, 0.845, 0.485
  b. 0.485, 0.845, 0.85, 0.8
  c. 0.485, 0.8, 0.845, 0.85
  d. None of these

Find the answer.

6. 3756 + 6577
  a. 9223
  b. 9333
  c. 10,223
  d. None of these

7. 8.323 + 11.45
  a. 8.468
  b. 19.873
  c. 19.773
  d. None of these

8. $9.85 + $3.60 + $.52
  a. $13.97
  b. $13.87
  c. $12.97
  d. None of these

9. 600 − 322
  a. 388
  b. 278
  c. 288
  d. None of these

10. 0.8 − 0.3562
  a. 0.4538
  b. 0.4548
  c. 0.4438
  d. None of these

11. $28.69 − 8.74
  a. $20.95
  b. $19.35
  c. $19.95
  d. None of these

12. 837 × 109
  a. 91,223
  b. 90,233
  c. 91,333
  d. None of these

13. 0.47 × 0.006
  a. 0.00282
  b. 0.0282
  c. 0.000282
  d. None of these

14. 30.314 × 0.73
  a. 22.12922
  b. 221.2922
  c. 2212.922
  d. None of these

Solve.

15. Jess worked 2.75 h on Monday, 3.5 h on Tuesday, and 4.25 h on Wednesday. He earns $3.10 an hour. How much did he earn in all?
  a. $31.55
  b. $32.55
  c. $21.55
  d. None of these

16. Paper plates cost $1.29 a package, and paper cups cost $.85 a package. How much will 5 packages of plates and 8 packages of cups cost?
  a. $10.70
  b. $9.70
  c. $10.60
  d. None of these

Find the answer.

17. $31\overline{)473}$
  a. 15 R18
  b. 15 R8
  c. 14 R8
  d. None of these

18. $8\overline{)16.56}$
  a. 2.07
  b. 20.7
  c. 2.70
  d. None of these

19. $24\overline{)1.248}$
  a. 0.52
  b. 0.042
  c. 0.052
  d. None of these

LANGUAGE and VOCABULARY REVIEW

Match each term with its description.

1. acute angle

2. perimeter

3. diameter

4. pentagon

5. right angle

6. octagon

7. obtuse angle

8. degree

A. a chord that passes through the center of a circle

B. an angle that has a measure greater than 90° and less than 180°

C. a five-sided polygon

D. unit of measure for angles

E. an eight-sided polygon

F. an angle that has a measure greater than 0° and less than 90°

G. the distance around a polygon

H. an angle that measures 90°

CPU: CONTROL UNIT

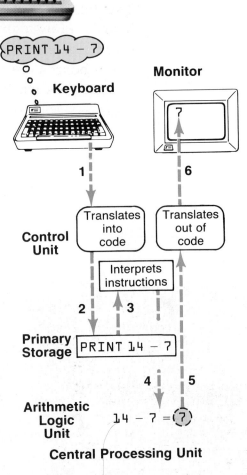

COMPUTER LITERACY

One part of the Central Processing Unit (CPU) is the Control Unit.

The Control Unit directs the flow of data through the computer. It performs these operations:

Translates characters into machine language or code.

Sends data into memory.

Interprets instructions.

Sends data to the Arithmetic Logic Unit. The data are used to do arithmetic or make comparisons.

Displays output.

Follow the steps in the diagram to see how the computer processes the instruction PRINT 14–7.

1. What part of the CPU translates the instruction PRINT 40 + 5900?

2. Do you think the ALU is used for the instruction, PRINT "HELLO"? Explain.

3. Use the diagram. List the steps to process the instruction, PRINT 4 + 10.

5

This lumber is stacked in groups of 56 boards. How many rows are in each stack? How many columns? How many boards are in 2 stacks? in 3 stacks? in 4 stacks?

NUMBER THEORY AND DEVELOPING FRACTIONS

DIVISIBILITY

A number is **divisible** by another number when the first number can be divided by the second number and the resulting quotient is a whole number.

On a calculator, quotients are shown as decimals or whole numbers.

42 ÷ 4 = 10.5   42 ÷ 6 = 7

42 is not divisible by 4.   42 is divisible by 6.

For certain divisors, you can use mental math to test for divisibility.

DIVISIBILITY TEST		EXAMPLES	DIVISIBLE
By 2:	Is the ones' digit 0, 2, 4, 6, or 8?	35	no
		60	yes
By 5:	Is the ones' digit 0 or 5?	85	yes
		30	yes
By 10:	Is the ones' digit 0?	25	no
		40	yes
By 4:	Is the number named by the last two digits divisible by 4?	124	yes
		213	no
By 3:	Is the sum of the digits divisible by 3?	45 → 4 + 5 = 9	yes
		90 → 9 + 0 = 9	yes
By 9:	Is the sum of the digits divisible by 9?	75 → 7 + 5 = 12	no
		126 → 1 + 2 + 6 = 9	yes

Numbers that are divisible by 2 are called **even** numbers.

50 is even.

Numbers that are not divisible by 2 are called **odd** numbers.

35 is odd.

CLASS EXERCISES

Is the first number divisible by the second? Write *yes* or *no*.

1. 88; 2   **2.** 154; 5   **3.** 245; 2   **4.** 300; 10

5. 128; 9   **6.** 231; 3   **7.** 345; 5   **8.** 1408; 4

PRACTICE

Write *2, 3, 4, 5, 9, 10,* or *none* to tell by which numbers the given number is divisible.

9. 457	**10.** 6582	**11.** 5000	**12.** 685
13. 1036	**14.** 1790	**15.** 726	**16.** 1028
17. 3332	**18.** 4064	**19.** 605	**20.** 1090
21. 2005	**22.** 963	**23.** 6103	**24.** 4122
25. 7062	**26.** 312	**27.** 4650	**28.** 6345

★ **29. Think:** What is the largest 3-digit number divisible by 4?

★ **30. Think:** What is the smallest 4-digit number divisible by 3?

Write *true* or *false.*

31. If a number is divisible by 10, it is also divisible by 2.

32. All odd numbers are divisible by 3.

★ **33.** If a number is divisible by 2 and 3, it is also divisible by 6.

Is the first number divisible by the second number? Write *yes* or *no.* Use a calculator or a divisibility test to help you decide.

CALCULATOR

34. 259 by 2	**35.** 1134 by 9	**36.** 2536 by 4
37. 3472 by 3	**38.** 4185 by 5	**39.** 2001 by 10

PROBLEM SOLVING APPLICATIONS
Nonroutine Problems

Solve.

40. A leap year is a year whose number is divisible by 4. A century is a leap year only when its number is divisible by 400. If you are born in a leap year and live to be eighty, how many leap years will you see?

★ **41.** Any number of 1000's is divisible by 8. Use this fact to devise a test for divisibility by 8.

FACTORS AND GREATEST COMMON FACTORS

When one number is divisible by another, the second is called a **factor** of the first.

$12 \div 1 = 12$	$12 \div 4 = 3$	$18 \div 1 = 18$	$18 \div 6 = 3$
$12 \div 2 = 6$	$12 \div 6 = 2$	$18 \div 2 = 9$	$18 \div 9 = 2$
$12 \div 3 = 4$	$12 \div 12 = 1$	$18 \div 3 = 6$	$18 \div 18 = 1$

Factors of 12: 1, 2, 3, 4, 6, 12   Factors of 18: 1, 2, 3, 6, 9, 18

Two numbers may have some factors that are the same. These factors are called **common factors.**

Common factors of 12 and 18: 1, 2, 3, 6

The **greatest common factor (GCF)** of 12 and 18 is 6.

You can use the divisibility tests to help you decide if one number is a factor of another. For example, is 3 a factor of 108?

Think: Is the sum of the digits divisible by 3?

$1 + 0 + 8 = 9$ ⇨ 3 is a factor of 108.

CLASS EXERCISES

Is the first number a factor of the second? Write *yes* or *no*.

1. 2; 8   **2.** 4; 15   **3.** 8; 24   **4.** 9; 36

5. 7; 54   **6.** 3; 25   **7.** 16; 64   **8.** 25; 100

9. 9; 108   **10.** 10; 75   **11.** 12; 108   **12.** 100; 200

Complete.

13. factors of 4: 1, 2, ▧
factors of 8: 1, 2, 4, ▧
common factors of 4 and 8:
▧, ▧, ▧
GCF of 4 and 8: ▧

14. factors of 16: 1, 2, 4, ▧, ▧
factors of 20: 1, 2, 4, ▧, ▧, ▧
common factors of 16 and 20:
▧, ▧, ▧
GCF of 16 and 20: ▧

PRACTICE

Write the GCF of the numbers.

15. 4 and 6   **16.** 9 and 12   **17.** 18 and 21   **18.** 10 and 35

19. 7 and 15   **20.** 14 and 21   **21.** 12 and 44   **22.** 16 and 18

23. 24 and 28   **24.** 24 and 42   **25.** 16 and 24   **26.** 28 and 32

27. 75 and 175   **28.** 60 and 105   **29.** 280 and 320

30. 250 and 300   ★ **31.** 20, 28, and 40   ★ **32.** 18, 36, and 27

★ **33.** 300, 600, and 800   ★ **34.** 360, 840, and 1290   ★ **35.** 252, 672, and 189

Use mental math to decide if the first number is a factor of both of the next two numbers. Write *yes* or *no*.

36. 2; 8, 16   **37.** 4; 15, 25   **38.** 5; 35, 40

39. 9; 108, 216   **40.** 10; 75, 95   **41.** 6; 63, 72

MENTAL MATH

42. Could you have used a calculator or estimation for Exercises 36–41? Explain your answer.

PROBLEM SOLVING APPLICATIONS
Logical Thinking

Solve.

43. A group of 72 players from Roundball Camp and 56 players from Central League met to play basketball. Each group must separate into teams with the same number of players. What is the greatest number of players that can be on each team?

44. You expect about 480 people to attend a camp talent show. If you can have 36 chairs in each row, how many rows of chairs should you set up?

★ **45.** I have nine factors. Two of my factors are 3 and 6. I am a two-digit number. The sum of my digits is 9 and the difference is 3. What number am I?

PRIMES AND COMPOSITES

Look at the table at the right. Notice that 2, 3, 5, and 7 have exactly 2 factors. Numbers that have exactly two factors are called **prime numbers.** A whole number that has more than two factors is called a **composite number.** In the table, 4, 6, and 8 are composite numbers. The numbers 0 and 1 are neither prime nor composite.

NUMBER	FACTORS
1	1
2	1, 2
3	1, 3
4	1, 2, 4
5	1, 5
6	1, 2, 3, 6
7	1, 7
8	1, 2, 4, 8

Every composite number can be written as a product of prime factors. Drawing a factor tree may help you find the prime factors of a number.

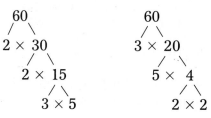

Notice that the prime factors of 60 are the same in either factor tree. Only the order of the factors is different.

$2 \times 2 \times 3 \times 5$ is called the **prime factorization** of 60.

Ⓜ You can check a prime factorization by multiplying mentally.
Think: $2 \times 2 \times 3 \times 5 = 60$

CLASS EXERCISES

Write the factors.

1. 9   **2.** 8   **3.** 5   **4.** 3   **5.** 28   **6.** 31

7. 29   **8.** 51   **9.** 73   **10.** 81   **11.** 94   **12.** 101

Is the number prime or composite? Write *prime* or *composite*.

13. 11   **14.** 19   **15.** 14   **16.** 22   **17.** 17   **18.** 35

19. 42   **20.** 43   **21.** 86   **22.** 151   **23.** 146   **24.** 205

PRACTICE

Complete the factor tree.

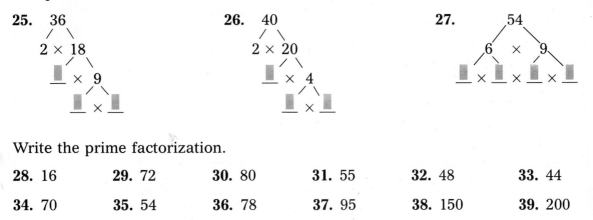

25. 36
    / \
   2 × 18
       / \
   __ × 9
       / \
    __ × __

26. 40
    / \
   2 × 20
       / \
   __ × 4
       / \
     __ × __

27.   54
       /   \
      6   ×   9
     / \   / \
   __ × __ × __ × __

Write the prime factorization.

28. 16   **29.** 72   **30.** 80   **31.** 55   **32.** 48   **33.** 44

34. 70   **35.** 54   **36.** 78   **37.** 95   **38.** 150   **39.** 200

Use mental math to find the error in the prime factorization.
Then write it correctly.

40. $24 = 2 \times 2 \times 3 \times 3$

41. $64 = 4 \times 16$

42. $81 = 3 \times 3 \times 3$

43. $120 = 2 \times 3 \times 3 \times 5$

MENTAL MATH

PROBLEM SOLVING APPLICATIONS
Choosing a Strategy

Solve.

44. The prime factors of a number n are 3 and 5. If $40 < n < 50$, what is n?

45. How many primes are there between 20 and 50? between 50 and 75?

46. A box to hold balloons in 24 separate compartments can be made in different rectangular shapes. What different arrangements of compartments can be made? (There is more than one answer.)

PROBLEM SOLVING
Strategy: Open-Ended Problems

Many problems have more than one correct answer.

Which coins, other than pennies, can you use to make change for a dollar?

Some answers are: 4 quarters

5 dimes, 2 quarters

2 dimes, 6 nickels, 2 quarters

Think: How many other answers can you think of?

Sometimes a problem can be solved by thinking about it in different ways.

Example: Find a pattern and write the next two numbers in the series. 2, 3, 5, 8, ▮, ▮

Pattern 1 — Each number in the series is the sum of the two previous numbers.

Solution: More than one pattern is possible with this set of numbers.

sum

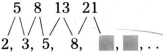

2, 3, 5, 8, ▮, ▮, . . .

Pattern 2 — The difference between two numbers in the pattern increases by one.

difference

1 2 3 4 5

/\\/\\/\\/\\/\\

2, 3, 5, 8, ▮, ▮, . . .

CLASS EXERCISES

1. List all the ways you can have 50¢ without using pennies or a half dollar.

Find a pattern and list the next two numbers in the series.

2. 1, 3, 5, ▮, ▮

3. 2, 4, 6, ▮, ▮

4. 2, 4, 8, ▮, ▮

5. 1, 4, 9 ▮, ▮

6. 1, 2, 4, 5, ▮, ▮

7. 0, 3, 1, 4, ▮, ▮

PRACTICE

Solve.

8. A customer ordered 15 pens. Pens come singly or in packages of 3 or 5. Describe five different ways you could fill the order.

9. Write names for the numbers 1 to 5 using only 4's. You may use only four 4's for each number. For example, $4 \div 4$ is one way to write 1.

10. You have 42 ft of fence. What are the dimensions, in whole feet, of all rectangular areas that can be enclosed with the fence? Which dimensions will give the greatest area?

11. In tic–tack–toe, you win by getting 3 of your marks in a row vertically, horizontally, or diagonally. Where should you place your first mark to have the most possible ways of winning?

12. José has six coins that total $1.15. He has no nickels and no pennies. What coins might he have?

13. Describe two ways in which you could cut rectangles that measure 3 in. by 5 in. from a rectangular piece of cardboard that measures 13 in. by 16 in. Which way will give you more rectangles? Drawing a picture may help.

14. Bonnie threw 5 darts and all 5 hit the target. Which of the following could be her score: 4, 17, 33, 59, 31, 28?

★ 15. There are a certain number of books and a certain number of shelves. If five books are put on each shelf, there will be five books left over. To put seven books on each shelf, 3 more books are needed. How many books and how many shelves are there?

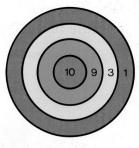

FRACTIONS

Each wheel of cheese is cut into 8 equal pieces at The Cheese Shop. Each piece is one eighth of a whole wheel.

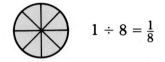

$$1 \div 8 = \frac{1}{8}$$

Three wheels are shared equally by 8 people. The amount for each person is $3 \div 8$, or $\frac{3}{8}$. Each person has three eighths of a wheel.

$\frac{3}{8}$ ◄─── number of wheels
   ◄─── number of people sharing

Last week 4 wheels of cheddar cheese were in the shop, but only 3 were sold. Three fourths of the wheels were sold.

$\frac{3}{4}$ ◄─── number of wheels sold
   ◄─── total number of wheels

The numbers $\frac{1}{8}$, $\frac{3}{4}$, and $\frac{3}{8}$ are called **fractions.**

In a fraction, we call the top number the **numerator** and the bottom number the **denominator.**

$\frac{1}{8}$ ◄─── numerator
   ◄─── denominator

CLASS EXERCISES

Complete.

1.

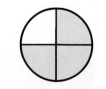

◄─── number of pieces shaded
◄─── total number of pieces

2.

◄─── number of ⬭ cheeses
◄─── total number of cheeses

PRACTICE

What fraction of all the cheeses in the gift package have the shape shown?

3. 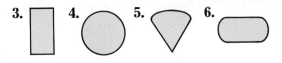 **4.** **5.** **6.**

Use the information from the inventory form. Write the fraction of the total for each type of cheese in the shop.

7. Blue   **8.** Cheddar

9. Edam   **10.** Gouda

11. Munster   **12.** Parmesan

13. Romano   **14.** Swiss

15. Romano and Parmesan

16. Edam and Gouda

INVENTORY	Date: 12-5
Cheese	**No. of Wheels**
Swiss	3
Edam	8
Cheddar	11
Romano	9
Parmesan	7
Munster	2
Blue	1
Gouda	6
TOTAL	47

Write the answer.

17. 6210
×7.02

18. 3003
+1999

19. 40,213
− 2,090

20. 135
×16.2

MIXED REVIEW

PROBLEM SOLVING APPLICATIONS
Choosing a Strategy

Solve.

21. The Cheese Shop is open 9 h a day. What fraction of the hours in a day is the shop open?

22. The school band has 42 brass, 12 woodwind, and 5 percussion instruments. What fraction is represented by each section?

EQUIVALENT FRACTIONS

Fractions can be pictured on a number line. The number lines below show that the fractions $\frac{3}{4}$, $\frac{6}{8}$, and $\frac{12}{16}$ name the same number.

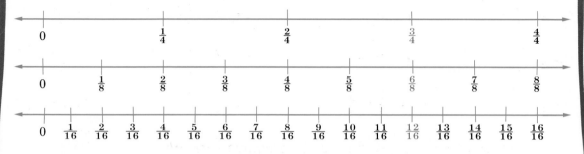

Fractions that name the same number are called **equivalent fractions.** To write equivalent fractions, multiply or divide by a fraction equal to 1.

$$\frac{3}{4} = \frac{3 \times 2}{4 \times 2} = \frac{6}{8} \qquad \frac{12}{16} = \frac{12 \div 4}{16 \div 4} = \frac{3}{4}$$

You can use **cross products** to check for equivalent fractions. Are $\frac{4}{18}$ and $\frac{6}{27}$ equivalent fractions? Use a calculator for a quick check.

$$\frac{4}{18} \diagdown\!\!\!\!\diagup \frac{6}{27}$$

4 ⌧ 27 🟰 108   18 ⌧ 6 🟰 108   cross products: 108, 108

When the cross products are equal, the fractions are equivalent. So, $\frac{4}{18}$ and $\frac{6}{27}$ are equivalent fractions.

CLASS EXERCISES

Complete.

1. $\frac{3}{4} = \frac{3 \times 3}{4 \times 3} = \blacksquare$

2. $\frac{7}{9} = \frac{7 \times 2}{9 \times 2} = \blacksquare$

3. $\frac{1}{12} = \frac{1 \times 3}{12 \times 3} = \blacksquare$

4. $\frac{4}{6} = \frac{4 \div 2}{6 \div 2} = \blacksquare$

5. $\frac{3}{9} = \frac{3 \div 3}{9 \div 3} = \blacksquare$

6. $\frac{10}{15} = \frac{10 \div 5}{15 \div 5} = \blacksquare$

PRACTICE

Complete.

7. $\frac{2}{9} = \frac{8}{\blacksquare}$

8. $\frac{3}{7} = \frac{15}{\blacksquare}$

9. $\frac{6}{7} = \frac{\blacksquare}{21}$

10. $\frac{2}{5} = \frac{\blacksquare}{15}$

11. $\frac{6}{9} = \frac{2}{\blacksquare}$

12. $\frac{25}{35} = \frac{5}{\blacksquare}$

13. $\frac{8}{72} = \frac{\blacksquare}{9}$

14. $\frac{35}{42} = \frac{\blacksquare}{6}$

15. $\frac{1}{2} = \frac{\blacksquare}{14}$

16. $\frac{12}{15} = \frac{4}{\blacksquare}$

17. $\frac{7}{12} = \frac{14}{\blacksquare}$

18. $\frac{28}{36} = \frac{\blacksquare}{9}$

19. $\frac{21}{45} = \frac{\blacksquare}{15}$

20. $\frac{1}{5} = \frac{9}{\blacksquare}$

21. $\frac{13}{15} = \frac{\blacksquare}{45}$

22. $\frac{18}{27} = \frac{2}{\blacksquare}$

Find the cross products. Are the fractions equivalent? Write *yes* or *no*. A calculator may be helpful.

CALCULATOR

23. $\frac{9}{15}, \frac{15}{25}$

24. $\frac{6}{27}, \frac{10}{45}$

25. $\frac{4}{12}, \frac{7}{24}$

26. $\frac{15}{21}, \frac{30}{42}$

27. $\frac{8}{18}, \frac{20}{45}$

28. $\frac{42}{49}, \frac{12}{17}$

PROBLEM SOLVING APPLICATIONS
Interpreting Answers

Solve.

29. "I spent 45 min cooking," said Sally. "It took me $\frac{3}{4}$ h to clean up," said Tim. Did they each spend the same amount of time?

30. Hannah got 18 out of 20 items correct on her first math test. She got 16 out of 18 correct on her second test. Did she receive the same score on each test?

★ **31.** Terry used $\frac{1}{2}$ dozen eggs to make a souffle. Barry had 8 eggs and used 4 to make omelets. Did the boys use an equivalent amount of eggs? Explain your answer.

LOWEST TERMS

On Monday, $\frac{5}{18}$ of the vessels entering the harbor were cruise vessels and $\frac{12}{18}$ were fishing vessels.

A fraction is in **lowest terms** when the numerator and the denominator are **relatively prime.** That is, their Greatest Common Factor (GCF) is 1.

GCF of 5 and 18: 1 $\frac{5}{18}$ is in lowest terms.

GCF of 12 and 18: 6 $\frac{12}{18}$ is not in lowest terms.

A quick way to write $\frac{12}{18}$ in lowest terms is to divide the numerator and denominator by the GCF.

$$\frac{12}{18} = \frac{12 \div 6}{18 \div 6} = \frac{2}{3}$$

You can divide by common factors to write fractions in lowest terms.

Think: What is the GCF of 8 and 10?

$8 \div 2 = 4$ $10 \div 2 = 5$ ▷ $\frac{8}{10} = \frac{4}{5}$

Another way to write a fraction in lowest terms is to divide first by one common factor, then by another.

$\frac{12}{18} = \frac{12 \div 2}{18 \div 2} = \frac{6}{9}$ ▷ $\frac{6}{9} = \frac{6 \div 3}{9 \div 3} = \frac{2}{3}$ ▷ $\frac{12}{18} = \frac{2}{3}$

CLASS EXERCISES

Write the GCF of the numerator and denominator.

1. $\frac{4}{12}$ 2. $\frac{6}{24}$ 3. $\frac{10}{12}$ 4. $\frac{15}{21}$ 5. $\frac{12}{60}$ 6. $\frac{24}{28}$

Is the fraction in lowest terms? Write *yes* or *no*.

7. $\frac{5}{15}$ 8. $\frac{2}{21}$ 9. $\frac{6}{18}$ 10. $\frac{2}{5}$ 11. $\frac{2}{10}$ 12. $\frac{27}{45}$

PRACTICE

Complete.

13. $\frac{12}{15} = \frac{4}{\blacksquare}$

14. $\frac{8}{24} = \frac{1}{\blacksquare}$

15. $\frac{9}{18} = \frac{\blacksquare}{2}$

16. $\frac{48}{60} = \frac{4}{\blacksquare}$

17. $\frac{15}{35} = \frac{3}{\blacksquare}$

18. $\frac{9}{15} = \frac{3}{\blacksquare}$

19. $\frac{18}{\blacksquare} = \frac{9}{11}$

20. $\frac{33}{42} = \frac{\blacksquare}{14}$

Write in the lowest terms.

21. $\frac{3}{9}$

22. $\frac{5}{20}$

23. $\frac{6}{10}$

24. $\frac{16}{20}$

25. $\frac{12}{26}$

26. $\frac{30}{36}$

27. $\frac{3}{12}$

28. $\frac{40}{100}$

29. $\frac{9}{21}$

30. $\frac{28}{32}$

31. $\frac{24}{30}$

32. $\frac{10}{35}$

33. $\frac{49}{56}$

34. $\frac{28}{48}$

35. $\frac{45}{81}$

36. $\frac{22}{88}$

37. $\frac{48}{72}$

38. $\frac{18}{48}$

★ **39.** $\frac{126}{210}$

★ **40.** $\frac{84}{140}$

★ **41.** $\frac{24}{184}$

★ **42.** $\frac{150}{210}$

★ **43.** $\frac{570}{690}$

★ **44.** $\frac{126}{2394}$

★ **45.** $\frac{2y}{4y}$

★ **46.** $\frac{4xc}{6}$

★ **47.** $\frac{4xnb}{12xb}$

★ **48.** $\frac{2xb}{2}$

★ **49.** $\frac{x}{x}$

★ **50.** $\frac{6xmxc}{9xmxc}$

PROBLEM SOLVING APPLICATIONS
Using Fractions

Write a fraction in lowest terms to answer the question.

51. It is 20 min to the beach. What part of an hour is this?

52. It is 660 ft around the school track. What part of a mile is this? (*Hint:* 5280 ft = 1 mi)

Solve.

★ **53.** A brick walk is being laid around a garden that is shaped like a regular hexagon. If the bricklayer begins on side A, on which side will she be when the walk is $\frac{3}{4}$ completed?

MULTIPLES AND LEAST COMMON MULTIPLES

The Flower Cart sells roses in bunches of 4 and daisies in bunches of 6. What is the least number of each that you can buy in order to have an equal number of roses and daisies?

When you multiply a number by 0, 1, 2, 3, 4, and so on, you get **multiples** of that number.

Roses are sold in multiples of 4. 0, 4, 8, 12, 16, 20, 24, 28, 32, 36, . . .

Daisies are sold in multiples of 6. 0, 6, 12, 18, 24, 30, 36, . . .

The **common multiples** of 4 and 6 are 12, 34, 36, ... When talking about common multiples, you do not include 0.

The **least common multiple (LCM)** of 4 and 6 is 12.

The least number you can buy to have an equal number of each kind is 12 roses and 12 daisies.

CLASS EXERCISES

List the next three multiples.

1. 0, 3, 6, 9, ■, ■, ■

2. 0, 8, 16, 24, ■, ■, ■

3. 0, 20, 40, 60, ■, ■, ■

4. 0, 30, 60, 90, ■, ■, ■

5. 0, 12, 24, 36, ■, ■, ■

6. 0, 15, 30, 45, ■, ■, ■

7. 0, 14, 28, 42, ■, ■, ■

8. 0, 19, 38, 57, ■, ■, ■

9. 0, 100, 200, 300, ■, ■, ■

10. 0, 125, 250, 375, ■, ■, ■

PRACTICE

Write the LCM of the numbers.

11. 2 and 5   **12.** 4 and 5   **13.** 5 and 7   **14.** 2 and 7

15. 3 and 6   **16.** 3 and 9   **17.** 4 and 12   **18.** 5 and 10

19. 6 and 8   **20.** 6 and 9   **21.** 8 and 12   **22.** 10 and 25

23. 3, 6, and 9   **24.** 2, 4, and 8   **25.** 2, 3, and 5   **26.** 2, 5, and 7

27. 2, 4, and 5   **28.** 3, 5, and 6   **29.** 4, 6, and 9   **30.** 6, 8, and 12

31. 5, 6, and 10   **32.** 5, 8, and 20   **33.** 3, 10, and 15   **34.** 6, 7, and 12

Write the answer.

35. 18×6 **36.** $4 \times 2 + 7$ **37.** $52 - 17$

38. $(43 + 7) \div 5$ **39.** $6 + 5 \times 12$ **40.** $49 \div 7 - 6$

MIXED REVIEW

PROBLEM SOLVING APPLICATIONS
Using Multiples

Solve.

41. Petunias are sold in flats of 6 plants. Pansies are sold in flats of 8 plants. You want to buy an equal number of petunias and pansies. What is the least number of each that you should buy?

42. A coleus plant needs water every 5 days. A jade plant needs water every 7 days. How often will they need water on the same day if you first water them on the same day?

★ **43.** Find two pairs of whole numbers whose LCM is 120 and whose GCF is 4.

COMPARING AND ORDERING FRACTIONS

Lulu checked two books when planning her vegetable garden. The first book said to leave $\frac{3}{8}$ yd space between rows of plants. The second said to leave $\frac{5}{8}$ yd. Which book calls for more space between rows?

You can use the number line to compare fractions.

On the number line, $\frac{5}{8}$ is to the right of $\frac{3}{8}$ so, $\frac{5}{8} > \frac{3}{8}$. The second book calls for more space.

To compare fractions with denominators that are the same, you compare their numerators.

$$\frac{5}{8} > \frac{3}{8} \quad \boxed{\textbf{Think:} \quad 5 > 3}$$

To compare fractions with different denominators, first rewrite the fractions as equivalent fractions with a **common denominator.** A common denominator is a common multiple of the denominators. The **least common denominator (LCD)** is the LCM of the denominators.

$$\frac{3}{5} \; ? \; \frac{1}{2}$$
$$\downarrow \qquad \downarrow$$
$$\frac{6}{10} \; ? \; \frac{5}{10} \qquad \frac{6}{10} > \frac{5}{10} \text{ so, } \frac{3}{5} > \frac{1}{2}$$

$\boxed{\textbf{Think:} \quad \text{The LCM of 5 and 2 is 10.}}$

CLASS EXERCISES

Write the LCD for the pair of fractions.

1. $\frac{5}{6}, \frac{11}{12}$
2. $\frac{1}{4}, \frac{3}{8}$
3. $\frac{1}{3}, \frac{2}{5}$
4. $\frac{1}{2}, \frac{4}{7}$
5. $\frac{1}{4}, \frac{3}{10}$

6. $\frac{1}{6}, \frac{2}{9}$
7. $\frac{1}{10}, \frac{4}{15}$
8. $\frac{3}{5}, \frac{4}{9}$
9. $\frac{1}{3}, \frac{2}{9}$
10. $\frac{3}{8}, \frac{5}{9}$

PRACTICE

Complete. Write > or <.

11. $\frac{7}{8} \blacksquare \frac{5}{8}$ **12.** $\frac{2}{7} \blacksquare \frac{6}{7}$ **13.** $\frac{5}{24} \blacksquare \frac{8}{24}$ **14.** $\frac{11}{36} \blacksquare \frac{1}{3}$

15. $\frac{2}{3} \blacksquare \frac{5}{9}$ **16.** $\frac{3}{4} \blacksquare \frac{11}{12}$ **17.** $\frac{13}{18} \blacksquare \frac{5}{9}$ **18.** $\frac{17}{24} \blacksquare \frac{6}{7}$

19. $\frac{1}{3} \blacksquare \frac{5}{6}$ **20.** $\frac{2}{7} \blacksquare \frac{1}{3}$ **21.** $\frac{2}{3} \blacksquare \frac{3}{5}$ **22.** $\frac{3}{7} \blacksquare \frac{4}{5}$

Order from least to greatest.

23. $\frac{2}{3}, \frac{3}{4}, \frac{5}{6}$ **24.** $\frac{1}{2}, \frac{3}{5}, \frac{3}{10}$ **25.** $\frac{7}{8}, \frac{15}{16}, \frac{3}{4}$ **26.** $\frac{3}{7}, \frac{5}{8}, \frac{1}{3}$

★**27.** $\frac{5}{21}, \frac{3}{14}, \frac{1}{6}$ ★**28.** $\frac{3}{8}, \frac{5}{12}, \frac{4}{9}$ ★**29.** $\frac{5}{11}, \frac{2}{3}, \frac{4}{21}$ ★**30.** $\frac{2}{3}, \frac{5}{7}, \frac{17}{21}$

PROBLEM SOLVING APPLICATIONS
Making Comparisons

Solve.

31. Louise spends $\frac{1}{4}$ of her pay on rent and $\frac{1}{5}$ on food. On which item does she spend more?

★**32.** Sam spent $\frac{3}{5}$ of a dollar. Later, he found 20¢. Did he find more or spend more? how much more?

CHECKPOINT 1

Write the GCF of the numbers.
(*pages 130–133*)

  1. 7 and 28   **2.** 9 and 12

Write the prime factorization.
(*pages 134–135*)

  3. 27   **4.** 20   **5.** 38

Complete. (*pages 138–143*)

  6. $\frac{5}{6} = \frac{30}{\blacksquare}$ **7.** $\frac{9}{12} = \frac{\blacksquare}{4}$

Write the LCM of the numbers.
(*pages 144–145*)

  8. 6 and 9   **9.** 3 and 7

Write > or < to compare the fractions. (*pages 146–147*)

  10. $\frac{7}{10} \blacksquare \frac{7}{12}$ **11.** $\frac{3}{4} \blacksquare \frac{5}{6}$

Extra Practice on page 440

MIXED NUMBERS

A baseball has a diameter of about $2\frac{3}{4}$ in.

A number such as $2\frac{3}{4}$ is called a **mixed number.** It means $2 + \frac{3}{4}$. A mixed number has two parts: a whole number and a fraction.

A whole number can be written as a fraction.

$$2 = \frac{?}{4} \qquad 2 = 8 \div 4 \qquad 2 = \frac{8}{4}$$

To write a mixed number as a fraction, first rewrite the whole number part as a fraction with the same denominator as the fractional part.

$$2\frac{3}{4} = 2 + \frac{3}{4} = \frac{8}{4} + \frac{3}{4} = \frac{11}{4}$$

Ⓜ You can use a shortcut to write a mixed number as a fraction.

$$3\frac{5}{6} = 3\frac{5}{6} \implies \frac{(6 \times 3) + 5}{6} = \frac{18 + 5}{6} = \frac{23}{6}$$

To write a fraction as a mixed number, divide the numerator by the denominator.

$$\frac{7}{4} \implies 4\overline{)7}^{\,1\,R3} \implies 1\frac{3}{4}$$

CLASS EXERCISES

Complete.

1. $1 = \frac{\blacksquare}{5}$

2. $3 = \frac{\blacksquare}{4}$

3. $\frac{9}{3} = \blacksquare$

4. $\frac{10}{5} = \blacksquare$

5. $3\frac{1}{2} = \frac{(2 \times 3) + \blacksquare}{2} = \frac{\blacksquare}{\blacksquare}$

6. $1\frac{3}{4} = \frac{(\blacksquare \times 1) + \blacksquare}{4} = \frac{\blacksquare}{\blacksquare}$

7. $\frac{9}{4} = 9 \div 4 = 2\frac{\blacksquare}{4}$

PRACTICE

Complete.

8. $1\frac{1}{8} = \frac{\blacksquare}{8}$

9. $2\frac{1}{5} = \frac{\blacksquare}{5}$

10. $4\frac{3}{7} = \frac{\blacksquare}{7}$

11. $3\frac{2}{5} = \frac{\blacksquare}{5}$

12. $\frac{6}{5} = 1\frac{\blacksquare}{5}$ **13.** $\frac{17}{7} = 2\frac{\blacksquare}{7}$ **14.** $\frac{7}{2} = 3\frac{\blacksquare}{2}$ **15.** $\frac{14}{3} = 4\frac{\blacksquare}{3}$

Write as a fraction.

16. $2\frac{7}{9}$ **17.** $4\frac{9}{10}$ **18.** $2\frac{5}{6}$ **19.** $3\frac{4}{7}$ **20.** $4\frac{2}{5}$ **21.** $5\frac{2}{3}$

22. $6\frac{3}{8}$ **23.** $7\frac{1}{9}$ **24.** $8\frac{4}{5}$ **25.** $19\frac{3}{5}$ **26.** $25\frac{3}{4}$ **27.** $13\frac{2}{9}$

Write as a whole number or a mixed number.

28. $\frac{8}{5}$ **29.** $\frac{10}{7}$ **30.** $\frac{18}{9}$ **31.** $\frac{12}{3}$ **32.** $\frac{26}{7}$ **33.** $\frac{15}{2}$

34. $\frac{26}{9}$ **35.** $\frac{21}{7}$ **36.** $\frac{17}{4}$ **37.** $\frac{132}{17}$ **38.** $\frac{280}{14}$ ★**39.** $\frac{190}{34}$

Use the shortcut and mental math to write as a fraction.

40. $1\frac{7}{8}$ **41.** $2\frac{5}{9}$ **42.** $3\frac{2}{3}$ **43.** $4\frac{1}{5}$ **44.** $5\frac{3}{4}$

45. $7\frac{5}{8}$ **46.** $8\frac{2}{5}$ **47.** $9\frac{3}{5}$ **48.** $10\frac{1}{2}$ **49.** $11\frac{2}{3}$

MENTAL MATH

PROBLEM SOLVING APPLICATIONS
Classifying Information

To prepare for a new baseball season, the D Street Dodgers are checking their equipment. All items must meet the new league rules.

Write the letter of the measurement that does *not* meet the rule given.

50. Baseballs must have a diameter less than $2\frac{3}{4}$ in.

   a. $2\frac{1}{2}$ in.   **b.** $2\frac{5}{8}$ in.   **c.** $2\frac{7}{8}$ in.   **d.** $2\frac{7}{16}$ in.

51. Baseballs must weigh more than $5\frac{1}{8}$ oz.

   a. $5\frac{1}{4}$ oz   **b.** $5\frac{3}{8}$ oz   **c.** $5\frac{1}{16}$ oz   **d.** $5\frac{3}{16}$ oz

52. Bats must be between $3\frac{1}{4}$ ft and $3\frac{1}{2}$ ft in length.

   a. $3\frac{3}{8}$ ft   **b.** $3\frac{5}{8}$ ft   **c.** $3\frac{5}{16}$ ft   **d.** $3\frac{7}{16}$ ft

FRACTIONS AND DECIMALS

One way to write a fraction as a decimal is to try to find an equivalent fraction whose denominator is a power of 10.

$$\frac{3}{4} = \frac{3 \times 25}{4 \times 25} = \frac{75}{100} = 0.75$$

Another way to change a fraction to a decimal is to divide the numerator by the denominator. In the example on the right, you get a remainder of zero and the division ends. The answer 0.625 is called a **terminating decimal.** Since $\frac{5}{8} = 0.625$, $1\frac{5}{8} = 1.625$.

$$\frac{5}{8} \Rightarrow \begin{array}{r} 0.625 \\ 8\overline{)5.000} \\ -4\,8 \\ \hline 20 \\ -16 \\ \hline 40 \\ -40 \\ \hline 0 \end{array}$$

$$\frac{1}{6} \Rightarrow \begin{array}{r} 0.166\ldots = 0.1\overline{6} \\ 6\overline{)1.000} \\ -6 \\ \hline 40 \\ -36 \\ \hline 40 \\ -36 \\ \hline 4 \end{array}$$

In the example on the left, the division does not give a remainder of zero. Instead, the digits in the quotient begin to repeat. The answer $0.1\overline{6}$ is called a **repeating decimal.** We show a repeating decimal by drawing a bar over the digit or digits that repeat.

On a calculator, you may see the repeating digits. When using repeating decimals, you may find rounding more convenient.

$$0.1666666 \Rightarrow 0.17$$

CLASS EXERCISES

Complete.

1. $\frac{1}{5} \longrightarrow 5\overline{)1.0}$ 0.■

   $2\frac{1}{5} = 2.\blacksquare$

2. $\frac{1}{20} \longrightarrow 20\overline{)1.00}$ 0.■■

   $7\frac{1}{20} = 7.\blacksquare\blacksquare$

3. $\frac{7}{40} \longrightarrow 40\overline{)7.000}$ 0.■■■

   $5\frac{7}{40} = 5.\blacksquare\blacksquare\blacksquare$

PRACTICE

Write as a decimal.

4. $\frac{2}{5}$ 5. $\frac{3}{5}$ 6. $\frac{1}{4}$ 7. $\frac{7}{20}$ 8. $\frac{3}{8}$ 9. $\frac{7}{8}$

10. $\frac{9}{50}$ **11.** $\frac{9}{20}$ **12.** $\frac{9}{40}$ **13.** $\frac{5}{16}$ **14.** $\frac{16}{25}$ **15.** $\frac{11}{80}$

16. $7\frac{1}{50}$ **17.** $4\frac{1}{25}$ **18.** $12\frac{1}{40}$ **19.** $3\frac{3}{16}$ **20.** $10\frac{7}{80}$ **21.** $6\frac{3}{50}$

Write as a decimal. Use a bar to show repeating digits.

22. $\frac{1}{3}$ **23.** $\frac{2}{3}$ **24.** $\frac{5}{9}$ **25.** $\frac{7}{9}$ **26.** $\frac{5}{6}$ **27.** $\frac{7}{15}$

28. $\frac{5}{11}$ **29.** $\frac{9}{11}$ **30.** $\frac{7}{12}$ **31.** $\frac{13}{30}$ **32.** $\frac{7}{22}$ **33.** $\frac{5}{33}$

Does the calculator display show the correct decimal for the given fraction? Write *yes* or *no*.

CALCULATOR

34. $7\frac{3}{100}$; `7.3`   **35.** $\frac{5}{6}$; `1.2`   **36.** $\frac{1}{45}$; `0.0222222`

37. $\frac{7}{8}$; `0.875`   **38.** $\frac{2}{11}$; `0.2727272`   ★ **39.** $\frac{3}{7}$; `0.4285714`

PROBLEM SOLVING APPLICATIONS
Using a Chart

Use the quality control reports for Exercises 40 and 41.

40. Write the fraction as a decimal. Round to the nearest thousandth if necessary.

★ **41.** Write the fraction for the number of good lures $\left(\frac{\text{no. good}}{\text{no. tested}}\right)$. Then write the fraction as a decimal rounded to the nearest thousandth.

GEE WHIZ TOYS QUALITY CONTROL REPORT

ITEM	$\frac{\text{NO. GOOD}}{\text{NO. TESTED}}$
yo-yo	$\frac{7}{8}$
magnet	$\frac{23}{25}$
microscope	$\frac{120}{125}$
flying saucer	$\frac{343}{385}$

GONE FISHIN' LURE CO. QC REPORT

LURE	NO. GOOD	NO. BAD
Windcheater	300	50
Pencil Popper	175	10
Skipper	489	111
Ranger	55	5

DECIMALS AND FRACTIONS

The Liberty Bell is at Independence Hall in Philadelphia. This bronze bell weighs about 0.5 metric ton.

You can write a terminating decimal as a fraction with a denominator that is a power of 10.

> Rewrite the fraction in lowest terms.

$$0.5 = 5 \text{ tenths} = \frac{5}{10} = \frac{1}{2}$$

$$0.47 = 47 \text{ hundredths} = \frac{47}{100}$$

$$0.019 = 19 \text{ thousandths} = \frac{19}{1000}$$

$$3.4 = 3 \text{ and } 4 \text{ tenths} = 3\frac{4}{10} = 3\frac{2}{5}$$

Think: Do 3.4 and $3\frac{2}{5}$ both round to the same whole number? Since $\frac{2}{5}$ is closer to 0 than to 1 on the number line, $\frac{2}{5}$ rounded to the nearest whole number is 0, and $3\frac{2}{5}$ rounds down to 3. You also round 3.4 down to 3.

$$0 \quad \frac{1}{5} \quad \frac{2}{5} \quad \frac{3}{5} \quad \frac{4}{5} \quad 1$$

CLASS EXERCISES

Complete.

1. $0.3 = \frac{\blacksquare}{10}$

2. $0.9 = \frac{9}{\blacksquare}$

3. $0.19 = \frac{\blacksquare}{100}$

4. $0.03 = \frac{\blacksquare}{100}$

5. $0.67 = \frac{67}{\blacksquare}$

6. $0.951 = \frac{951}{\blacksquare}$

7. $0.009 = \frac{9}{\blacksquare}$

8. $0.017 = \frac{17}{\blacksquare}$

9. $8.3 = 8\frac{\blacksquare}{10}$

10. $4.71 = 4\frac{\blacksquare}{100}$

11. $1.007 = 1\frac{7}{\blacksquare}$

12. $4.01 = 4\frac{1}{\blacksquare}$

13. $2.6 = 2\blacksquare$

14. $7.04 = 7\blacksquare$

15. $10.379 = 10\blacksquare$

16. $9.081 = 9\blacksquare$

PRACTICE

Write as a fraction or a mixed number.

17. 0.7   **18.** 0.23   **19.** 0.623   **20.** 0.01   **21.** 0.007   **22.** 0.039

23. 5.8   **24.** 3.9   **25.** 1.19   **26.** 1.03   **27.** 4.179   **28.** 6.003

Write as a fraction in lowest terms.

29. 0.4   **30.** 0.8   **31.** 0.25   **32.** 0.75   **33.** 0.005   **34.** 0.002

35. 0.04   **36.** 0.6   **37.** 0.015   **38.** 0.025   **39.** 0.125   **40.** 0.175

Round to the nearest whole number.

41. $\frac{1}{5}$ **42.** $\frac{4}{5}$ **43.** $\frac{7}{9}$ **44.** $3\frac{5}{8}$ **45.** $1\frac{6}{15}$

46. $9\frac{11}{20}$ **47.** $2\frac{8}{13}$ **48.** 6.8   **49.** 7.43   **50.** 10.81

ESTIMATE

PROBLEM SOLVING APPLICATIONS
Using a Circle Graph

51. Pat and Sue worked on a science report. Pat wrote the report and Sue made the graphs. Use Pat's report to complete the labels for the circle graph.

Smog is a type of air pollution. It occurs when pollutants in the atmosphere combine with moisture to form a blanket of murky air over cities. It is usually the result of using fuels with high sulphur content. About $\frac{21}{50}$ of smog is the result of emissions from various forms of transportation. Another $\frac{7}{20}$ is caused by fuels burned in power and industrial plants. Forest fires contribute $\frac{1}{11}$ of the pollutants, and the remaining $\frac{7}{50}$ results from other sources.

PROBLEM SOLVING
Strategy: Estimation with Fractions

1. Understand
2. Plan
3. Work
4. Answer/ Check

You often use fractions to estimate an amount or quantity. For example, "We have about a half a loaf of bread. The car has about a half a tank of gas. We are about three fourths finished with our Social Studies project." Sometimes you need to round the numerator or the denominator so that you can write a simpler fraction.

A class of 31 students was asked to complete a question-naire about career plans. Five students said they planned to become teachers. What fraction of the students plan to become teachers?

Think: How can the numbers be rounded so that the numerator and denominator have a common factor?

$$\frac{5}{31} \approx \frac{5}{30} = \frac{1}{6}$$

Write in lowest terms.

About $\frac{1}{6}$ of the students plan to become teachers.

CLASS EXERCISES

Use the diagram at the right to answer.

1. How much of the cheese was eaten?

2. How much of the window is open?

3. What part of an hour past 3 o'clock is it?

4. What part of the billboard is painted?

Round the numbers so the numerator and denominator have a common factor. Then write the fraction in lowest terms.

5. $\frac{6}{17}$
6. $1\frac{81}{125}$
7. $5\frac{42}{99}$
8. $\frac{19}{28}$
9. $\frac{53}{72}$
10. $4\frac{248}{499}$

PRACTICE

Estimate.

11. It takes 41 min to walk to the park. About what part of an hour is this?

12. On a 100 mi trip, you have traveled 60 mi. Have you completed half the trip?

13. There are 42 min to hear 9 book reports. About how many minutes will each report have?

14. Herb received 311 out of 625 votes. About what part of the total votes did he receive?

15. It is 885 ft around a track. If you have run about half way around the track, about how many feet have you run?

16. A filing clerk has 235 papers to be filed. About how many papers will be filed when the job is three quarters finished?

★17. A 9 ft by 12 ft room is being tiled. After 144 nine-inch square tiles have been laid, about how much of the room will be covered?

CHECKPOINT 2

Write as a fraction. *(pages 148–149)*

1. $2\frac{1}{3}$

2. $10\frac{2}{5}$

3. $6\frac{8}{9}$

4. $11\frac{3}{8}$

Write as a whole number or as a mixed number. *(pages 148–149)*

5. $\frac{7}{5}$

6. $\frac{7}{2}$

7. $\frac{21}{7}$

8. $\frac{15}{8}$

Write as a decimal. Use a bar to show repeating digits. *(pages 150–153)*

9. $\frac{3}{5}$

10. $4\frac{2}{3}$

11. $7\frac{19}{20}$

12. $\frac{5}{9}$

Estimate. *(pages 154–155)*

13. Josephine ran 12 mi in a 26 mi marathon. About how much of the race did she run?

Extra Practice on page 440

CHAPTER 5 TEST

Write the factors of each number. Then write the GCF of each pair of numbers. *(pages 130–133)*

1. 10 and 25 **2.** 21 and 49 **3.** 27 and 36

Is the number prime or composite?
Write *prime* or *composite*. *(pages 134–135)*

4. 19 **5.** 39 **6.** 47 **7.** 51

Compare. Write > or <. *(pages 138–147)*

8. $\frac{5}{7}$ ▢ $\frac{3}{7}$ **9.** $\frac{5}{8}$ ▢ $\frac{5}{6}$ **10.** $\frac{7}{9}$ ▢ $\frac{11}{12}$ **11.** $\frac{4}{5}$ ▢ $\frac{7}{8}$

Write as a fraction. *(pages 148–149)*

12. $1\frac{5}{8}$ **13.** $3\frac{2}{9}$ **14.** $2\frac{2}{5}$ **15.** $11\frac{4}{7}$

Write as a mixed number. *(pages 148–149)*

16. $\frac{11}{7}$ **17.** $\frac{5}{4}$ **18.** $\frac{35}{6}$ **19.** $\frac{101}{9}$

Write as a decimal. Use a bar to show repeating digits. *(pages 150–151)*

20. $\frac{4}{5}$ **21.** $\frac{1}{6}$ **22.** $11\frac{4}{9}$ **23.** $\frac{5}{8}$

Write as a fraction in lowest terms. *(pages 152–153)*

24. 0.13 **25.** 0.862 **26.** 0.049 **27.** 0.215

Solve. *(pages 154–155)*

28. The North Shore train makes 26 stops between the beginning and end of the line. About how much of the trip is completed by the fifth stop?

Extra Practice on page 441

MATHEMATICS and SOCIAL STUDIES

Companies sell stock to raise money. When you buy a share of stock, you own a part of a company.

Stock prices are listed in the business pages of many newspapers. Stock prices are quoted in fractions of a dollar.

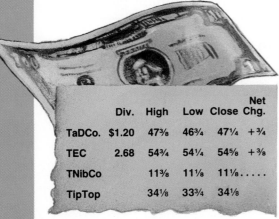

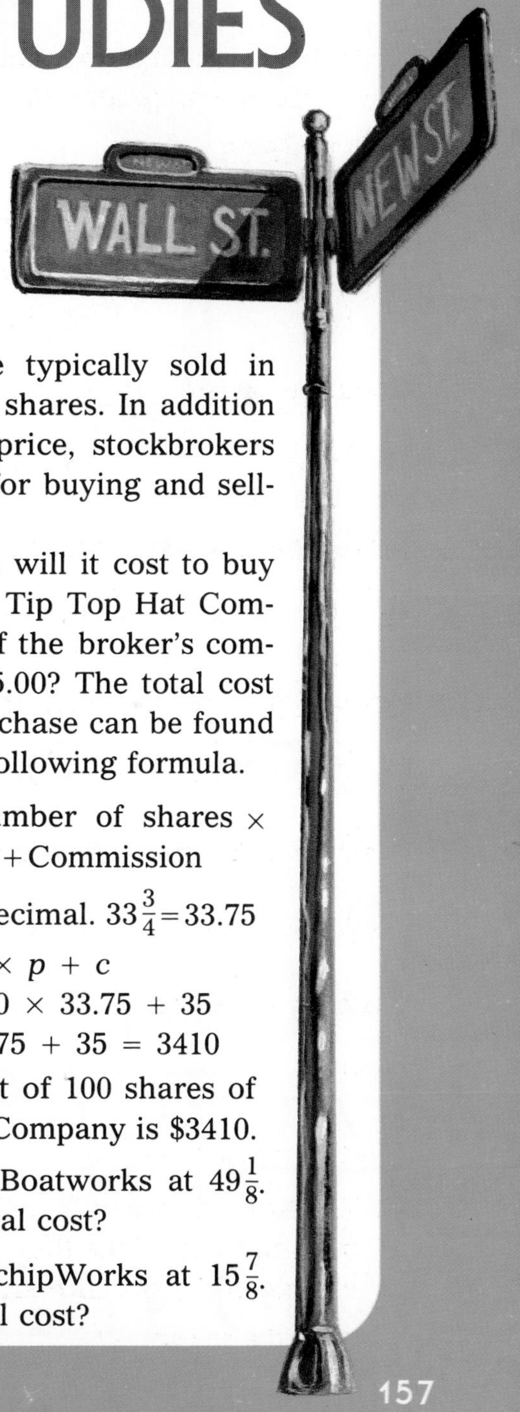

	Div.	High	Low	Close	Net Chg.
TaDCo.	$1.20	47⅜	46¾	47¼	+¾
TEC	2.68	54¾	54¼	54⅝	+⅜
TNibCo		11⅜	11⅛	11⅛	.....
TipTop		34⅛	33¾	34⅛	

ARE YOU TAKING STOCK?

Stocks are typically sold in blocks of 100 shares. In addition to the stock price, stockbrokers charge a fee for buying and selling stock.

How much will it cost to buy 100 shares of Tip Top Hat Company at $33\frac{3}{4}$ if the broker's commission is $35.00? The total cost of a stock purchase can be found by using the following formula.

Total cost = Number of shares × Price per share + Commission

First write $33\frac{3}{4}$ as a decimal. $33\frac{3}{4} = 33.75$

$$t = n \times p + c$$
$$= 100 \times 33.75 + 35$$
$$= 3375 + 35 = 3410$$

The total cost of 100 shares of Tip Top Hat Company is $3410.

1. Alice Arnez bought 3000 shares of Catfish Boatworks at $49\frac{1}{8}$. The commission was $2950. What was the total cost?

2. Jon Weinstein bought 500 shares of MicrochipWorks at $15\frac{7}{8}$. The commission was $320. What was the total cost?

157

Enrichment

It is often easier to calculate the greatest common factor by using prime factors, especially if the numbers are large.

For example, this is how you would use prime factors to calculate the GCF of 90 and 108.

$90 = 2 \times 3 \times 3 \times 5$ $108 = 2 \times 2 \times 3 \times 3 \times 3$ $GCF = 2 \times 3 \times 3 = 18$	Multiply the common prime factors. Use each factor the number of times that it appears as a common factor.

The GCF of 90 and 108 is 18.

Here is an example using exponents.

$80 = 2 \times 2 \times 2 \times 2 \times 5 = 2^4 \times 5$ $300 = 2 \times 2 \times 3 \times 5 \times 5 = 2^2 \times 3 \times 5^2$ $GCF = 2^2 \times 5 = 20$	Multiply the common prime factors. Use the least powers of the common factors.

The GCF of 80 and 300 is 20.

Write the GCF of the numbers.

1. $2 \times 3 \times 3 \times 5$
   $2 \times 2 \times 3 \times 5 \times 7$

2. $2 \times 5 \times 5 \times 7$
   $3 \times 5 \times 7 \times 7$

3. $2 \times 3 \times 5^2$
   $2 \times 3^2 \times 5 \times 7$

4. $2 \times 2 \times 3 \times 5$
   $2 \times 3 \times 5 \times 5$
   $3 \times 5 \times 5 \times 7$

5. $2 \times 3^3 \times 5 \times 7$
   $2 \times 3 \times 5^3$
   $2^3 \times 5 \times 7$

USING PRIME FACTORS TO FIND THE GCF AND THE LCM

6. 48 and 168   **7.** 84 and 112   **8.** 98 and 147

9. 20, 28, 40   **10.** 56, 84, 140   **11.** 42, 63, 105

You can also use prime factors to calculate the least common multiple. Again you may find this method especially helpful if the numbers are large.

Here is an example of using prime factors to find the LCM of 24 and 90.

$$24 = 2 \times 2 \times 2 \times 3$$
$$90 = 2 \times 3 \times 3 \times 5$$
$$\text{LCM} = 2 \times 2 \times 2 \times 3 \times 3 \times 5 = 360$$

Use each factor the greatest number of times that it appears.

The LCM of 24 and 90 is 360.

Here is an example using exponents.

$$54 = 2 \times 3 \times 3 \times 3 = 2 \times 3^3$$
$$60 = 2 \times 2 \times 3 \times 5 = 2^2 \times 3 \times 5$$
$$\text{LCM} = 2^2 \times 3^3 \times 5 = 540$$

Use the greatest power of each factor that appears.

The LCM of 54 and 60 is 540.

Write the LCM of the numbers.

12. $2 \times 2 \times 2$
$2 \times 2 \times 3$
$2 \times 3 \times 5$

13. $2^3 \times 3$
$2^2 \times 3^2$
$2^2 \times 3 \times 5$

14. $2 \times 3^2 \times 5$
$2^2 \times 5^2$
$2 \times 3 \times 5 \times 7$

15. 54 and 84   **16.** 48 and 80   **17.** 25 and 36

18. 39 and 130   **19.** 54 and 180   **20.** 75 and 175

21. 10, 15, 25   **22.** 18, 21, 36   **23.** 18, 24, 28

CUMULATIVE REVIEW

Choose the correct answer. Write a, b, c, or d.

Choose the best estimate.

1. 5213×78
  a. 40,014
  b. 4034
  c. 400,000
  d. 45,000

2. 9.32×5.61
  a. 5.4
  b. 54
  c. 0.54
  d. 0.0054

3. 13.6×0.8
  a. 0.08
  b. 8
  c. 0.8
  d. 80

Choose the number with the matching value.

4. $9 \times 9 \times 9 \times 9$
  a. 9^1
  b. 9^3
  c. 9^4
  d. None of these

5. 852
  a. $(8 \times 10^2) + (5 \times 10^1) + (2 \times 10^0)$
  b. $(8 \times 10^8) + (5 \times 10^5) + (2 \times 10^2)$
  c. $(5 \times 10^3) + (8 \times 10^2) + (2 \times 10^1)$
  d. None of these

6. 7^0
  a. 0
  b. 7
  c. 1
  d. None of these

7. 8^3
  a. 24
  b. 32
  c. 512
  d. None of these

8. 5^4
  a. 625
  b. 54
  c. 20
  d. None of these

Find the answer.

9. 2.61×10
  a. 0.261
  b. 2.61
  c. 26.1
  d. None of these

10. 7.93×100
  a. 79.3
  b. 793
  c. 0.0793
  d. None of these

11. $245.8 \div 1000$
  a. 24.58
  b. 0.02458
  c. 0.2458
  d. None of these

12. $0.8)\overline{10.4}$
  a. 13
  b. 1.3
  c. 0.013
  d. None of these

13. $0.27)\overline{0.837}$
  a. 31
  b. 0.31
  c. 3.1
  d. None of these

14. $5.9)\overline{261.96}$
  a. 444
  b. 44.4
  c. 4.44
  d. None of these

Estimate the quotient.

15. $85\overline{)5355}$
   a. 80
   b. 600
   c. 60
   d. 800

16. $191\overline{)81,386}$
   a. 300
   b. 400
   c. 3300
   d. 4000

17. $2.37\overline{)5.77}$
   a. 0.3
   b. 30
   c. 3
   d. 0.03

18. $642 \div 21$
   a. 30
   b. 3.0
   c. 0.03
   d. 300

19. $357.6 \div 81$
   a. 0.4
   b. 400
   c. 4
   d. 4000

20. $4883 \div 5.44$
   a. 98
   b. 1000
   c. 110
   d. 10

Solve using estimation.

21. Andy delivers 77 newspapers in 2 hours. About how many minutes does he spend on each delivery?
   a. 15 min
   b. 2 min
   c. 40 min
   d. None of these

22. Molly earns $42.50 a week. She wants to buy a plane ticket that costs $137.00. About how many weeks must she save her paycheck to be able to buy the ticket?
   a. 3 weeks
   b. 2 weeks
   c. 30 weeks
   d. None of these

LANGUAGE and VOCABULARY REVIEW

Choose the correct terms to complete.

standard form   mixed number   composite number
supplementary angles   complementary angles   expanded form

1. A _____?_____ has more than two factors.

2. Two angles whose sum is 180° are called _____?_____.

3. A fraction greater than 1 can be written as a _____?_____.

4. The number 486,029 is written in _____?_____.

5. Two angles whose sum is 90° are called _____?_____.

COMPUTER
LITERACY

COMPUTER LOGIC

Sentences with IF . . . THEN are called conditional statements. They show that a decision should be made by the computer.

If the sum of the measures of two angles is 90°,
then write "The angles are complementary."

If the condition is true, the event will occur. If the condition is false, the computer will go to the next line of the program. For the sentence above, *true* means the computer has been given the measures of two angles whose sum is 90°; *false* means the computer has been given the measures of two angles whose sum is not 90°.

Sometimes a condition has two parts, joined by **and** or **or.**

If a figure has four right angles *and* four congruent sides, then write "The figure is a square."

One part is false.
The computer does not complete the action.

If a figure is an equilateral triangle *or* a square, then write "The figure is a regular polygon."

One part is true.
The computer does the action.

For each input tell if the condition is *true* or *false.* If true, then give the output.

Conditional Statement	Input	Output
1. If the sum of the measure of two angles is 180° then write "supplementary."	**a.** 96°, 74°	?
	b. 143°, 37°	?
2. If a number is less than 99 or equal to 99, then write "no hundreds."	**a.** 101	?
	b. 56	?
3. If a number is greater than 1.5 and less than 2, then round the number to 2.	**a.** 1.7	?
	b. 2.4	?

Which would make a wider column, one plank $3\frac{1}{2}$ in. wide or three planks $1\frac{1}{2}$ in. wide fastened together?

ADDITION AND SUBTRACTION OF FRACTIONS

ADDITION AND SUBTRACTION OF FRACTIONS

To add or subtract fractions with the same denominators, write the sum or difference of the numerators over the common denominator. Then write this answer in lowest terms.

A tote bag takes $\frac{5}{8}$ yd of fabric for the bag alone. The straps need $\frac{1}{8}$ yd of fabric. How much fabric will it take in all? Add to find out.

$$\frac{5}{8} + \frac{1}{8} = \frac{5+1}{8} = \frac{6}{8} = \frac{3}{4}$$

It takes $\frac{3}{4}$ yd of fabric.

How much more fabric does it take to make the bag than to make the straps? Subtract to find out.

$$\frac{5}{8} - \frac{1}{8} = \frac{4}{8} = \frac{1}{2}$$

It takes $\frac{1}{2}$ yd more.

The properties of addition apply to fractions also. To help you add fractions mentally, look for addends that will give a fractional sum equal to 1.

To add: $\frac{3}{8} + \frac{1}{8} + \frac{5}{8}$ **Think:** $\frac{3}{8} + \frac{1}{8} + \frac{5}{8} = \frac{8}{8} + \frac{1}{8} = 1\frac{1}{8}$

CLASS EXERCISES

Complete.

1. $\frac{5}{9} + \frac{2}{9} = \frac{\blacksquare + 2}{9}$

2. $\frac{4}{5} - \frac{3}{5} = \frac{4 - \blacksquare}{5}$

3. $\frac{3}{7} + \frac{1}{7} + \frac{2}{7} = \frac{3 + \blacksquare + 2}{7}$

4. $\frac{3}{5} + \frac{1}{5} = \frac{\blacksquare + 1}{\blacksquare}$

5. $\frac{5}{7} - \frac{2}{7} = \frac{5 - \blacksquare}{\blacksquare}$

6. $\frac{8}{11} + \frac{\blacksquare}{11} = \frac{\blacksquare + 2}{\blacksquare}$

PRACTICE

Add or subtract. Write the answer in lowest terms.

7. $\frac{8}{9} - \frac{1}{9}$

8. $\frac{5}{10} + \frac{3}{10}$

9. $\frac{10}{11} - \frac{4}{11}$

10. $\frac{5}{16} + \frac{7}{16}$

11. $\frac{4}{9} + \frac{2}{9}$

12. $\frac{9}{16} - \frac{5}{16}$

13. $\frac{9}{10} + \frac{3}{10}$

14. $\frac{9}{20} - \frac{3}{20}$

15. $\frac{3}{16} + \frac{1}{16} + \frac{5}{16}$

16. $\frac{7}{20} + \frac{9}{20} + \frac{1}{20}$

★ **17.** $\frac{21}{81} + \frac{4}{81} - \frac{2}{81} - \frac{6}{81}$

★ **18.** $\frac{51}{108} + \frac{25}{108} - \frac{27}{108} + \frac{5}{108}$

Solve for *n*.

19. $\frac{4}{7} + \frac{2}{7} = n$

20. $\frac{4}{11} + \frac{5}{11} = n$

★ **21.** $\frac{6}{7} - n = \frac{3}{7}$

★ **22.** $\frac{5}{8} - n = \frac{3}{8}$

★ **23.** $n + \frac{5}{12} = \frac{11}{12}$

★ **24.** $n - \frac{1}{9} = \frac{5}{9}$

Use mental math to add. Write the answer in lowest terms.

25. $\frac{3}{4} + \frac{3}{4} + \frac{1}{4}$

26. $\frac{5}{8} + \frac{7}{8} + \frac{3}{8}$

MENTAL MATH

27. $\frac{6}{15} + \frac{3}{15} + \frac{9}{15} + \frac{2}{15}$

★ **28.** $\frac{7}{12} + \frac{5}{12} + \frac{11}{12} + \frac{5}{12} + \frac{1}{12}$

PROBLEM SOLVING APPLICATIONS
Choosing the Operation

Solve. Write the answer in lowest terms.

29. A piece of wood is $\frac{11}{16}$ in. thick. How much needs to be shaved off so the piece is $\frac{7}{16}$ in. thick?

30. Dan is trimming a strip of leather to make a belt. He first trimmed $\frac{7}{8}$ in., then another $\frac{5}{8}$ in. How much did he trim in all?

★ **31.** A board is 2 ft long. Is there enough to cut a shelf 10 in. long and a second one $\frac{1}{2}$ ft long?

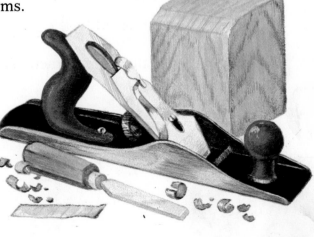

ADDITION OF FRACTIONS: DIFFERENT DENOMINATORS

A park service rents canoes and also gives canoeing lessons. Of all the visitors to the park, $\frac{2}{9}$ rent canoes and take the lessons, and $\frac{1}{6}$ only rent canoes. What fraction of the visitors rent canoes?

To add fractions with different denominators, first rewrite each fraction as an equivalent fraction with the least common denominator (LCD). Then add the numerators and write the sum over the common denominator.

Think: Is the LCD also the least common multiple (LCM) of the two denominators?

$$\frac{2}{9} = \frac{4}{18}$$
$$+\frac{1}{6} = +\frac{3}{18}$$
$$\frac{7}{18}$$

Canoes are rented by $\frac{7}{18}$ of the visitors.

Your work will probably be simpler if you use the LCD, but any common multiple of the denominators can be used as a common denominator. A quick way to find a common denominator of two fractions is to multiply the denominators.

$$\frac{7}{9} + \frac{5}{6} = \frac{42}{54} + \frac{45}{54} = \frac{87}{54} = 1\frac{33}{54} = 1\frac{11}{18}$$

CLASS EXERCISES

Write the LCD for the pair of fractions.

1. $\frac{3}{4}, \frac{1}{3}$

2. $\frac{5}{6}, \frac{5}{8}$

3. $\frac{1}{9}, \frac{1}{3}$

4. $\frac{2}{3}, \frac{3}{8}$

5. $\frac{4}{15}, \frac{1}{6}$

Complete.

6. $\frac{1}{2} = \frac{\blacksquare}{4}$
$+\frac{1}{4} = +\frac{\blacksquare}{4}$
$\frac{\blacksquare}{4}$

7. $\frac{2}{15} = \frac{\blacksquare}{15}$
$+\frac{3}{5} = +\frac{\blacksquare}{15}$
$\frac{\blacksquare}{15}$

8. $\frac{1}{4} = \frac{\blacksquare}{20}$
$+\frac{2}{5} = +\frac{\blacksquare}{20}$
$\frac{\blacksquare}{20}$

9. $\frac{1}{6} = \frac{\blacksquare}{12}$
$+\frac{7}{12} = +\frac{\blacksquare}{12}$
$\frac{\blacksquare}{12} = \frac{\blacksquare}{4}$

PRACTICE

Add. Write the answer in lowest terms.

10. $\dfrac{2}{3}$
$+\dfrac{1}{6}$

11. $\dfrac{1}{4}$
$+\dfrac{3}{8}$

12. $\dfrac{1}{2}$
$+\dfrac{5}{12}$

13. $\dfrac{2}{3}$
$+\dfrac{2}{9}$

14. $\dfrac{5}{16}$
$+\dfrac{3}{8}$

15. $\dfrac{3}{4}$
$+\dfrac{1}{3}$

16. $\dfrac{5}{6}$
$+\dfrac{1}{4}$

17. $\dfrac{5}{12}$
$+\dfrac{3}{8}$

18. $\dfrac{3}{4}$
$+\dfrac{3}{5}$

19. $\dfrac{5}{6}$
$+\dfrac{3}{8}$

20. $\dfrac{3}{4} + \dfrac{2}{3} + \dfrac{5}{6}$

21. $\dfrac{2}{5} + \dfrac{3}{4} + \dfrac{1}{2}$

22. $\dfrac{5}{6} + \dfrac{3}{5} + \dfrac{2}{3}$

23. $\dfrac{5}{16} + \dfrac{2}{3} + \dfrac{1}{4}$

24. $\dfrac{7}{10} + \dfrac{7}{15} + \dfrac{1}{6}$

25. $\dfrac{3}{5} + \dfrac{1}{8} + \dfrac{3}{7}$

Write as a mixed number in lowest terms.

26. $\dfrac{37}{5}$

27. $\dfrac{26}{4}$

28. $\dfrac{28}{6}$

29. $\dfrac{39}{7}$

30. $\dfrac{83}{15}$

31. $\dfrac{187}{23}$

32. $\dfrac{415}{32}$

33. $\dfrac{110}{12}$

MIXED REVIEW

PROBLEM SOLVING APPLICATIONS
Using Information from a Table

Solve.

34. What fraction of the total were the Child and Senior Citizen admissions together?

35. Were more children admitted to the park than senior citizens?

★ **36.** Explain why you would expect the sum of the fractions in the table to be 1.

STATE PARK ADMISSIONS	
Type of Admission	**Fraction of Total Visitors**
General	$\dfrac{1}{4}$
Child	$\dfrac{1}{2}$
Senior Citizen	$\dfrac{1}{8}$
Complimentary	$\dfrac{1}{8}$

SUBTRACTION OF FRACTIONS: DIFFERENT DENOMINATORS

There is $\frac{3}{4}$ c of milk in a carton. A muffin recipe needs $\frac{1}{3}$ c of milk. How much milk will be left? Subtract to find the amount.

First rewrite the fractions as equivalent fractions with a common denominator. Then subtract the numerators and write the difference over the denominator.

$$\frac{3}{4} = \frac{9}{12}$$
$$-\frac{1}{3} = -\frac{4}{12}$$
$$\frac{5}{12}$$

There will be $\frac{5}{12}$ c of milk left.

You can use the calculator to compute with fractions with the help of a memory key. For example, on some calculators you press **M+** to store a number in memory and **MR** to recall the number from memory. To calculate $\frac{7}{8} - \frac{5}{8}$ you enter:

5 ÷ 8 = M+ 7 ÷ 8 = − MR = 0.25

Of course, fractions will appear as decimals when you use a calculator.

CLASS EXERCISES

Write the LCD for the pair of fractions.

1. $\frac{7}{8}, \frac{1}{6}$ 2. $\frac{7}{10}, \frac{2}{5}$ 3. $\frac{3}{4}, \frac{9}{20}$ 4. $\frac{4}{15}, \frac{1}{3}$ 5. $\frac{5}{12}, \frac{1}{9}$

Complete.

6. $\frac{2}{3} = \frac{\blacksquare}{12}$
   $-\frac{1}{4} = -\frac{\blacksquare}{12}$
   $\frac{\blacksquare}{12}$

7. $\frac{1}{2} = \frac{\blacksquare}{6}$
   $-\frac{1}{3} = -\frac{\blacksquare}{6}$
   $\frac{\blacksquare}{6}$

8. $\frac{5}{6} = \frac{\blacksquare}{24}$
   $-\frac{3}{8} = -\frac{\blacksquare}{24}$
   $\frac{\blacksquare}{24}$

9. $\frac{4}{9} = \frac{\blacksquare}{18}$
   $-\frac{1}{6} = -\frac{\blacksquare}{18}$
   $\frac{\blacksquare}{18}$

PRACTICE

Subtract. Write the answer in lowest terms.

10. $\frac{7}{9}$
$-\frac{1}{3}$

11. $\frac{3}{4}$
$-\frac{5}{8}$

12. $\frac{17}{20}$
$-\frac{1}{4}$

13. $\frac{5}{9}$
$-\frac{7}{18}$

14. $\frac{11}{12}$
$-\frac{1}{4}$

15. $\frac{2}{3}$
$-\frac{3}{5}$

16. $\frac{4}{5}$
$-\frac{1}{4}$

17. $\frac{3}{8}$
$-\frac{1}{5}$

18. $\frac{5}{7}$
$-\frac{2}{3}$

19. $\frac{3}{4}$
$-\frac{5}{9}$

20. $\frac{8}{9} - \frac{1}{6}$

21. $\frac{7}{12} - \frac{2}{9}$

22. $\frac{5}{8} - \frac{1}{6}$

23. $\frac{5}{6} - \frac{7}{10}$

★**24.** $\frac{5}{6} - \frac{2}{3} + \frac{3}{4}$

★**25.** $\frac{3}{4} + \frac{2}{5} - \frac{1}{2}$

★**26.** $\frac{1}{6} + \frac{3}{5} - \frac{2}{3}$

★**27.** $\frac{3}{4} - \frac{8}{11} + \frac{2}{3}$

Write the answer as a decimal. Use a calculator if you wish.

CALCULATOR

28. $\frac{5}{8} - \frac{3}{8}$

29. $\frac{3}{4} - \frac{1}{4}$

30. $\frac{7}{10} - \frac{3}{10}$

31. $\frac{22}{25} - \frac{17}{25}$

32. $\frac{11}{16} - \frac{5}{16}$

33. $\frac{27}{32} - \frac{13}{32}$

PROBLEM SOLVING APPLICATIONS
Too Much Information

Solve.

Ana is planning to make stuffed acorn squash. Use the measures shown on her recipe to answer the question.

34. Ana has $\frac{1}{4}$ c brown rice. How much more does she need?

35. She has $\frac{1}{2}$ c minced onion. How much will she have left after she makes the recipe?

★**36.** She has $\frac{2}{3}$ c grated cheese. Is this more or less than she needs?

Stuffed Acorn Squash

2 acorn squash
⅓ cup minced onion
½ cup chopped walnuts
¾ cup brown rice
1 egg
1 tablespoon melted butter or margarine
¾ cup grated cheese
seasoning to taste

see back for cooking directions

PROBLEM SOLVING
Strategy: Reasonable Answers

1. Understand
2. Plan
3. Work
4. Answer/Check

Sometimes an answer to a problem may make you ask, "Is this reasonable?" That is when you should go over your computation to look for a mistake. For example, a clue may be an answer that is a decimal when it can only be a whole number.

Kelly paid $66 for a few throw rugs. How many did she buy if each rug cost $16.50?

You use a calculator to divide.

$$66 \div 16.5 = 0.4$$

The answer, 0.4, isn't reasonable. The answer should be a whole number. You check your computation for an error. You find that the correct answer is 4 rugs.

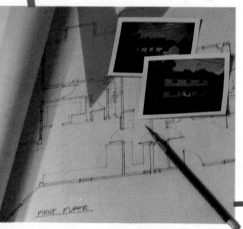

Thompson Constructions is building 2 houses, one on $\frac{1}{2}$ acre of land and the other on $\frac{1}{4}$ acre of land. How many acres in all is this? You calculate:

$$\frac{1}{2} - \frac{1}{4} = \frac{2}{4} - \frac{1}{4} = \frac{1}{4}$$

You know that $\frac{1}{4}$ acre is not reasonable. The total should be more than either part. You check your computation to find that you should have added. The correct answer is $\frac{3}{4}$ acre.

CLASS EXERCISES

What would be a reasonable answer? Write *a* or *b*.

1. Arlo biked $\frac{3}{8}$ mi before lunch and $\frac{2}{5}$ mi after lunch. How many miles in all did he bike?
   a. less than 1 mi   **b.** more than 1 mi

2. The French Club paid $103.20 for 86 bus tickets. What is the cost of one ticket?
   a. more than $2   **b.** less than $2

PRACTICE

Is the answer reasonable or unreasonable? Write *R* or *U*.
If unreasonable, find the correct answer.

3. The muffin recipe calls for $\frac{3}{4}$ c of flour. The bread recipe calls for $\frac{1}{2}$ c of flour. How much more flour does the muffin recipe need? *Answer:* $\frac{1}{2}$ c

4. A potter used $\frac{2}{3}$ of the clay to make plates and $\frac{1}{5}$ of it to make bowls. Is there any clay left over?
Answer: Yes

5. Karen bought some pork at $2.10 a pound and a pack of dinner rolls for $1.89. The bill came to $6.09. How many pounds of pork did Karen buy? *Answer:* 3 lb

6. Ralph bought some apples for 45¢ each. He also bought a bag of potatoes for $.89. How many apples did Ralph buy if the apples and potatoes together cost $3.59?
Answer: 60 apples

7. A clover leaf weevil is $\frac{5}{16}$ in. long. About how many weevils can fit end-to-end on a leaf 1 in. long?
Answer: about 3 weevils

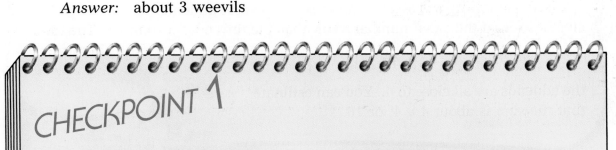

CHECKPOINT 1

Add or subtract. Write the answer in lowest terms. *(pages 164–169)*

1. $\frac{7}{9} + \frac{5}{9}$ 2. $\frac{8}{11} - \frac{3}{11}$

3. $\frac{2}{3} + \frac{7}{8}$ 4. $\frac{3}{4} - \frac{1}{6}$

5. $\frac{3}{4} + \frac{4}{5} + \frac{2}{3}$ 6. $\frac{7}{9} - \frac{3}{8} - \frac{2}{8}$

Is the answer reasonable? If not, find the correct answer.
(pages 170–171)

7. Natalie practiced her flute for $\frac{1}{2}$ h, $\frac{1}{4}$ h, $\frac{3}{4}$ h, and $\frac{1}{2}$ h this week. How many hours did she practice in all? *Answer:* $1\frac{1}{4}$ h

Extra Practice on page 442

ADDITION OF MIXED NUMBERS

Here's how you can add mixed numbers.

First rewrite all the fractions as equivalent fractions with a common denominator.

$$4\frac{1}{2} = \quad 4\frac{5}{10}$$
$$+2\frac{3}{5} = +2\frac{6}{10}$$

Then add the fractions. Add the whole numbers. Write the answer as a mixed number in lowest terms.

$$4\frac{5}{10}$$
$$+2\frac{6}{10}$$
$$6\frac{11}{10} = 6 + 1\frac{1}{10} = 7\frac{1}{10}$$

You can make quick mental estimates when adding mixed numbers. Round up if the fractional part of the mixed number is one half or more. Round down if it is less than one half. In the example above, you can estimate that $4\frac{1}{2} + 2\frac{3}{5}$ is about $5 + 3$, or 8.

Think: Since both numbers were rounded up, is the actual sum more or less than the estimated sum?

Here is one way to use estimation when several addends cluster around the same number. For example, in

$$3\frac{1}{2} + 4\frac{2}{5} + 3\frac{7}{8} + 3\frac{3}{4}$$

the addends are all close to 4. You can estimate that the sum is about 4×4, or 16.

CLASS EXERCISES
Complete.

1. $4\frac{9}{8} = 4 + \blacksquare\frac{1}{8}$

2. $3\frac{7}{6} = 3 + 1\frac{\blacksquare}{6}$

3. $7\frac{9}{5} = 7 + \blacksquare\frac{4}{5}$

4. $5\frac{7}{4} = 5 + \blacksquare\frac{3}{4} = \blacksquare$

5. $3\frac{11}{8} = 3 + 1\frac{\blacksquare}{8} = \blacksquare$

6. $6\frac{8}{3} = 6 + \blacksquare\frac{2}{3} = \blacksquare$

7. $12\frac{16}{10} = 13\frac{\blacksquare}{10} = 13\frac{\blacksquare}{5}$

8. $9\frac{12}{8} = 10\frac{\blacksquare}{8} = 10\frac{\blacksquare}{2}$

PRACTICE

Add. Write the answer in lowest terms.

9. $1\frac{6}{7}$
$+3\frac{3}{7}$

10. $4\frac{8}{9}$
$+2\frac{5}{9}$

11. $6\frac{2}{3}$
$+7\frac{2}{3}$

12. $10\frac{3}{5}$
$+\frac{4}{5}$

13. $12\frac{4}{7}$
$+\frac{5}{7}$

14. $5\frac{2}{3}$
$+4\frac{1}{4}$

15. $6\frac{7}{8}$
$+4\frac{2}{5}$

16. $8\frac{3}{5}$
$+2\frac{3}{4}$

17. $9\frac{8}{9}$
$+2\frac{1}{3}$

18. $2\frac{5}{6}$
$+3\frac{2}{3}$

19. $6\frac{7}{8}$
$+8\frac{5}{12}$

20. $8\frac{1}{2}$
$+7\frac{3}{5}$

21. $3\frac{1}{2}$
$+4\frac{2}{3}$

22. $7\frac{3}{4}$
$+8\frac{5}{6}$

23. $18\frac{5}{9}$
$+2\frac{3}{4}$

24. $5\frac{5}{8} + 6\frac{1}{2} + 3\frac{1}{4}$

25. $7\frac{2}{9} + 5\frac{1}{3} + 2\frac{1}{2}$

26. $9\frac{2}{5} + 7\frac{1}{8} + 5\frac{3}{4}$

★ 27. $3\frac{1}{6} + 4\frac{2}{5} + 1\frac{5}{9}$

★ 28. $3\frac{3}{8} + 4\frac{7}{15} + 1\frac{5}{6}$

★ 29. $5\frac{5}{12} + 7\frac{7}{8} + 2\frac{9}{16}$

Estimate. Answer the question.

30. $\frac{1}{2} + \frac{4}{5} + \frac{3}{5}$ Is the sum more than 3?

31. $5\frac{1}{2} + 4\frac{2}{5} + 3\frac{2}{7}$ Is the sum less than 12?

32. $4\frac{3}{5} + 5\frac{1}{8} + 5\frac{1}{4}$ Is the sum about 3×5 or 3×4?

ESTIMATE

PROBLEM SOLVING APPLICATIONS
Choosing a Strategy

Solve.

33. A rhombus measures $4\frac{5}{7}$ ft on each side. What is the perimeter?

34. A rectangular tablecloth measures $4\frac{1}{4}$ yd by $2\frac{3}{8}$ yd. Will 13 yd of lace be enough to border the tablecloth?

★ 35. If a roast takes $2\frac{1}{2}$ h to cook, when should you put it in the oven to be ready at 6:10 P.M.?

SUBTRACTION OF MIXED NUMBERS WITHOUT RENAMING

One of the largest living species of birds is the wandering albatross. It has an average wingspan of $10\frac{1}{3}$ ft. There is a record of one albatross that had a wingspan of $11\frac{5}{6}$ ft. You subtract to find how much wider than the average this was.

Write equivalent fractions with the least common denominator (LCD).

Subtract the fractions.

Subtract the whole numbers.

$$11\frac{5}{6} = \quad 11\frac{5}{6}$$
$$-10\frac{1}{3} = -10\frac{2}{6}$$

$\Rightarrow$

$$11\frac{5}{6}$$
$$-10\frac{2}{6}$$
$$\overline{\quad\frac{3}{6}}$$

$\Rightarrow$

$$11\frac{5}{6}$$
$$-10\frac{2}{6}$$
$$\overline{1\frac{3}{6} = 1\frac{1}{2}}$$

The record wingspan was $1\frac{1}{2}$ ft wider than the average.

To find the LCD you can think of multiples of the larger denominator until you find one that is also a multiple of the smaller denominator.

Name the LCD of $\frac{3}{8}$ and $\frac{5}{6}$.

Think: The multiples of 8 are: 8, 16, 24, . . . Since 24 is also a multiple of 6 the LCD is 24.

CLASS EXERCISES

Write equivalent fractions or mixed numbers with the LCD.

1. $\frac{3}{4}, \frac{9}{10}$

2. $\frac{5}{6}, \frac{7}{9}$

3. $\frac{4}{5}, \frac{2}{3}$

4. $\frac{3}{4}, \frac{1}{3}$

5. $1\frac{5}{6}, 3\frac{1}{4}$

6. $4\frac{3}{4}, 1\frac{5}{7}$

7. $8\frac{5}{6}, 2\frac{7}{9}$

8. $6\frac{7}{15}, 3\frac{3}{10}$

PRACTICE

Subtract. Write the answer in lowest terms.

9. $7\frac{4}{5}$
$-\ \frac{1}{5}$

10. $10\frac{5}{7}$
$-\ \frac{2}{7}$

11. $13\frac{7}{8}$
$-\ 4$

12. $12\frac{4}{5}$
$-\ \frac{2}{5}$

13. $11\frac{2}{3}$
$-\ 7$

14. $7\frac{3}{4}$
$-2\frac{2}{3}$

15. $9\frac{4}{5}$
$-3\frac{1}{2}$

16. $11\frac{2}{3}$
$-\ 7\frac{3}{5}$

17. $10\frac{5}{9}$
$-\ 6\frac{1}{2}$

18. $11\frac{3}{7}$
$-\ 2\frac{2}{5}$

19. $8\frac{5}{12}$
$-4\frac{3}{8}$

20. $6\frac{3}{4}$
$-4\frac{3}{10}$

21. $7\frac{3}{8}$
$-5\frac{1}{6}$

22. $5\frac{9}{10}$
$-4\frac{1}{6}$

23. $20\frac{5}{6}$
$-10\frac{3}{4}$

24. $12\frac{3}{8} - 11\frac{1}{5}$

25. $13\frac{3}{4} - 6\frac{1}{20}$

26. $10\frac{5}{6} - 3\frac{7}{9}$

27. $14\frac{2}{3} - 7\frac{1}{9}$

★ **28.** $18\frac{4}{15} - 2\frac{1}{11}$

★ **29.** $21\frac{14}{17} - 3\frac{1}{3}$

★ **30.** $10\frac{11}{18} - 2\frac{1}{5}$

★ **31.** $13\frac{16}{17} - 3\frac{3}{7}$

Write the answer.

32. $432 \div 12$

33. $504 - 486$

34. 8×135

35. $875 + 203$

36. $256 \div 8$

37. $1092 \div 52$

MIXED REVIEW

PROBLEM SOLVING APPLICATIONS
Choosing the Operation

Solve.

38. The black-headed grosbeak measures from $6\frac{1}{2}$ in. to $7\frac{3}{4}$ in. from head to tail. What is the difference in length between the longest grosbeak and the shortest?

39. Dana bought 3 books on birds. The first book is $1\frac{3}{4}$ in. thick, the second is $2\frac{1}{8}$ in. thick, and the third is $1\frac{5}{8}$ in. thick. How much shelf space will Dana need to place the three books side-by-side?

SUBTRACTION OF MIXED NUMBERS FROM WHOLE NUMBERS

Chuck Cooper bought a 25 yd bolt of fabric and sold $21\frac{3}{4}$ yd at the regular price. He will sell the rest as a remnant at a reduced price. He subtracts to find how much fabric will be in the remnant.

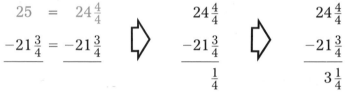

First write 25 as a mixed number.

$$25 = 24\frac{4}{4}$$
$$-21\frac{3}{4} = -21\frac{3}{4}$$

Subtract the fractions.

$$24\frac{4}{4}$$
$$-21\frac{3}{4}$$
$$\overline{\frac{1}{4}}$$

Subtract the whole numbers.

$$24\frac{4}{4}$$
$$-21\frac{3}{4}$$
$$\overline{3\frac{1}{4}}$$

There will be $3\frac{1}{4}$ yd of fabric in the remnant.

CLASS EXERCISES

Complete.

1. $4 = 3\frac{\blacksquare}{6}$

2. $9 = 8\frac{\blacksquare}{4}$

3. $6 = 5\frac{\blacksquare}{10}$

4. $13 = 12\frac{\blacksquare}{8}$

5. $10 = \blacksquare\frac{12}{12}$

6. $15 = \blacksquare\frac{9}{9}$

7. $20 = \blacksquare\frac{6}{6}$

8. $2 = \blacksquare\frac{18}{18}$

9. $\blacksquare = 3\frac{15}{15}$

10. $\blacksquare = 5\frac{8}{8}$

11. $\blacksquare = 6\frac{20}{20}$

12. $\blacksquare = 8\frac{10}{10}$

PRACTICE

Subtract.

13. $\begin{aligned} 7 \\ -2\frac{2}{3} \end{aligned}$

14. $\begin{aligned} 9 \\ -3\frac{1}{2} \end{aligned}$

15. $\begin{aligned} 11 \\ -7\frac{3}{5} \end{aligned}$

16. $\begin{aligned} 10 \\ -6\frac{1}{2} \end{aligned}$

17. $\begin{aligned} 11 \\ -2\frac{2}{5} \end{aligned}$

Subtract. Write the answer in lowest terms.

18. $\begin{array}{r} 6 \\ -4\frac{3}{10} \\ \hline \end{array}$
19. $\begin{array}{r} 7 \\ -5\frac{1}{6} \\ \hline \end{array}$
20. $\begin{array}{r} 17 \\ -\ 2\frac{5}{8} \\ \hline \end{array}$
21. $\begin{array}{r} 20 \\ -\ \frac{7}{10} \\ \hline \end{array}$
22. $\begin{array}{r} 14 \\ -\ 9\frac{3}{16} \\ \hline \end{array}$

23. $\begin{array}{r} 19 \\ -15\frac{1}{2} \\ \hline \end{array}$
24. $\begin{array}{r} 15 \\ -\ 9\frac{11}{16} \\ \hline \end{array}$
25. $\begin{array}{r} 23 \\ -14\frac{5}{6} \\ \hline \end{array}$
26. $\begin{array}{r} 19 \\ -\ \frac{2}{7} \\ \hline \end{array}$
27. $\begin{array}{r} 25 \\ -\ \frac{3}{7} \\ \hline \end{array}$

28. $10 - 6\frac{2}{5}$
29. $8 - 3\frac{1}{3}$
30. $14 - 10\frac{1}{7}$
31. $15 - 9\frac{1}{6}$

32. $20 - \frac{5}{16}$
33. $4 - \frac{9}{16}$
34. $7 - \frac{2}{3}$
35. $1 - \frac{7}{8}$

★ **36.** $10 - 1\frac{3}{14} + 2\frac{7}{8}$
★ **37.** $15 - 7\frac{1}{2} - 5\frac{1}{40}$
★ **38.** $25 - 8\frac{7}{9} + 4\frac{2}{13}$

Solve for x.

39. $2 - 1\frac{3}{4} = x$
40. $5 - 4\frac{7}{8} = x$
41. $15 - 11\frac{3}{4} = x$

★ **42.** $7 - x = 3\frac{1}{2}$
★ **43.** $x - 2\frac{1}{4} = 3\frac{3}{4}$
★ **44.** $19 - x = 6\frac{5}{6}$

PROBLEM SOLVING APPLICATIONS
Choosing a Strategy

Solve.

45. One customer bought a 3 yd remnant of fabric. She needs $2\frac{2}{3}$ yd to make a skirt. How much fabric will be left to trim a jacket?

46. Priscilla is installing speakers for her stereo upstairs and downstairs. Upstairs she used 24 ft of wire. Downstairs she used $16\frac{2}{3}$ ft. How much more wire did she use upstairs?

★ **47.** A stock started the day at a price of 57, fell $2\frac{1}{2}$ points, then rose $3\frac{1}{4}$ points by closing time. What was the closing price of the stock?

SUBTRACTION OF MIXED NUMBERS WITH RENAMING

Wilma's flight to London took $8\frac{1}{4}$ h. The return flight took $6\frac{3}{4}$ h. How much shorter is the return flight?

Since it is not possible to subtract $\frac{3}{4}$ from $\frac{1}{4}$, you need to rename $8\frac{1}{4}$. Use the fact that 8 equals $7\frac{4}{4}$ to rename.

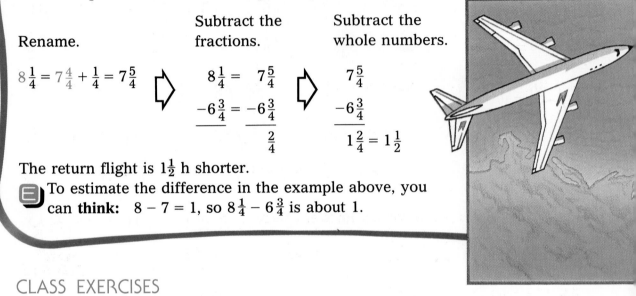

Rename.

$8\frac{1}{4} = 7\frac{4}{4} + \frac{1}{4} = 7\frac{5}{4}$

Subtract the fractions.

$$8\frac{1}{4} = 7\frac{5}{4}$$
$$-6\frac{3}{4} = -6\frac{3}{4}$$
$$\overline{\frac{2}{4}}$$

Subtract the whole numbers.

$$7\frac{5}{4}$$
$$-6\frac{3}{4}$$
$$\overline{1\frac{2}{4} = 1\frac{1}{2}}$$

The return flight is $1\frac{1}{2}$ h shorter.

To estimate the difference in the example above, you can **think:** $8 - 7 = 1$, so $8\frac{1}{4} - 6\frac{3}{4}$ is about 1.

CLASS EXERCISES

Is renaming necessary before subtracting? Write *yes* or *no*.

1. $9\frac{1}{5} - 4\frac{3}{5}$ **2.** $5\frac{4}{7} - 3\frac{6}{7}$ **3.** $15\frac{3}{4} - 4\frac{1}{4}$ **4.** $20\frac{9}{11} - 15\frac{10}{11}$

Complete.

5.
$$9\frac{1}{5} = 8\frac{\blacksquare}{5}$$
$$-1\frac{3}{5} = -1\frac{3}{5}$$
$$\overline{7\frac{\blacksquare}{5}}$$

6.
$$6\frac{2}{9} = 5\frac{\blacksquare}{9}$$
$$-2\frac{7}{9} = -2\frac{7}{9}$$
$$\overline{3\frac{\blacksquare}{9}}$$

7.
$$7\frac{1}{3} = 6\frac{\blacksquare}{3}$$
$$-5\frac{2}{3} = -5\frac{2}{3}$$
$$\overline{1\frac{\blacksquare}{3}}$$

8.
$$4\frac{1}{6} = 3\frac{\blacksquare}{6}$$
$$-1\frac{5}{6} = -1\frac{5}{6}$$
$$\overline{2\frac{\blacksquare}{6} = 2\frac{\blacksquare}{3}}$$

9.
$$7\frac{3}{8} = 6\frac{\blacksquare}{8}$$
$$-5\frac{7}{8} = -5\frac{7}{8}$$
$$\overline{1\frac{\blacksquare}{8} = 1\frac{\blacksquare}{2}}$$

10.
$$7\frac{3}{10} = 6\frac{\blacksquare}{10}$$
$$-2\frac{7}{10} = -2\frac{7}{10}$$
$$\overline{4\frac{\blacksquare}{10} = 4\frac{\blacksquare}{5}}$$

PRACTICE

Subtract. Write the answer in lowest terms.

11. $8\frac{1}{7}$
$-1\frac{3}{7}$

12. $6\frac{2}{9}$
$-1\frac{5}{9}$

13. $7\frac{1}{5}$
$-2\frac{4}{5}$

14. $4\frac{1}{6}$
$-1\frac{5}{6}$

15. $7\frac{3}{8}$
$-5\frac{7}{8}$

16. $9\frac{2}{5}$
$-3\frac{9}{10}$

17. $9\frac{3}{7}$
$-2\frac{1}{2}$

18. $12\frac{2}{5}$
$-\ 4\frac{5}{6}$

19. $7\frac{1}{4}$
$-2\frac{1}{3}$

20. $3\frac{1}{4}$
$-2\frac{9}{10}$

21. $10\frac{1}{8} - 2\frac{3}{8}$

22. $7\frac{1}{10} - 4\frac{3}{5}$

23. $5\frac{2}{5} - 4\frac{1}{2}$

24. $10\frac{1}{8} - 2\frac{3}{8}$

25. $11\frac{3}{4} - 5\frac{9}{10}$

26. $6\frac{1}{5} - 2\frac{9}{10}$

27. $4\frac{1}{3} - 3\frac{7}{8}$

28. $6\frac{4}{5} - 2\frac{3}{10}$

★29. $10\frac{1}{2} - 4\frac{5}{4} + 2\frac{1}{6}$

★30. $7\frac{3}{8} - 5\frac{13}{6} + 3\frac{7}{12}$

★31. $53\frac{4}{9} - 47\frac{5}{6} - \frac{20}{18}$

Estimate to choose the correct answer. Write a, b, or c.

32. $6\frac{1}{8} - 4\frac{3}{8}$ **a.** $1\frac{3}{4}$ **b.** $2\frac{3}{4}$ **c.** $3\frac{3}{4}$

33. $11\frac{1}{3} - 5\frac{1}{6}$ **a.** $6\frac{1}{6}$ **b.** $5\frac{1}{6}$ **c.** $4\frac{1}{6}$

ESTIMATE

PROBLEM SOLVING APPLICATIONS
Using a Chart

The price of a share of stock is often listed as a mixed number. The increase and decrease in value of a stock are also listed as fractions.

Complete the chart at the right.

	COMPANY	STARTING PRICE	CHANGE	CLOSING PRICE
34.	Atlantis	$75\frac{3}{4}$	up $\frac{1}{2}$	?
35.	Daytron	$38\frac{7}{8}$	down $\frac{1}{4}$	?
36.	Eksonn	$89\frac{5}{8}$	up $1\frac{1}{2}$	?
37.	NY Tesco	100	down $\frac{1}{8}$	?

PROBLEM SOLVING
Strategy: Interpreting Answers

In division problems with remainders you may need to interpret the results to give a reasonable answer. In general, common sense tells you how best to express the answer.

105 people signed up for the outing. Each bus can carry 60 passengers. How many buses are needed?

$$105 \div 60 = 1 \text{ R45}$$

Answer: 2 buses

The film lasts 105 min. How many hours is this?

$$105 \div 60 = 1\frac{3}{4}$$

Answer: $1\frac{3}{4}$ h

The toll booth collects $105 from 60 cars. How much is the toll for each car?

$$105 \div 60 = 1.75$$

Answer: $1.75

The group prepared 105 gifts. If 60 children show up, how many gifts will be given to each child?

$$105 \div 60 = 1 \text{ R45}$$

Answer: 1 gift

CLASS EXERCISES

Which is the most reasonable way to express the answer? Write *a*, *b*, *c*, or *d*.

1. You have 800 bulbs to pack into 12 boxes. How many bulbs is that per box?

   a. $66\frac{1}{100}$ bulbs   **b.** 66.67 bulbs   **c.** 66 bulbs   **d.** 66 R8

2. Alfred paid $122.50 for 7 tickets to the musical. How much was each ticket?

   a. $17\frac{1}{2}$ **b.** $17.50   **c.** $17   **d.** $18

3. On each trip the ski lift can carry 4 people only. How many trips must it make to carry 27 people?

   a. 6 trips   **b.** 6.75 trips   **c.** 7 trips   **d.** $6\frac{3}{4}$ trips

PRACTICE

Solve.

4. There are 3 tennis balls in a can. Each player is to have 2 tennis balls for a practice session. If there are 37 players, how many cans of tennis balls will they need?

5. A group of 18 students and 2 advisors went on a trip to the museum. They spent a total of $100 for bus fare and admission. Admission to the museum was $45. How much was the bus fare for each person?

6. There are 36 lb of clay to be divided evenly among a ceramic class of 24 people. How much clay will each person get?

7. A telephone directory lists 460 numbers on a page. How many pages will there be in a directory of 25,000 names?

★ 8. The special fruit baskets on sale this week contain 4 apples, 4 oranges, and 2 grapefruits. How many baskets can be made with 175 apples, 130 oranges, and 75 grapefruits?

★ 9. Light bulbs are packed in packages of 2, 4, and 8. What is the least number of packages needed to pack 126 light bulbs?

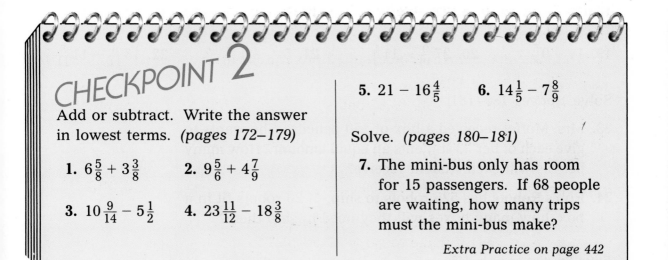

CHECKPOINT 2

Add or subtract. Write the answer in lowest terms. *(pages 172–179)*

1. $6\frac{5}{8} + 3\frac{3}{8}$ 2. $9\frac{5}{6} + 4\frac{7}{9}$

3. $10\frac{9}{14} - 5\frac{1}{2}$ 4. $23\frac{11}{12} - 18\frac{3}{8}$

5. $21 - 16\frac{4}{5}$ 6. $14\frac{1}{5} - 7\frac{8}{9}$

Solve. *(pages 180–181)*

7. The mini-bus only has room for 15 passengers. If 68 people are waiting, how many trips must the mini-bus make?

Extra Practice on page 442

Write the answer in lowest terms. *(pages 164–169)*

1. $\frac{5}{9} - \frac{4}{9}$ **2.** $\frac{7}{11} + \frac{5}{11}$ **3.** $\frac{7}{8} - \frac{5}{6}$ **4.** $\frac{4}{5} + \frac{1}{4}$

5. $\frac{1}{3} + \frac{1}{6}$ **6.** $\frac{9}{10} - \frac{3}{5}$ **7.** $\frac{17}{20} - \frac{3}{4}$ **8.** $\frac{2}{15} + \frac{4}{45}$

Is the answer reasonable or unreasonable? Write *R* or *U*. If unreasonable, find the correct answer. *(pages 170–171)*

9. A yogurt recipe calls for $\frac{5}{8}$ c milk. A custard recipe calls for $\frac{1}{4}$ c milk. How much more milk is needed for yogurt?
Answer: $\frac{7}{8}$ c

10. Hank studied $\frac{1}{4}$ h in the morning, $\frac{1}{2}$ h in the afternoon, and $\frac{3}{4}$ h in the evening. How long did he study in all?
Answer: 2 h

Write the answer in lowest terms. *(pages 172–173)*

11. $5\frac{3}{5} + 7\frac{4}{5}$ **12.** $4\frac{2}{5} + 3\frac{7}{8}$ **13.** $8\frac{5}{9} + \frac{5}{6}$ **14.** $2\frac{3}{4} + 6\frac{5}{6}$

Write the answer in lowest terms. *(pages 174–179)*

15. $9\frac{7}{9} - \frac{2}{9}$ **16.** $7\frac{7}{12} - 3\frac{3}{8}$ **17.** $8 - 2\frac{3}{4}$ **18.** $5\frac{1}{8} - 2\frac{3}{10}$

19. $14 - 9\frac{5}{8}$ **20.** $27\frac{9}{14} - 11\frac{1}{2}$ **21.** $5\frac{7}{10} - 1\frac{9}{10}$ **22.** $13\frac{9}{11} - 11\frac{5}{11}$

Solve. *(pages 180–181)*

23. Mrs. Moffet received a box of 150 pencils. She wants to give each of her 33 students an equal amount. How many pencils will each student receive?

24. Rob's Robots has 525 robots to ship. If 20 robots fit in a box, how many boxes will they need to ship them?

Extra Practice on page 443

MATHEMATICS and SHOP

You would expect a 2×4 (read *two by four*) plank to be 2 in. high and 4 in. wide, but standard lumber sizes don't quite measure up to their names. This is because sawmills plane planks smooth after the planks have been cut, and in the process the planks become thinner and narrower. The chart shows the plank names and the actual dimensions of standard lumber sizes.

1. How high would a stack of three 2 × 12 planks be?

2. Julie built an open cabinet using 1×10 planks. The cabinet stands 60 in. high and is 24 in. wide. What are the height and the width of the space inside the cabinet?

PLANKS A MILLION!

3. You want to make a rectangular picture frame using a 1×2 plank. The inside dimensions must measure 10 in. by 12 in. Will 40 in. of the 1×2 plank be enough? Explain.

STANDARD LUMBER SIZES
(ACTUAL SIZE)

1 x 2	(¾ x 1½″)
1 x 3	(¾ x 2½″)
1 x 4	(¾ x 3½″)
1 x 5	(¾ x 4½″)
1 x 6	(¾ x 5½″)
1 x 8	(¾ x 7¼″)
1 x 10	(¾ x 9¼″)
1 x 12	(¾ x 11¼″)
2 x 2	(1½ x 1½″)
2 x 3	(1½ x 2½″)
2 x 4	(1½ x 3½″)
2 x 6	(1½ x 5½″)
2 x 8	(1½ x 7¼″)
2 x 10	(1½ x 9¼″)
2 x 12	(1½ x 11¼″)

Enrichment

There are many times that one quantity depends on another. For example, the cost of a phone call to your friend in another state depends on the time of day that you make the call.

x = time of day
y = cost of a 5 min phone call

x	7:30 A.M.	9:30 A.M.	11:30 A.M.	1:30 P.M.	3:30 P.M.	5:30 P.M.	7:30 P.M.	9:30 P.M.	11:30 P.M.
y	$.80	$1.94	$1.94	$1.94	$1.94	$1.28	$1.28	$1.28	$.80

When the value of y depends on the value of x, we say that y is a **function** of x. A function can have only one value of y for each value of x.

The cost of your phone call is a function of the time that you make the call.

Does the chart show a function? Write *yes* or *no*.

1. x = cost of an item
y = amount of sales tax

x	0¢ to 29¢	30¢ to 49¢	50¢ to 69¢	70¢ to 89¢
y	1¢	2¢	3¢	4¢

2. x = sock size
y = shoe size

x	$9\frac{1}{2}$	10	$10\frac{1}{2}$	11
y	$5-5\frac{1}{2}$	$6-6\frac{1}{2}$	$7-7\frac{1}{2}$	$8-8\frac{1}{2}$

Is y a function of x? Write *yes* or *no*.

3. x = number of minutes you talk
y = cost of a long-distance phone call

4. x = temperature
y = cost of a long-distance phone call

5. x = color of the package
y = cost of mailing the package

6. x = weight of the package
y = cost of mailing the package

FUNCTIONS

Here is another example of a function.

You know that it will take you one hour to make dinner tonight. The time that you can serve dinner is a function of the time that you start to make dinner.

x = time that you start to make dinner
y = time that you can serve dinner

x	5:00	5:15	5:30	5:45	6:00	6:15	6:30
y	6:00	6:15	6:30	6:45	7:00	7:15	7:30

In this function, each value of y is exactly one hour greater than the related value of x.

x = time that you start to make dinner
y = time that you can serve dinner
$x + 1$ (hour) $= y$

Write an equation for the rule of the function.

7.

x	2	4	6	8	10	12	14
y	4	8	12	16	20	24	28

8.

x	9	12	15	18	21	24	27
y	3	6	9	12	15	18	21

9.

x	1	2	3	4	5	6	7
y	3	5	7	9	11	13	15

10.

x	1	2	3	4	5	6	7
y	1	4	9	16	25	36	49

11. You must be at Jill's house one hour before she leaves.
x = time that Jill leaves
y = time that you must be there

12. You earn money mowing lawns at $2 an hour.
x = hours you work
y = total amount you earn

13. You need 45 min to deliver papers on your route.
x = time that you start
y = time that you finish

14. Two friends will share the profits of the car wash equally.
x = total profits
y = amount of each share

CUMULATIVE REVIEW

Choose the correct answer. Write *a*, *b*, *c*, or *d*.

Find the answer.

1. 3648×205
  a. 91,200
  b. 747,740
  c. 747,840
  d. None of these

2. 0.0051×0.036
  a. 0.01836
  b. 0.001836
  c. 0.0001836
  d. None of these

3. $\$22.90 \times 0.7$
  a. $16.03
  b. $16.30
  c. $15.03
  d. None of these

Find the answer.

4. $52\overline{)4481}$
  a. 88 R15
  b. 86 R9
  c. 85 R41
  d. None of these

5. $6\overline{)21.708}$
  a. 3.618
  b. 36.18
  c. 361.80
  d. None of these

6. $3.9\overline{)0.234}$
  a. 0.6
  b. 0.06
  c. 0.0006
  d. None of these

Find the perimeter or circumference.

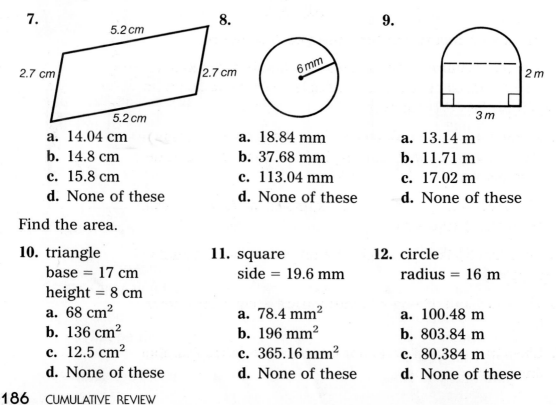

7.
  5.2 cm
  2.7 cm
  2.7 cm
  5.2 cm
  a. 14.04 cm
  b. 14.8 cm
  c. 15.8 cm
  d. None of these

8.
  6 mm
  a. 18.84 mm
  b. 37.68 mm
  c. 113.04 mm
  d. None of these

9.
  2 m
  3 m
  a. 13.14 m
  b. 11.71 m
  c. 17.02 m
  d. None of these

Find the area.

10. triangle
  base = 17 cm
  height = 8 cm
  a. 68 cm^2
  b. 136 cm^2
  c. 12.5 cm^2
  d. None of these

11. square
  side = 19.6 mm

  a. 78.4 mm^2
  b. 196 mm^2
  c. 365.16 mm^2
  d. None of these

12. circle
  radius = 16 m

  a. 100.48 m
  b. 803.84 m
  c. 80.384 m
  d. None of these

Use a formula to solve the problem.

13. What is the perimeter of a door-
    way that is 8 ft high and 3 ft wide?
    a. 11 ft
    b. 22 ft
    c. 24 ft
    d. None of these

14. What is the circumference of the
    lid of a can whose radius is 9 in.?
    a. 81 in.
    b. 28.53 in.
    c. 565.20 in.
    d. None of these

15. What is the area of a triangular
    banner 22 cm high and 10 cm
    wide?
    a. 220 cm^2
    b. 16 cm^2
    c. 110 cm^2
    d. None of these

16. A circular rug has a diameter of
    12 ft. What is the area of the
    smallest square room in which
    the rug will fit?
    a. 144 ft^2
    b. 121 ft^2
    c. 169 ft^2
    d. None of these

LANGUAGE and VOCABULARY REVIEW

Choose the correct term to complete each sentence.

1. The least common denominator of a pair of fractions is
   also the (greatest common multiple, least common multiple) of the denominators.

2. A fraction is in lowest terms when the (greatest common
   factor, least common multiple) of the numerator and denominator is 1.

3. The fractions $\frac{3}{4}$ and $\frac{9}{12}$ are examples of (lowest term,
   equivalent) fractions.

4. The term $3\frac{7}{8}$ is an example of a (mixed number, common
   number).

5. The basic unit of length in the metric system is the (meter,
   liter).

6. Lines in a plane that do not intersect are called (parallel
   lines, line segments).

FLOWCHARTS

COMPUTER
LITERACY

Computer programmers often use flowcharts to plan programs. A **flowchart** is a diagram that shows the sequence of steps for solving a problem.

Flowcharts are made up of instructions placed inside different shapes. Connecting lines show the order in which the computer will process each instruction.

This flowchart shows the plan for a computer program. The program will decide if a number is divisible by 9. The loop allows the computer to repeat the steps in order to test more than one number.

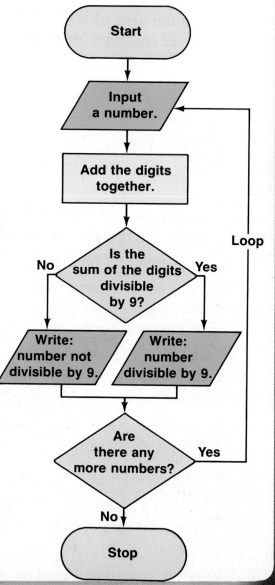

Use the flowchart to write the output for each line of data.

1. Data:
509   1125   5409   14,076

2. Data:
2083   67,123   331,839   3,031,848

3. Draw a flowchart that shows how to decide whether a number is even or odd.

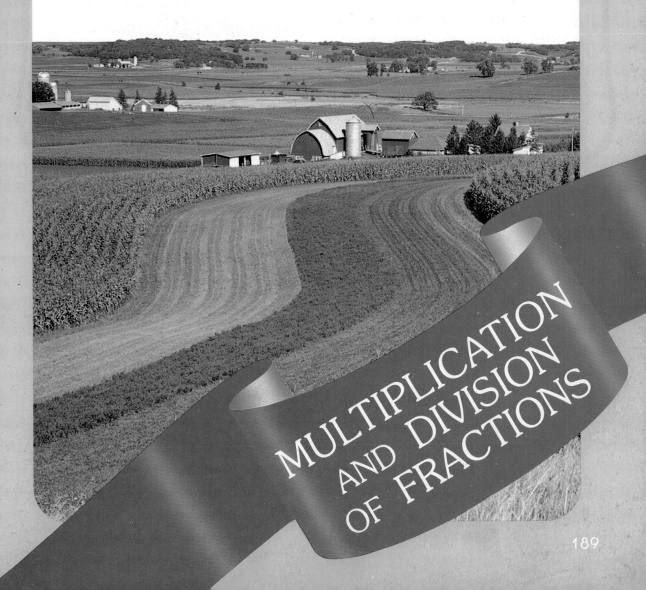

One third of this 300-acre farm is planted in corn. How many acres are planted in corn?

7

MULTIPLICATION AND DIVISION OF FRACTIONS

MULTIPLYING FRACTIONS AND WHOLE NUMBERS

A giant turtle weighs about $\frac{1}{5}$ t. About how much would 8 giant turtles weigh? Multiply, since you want $\frac{1}{5}$ eight times.

$$8 \times \frac{1}{5} = \frac{8 \times 1}{5} = \frac{8}{5} = 1\frac{3}{5}$$

Eight giant turtles weigh about $1\frac{3}{5}$ t.

M When the numerator is 1, you can use mental math to multiply fractions. Here are two examples.

$$\frac{1}{9} \times 27 \ \Rightarrow \ 27 \div 9 = 3$$

$$36 \times \frac{1}{5} \ \Rightarrow \ \frac{36}{5} = 7\frac{1}{5}$$

CLASS EXERCISES

Complete.

1. $2 \times \frac{1}{6} = \frac{\blacksquare \times \blacksquare}{6} = \frac{2}{6} = \frac{1}{3}$

2. $\frac{1}{5} \times 10 = \frac{\blacksquare \times \blacksquare}{5} = \frac{10}{5} = 2$

3. $5 \times \frac{5}{6} = \frac{\blacksquare \times \blacksquare}{6} = \frac{25}{6} = 4\frac{1}{6}$

4. $8 \times \frac{3}{4} = \frac{\blacksquare \times \blacksquare}{\blacksquare} = \frac{24}{4} = 6$

5. $\frac{1}{5} \times 3 = \frac{\blacksquare \times \blacksquare}{5} = \frac{\blacksquare}{5}$

6. $2 \times \frac{1}{4} = \frac{\blacksquare \times \blacksquare}{4} = \frac{\blacksquare}{\blacksquare} = \frac{1}{2}$

7. $2 \times \frac{3}{8} = \frac{2 \times \blacksquare}{\blacksquare} = \frac{\blacksquare}{\blacksquare} = \frac{3}{4}$

8. $\frac{4}{9} \times 2 = \frac{\blacksquare \times \blacksquare}{\blacksquare} = \frac{\blacksquare}{\blacksquare}$

PRACTICE

Multiply. Write the product in lowest terms.

9. $\frac{1}{7} \times 21$

10. $\frac{1}{8} \times 40$

11. $8 \times \frac{1}{2}$

12. $24 \times \frac{1}{8}$

13. $12 \times \frac{1}{3}$

14. $4 \times \frac{3}{14}$ **15.** $3 \times \frac{1}{7}$ **16.** $5 \times \frac{3}{16}$ **17.** $5 \times \frac{1}{9}$ **18.** $7 \times \frac{2}{15}$

19. $16 \times \frac{3}{4}$ **20.** $42 \times \frac{6}{7}$ **21.** $36 \times \frac{5}{9}$ **22.** $48 \times \frac{5}{6}$ **23.** $\frac{3}{4} \times 12$

24. $\frac{2}{9} \times 5$ **25.** $\frac{4}{5} \times 3$ **26.** $\frac{3}{8} \times 7$ **27.** $\frac{5}{9} \times 4$ **28.** $\frac{3}{7} \times 8$

29. $25 \times \frac{5}{6}$ **30.** $\frac{7}{12} \times 33$ **31.** $\frac{3}{10} \times 45$ **32.** $\frac{1}{4} \times 30$ **33.** $\frac{1}{6} \times 92$

★ **34.** $\left(16 \times \frac{3}{4}\right) \times \frac{1}{2}$ ★ **35.** $\left(15 \times \frac{2}{5}\right) \times \frac{3}{4}$ ★ **36.** $\left(12 \times \frac{2}{3}\right) \times \frac{1}{5}$ ★ **37.** $\left(27 \times \frac{4}{9}\right) \times \frac{3}{5}$

Use mental math to multiply.

38. $\frac{1}{4} \times 16$ **39.** $\frac{1}{3} \times 24$ **40.** $\frac{1}{6} \times 12$

MENTAL MATH

41. $8 \times \frac{1}{2}$ **42.** $35 \times \frac{1}{5}$ **43.** $63 \times \frac{1}{7}$

44. $\frac{1}{8} \times 96$ ★ **45.** $\frac{1}{9} \times 486$ ★ **46.** $260 \times \frac{1}{13}$

PROBLEM SOLVING APPLICATIONS
Multi-Step Problems

Solve.

47. Marilyn's family room measures 13 ft by 15 ft. How much carpeting does she need to cover $\frac{2}{3}$ of the room?

48. Fencing costs $2.00 per foot. Will it cost more than $50 to fence in a rectangular garden that is 5 ft long and 8 ft wide?

★ **49.** A rectangular wing measuring 75 ft by 100 ft is being added to the Field School. A media center will occupy half the space. A photography lab will occupy two fifths of the space. The remaining area will be used for storage. How many square feet will be used for each purpose?

MULTIPLYING FRACTIONS

A market research company is looking for volunteers to test two new brands of orange juice. In the seventh grade $\frac{3}{4}$ of the students volunteer.

Of the volunteers, $\frac{1}{2}$ will try Brand X, and $\frac{1}{2}$ will try Brand Y. What fraction of the seventh grade students will try Brand X? Multiply to find $\frac{1}{2}$ of $\frac{3}{4}$.

To multiply fractions, multiply the numerators. Then multiply the denominators. Write the resulting fraction in lowest terms.

$$\frac{1}{2} \times \frac{3}{4} = \frac{1 \times 3}{2 \times 4} = \frac{3}{8}$$

You can sometimes simplify the multiplication by looking for common factors. First, divide the numerators and the denominators by the common factors and then multiply.

$$\frac{\overset{1}{\cancel{3}}}{\underset{1}{\cancel{6}}} \times \frac{\overset{1}{\cancel{5}}}{\underset{3}{\cancel{9}}} = \frac{1}{3}$$

Think: What common factors were found in the example above?

CLASS EXERCISES

Complete.

1. $\frac{5}{6} \times \frac{1}{4} = \frac{5 \times \blacksquare}{6 \times \blacksquare} = \frac{5}{24}$

2. $\frac{1}{4} \times \frac{3}{8} = \frac{\blacksquare \times 3}{\blacksquare \times 8} = \frac{3}{32}$

3. $\frac{2}{5} \times \frac{3}{7} = \frac{\blacksquare \times \blacksquare}{5 \times 7} = \frac{6}{35}$

4. $\frac{2}{7} \times \frac{2}{3} = \frac{2 \times 2}{\blacksquare \times \blacksquare} = \frac{4}{21}$

5. $\frac{2}{7} \times \frac{1}{9} = \frac{\blacksquare \times \blacksquare}{\blacksquare \times \blacksquare} = \frac{\blacksquare}{\blacksquare}$

6. $\frac{1}{2} \times \frac{5}{9} = \frac{\blacksquare \times \blacksquare}{\blacksquare \times \blacksquare} = \frac{\blacksquare}{\blacksquare}$

7. $\frac{6}{7} \times \frac{1}{7} = \frac{\blacksquare \times \blacksquare}{\blacksquare \times \blacksquare} = \frac{\blacksquare}{49}$

8. $\frac{1}{2} \times \frac{1}{8} = \frac{\blacksquare \times \blacksquare}{\blacksquare \times \blacksquare} = \frac{\blacksquare}{\blacksquare}$

PRACTICE

Multiply. Write the product in lowest terms.

9. $\frac{3}{8} \times \frac{1}{7}$ **10.** $\frac{2}{3} \times \frac{7}{9}$ **11.** $\frac{3}{4} \times \frac{3}{8}$ **12.** $\frac{4}{5} \times \frac{2}{9}$ **13.** $\frac{3}{5} \times \frac{1}{8}$

14. $\frac{7}{12} \times \frac{5}{8}$ **15.** $\frac{7}{10} \times \frac{3}{5}$ **16.** $\frac{3}{4} \times \frac{5}{7}$ **17.** $\frac{5}{6} \times \frac{5}{7}$ **18.** $\frac{3}{4} \times \frac{5}{12}$

19. $\frac{7}{10} \times \frac{5}{9}$ **20.** $\frac{1}{10} \times \frac{15}{16}$ **21.** $\frac{9}{20} \times \frac{10}{16}$ **22.** $\frac{3}{4} \times \frac{4}{5}$ **23.** $\frac{5}{6} \times \frac{3}{5}$

24. $\frac{5}{9} \times \frac{2}{7} \times \frac{3}{10}$ **25.** $\frac{5}{8} \times \frac{3}{7} \times \frac{4}{15}$ **26.** $\frac{4}{5} \times \frac{2}{9} \times \frac{6}{16}$

★ **27.** $\frac{26}{25} \times \frac{35}{39} \times \frac{45}{7}$ ★ **28.** $\frac{57}{20} \times \frac{35}{38} \times \frac{22}{27}$ ★ **29.** $\frac{60}{51} \times \frac{17}{24} \times \frac{4}{5}$

Write the answer.

30. $1\frac{1}{2} + 6\frac{7}{8}$ **31.** $5\frac{7}{8} - 2\frac{9}{10}$ **32.** $8.7 + 6.9 + 15.2$

33. $18.08 - 7.91$ **34.** 15.9×7.0 **35.** $300.8 \div 0.2$

MIXED REVIEW

PROBLEM SOLVING APPLICATIONS
Consumer Topics

The seventh grade cooking class made this recipe.

36. The cooking class doubled this recipe. How much of each ingredient did they use?

37. Jamie wants to make half of this recipe to serve her family. How much of each ingredient should she use?

38. Suppose the only measuring cups you have are for $\frac{1}{2}$ c and $\frac{1}{3}$ c. Write and solve a problem about using these to measure ingredients for Potatoes Florentine.

POTATOES FLORENTINE

1 10-oz pkg frozen spinach $\frac{1}{4}$ c butter
3 c dried potato flakes 2 eggs
3 c hot water $\frac{1}{3}$ c grated cheese

Thaw and drain spinach. Mix potato flakes and hot water in large bowl. Let stand until water is absorbed. Add butter, eggs, and cheese. Mix well. Fold in spinach. Pour into greased baking pan. Bake at 350° for 40 min. Makes 8 servings.

MULTIPLYING MIXED NUMBERS

The New Age Dance Troupe needs costumes for its production of *The Nutcracker*. For each toy soldier costume $2\frac{1}{8}$ yd of blue cloth is needed. If there are 12 toy soldiers, how much blue cloth is needed for the toy soldier costumes?

To multiply mixed numbers, first write the mixed number as a fraction. Then multiply the fractions.

$$12 \times 2\frac{1}{8} = \overset{3}{\cancel{12}} \times \frac{17}{\underset{2}{\cancel{8}}}$$

$$= \frac{51}{2} = 25\frac{1}{2}$$

For the toy soldier costumes, $25\frac{1}{2}$ yd of blue cloth is needed.

E You can use estimation when multiplying mixed numbers to check the reasonableness of an answer. For example:

$$2\frac{3}{4} \times 2\frac{1}{3} = \frac{11}{4} \times \frac{7}{3} = \frac{77}{12} = 6\frac{5}{12}$$

Think: $3 \times 2 = 6$

The answer $6\frac{5}{12}$ is reasonable.

CLASS EXERCISES

Complete.

1. $3\frac{1}{4} = \frac{\blacksquare}{4} + \frac{1}{4} = \frac{\blacksquare}{4}$

2. $3\frac{5}{8} = \frac{\blacksquare}{8} + \frac{5}{8} = \frac{\blacksquare}{8}$

3. $2\frac{3}{5} = \frac{\blacksquare}{5} + \frac{\blacksquare}{5} = \frac{\blacksquare}{5}$

4. $2\frac{1}{2} = \frac{\blacksquare}{2}$

5. $4\frac{3}{5} = \frac{\blacksquare}{5}$

6. $5\frac{3}{4} = \frac{\blacksquare}{4}$

7. $\frac{3}{5} \times 2\frac{1}{7} = \frac{3}{5} \times \frac{\blacksquare}{7}$

8. $2\frac{2}{7} \times 4\frac{1}{4} = \frac{\blacksquare}{7} \times \frac{\blacksquare}{4}$

9. $2\frac{1}{5} \times 3\frac{1}{2} = \frac{\blacksquare}{5} \times \frac{\blacksquare}{2}$

PRACTICE

Multiply. Write the product in lowest terms.

10. $1\frac{4}{5} \times 2\frac{2}{9}$ **11.** $6\frac{2}{9} \times 1\frac{5}{8}$ **12.** $4\frac{2}{5} \times 1\frac{7}{8}$ **13.** $8\frac{1}{3} \times 2\frac{1}{10}$

14. $4\frac{2}{3} \times 3\frac{3}{8}$ **15.** $5\frac{1}{4} \times 2\frac{1}{8}$ **16.** $3\frac{1}{9} \times 1\frac{1}{4}$ **17.** $2\frac{1}{3} \times 1\frac{1}{5}$

18. $9\frac{1}{3} \times 2\frac{1}{4}$ **19.** $1\frac{3}{4} \times 1\frac{7}{8}$ **20.** $3\frac{1}{9} \times 1\frac{1}{14}$ **21.** $3\frac{3}{4} \times 1\frac{1}{9}$

22. $4\frac{7}{8} \times 3\frac{2}{7}$ **23.** $3\frac{5}{6} \times 9$ **24.** $8\frac{1}{2} \times 4\frac{3}{16}$ **25.** $7\frac{2}{3} \times 6$

26. $1\frac{1}{2} \times 3\frac{2}{5} \times 6\frac{1}{4}$ **27.** $4\frac{9}{10} \times 3 \times \frac{1}{2}$ **28.** $3\frac{1}{2} \times 2\frac{1}{5} \times 3\frac{3}{4}$

★**29.** $1\frac{11}{13} \times 4\frac{7}{8} + 3\frac{1}{2}$ ★**30.** $7\frac{3}{7} \times 2\frac{2}{13} + 3\frac{5}{169}$ ★**31.** $1\frac{2}{3} + 4\frac{2}{7} \times 1\frac{2}{5}$

Estimate. Choose the best answer. Write *a*, *b*, or *c*.

32. $3\frac{1}{5} \times 2\frac{1}{8}$ **a.** less than 10
                        b. between 10 and 20
                        c. greater than 20

33. $6\frac{2}{3} \times 5\frac{1}{4}$ **a.** less than 10
                        b. between 10 and 20
                        c. greater than 20

ESTIMATE

PROBLEM SOLVING APPLICATIONS
Using Formulas

Solve. Write your answer in lowest terms.

34. The formula for the area of a square is $A = s^2$. If a square has a side measuring $2\frac{3}{4}$ ft, what is its area?

35. The formula for the area of a triangle is $A = \frac{1}{2} \times b \times h$. If a triangle has a base of $10\frac{3}{4}$ in. and a height of $15\frac{3}{4}$ in., what is its area?

★**36.** The crankcase of a motor holds $5\frac{3}{4}$ qt of oil. If the oil level has dropped to $\frac{3}{5}$ of its original amount, how many quarts of oil should be added to fill the crankcase?

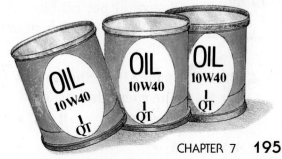

PROBLEM SOLVING
Strategy: Working Backwards

1. Understand
2. Plan
3. Work
4. Answer/Check

Working backwards may be the easiest way to solve a problem such as the one below where you are given an end result and asked to find a missing fact.

Jay paid $6.70 for taxi fare from his home to the airport including a $1 tip. City Cab charges $1.80 for the first mile plus $.15 for each additional $\frac{1}{6}$ mi. How many miles is Jay's home from the airport?

5 3 miles

$ 06 70

Subtract the tip and the amount for the first mile.	Divide to find how many $\frac{1}{6}$ mi.	Multiply and write as a mixed number.	Add the first mile.
$6.70 - $2.80 = $3.90	$3.90 ÷ $.15 = 26	$26 \times \frac{1}{6} = \frac{26}{6} = 4\frac{1}{3}$	$4\frac{1}{3} + 1 = 5\frac{1}{3}$

Jay's house is $5\frac{1}{3}$ mi from the airport.

CLASS EXERCISES

Name the steps you will use to solve the problem. Then solve the problem.

1. Craig had several pet rabbits. He gave $\frac{1}{2}$ of them away and now has 4 rabbits. How many rabbits did Craig have to begin with?

2. Barbara spent $165. She bought a skirt for $45 and shoes for $40. She spent the rest on a coat. How much did she pay for the coat?

PRACTICE

Solve.

3. Laurie's plane leaves at 4:35 P.M. It takes 35 min to get to the airport from her house. If she allows 30 min for check-in and getting to the gate, what time should she leave her house?

4. James had a certain amount of money in his checking account. He wrote checks for $32, $29, and $57. James then had a balance of $125. How much did he have to begin with?

5. In the last six months, Gus the gorilla gained $2\frac{1}{2}$ lb, lost $1\frac{1}{2}$ lb, and then gained $3\frac{1}{4}$ lb. He now weighs 24 lb. How much did Gus weigh to begin with?

★6. A drama club needs $300 for sets and costumes. They have decided to have a car wash and charge $2 per car. They can wash 2 cars at a time. Each car takes $4\frac{1}{2}$ min to wash and $3\frac{1}{2}$ min to dry. How long will it take to make the amount of money they need?

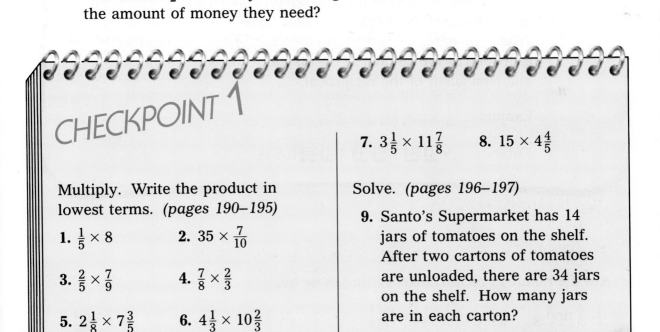

CHECKPOINT 1

Multiply. Write the product in lowest terms. *(pages 190–195)*

1. $\frac{1}{5} \times 8$

2. $35 \times \frac{7}{10}$

3. $\frac{2}{5} \times \frac{7}{9}$

4. $\frac{7}{8} \times \frac{2}{3}$

5. $2\frac{1}{8} \times 7\frac{3}{5}$

6. $4\frac{1}{3} \times 10\frac{2}{3}$

7. $3\frac{1}{5} \times 11\frac{7}{8}$

8. $15 \times 4\frac{4}{5}$

Solve. *(pages 196–197)*

9. Santo's Supermarket has 14 jars of tomatoes on the shelf. After two cartons of tomatoes are unloaded, there are 34 jars on the shelf. How many jars are in each carton?

Extra Practice on page 444

RECIPROCALS

Reciprocals are pairs of numbers whose product is 1.

$$3 \times \frac{1}{3} = 1 \qquad \frac{5}{6} \times \frac{6}{5} = 1 \qquad \frac{7}{8} \times \frac{8}{7} = 1$$

These numbers are reciprocals of each other:

$$3 \text{ and } \frac{1}{3} \qquad \frac{5}{6} \text{ and } \frac{6}{5} \qquad \frac{7}{8} \text{ and } \frac{8}{7}$$

Since $1 \times 1 = 1$, the number 1 is its own reciprocal.

The product of 0 and any number is 0. Therefore the number 0 does not have a reciprocal.

To write a reciprocal for a mixed number, first write the mixed number as a fraction.

$$5\frac{1}{4} = \frac{21}{4} \quad \Rightarrow \quad \frac{21}{4} \times \frac{4}{21} = 1 \qquad \text{So, } \frac{4}{21} \text{ is the reciprocal of } 5\frac{1}{4}.$$

Some calculators have a reciprocal key. It looks like $\boxed{1/x}$. You can use this key to find the reciprocal of a whole number or to calculate with fractions that have a numerator of 1. When you enter a number and then the $\boxed{1/x}$ key, the number 1 is divided by the number in the display. You will see the decimal equivalent of the reciprocal.

Example: $\frac{1}{4} + \frac{1}{5} + \frac{1}{8}$

Enter: $4 \boxed{1/x} \boxed{+} 5 \boxed{1/x} \boxed{+} 8 \boxed{1/x} \boxed{=} \ 0.575$

CLASS EXERCISES

Are the numbers reciprocals? Write *yes* or *no*.

1. $\frac{8}{9}$ and $\frac{9}{8}$ **2.** $5\frac{1}{4}$ and $2\frac{1}{4}$ **3.** $3\frac{1}{6}$ and $\frac{6}{19}$ **4.** $\frac{1}{5}$ and 5

5. 8 and $\frac{8}{1}$ **6.** $2\frac{1}{2}$ and $\frac{5}{2}$ **7.** $\frac{9}{12}$ and $\frac{4}{3}$ **8.** $\frac{12}{16}$ and $\frac{3}{4}$

PRACTICE

Write the reciprocal.

9. $\frac{1}{5}$ **10.** $\frac{7}{9}$ **11.** $\frac{4}{5}$ **12.** $\frac{5}{9}$ **13.** $\frac{8}{11}$ **14.** $\frac{5}{7}$

15. $\frac{3}{4}$ **16.** $\frac{12}{13}$ **17.** $\frac{11}{14}$ **18.** $\frac{12}{21}$ **19.** $\frac{19}{20}$ **20.** $\frac{13}{14}$

21. $\frac{3}{5}$ **22.** $\frac{4}{7}$ **23.** 8   **24.** 16   **25.** 25   **26.** 141

Write the mixed number as a fraction. Then write the reciprocal.

27. $3\frac{1}{9}$ **28.** $1\frac{1}{5}$ **29.** $8\frac{7}{9}$ **30.** $4\frac{1}{5}$ **31.** $10\frac{1}{7}$ **32.** $14\frac{7}{8}$

33. $17\frac{1}{2}$ **34.** $25\frac{1}{6}$ **35.** $20\frac{3}{8}$ **36.** $15\frac{5}{9}$ **37.** $2\frac{8}{13}$ **38.** $12\frac{5}{8}$

Solve. A calculator with the ⅟ₓ key may be helpful.

39. $\frac{1}{8} + \frac{1}{7} = a$ **40.** $\frac{1}{15} + \frac{1}{9} = x$ **41.** $\frac{1}{12} + \frac{1}{3} = y$

42. $\frac{1}{5} - \frac{1}{10} = b$ **43.** $\frac{1}{3} - \frac{1}{9} = z$ **44.** $\frac{1}{6} - \frac{1}{8} = w$

CALCULATOR

PROBLEM SOLVING APPLICATIONS
Estimation, Mental Math, or Calculator

Solve. Choose estimation (*E*), mental math (*M*), or a calculator (*C*).

45. A play consists of 3 acts with a ten-minute intermission between acts. If the whole production takes 2 h 20 min, what is the average length of each act in minutes?

46. Harry made 8 out of 20 shots in a basketball game. Jay made 10 out of 22 shots. Who made a greater fraction of his shots?

47. Would you estimate the difference between $15\frac{4}{5}$ and $20\frac{1}{10}$ to be closest to 4, 5, or 6? Check your estimation by subtracting.

48. Greg traveled $1\frac{1}{8}$ mi from home to school, $\frac{5}{6}$ mi from school to the skating rink, $\frac{2}{3}$ mi from the skating rink to work, and $\frac{5}{16}$ mi from work to his home. How many miles did Greg travel?

DIVIDING FRACTIONS AND WHOLE NUMBERS

Each of four logs is cut in half to make two fence posts.

How many fence posts will there be? $4 \times 2 = 8$

How many halves are there in 4? $4 \div \frac{1}{2} = 8$

There will be 8 fence posts. There are 8 halves in 4.

To divide by a fraction, multiply by the reciprocal of the divisor. Here is another example.

Suppose $\frac{2}{3}$ of a barn is being partitioned into 4 stalls. How much of the barn will each stall occupy?

$$\frac{2}{3} \div 4 = \frac{2}{3} \times \frac{1}{4} = \frac{2}{12} = \frac{1}{6}$$

Each stall will occupy $\frac{1}{6}$ of the barn.

CLASS EXERCISES

Complete.

1.

How many fourths are in 3?

$$3 \div \frac{1}{4} = 3 \times \frac{\blacksquare}{1} = \blacksquare$$

2.

How many eighths are in 4?

$$4 \div \frac{1}{8} = 4 \times \frac{8}{\blacksquare} = \blacksquare$$

3.

$$\frac{1}{4} \div 2 = \frac{1}{4} \times \frac{\blacksquare}{2} = \frac{\blacksquare}{\blacksquare}$$

4.

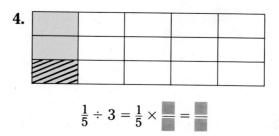

$$\frac{1}{5} \div 3 = \frac{1}{5} \times \frac{\blacksquare}{\blacksquare} = \frac{\blacksquare}{\blacksquare}$$

PRACTICE

Divide. Write the quotient in lowest terms.

5. $8 \div \frac{2}{3}$

6. $\frac{3}{4} \div 9$

7. $\frac{8}{9} \div 4$

8. $6 \div \frac{2}{3}$

9. $\frac{6}{7} \div 12$

10. $9 \div \frac{9}{10}$

11. $\frac{5}{6} \div 10$

12. $12 \div \frac{7}{8}$

13. $\frac{3}{14} \div 7$

14. $15 \div \frac{9}{10}$

15. $16 \div \frac{5}{8}$

16. $\frac{3}{5} \div 15$

17. $18 \div \frac{3}{5}$

18. $\frac{7}{8} \div 14$

19. $30 \div \frac{2}{3}$

20. $20 \div \frac{15}{16}$

★21. $\frac{4}{5} \div \left(\frac{3}{4} \div \frac{1}{8}\right)$

★22. $12 \div \left(\frac{4}{5} \times \frac{6}{7}\right)$

★23. $18 \div \left(\frac{1}{6} + \frac{1}{3}\right)$

★24. $\frac{15}{16} \div \left(\frac{20}{3} - \frac{56}{12}\right)$

Solve.

25. $40 + x = 55$

26. $y - 15 = 20$

27. $n \times 10 = 120$

28. $a \div 5 = 9$

29. $14 + z = 25$

30. $12 \times r = 48$

MIXED REVIEW

PROBLEM SOLVING APPLICATIONS
Using a Table

What does your locker say about you? You have these items in your locker. Solve the equation for each item, and then get a total score for the exercise. (You may use the table to find your rating.)

31. homework $\quad 15.2 + 139.6 = x$

32. computer book $\quad 1598 \div 8 = y$
comic book $\quad\quad 400 - (175 \times 2) + 1 = q$

33. take-out menu $\quad 0.35 \div 5 = p$
calculator $\quad\quad\quad 12^2 = a$
gym shoes $\quad\quad\quad 13.6 \times 2.2 = m$

34. cassette tape $\quad 45 + 2 - (4^2) = b$
school book $\quad\quad 3.14 \times 6^2 = n$
graph paper $\quad\quad \frac{500}{y} = 5$

35. moldy food $\quad 13.9 + 12.5 + 6.08 = x$

For Each Solution	Score
greater than 101	100
between 50 and 100	50
between 0 and 49	10

Score	Rating
0–50	Do you really have a locker?
51–150	Well-rounded student
Over 150	Future Einstein

DIVIDING FRACTIONS

Paul needs $\frac{3}{8}$ yd of fabric to make part of a banner. If he has $\frac{7}{8}$ yd of fabric, how many parts can he make?

Divide to find how many $\frac{3}{8}$ yd pieces there are in $\frac{7}{8}$ yd.

To divide by a fraction, multiply by the reciprocal of the divisor.

$$\frac{7}{8} \div \frac{3}{8} = \frac{7}{8} \times \frac{8}{3}$$

$$= \frac{7}{\underset{1}{\cancel{8}}} \times \frac{\overset{1}{\cancel{8}}}{3}$$

$$= \frac{7 \times 1}{1 \times 3} = \frac{7}{3} = 2\frac{1}{3}$$

Paul has enough fabric to make two parts.

You can use a calculator to divide fractions. Of course, the answer on the calculator will be in decimal form.

Think: How will you enter a division example?

$$\frac{3}{8} \div \frac{2}{3} = \frac{3}{8} \times \frac{3}{2} \quad \Rightarrow \quad 3 \div 8 \times 3 \div 2 = 0.5625$$

CLASS EXERCISES

Complete.

1. $\frac{1}{7} \div \frac{2}{3} = \frac{1}{7} \times \blacksquare = \blacksquare$

2. $\frac{2}{3} \div \frac{3}{4} = \frac{2}{3} \times \blacksquare = \blacksquare$

3. $\frac{4}{7} \div \frac{3}{5} = \frac{4}{7} \times \blacksquare = \blacksquare$

4. $\frac{5}{8} \div \frac{2}{3} = \frac{5}{8} \times \blacksquare = \blacksquare$

PRACTICE

Divide. Write the quotient in lowest terms.

5. $\frac{3}{4} \div \frac{7}{8}$

6. $\frac{1}{5} \div \frac{9}{10}$

7. $\frac{2}{3} \div \frac{7}{9}$

8. $\frac{5}{8} \div \frac{7}{12}$

9. $\frac{4}{4} \div \frac{2}{3}$

10. $\frac{5}{12} \div \frac{5}{7}$

11. $\frac{7}{10} \div \frac{11}{15}$

12. $\frac{3}{8} \div \frac{9}{10}$

13. $\frac{5}{9} \div \frac{5}{6}$

14. $\frac{9}{14} \div \frac{6}{7}$

15. $\frac{5}{8} \div \frac{2}{3}$

16. $\frac{7}{8} \div \frac{21}{22}$

17. $\frac{3}{5} \div \frac{3}{10}$

18. $\frac{3}{8} \div \frac{6}{10}$

19. $\frac{8}{9} \div \frac{2}{3}$

20. $\frac{9}{16} \div \frac{2}{4}$

21. $\frac{3}{8} \div \frac{7}{12}$

22. $\frac{9}{10} \div \frac{3}{20}$

23. $\frac{4}{5} \div \frac{14}{15}$

24. $\frac{8}{15} \div \frac{16}{25}$

25. $\frac{4}{7} \div 4$

★ 26. $\frac{d}{6} \div d$

★ 27. $\frac{5}{m} \div 10$

★ 28. $\frac{x}{4} \div x$

Show the sequence of steps necessary to do the arithmetic on the calculator.

29. $\frac{3}{4} \times \frac{2}{5}$

30. $\frac{2}{7} \times \frac{9}{10}$

31. $\frac{4}{5} \div \frac{2}{3}$

CALCULATOR

32. $\frac{5}{8} \times \frac{3}{10}$

33. $\frac{8}{9} \div \frac{4}{7}$

34. $\frac{3}{5} \div \frac{5}{6}$

35–40. Fractions will appear as decimals when you use a calculator to solve. Write the answers to Exercises 29–34 as decimals. Round to the nearest thousandth.

PROBLEM SOLVING APPLICATIONS
Choosing the Operation

Solve.

41. If you draw lines $\frac{5}{16}$ in. apart on a 15 in. long sheet of paper, how many equal spaces will you have? Assume the first line is drawn $\frac{5}{16}$ in. from the edge of the paper.

42. A recipe for French toast calls for $\frac{3}{4}$ c of milk. If you want to make only $\frac{2}{3}$ of the recipe, how much milk should you use?

43. A board $\frac{1}{4}$ in. thick is placed on top of a board $\frac{5}{8}$ in. thick. What is the total thickness of the two boards?

★ 44. At a party the guests ate $\frac{3}{4}$ of a cheese wheel that weighed 2 lb. How many ounces of cheese are left?

DIVIDING MIXED NUMBERS

At the Jolly Roller Rink the music at the snack bar plays constantly. Each tape takes about $1\frac{1}{4}$ h. How many tapes does it take to keep the music going for 10 h? To answer the question you divide 10 by $1\frac{1}{4}$.

$$10 \div 1\frac{1}{4} = 10 \div \frac{5}{4}$$

Write the mixed number as a fraction.

$$= 10 \times \frac{4}{5}$$

$$= \frac{\overset{2}{\cancel{10}}}{1} \times \frac{4}{\cancel{5}} = 8$$

It takes 8 tapes.

Is this answer reasonable?

Think: $10 \div 1\frac{1}{4}$ is about $10 \div 1$, or 10.

Since 8 is close to 10, the answer is reasonable.

CLASS EXERCISES

Write as a fraction.

1. $1\frac{2}{7}$ **2.** $3\frac{5}{9}$ **3.** $6\frac{2}{5}$ **4.** $2\frac{7}{8}$

Explain each step you will take to divide.

5. $2\frac{1}{2} \div 1\frac{3}{4}$ **6.** $5\frac{1}{3} \div 7\frac{2}{5}$ **7.** $1\frac{1}{8} \div 3\frac{2}{3}$ **8.** $10\frac{2}{3} \div 5\frac{4}{5}$

PRACTICE

Divide. Write the quotient in lowest terms.

9. $4\frac{1}{2} \div 3$ **10.** $7\frac{4}{5} \div 13$ **11.** $13\frac{3}{4} \div 11$ **12.** $5\frac{2}{3} \div 17$

13. $8\frac{1}{8} \div \frac{5}{16}$ **14.** $13\frac{1}{3} \div \frac{3}{4}$ **15.** $5\frac{3}{5} \div \frac{7}{10}$ **16.** $3\frac{5}{9} \div \frac{8}{12}$

17. $2\frac{4}{5} \div 1\frac{1}{3}$ **18.** $1\frac{1}{8} \div 1\frac{1}{16}$ **19.** $2\frac{5}{6} \div 2\frac{1}{2}$ **20.** $3\frac{2}{3} \div 1\frac{2}{9}$

21. $8\frac{4}{5} \div 2\frac{3}{4}$ **22.** $10\frac{2}{3} \div 2\frac{1}{6}$ **23.** $9\frac{2}{7} \div 1\frac{1}{4}$ **24.** $12\frac{1}{2} \div 2\frac{1}{2}$

25. $9\frac{4}{5} \div 1\frac{1}{3}$ **26.** $2\frac{1}{6} \div 1\frac{1}{2}$ **27.** $14\frac{2}{3} \div 10\frac{1}{6}$ **28.** $13\frac{2}{3} \div 11\frac{2}{9}$

Estimate to see if the answer is reasonable. If it is not, divide
to obtain an exact answer. Write *yes* or *no*.

29. $7\frac{1}{2} \div 5 = 90$ **30.** $9 \div 4\frac{1}{2} = 2$ **31.** $3\frac{3}{4} \div 1\frac{2}{8} = 2$

ESTIMATE

32. $8\frac{3}{4} \div 2\frac{3}{4} = 3\frac{2}{11}$ **33.** $1\frac{4}{5} \div 2\frac{7}{10} = 1\frac{1}{2}$ **34.** $6\frac{1}{3} \div 2\frac{1}{2} = 5$

PROBLEM SOLVING APPLICATIONS
Reasonable Answers

Solve. Then estimate to check the reasonableness
of your answer.

35. Martha typed 66 pages in $7\frac{1}{2}$ h. How many
pages can she type in one hour?

36. If $12\frac{1}{2}$ yd of rope is to be divided into $1\frac{1}{4}$ ft
lengths, how many lengths will there be?

★ **37.** Mr. Jackson gives music lessons from 9:15
A.M. to 11:45 A.M. and 1:30 P.M. to 3:30 P.M.
each day. If each lesson is $\frac{3}{4}$ h long, how many
lessons does he give?

★ **38.** Kipp is building a dock. It
will be made from 8 planks,
each $7\frac{5}{8}$ in. wide. The total
width of the dock will be
70 in. If there are equal
spaces between adjacent
planks, about how wide
must each space be?

PROBLEM SOLVING
Strategy: Choosing the Operation

1. Understand
2. Plan
3. Work
4. Answer / Check.

You must read a problem carefully before deciding on a method of solution. Understanding the question asked will help you make a plan.

On a recent fishing trip, Mario caught 1008 lb of fish. About $\frac{1}{6}$ of the fish were too small to sell. About how many pounds of the fish were too small to sell?

What do you know? $\frac{1}{6}$ of the fish were too small to sell. 1008 lb of fish were caught. What do you want to know? Number of pounds of fish too small to sell.

- *Plan:* Find the product of $\frac{1}{6}$ and 1008.
- *Operation:* Multiplication
- *Work:* $\frac{1}{6} \times 1008 = 168$

About 168 lb of fish were too small to sell.

CLASS EXERCISES

What operation would you use to solve the problem? List as many operations as necessary.

1. How can you find the total number of students in your school if you know the number in each grade?

2. If you know the price of a record and the amount of money you have to spend, how can you figure out your change?

3. You know how far you've traveled and how long it took to reach your destination. How can you figure out your average speed?

4. You know the regular prices of tennis balls, sweat socks, and sun screen. How can you find the total price of the items when on sale for $\frac{1}{3}$ off?

PRACTICE

Solve.

5. You want to submit a story you wrote to seven magazines. The story is 23 pages long. If it costs $.03 per page to make photocopies, how much will it cost to make enough copies for all the magazines?

6. Natalie bought $3\frac{1}{4}$ lb of cherries and $2\frac{5}{8}$ lb of peaches. How much fruit did she buy altogether?

7. Michele jogged $\frac{7}{8}$ mi. Mary jogged $\frac{7}{10}$ mi. Who jogged farther? how much farther?

8. The odometer on Tom's car showed 16,045.7 before a trip to the snowmobile races. When he returned home the odometer showed 16,261.1. How many miles did Tom travel?

9. Mona spent $6.50 on decorations for a party. She also spent $11.75 for refreshments and $5.15 for prizes. There were 10 guests. What was the cost per guest?

CHECKPOINT 2

Divide. Write the quotient in lowest terms. *(pages 198–205)*

1. $\frac{1}{5} \div 8$

2. $8 \div \frac{3}{4}$

3. $\frac{3}{5} \div \frac{6}{7}$

4. $\frac{5}{9} \div \frac{10}{21}$

5. $6\frac{7}{8} \div 2\frac{1}{2}$

6. $8\frac{1}{4} \div 3\frac{6}{7}$

Solve. *(pages 206–207)*

7. Together, 3 friends collected $42\frac{3}{4}$ lb of litter. What was the average amount collected by each friend?

8. Americans produce about 2.5 kg of trash per person each day. How much is this in one week? in one year?

Extra Practice on page 444

Write the answer in lowest terms. *(pages 190–195)*

1. $\frac{1}{3} \times 15$

2. $56 \times \frac{3}{8}$

3. $\frac{3}{4} \times \frac{1}{9}$

4. $\frac{2}{5} \times \frac{7}{8} \times \frac{1}{10}$

5. $2\frac{1}{7} \times 1\frac{2}{3}$

6. $7\frac{3}{10} \times 2\frac{2}{9}$

7. $4\frac{3}{4} \times 8$

8. $3\frac{1}{3} \times 2\frac{1}{6} \times 4\frac{1}{2}$

Work backwards to solve. *(pages 196–197)*

9. Debra had a certain amount of money in her savings account. She spent $\frac{1}{3}$ of the money and deposited $55 more. Debra now has a balance of $75. How much did she have to begin with?

10. In the last three months Jake the wrestler lost $5\frac{1}{2}$ lb, gained $2\frac{1}{4}$ lb, and then lost $3\frac{3}{4}$ lb. Jake now weighs 210 lb. How much did Jake weigh to begin with?

Write the reciprocal. *(pages 198–199)*

11. $\frac{1}{4}$

12. $\frac{9}{11}$

13. 36

14. $6\frac{1}{3}$

15. 7

16. $3\frac{4}{5}$

17. $81\frac{1}{2}$

18. $40\frac{3}{7}$

Write the answer in lowest terms. *(pages 200–205)*

19. $8 \div \frac{4}{7}$

20. $\frac{7}{16} \div 35$

21. $\frac{2}{3} \div \frac{2}{9}$

22. $\frac{7}{12} \div \frac{14}{15}$

23. $6 \div 1\frac{1}{5}$

24. $3\frac{3}{8} \div 9$

25. $1\frac{2}{3} \div 1\frac{4}{9}$

26. $5\frac{3}{4} \div 3\frac{1}{2}$

Solve. *(pages 206–207)*

27. Peggy walked $\frac{1}{6}$ mi to the store and then $\frac{2}{3}$ mi to the bank. How far did she walk altogether?

28. Concert tickets usually cost $12. For the Saturday matinee they are specially priced at $\frac{1}{6}$ off. How much will 6 tickets cost?

Extra Practice on page 445

MATHEMATICS and HISTORY

Settlement of the nation's frontier accelerated as travel and communication became faster and easier. Distances seemed to shrink because journeys took less time.

1. In 1849, gold miners often traveled by sea from New York to San Francisco. The voyage around South America often took 150 days. The fastest ships of the era, the Clipper Ships, could reduce this time by $\frac{1}{3}$. How long would the shorter voyage last?

2. The transcontinental railroad was opened in 1869. The journey from Omaha, Nebraska, to Sacramento, California, could take 6 months (180 days) for settlers traveling by covered wagon. By train, the journey took about $\frac{1}{25}$ the time. How many days was the trip by train?

HOW CLOSE IS EAST TO WEST?

★ 3. The Pony Express carried mail 2000 mi between St. Joseph, Missouri, and Sacramento, California, in 10 days. This cut in half the fastest previous record. A rider carried a 15 lb satchel of mail. It cost $5 to mail $\frac{1}{2}$ oz by Pony Express. How much was charged to carry the 15 lb of mail?

Enrichment

In the base ten number system we use the digits from 0 through 9 and group in powers of ten. The base two system uses only the digits 0 and 1 and groups in powers of two.

The chart on the left below shows the expanded form of the base ten numeral 21. The chart on the right shows the conversion of the base two numeral 10101_{two} to base ten.

BASE TEN			
10^3	10^2	10^1	10^0
1000's	100's	10's	1's
		2	1

BASE TWO						
2^6	2^5	2^4	2^3	2^2	2^1	2^0
64's	32's	16's	8's	4's	2's	1's
		1	0	1	0	1

$21_{ten} = (2 \times 10^1) + (1 \times 10^0)$
$= 20 + 1$
$= 21_{ten}$

$10101_{two} = (1 \times 2^4) + 0 + (1 \times 2^2) +$
$0 + (1 \times 2^0)$
$= 16 + 4 + 1$
$= 21_{ten}$

The base two number 10101_{two} is read *one zero one zero one, base two*.

Complete the chart.

	BASE TWO NUMERAL	2^4	2^3	2^2	2^1	2^0	BASE TEN NUMERAL
		16's	8's	4's	2's	1's	
1.	111_{two}			1	1	1	?
2.	1101_{two}		1	1	0	1	?
3.	11011_{two}	1	1	0	1	1	?
4.	11111_{two}	1	1	1	1	1	?

BASE TWO AND BASE EIGHT

As you might expect, the base eight number system uses the digits from 0 through 7 and groups in powers of 8.

This number is read,
five six seven, base eight.

$$567_{eight} = (5 \times 8^2) + (6 \times 8^1) + (7 \times 8^0)$$
$$= (5 \times 64) + (6 \times 8) + (7 \times 1)$$
$$= 320 + 48 + 7$$
$$= 375_{ten}$$

Complete the chart.

	BASE EIGHT NUMERAL	8^3 512's	8^2 64's	8^1 8's	8^0 1's	BASE TEN NUMERAL
5.	56_{eight}			5	6	?
6.	135_{eight}		1	3	5	?
7.	714_{eight}		7	1	4	?
8.	1047_{eight}	1	0	4	7	?
9.	312_{eight}		3	1	2	?
10.	210_{eight}		2	1	0	?

Think of a base five system.

11. What digits would be used?

12. How would numbers be grouped?

13. Make a place value chart for a base five system.

14. Use your place value chart to write these base five numbers in base ten.

40_{five} 34_{five} 233_{five} 1032_{five}

CUMULATIVE REVIEW

Choose the best answer. Write *a*, *b*, *c*, or *d*.

Choose the correct answer.

1. numbers all
divisible by 5
  a. 25, 30, 33, 35
  b. 5, 1, 15, 20
  c. 10, 20, 30, 95
  d. None of these

2. the GCF of
24 and 32
  a. 12
  b. 4
  c. 8
  d. None of these

3. numbers that
are all composite
  a. 9, 10, 13, 15
  b. 4, 5, 6, 7
  c. 2, 4, 6, 8
  d. None of these

Compare the fractions.

4. $\frac{11}{25}$ ▆ $\frac{7}{25}$
  a. >   **b.** <   **c.** =
  d. None of these

5. $\frac{9}{32}$ ▆ $\frac{9}{16}$
  a. >   **b.** <   **c.** =
  d. None of these

6. $\frac{6}{24}$ ▆ $\frac{3}{12}$
  a. >   **b.** <   **c.** =
  d. None of these

Order the fractions from least to greatest.

7. $\frac{1}{6}$ $\frac{1}{8}$ $\frac{1}{7}$
  a. $\frac{1}{8}$ $\frac{1}{7}$ $\frac{1}{6}$
  b. $\frac{1}{6}$ $\frac{1}{7}$ $\frac{1}{8}$
  c. $\frac{1}{8}$ $\frac{1}{6}$ $\frac{1}{7}$
  d. None of these

8. $\frac{3}{8}$ $\frac{3}{5}$ $\frac{3}{10}$
  a. $\frac{3}{10}$ $\frac{3}{5}$ $\frac{3}{8}$
  b. $\frac{3}{5}$ $\frac{3}{8}$ $\frac{3}{10}$
  c. $\frac{3}{8}$ $\frac{3}{10}$ $\frac{3}{5}$
  d. None of these

9. $\frac{5}{6}$ $\frac{2}{3}$ $\frac{7}{8}$
  a. $\frac{2}{3}$ $\frac{5}{6}$ $\frac{7}{8}$
  b. $\frac{5}{6}$ $\frac{7}{8}$ $\frac{2}{3}$
  c. $\frac{7}{8}$ $\frac{5}{6}$ $\frac{2}{3}$
  d. None of these

Find the terms with the matching values.

10. $\frac{22}{9}$
  a. $2\frac{1}{3}$
  b. $3\frac{4}{9}$
  c. $2\frac{2}{9}$
  d. None of these

11. $1\frac{3}{8}$
  a. $\frac{8}{8}$
  b. $\frac{11}{8}$
  c. $\frac{5}{8}$
  d. None of these

12. $6\frac{4}{7}$
  a. $\frac{42}{7}$
  b. $\frac{46}{7}$
  c. $\frac{31}{7}$
  d. None of these

Find the term with the matching value.

13. $\frac{4}{5}$ **14.** $\frac{21}{30}$ **15.** 0.692

a. 0.8   **a.** 0.07   **a.** $\frac{173}{250}$

b. 0.08   **b.** 0.77   **b.** $\frac{341}{500}$

c. 0.008   **c.** 0.7   **c.** $\frac{0.692}{1000}$

d. None of these   **d.** None of these   **d.** None of these

Estimate.

16. A total of 212 students out of 800 signed up for basketball camp. About what fraction of the group signed up?

     a. About $\frac{1}{3}$ **b.** About $\frac{1}{4}$ **c.** About $\frac{1}{2}$ **d.** None of these

17. Madeline went to hockey practice 21 out of 26 times. About what fraction of the time did she attend practice?

     a. About $\frac{7}{9}$ **b.** About $\frac{1}{2}$ **c.** About $\frac{1}{5}$ **d.** None of these

LANGUAGE and VOCABULARY REVIEW

Choose the correct word to complete.

1. (Reciprocals, Fractions) are pairs of numbers whose product is 1.

2. To divide a fraction, multiply by the reciprocal of the (quotient, divisor).

3. The numbers $\frac{1}{4}$, $\frac{5}{8}$, and $\frac{7}{9}$ are called (decimals, fractions).

4. We can use (cross products, common factors) to determine whether two fractions are equivalent.

5. An angle with a measure of 90° is called a (complementary, right) angle.

6. A (triangle, trapezoid) is a quadrilateral with only one pair of parallel sides.

7. When we write 3^4 the number 3 is the (exponent, base).

PLANNING A PROGRAM

COMPUTER LITERACY

Programmers make detailed plans before writing a program. They often show the details of the plan in a flowchart.

Problem: Convert measurements given in centimeters to millimeters and millimeters to centimeters.

Solution Steps:

1. Ask for a metric measurement in centimeters or millimeters.

2. Determine the metric unit being used.

3. Use a formula to convert the measurement.

4. Write the output.

5. Stop.

Use the flowchart to answer.

1. What decisions are shown in the flowchart?

2. What will the computer do if the measurement is in meters?

Test the flowchart. Write the output.

3. Input: 95 mm
4. Input: 85 cm
5. Input: 63 cm
6. Input: 9 mm
7. Input: 104 mm
8. Input: 5 cm
9. Input: 15.9 mm
10. Input: 100 m

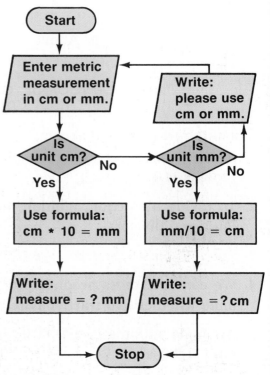

214

During launch, Shuttle passengers feel 3 times heavier than normal. Using $w = 3n$, replace n with your normal weight to find how heavy you'd feel.

PRE-ALGEBRA: EQUATIONS

MATHEMATICAL EXPRESSIONS

Numbers, variables, and operation symbols are often combined to form **mathematical expressions.**

In mathematical expressions with variables, the multiplication symbol is usually omitted.

$2n$ means $2 \times n$

abc means $a \times b \times c$

WORD EXPRESSION	MATHEMATICAL EXPRESSION
eight plus fifteen	$8 + 15$
six subtracted from a number x	$x - 6$
seven times a number n	$7 \times n$ or $7n$
a number z divided by 21	$z \div 21$, or $\frac{z}{21}$

CLASS EXERCISES

Choose the correct mathematical expression. Write a, b, or c.

1. the product of six and fifty
   a. $6 + 50$ **b.** $50 - 6$ **c.** 6×50

2. the sum of 18 and 5
   a. 5×18 **b.** $18 + 5$ **c.** $18 - 5$

3. fifteen times a number s
   a. $15 + s$ **b.** $15 - s$ **c.** $15s$

4. a number q increased by 37
   a. $q + 37$ **b.** $q - 37$ **c.** $q \div 37$

5. seventeen less than a number d
   a. $d - 17$ **b.** $17 - d$ **c.** $\frac{d}{17}$

6. the quotient of a number y and 48
   a. $y + 48$ **b.** $48y$ **c.** $\frac{y}{48}$

PRACTICE

Write as a mathematical expression.

7. eighteen minus seven

8. forty-six times nine

9. seven more than a number p

10. fourteen less than a number q

11. a number b divided by 4

12. a number n multiplied by 12

13. a number g decreased by 3

14. a number w increased by 11

15. the sum of a number x and 13

16. the product of a number x and 5

17. the sum of a number x and a number y

18. the product of a number x and a number y

Write as a word expression.

19. $27 + 19$

20. $\frac{8}{13}$

21. $40 - 37$

22. 3×51

23. $a - 15$

24. $3v$

25. $\frac{z}{10}$

26. $18 - c$

27. $\frac{48}{h}$

28. $56 + y$

29. $35b$

30. $x + y$

31. $x - y$

32. xy

33. $\frac{x}{y}$

PROBLEM SOLVING APPLICATIONS
Choosing the Operation

Match the statement with the mathematical expression.

34. The group was divided into five teams.

A. $7m$

35. Suzanna tripled the recipe.

B. $k - 3$

36. Seven new members joined the computer club.

C. $3x$

37. Tom gave away three kittens.

D. $a + 7$

38. The Jordans planned to hike about seven miles each day.

E. $\frac{g}{5}$

39. One year later the profits increased to five times their original investment.

F. $5g$

40. The class raised $30 more after the bake sale.

G. $d + 30$

EVALUATING
MATHEMATICAL EXPRESSIONS

Each lap around the track measures 400 m. The expression $400n$ represents the total number of meters that a student runs in laps.

NUMBER OF LAPS (n)	TOTAL DISTANCE IN METERS ($400n$)
1	$400 \times 1 = 400$
2	$400 \times 2 = 800$
3	$400 \times 3 = 1200$

To **evaluate** an expression for a given number, replace the variable in the expression with the number and then do the indicated arithmetic.

You can evaluate many expressions mentally. Evaluate the expression $5n$ when $n = 5$, when $n = 7$, and when $n = 12$.

Think: $5n = 5 \times 5 = 25$
$5n = 5 \times 7 = 35$
$5n = 5 \times 12 = 60$

Frank 400
Susan 800
Rita 1200

CLASS EXERCISES

Evaluate $n + 12$ for the given value.

1. $n = 5$ **2.** $n = 49$ **3.** $n = 0$ **4.** $n = 18$ **5.** $n = 50$ **6.** $n = 12$

Evaluate $\frac{45}{n}$ for the given value.

7. $n = 9$ **8.** $n = 45$ **9.** $n = 15$ **10.** $n = 3$ **11.** $n = 1$ **12.** $n = 5$

PRACTICE

Evaluate the expression. Use $a = 14$ and $b = 5$.

13. $b - 3$ **14.** $3a$ **15.** $\frac{b}{5}$ **16.** $21 - a$ **17.** $38 + b$

18. $\frac{56}{a}$ **19.** $5b$ **20.** $a - b$ **21.** ab **22.** $\frac{a}{b}$

Evaluate the expression. Use $x = 6$, $y = 12$, and $z = 24$.

23. $x + 15$ **24.** $y - 12$ **25.** $3z$ **26.** $\frac{y}{2}$ **27.** $32 - z$

28. $34 + y$ **29.** $\frac{x}{6}$ **30.** $9x$ **31.** $y - x$ **32.** $z - x$

33. $\frac{z}{x}$ **34.** $\frac{z}{y}$ **35.** $x + y + z$ **36.** xyz **37.** $3xy$

38. $2yz$ **39.** $2x + 2y - z$ **40.** $\frac{y}{2} + \frac{z}{4}$ **41.** $2x + y$ **42.** $5x - 2y$

Evaluate the expression using the given value for the variable.

43. $3m$; $m = 17$ **44.** $4x + 7$; $x = 25$ **45.** $12 - 2y$; $y = 5$

46. $\frac{2a}{15}$; $a = 5$ ★ **47.** $6(3a + 5)$; $a = 8$ ★ **48.** $10(5x - 7)$; $x = 15$

Evaluate the expression mentally. Use $r = 5$.

49. $5r$ **50.** $r + 8$ **51.** $r - 2$ **52.** $(2r) + 5$

53. $6r - 5$ **54.** $\frac{r}{10}$ **55.** $\frac{25}{r}$ **56.** $50\left(\frac{5}{r}\right)$

MENTAL MATH

PROBLEM SOLVING APPLICATIONS
Evaluating Expressions

Use the information to write and evaluate an expression for each statement.

a decade = 10 years   a score of years = 20 years   a century = 100 years
            $d = 10$ $s = 20$ $c = 100$

57. "Four score and seven years ago" is the beginning of the Gettysburg Address.

58. Bill's grandfather is seven decades old.

59. The Masons bought a house that is $\frac{3}{4}$ decade old.

60. The first printing press was used about five centuries and three decades ago.

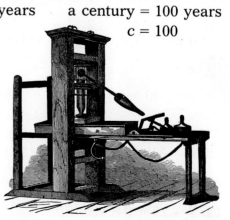

EQUATIONS

An **equation** is a statement that two numbers or quantities are equal. Equations often contain variables.

$$8 + 3 = 5 + 6 \qquad s + 4 = 7 \qquad 5x + 3 = 20$$

You can solve some equations by replacing the variable with trial numbers. This is called **substitution.** A number that makes a true equation is a **solution.**

Solve: $16 + x = 100$

Think: What number can I substitute for x to make a true equation?

Try 90: $16 + 90 = 106$ False
Try 84: $16 + 84 = 100$ True

The number 84 is a solution of the equation $16 + x = 100$.

Ⓜ Some equations can be solved mentally.

Solve: $a + 3 = 8$

Think: $5 + 3 = 8$, so $a = 5$.

CLASS EXERCISES

Is the equation true or false? Write *true* or *false*.

1. $5 + 3 = 8$ **2.** $7 - 2 = 4$ **3.** $20 + 30 = 50$ **4.** $120 - 85 = 60$

5. $\frac{12}{6} = 3$ **6.** $9 \times 3 = 27$ **7.** $8 + 6 = 7 - 2$ **8.** $15 + 10 = 35 - 10$

9. $60 + 40 = 50 + 50$ **10.** $81 + 72 = 58 + 65$ **11.** $\frac{15}{45} + 3 = 3 + \frac{12}{36}$

PRACTICE

Is the given number the solution of the equation? Write *yes* or *no*.

12. $z + 25 = 94$; 79   **13.** $a - 46 = 35$; 81   **14.** $9p = 171$; 19

15. $\frac{c}{7} = 147$; 21 $\qquad$ **16.** $\frac{76}{x} = 19$; 4 $\qquad$ **17.** $12h = 96$; 84

Choose the solution of the equation. Write a, b, or c.

18. $m + 23 = 72$
    a. 95 $\qquad$ **b.** 55 $\qquad$ **c.** 49

19. $x - 14 = 27$
    a. 13 $\qquad$ **b.** 41 $\qquad$ **c.** 31

20. $3t = 87$
    a. 261 $\qquad$ **b.** 84 $\qquad$ **c.** 29

21. $\frac{r}{5} = 21$
    a. $4\frac{1}{5}$ $\qquad$ **b.** 105 $\qquad$ **c.** 26

22. $125 - d = 46$
    a. 79 $\qquad$ **b.** 171 $\qquad$ **c.** 81

23. $77 + q = 138$
    a. 215 $\qquad$ **b.** 161 $\qquad$ **c.** 61

24. $\frac{120}{y} = 8$
    a. 112 $\qquad$ **b.** 15 $\qquad$ **c.** 960

25. $6g = 108$
    a. 18 $\qquad$ **b.** 648 $\qquad$ **c.** 102

Solve the equation mentally.

26. $x + 5 = 8$ $\qquad$ **27.** $3a = 12$ $\qquad$ **28.** $\frac{15}{y} = 5$

29. $7 + z = 14$ $\qquad$ **30.** $y \div 3 = 6$ $\qquad$ **31.** $2c = 20$

MENTAL MATH

PROBLEM SOLVING APPLICATIONS
Using Formulas

Use the distance formula to solve the problem.

$$\text{Distance} = \text{rate} \times \text{time}$$
$$D = rt$$

32. A train traveled for four hours at 110 mi/h. How far did it travel?

33. A cyclist pedaled for five hours at a rate of 12.5 mi/h. How far did she travel?

34. A canoe traveled 20 mi in three hours. How fast was the canoe traveling?

★ **35.** Hal left his house at 8:00 A.M. He drove at 50 mi/h until he stopped at 12:00 P.M. for lunch. How far did Hal travel?

INVERSE OPERATIONS
ADDITION AND SUBTRACTION

Addition and subtraction of the same number are called **inverse operations.** This means that one operation "undoes" the other.

$$5 + 9 = 14 \quad \Rightarrow \quad 14 - 9 = 5$$

You can use inverse operations to rewrite an equation. Often this makes it easier to see the solution.

$$
\begin{aligned}
y + 14 &= 43 \\
y + 14 - 14 &= 43 - 14 \\
y + 0 &= 29 \\
y &= 29
\end{aligned}
$$

Solution: 29

$$
\begin{aligned}
a - 28 &= 95 \\
a - 28 + 28 &= 95 + 28 \\
a - 0 &= 123 \\
a &= 123
\end{aligned}
$$

Solution: 123

Substitute to check the solution in the original equation.

$$
\begin{aligned}
y + 14 &= 43 \\
29 + 14 &= 43 \quad \text{True}
\end{aligned}
\qquad
\begin{aligned}
a - 28 &= 95 \\
123 - 28 &= 95 \quad \text{True}
\end{aligned}
$$

When you use inverse operations to solve an equation, it is very important to do the same thing to both sides of the equation.

CLASS EXERCISES

What number should be subtracted from each side to solve the equation?

1. $y + 4 = 16$ **2.** $r + 46 = 95$ **3.** $x + 24 = 49$ **4.** $d + 19 = 91$

5. $m + 86 = 102$ **6.** $s + 55 = 127$ **7.** $b + 66 = 155$ **8.** $t + 15 = 108$

What number should be added to each side to solve the equation?

9. $n - 5 = 12$ **10.** $t - 36 = 57$ **11.** $a - 84 = 107$ **12.** $w - 60 = 89$

13. $b - 99 = 123$ **14.** $p - 48 = 102$ **15.** $d - 38 = 115$ **16.** $s - 87 = 142$

PRACTICE

Complete.

17. $z + 15 = 22$
$z + 15 - 15 = 22 - \blacksquare$
$z = \blacksquare$

18. $c - 27 = 48$
$c - 27 + \blacksquare = 48 + \blacksquare$
$c = \blacksquare$

19. $b + 35 = 68$
$b + 35 - \blacksquare = 68 - \blacksquare$
$b = \blacksquare$

Solve the equation.

20. $b + 18 = 21$ **21.** $g + 9 = 23$ **22.** $x + 15 = 42$ **23.** $m - 19 = 31$

24. $c - 28 = 49$ **25.** $a + 24 = 93$ **26.** $d - 51 = 14$ **27.** $h - 130 = 47$

28. $y + 1.2 = 1.89$ **29.** $x - 5.9 = 11.8$ **30.** $z + 0.52 = 1.91$ **31.** $v - 6.13 = 17.06$

★**32.** $t - \frac{4}{9} = \frac{1}{9}$ ★**33.** $c + 2\frac{1}{3} = 4\frac{2}{3}$ ★**34.** $n + 4\frac{7}{11} = 9$ ★**35.** $w - 6\frac{4}{5} = 15\frac{1}{5}$

Are the fractions equivalent? Write *yes* or *no*.

36. $\frac{3}{4}, \frac{9}{12}$ **37.** $\frac{1}{5}, \frac{4}{20}$ **38.** $\frac{15}{20}, \frac{10}{14}$ **39.** $\frac{8}{20}, \frac{10}{25}$

MIXED REVIEW

Complete.

40. $\frac{1}{9} = \frac{\blacksquare}{18}$ **41.** $\frac{3}{7} = \frac{12}{\blacksquare}$ **42.** $\frac{5}{7} = \frac{\blacksquare}{21}$ **43.** $\frac{1}{3} = \frac{6}{\blacksquare}$

PROBLEM SOLVING APPLICATIONS
Nonroutine Problems

Solve.

44. A chicken and a half lays an egg and a half in one day. How many eggs will five chickens lay in 6 days?

45. There are two numbers that do not have zero as a digit, and whose product is one million. Find the two numbers.

★**46.** What is the greatest amount of money you can have in a combination of quarters, dimes, nickels, and pennies and still not have change for $1.00?

★**47.** Selma has a bag of apples. If the number of apples is divided by 3, 4, or 9 the remainder is 2. How many apples are in the bag?

INVERSE OPERATIONS MULTIPLICATION AND DIVISION

Multiplication and division by the same number are inverse operations.

$$7 \times 8 = 56 \quad \Rightarrow \quad 56 \div 8 = 7$$

You can use inverse operations to solve equations. Always remember to do the same thing to both sides of the equation.

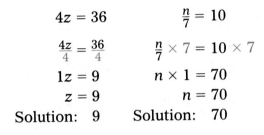

$$4z = 36 \qquad\qquad \frac{n}{7} = 10$$

$$\frac{4z}{4} = \frac{36}{4} \qquad\qquad \frac{n}{7} \times 7 = 10 \times 7$$

$$1z = 9 \qquad\qquad n \times 1 = 70$$

$$z = 9 \qquad\qquad n = 70$$

Solution: 9   Solution: 70

Substitute to check the solution in the original equation.

$$4z = 36 \qquad\qquad \frac{n}{7} = 10$$

$$4 \times 9 = 36 \quad \text{True} \qquad \frac{70}{7} = 10 \quad \text{True}$$

You can use a calculator to solve equations.

Solve: $45x = 765$ Enter 765 ÷ 45 = 17   Solution: 17

Solve: $\frac{a}{38} = 93$ Enter 93 × 38 = 3534   Solution: 3534

CLASS EXERCISES

What can you do to both sides of the equation to find a solution?

1. $6y = 78$

2. $\frac{d}{4} = 17$

3. $5m = 125$

4. $\frac{k}{6} = 9$

5. $7w = 56$

6. $\frac{a}{10} = 30$

7. $8m = 160$

8. $12z = 144$

Solve the equation.

9. $5k = 75$ **10.** $6x = 90$ **11.** $4c = 92$ **12.** $\frac{y}{2} = 16$

13. $\frac{n}{4} = 14$ **14.** $\frac{w}{3} = 32$ **15.** $2b = 78$ **16.** $\frac{a}{6} = 17$

17. $8z = 104$ **18.** $\frac{m}{5} = 11$ **19.** $\frac{s}{2} = 46$ **20.** $7q = 91$

21. $3g = 96$ **22.** $\frac{p}{7} = 15$ **23.** $12w = 144$ **24.** $\frac{a}{10} = 15$

25. $\frac{x}{14} = 14$ **26.** $15y = 165$ **27.** $11j = 121$ **28.** $\frac{t}{19} = 12$

Solve the equation. A calculator may be helpful.

29. $25x = 425$ **30.** $\frac{y}{48} = 48$ **31.** $621a = 1863$

32. $5.06t = 1.6698$ **33.** $\frac{b}{20.5} = 0.8$ **34.** $0.95w = 0.57$

CALCULATOR

35. Which of Exercises 29–34 can be done using mental math?

PROBLEM SOLVING APPLICATIONS
Working Backwards

Remember that a magic square is a square array of numbers in which each row, column, and diagonal has the same sum.

Solve the equation. Then replace the variable in the square with the solution of the equation. If your work is correct, the solutions will form a magic square.

a	b	c
d	e	f
g	h	j

36. $a + 28 = 44$ **37.** $\frac{b}{6} = 6$ **38.** $13c = 104$

39. $d + 89 = 101$ **40.** $e - 2 = 18$ **41.** $\frac{f}{2} = 14$

42. $g - 19 = 13$ **43.** $h + 58 = 62$ **44.** $7j = 168$

WRITING AND SOLVING EQUATIONS

Due to bad weather and a lack of money, it took sculptors 14 years to complete the Mt. Rushmore Memorial. Actual construction time amounted to about 6 years. How much time was lost due to bad weather and lack of money?

You can write an equation to describe the problem. Let t = time lost.

time lost	plus	construction time	equals	total time
t	+	6	=	14

Use the inverse operation to solve the equation.

$$t + 6 = 14$$
$$t + 6 - 6 = 14 - 6$$
$$t = 8$$

8 years were lost.

Use substitution to check the solution.

$$t + 6 = 14$$
$$8 + 6 = 14 \quad \text{True}$$

E For some equations, you can estimate to see if a solution is reasonable.

Solve: $w = \frac{5724}{4}$

$$w = 1431$$

Estimate: $\frac{5724}{4} \approx \frac{6000}{4} = 1500$

Since 1431 is close to 1500, the solution is reasonable.

CLASS EXERCISES

Choose an equation to describe the situation. Write a, b, c, or d.

1. The product of a number and 8 is 112.

   a. $\frac{n}{8} = 112$ **b.** $8n = 112$

   c. $n = 8 \times 112$ **d.** $112n = 8$

2. A number divided by 3 equals 42.

   a. $\frac{n}{3} = 42$ **b.** $\frac{3}{n} = 42$

   c. $3n = 42$ **d.** $n = \frac{42}{3}$

PRACTICE

Use a variable to write an equation. Solve.

3. What number times 9 is 189?

4. Twice what number is 58?

5. What number divided by 3 is 24?

6. Triple what number is 48?

7. The product of what number and 6 is 96?

8. What number shared equally by 5 is 125?

9. One half of what number is 35?

10. One fourth of what number is 14?

Use a variable to write an equation. Estimate the solution.

ESTIMATE

11. 3589 decreased by a number is 981.

12. The sum of 58 and a number is 310.

★ 13. The average of 3 numbers whose sum is 6189.

★ 14. 681 is the average of what number of addends whose sum is 3405?

PROBLEM SOLVING APPLICATIONS
Writing an Equation

Use a variable to write an equation. Solve.

15. The nose on each face carved in Mt. Rushmore is about 20 ft high. Each face is about three times as high as its nose. What is the approximate height of each face?

16. About 1 million people visit Mt. Rushmore each year. What is the average daily attendance? weekly attendance? (An estimated answer is sufficient.)

17. Mt. Rushmore is about 25 mi from Rapid City, South Dakota. It's also about 3 mi from Keystone, South Dakota. You pass through Keystone from Rapid City to Mt. Rushmore. About how far apart are the cities?

PROBLEM SOLVING
Strategy: Trial and Error

Sometimes you need a combination of logical thinking and trial and error to solve a problem.

Janna bought three items for snacks. She spent $1.75. Which three items did she buy?

Here's one set of steps to solve the problem.

juice	$.45	strawberries	$3.75
milk	$.65	pineapple	$2.65
bagel	$.95	yogurt	$.80
toast	$.50	cheeseplate	$4.85

STEP	RESULT
1. Eliminate the items that cost more than the total.	Not strawberries, not pineapples, not cheese plate.
2. Look at the digit in the ones' place in the total.	The ones' digit is 5, so the ones' digits of the three items must add to 5.
3. Look at the ones' digits of the remaining menu items.	The digits are 5's or 0's, so the sum must be three 5's or one 5 and two 0's.
4. Try the possible combinations.	juice $ .45 milk .65 bagel .95 _____ $2.05 NO juice $ .45 toast .50 yogurt .80 _____ $1.75 YES

A calculator may be helpful when solving problems by trial and error.

CLASS EXERCISE

Complete the table to solve the problem. A calculator may be helpful.

1. Two even numbers have a difference of 12 and a product of 160. What are the two numbers?

TRIAL	NUMBERS	DIFFERENCE	PRODUCT
1	14, 2	12	28
2	16, ▨	12	▨
3	▨, ▨	12	▨
▨	▨, ▨	▨	▨

PRACTICE

Solve. A calculator may be helpful.
Use the sale poster for Exercises 2–4.

2. Alice bought four items and spent $39.42. What did she buy?

3. "I spent $24.96 for four items," said Ralph. What did Ralph buy?

4. "I spent $10.47 in the morning, and $20.47 in the afternoon," said Leroy. "Guess what six things I bought."

5. The product of two consecutive, three-digit numbers is 49,506. Find the numbers.

★ 6. In the National Hockey League, a team gets 2 points for a win, 1 point for a tie, and no points for a loss. One team lost 14 of their 80 games. They ended the season with 113 points. How many games did they win?

Sam's
Super Sale

Record albums	$ 7.99
Cassette tapes	8.99
Posters	3.49
Computer games	19.95

ONE DAY ONLY

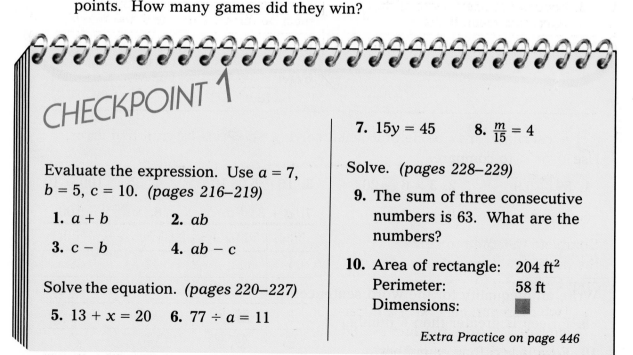

CHECKPOINT 1

Evaluate the expression. Use $a = 7$, $b = 5$, $c = 10$. (pages 216–219)

1. $a + b$
2. ab
3. $c - b$
4. $ab - c$

Solve the equation. (pages 220–227)

5. $13 + x = 20$
6. $77 \div a = 11$

7. $15y = 45$
8. $\frac{m}{15} = 4$

Solve. (pages 228–229)

9. The sum of three consecutive numbers is 63. What are the numbers?

10. Area of rectangle: 204 ft²
    Perimeter: 58 ft
    Dimensions: ■

Extra Practice on page 446

INEQUALITIES

Jake has 7 kinds of butterflies in his collection. When he finds a certain number of other varieties, his collection will include more than 10 kinds of butterflies.

You can write an inequality using variables. Let y be the number of varieties of butterflies Jake needs.

A number $7 + y$ is greater than 10.

$$7 + y > 10$$

The graph of an inequality can be shown on a number line.

This number line shows the graph of the inequality $25 < x < 30$ which means that x is between 25 and 30.

This number line shows the graph of the inequality $y < 6$.

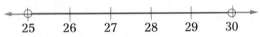

The open dot shows that a number is not included in the graph.

CLASS EXERCISES

Use $>$ or $<$ to compare.

1. 59 ▓ 5.9　　**2.** 3×6 ▓ 20　　**3.** $16 - 5$ ▓ 10　　**4.** 35 ▓ $100 \div 10$

5. x ▓ $x + 1$　　**6.** $y - 3$ ▓ y　　**7.** $a + 3$ ▓ a　　**8.** x ▓ $x - 100$

PRACTICE

Write an inequality for the word sentence.

9. Fifteen is greater than a number x.

10. Four is less than a number a.

11. A number y is greater than forty.

12. A number x is between fifteen and twenty-one.

13. A number p is less than the sum of p and three.

14. A number j is greater than the product of three and five.

15. Four is less than a number x and greater than a number y.

16. The sum of a number x and 2 is less than 20.

★ **17.** Twenty is between x and y and x is greater than y.

★ **18.** A number r is between zero and eight and a number s is between eight and fifteen.

Write an inequality for the graph. Use x for a variable.

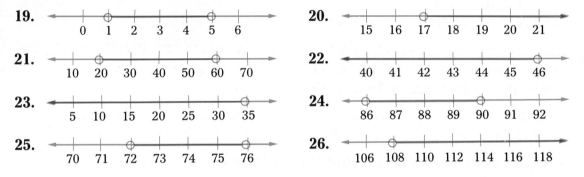

19.
0 1 2 3 4 5 6

20.
15 16 17 18 19 20 21

21.
10 20 30 40 50 60 70

22.
40 41 42 43 44 45 46

23.
5 10 15 20 25 30 35

24.
86 87 88 89 90 91 92

25.
70 71 72 73 74 75 76

26.
106 108 110 112 114 116 118

PROBLEM SOLVING APPLICATIONS
Open-Ended Problems

Write plus signs between some digits to make a true sentence.

27. 8　8　8　8　8　8　8　8 > 1000

28. 8　8　8　8　8　8　8　8 = 1000

29. 8　8　8　8　8　8　8　8 < 1000

30. 4　4　4　4　4　4　4 = 100

31. 4　4　4　4　4　4　4 > 100

32. 4　4　4　4　4　4　4 < 100

★ **33.** 4　4　4　4　4　4　4　4　4　4　4　4　4　4　4　4 = 1000

SOLVING INEQUALITIES

You can use inverse operations to find solutions of inequalities.

$$n + 14 > 55 \qquad\qquad x - 73 < 10$$
$$n + 14 - 14 > 55 - 14 \qquad x - 73 + 73 < 10 + 73$$
$$n > 41 \qquad\qquad x < 83$$

$\boxed{M}$ You can use mental math to solve many inequalities.

Solve: $x + 8 > 14$

Think: You know that $6 + 8 = 14$, so any number greater than 6 is a solution.

CLASS EXERCISES

Complete. Use $+$, $-$, $\times$, or $\div$ to make a true statement.

1. $19 \ \blacksquare \ 5 = 24$

2. $12 \ \blacksquare \ 6 = 2$

3. $27 \ \blacksquare \ 9 = 3$

4. $32 \ \blacksquare \ 3 = 96$

5. $71 \ \blacksquare \ 20 = 51$

6. $84 \ \blacksquare \ 19 = 65$

7. $14 \ \blacksquare \ 3 < 8$

8. $14 \ \blacksquare \ 8 > 40$

9. $24 \ \blacksquare \ 6 < 5$

10. $17 \ \blacksquare \ 6 < 10$

11. $36 \ \blacksquare \ 8 < 6$

12. $27 \ \blacksquare \ 5 > 133$

PRACTICE

Is the given value a solution of the inequality? Write *yes* or *no*.

13. $x + 25 > 30$; 10

14. $a - 17 < 29$; 49

15. $y + 68 < 101$; 50

16. $a + 8 > 8$; 3

17. $m + 0 > 8$; 15

18. $r + 13 < 40$; 25

Solve.

19. $y + 22 < 50$

20. $n - 75 > 113$

21. $b < 68 + 77$

22. $84 - 17 > y$

23. $q + 39 > 61$

24. $g - 52 > 52$

25. $z + 103 < 727$

26. $k + 46 > 83$

27. $a - 112 > 69$

28. $a + 432 > 1000$

29. $b - 375 > 99$

30. $c - 77 > 319$

★ 31. $c + 6.2 > 8.7$

★ 32. $k + 4.6 < 11.5$

★ 33. $m - 3.4 > 7.2$

★ 34. $a - 104.9 > 86$

★ 35. $w + 73.48 > 100.5$

★ 36. $b - 6.8 < 27.8$

★ 37. $\frac{1}{7} + m < \frac{6}{7}$

★ 38. $t - \frac{1}{11} > \frac{4}{11}$

★ 39. $d - \frac{18}{35} > \frac{11}{35}$

★ 40. $g + \frac{2}{15} < \frac{13}{15}$

★ 41. $k + \frac{20}{67} > \frac{41}{67}$

★ 42. $p - \frac{6}{53} < \frac{13}{53}$

Use mental math to solve.

43. $b + 5 > 8$

44. $a - 3 > 12$

45. $m + 2 > 5$

46. $q - 2 > 1$

47. $b + 4 > 10$

48. $y + 9 < 11$

49. $x - 1 > 0$

50. $s + 7 < 15$

51. $b - 11 > 11$

MENTAL MATH

PROBLEM SOLVING APPLICATIONS
Writing an Inequality

Write an inequality to describe the problem.

52. Bill volunteered to work for three hours at the carnival. Sharon agreed to work more hours than Bill. Let h equal the number of hours Sharon agreed to work.

53. Tickets to the Fun House cost less than $3.75. Let c equal the cost of one ticket.

54. The students in the seventh grade had $180 in the class fund. The amount earned at the carnival brought the fund to over $500. Let m equal the amount of money earned at the carnival.

★ 55. The students in Room 202 inflated helium balloons for a carnival. After two dozen were sold, there were less than five dozen left. Let b equal the original number of balloons.

EQUATIONS IN TWO VARIABLES

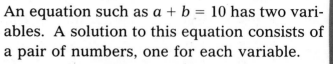

An equation such as $a + b = 10$ has two variables. A solution to this equation consists of a pair of numbers, one for each variable.

One way to find solutions of an equation in two variables is to substitute a value for one variable. Then you can solve for the other variable. Here are some of the solutions to the equation $a + b = 10$.

Let $a = 0$, then $0 + b = 10$
$$b = 10$$

Let $a = 2$, then $2 + b = 10$
$$b = 8$$

You can write the solutions as **ordered pairs** of numbers, (a,b). It is useful to organize solutions in a chart.

a	b	(a,b)
0	10	(0,10)
2	8	(2,8)
5	5	(5,5)

The first variable that appears in the equation is the first variable named in the ordered pair.

CLASS EXERCISES

Is the ordered pair a solution of the equation? Write *yes* or *no*.

1. $x + y = 11$; (5,6)

2. $x - y = 2$; (6,4)

3. $x \div y = 3$; (10,5)

4. $2x + y = 7$; (3,1)

5. $x + y = 12$; (7,5)

6. $2x - y = 4$; (5,6)

7. $x + 2y = 9$; (1,5)

8. $x \div 2y = 2$; (8,2)

9. $2x + 2y = 10$; (2,3)

PRACTICE

Complete the chart.

10. $x + 5 = y$

x	y	(x,y)
0	5	(?,?)
1	6	(1,?)
?	7	(?,7)
3	?	(?,?)
?	9	(?,?)
5	?	(?,?)

11. $m - 6 = n$

m	n	(m,n)
6	0	(?,?)
8	?	(8,?)
10	?	(?,?)
?	6	(?,?)
14	?	(14,?)
?	10	(?,?)

12. $4a = b$

a	b	(a,b)
0	?	(0,?)
3	?	(3,?)
?	24	(?,?)
?	36	(?,?)
12	?	(?,?)
?	60	(?,?)

Write the answer.

13. 48×29

14. $1182 + 279 + 3759$

15. $32\overline{)1176}$

16. 33.7×0.2

17. $3000 - 223$

18. $1.8\overline{)22.355}$

MIXED REVIEW

PROBLEM SOLVING APPLICATIONS
Organizing Information

Complete the equation. Then use the equation to complete the chart.

19. The temperature at home is 3°F higher than it is at camp.

c = temperature in °F at camp
h = temperature in °F at home
$c + \blacksquare = h$

c	79	80	81	82	83	84
h	?	?	?	?	?	?

20. The weight of a camper is usually 4 lb less after camping for a week.

b = weight in lb before camping
a = weight in lb after camping
$b - \blacksquare = a$

b	135	138	141	144	147	150
a	?	?	?	?	?	?

21. Three campers will share the cost.

t = total cost in dollars
e = cost in dollars for each camper

$\dfrac{t}{\blacksquare} = e$

t	90	96	102	108	114	120
e	?	?	?	?	?	?

GRAPHING COORDINATES

You can locate a point on a grid by naming an ordered pair of numbers.

The **coordinates** of point A at the right are (1,5).

To graph (4,2) start at 0 and move 4 units to the right. Then move up 2 units.

Think: How do you graph (2,4)? Are (4,2) and (2,4) the same point?

CLASS EXERCISES

Write the coordinates for these directions. Start at 0.

1. 3 units right and 6 units up

2. 8 units right and 3 units up

3. 1 unit right and 8 units up

4. 5 units right and 2 units up

5. 1 unit right and 0 units up

6. 0 units right and 6 units up

PRACTICE

Write the letter that names the coordinates.

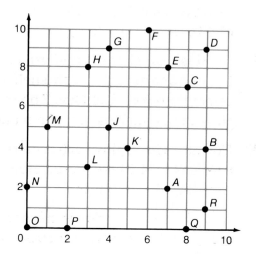

7. (7,2)   **8.** (3,8)

9. (6,10)   **10.** (9,1)

11. (4,5)   **12.** (5,4)

13. (3,3)   **14.** (9,9)

15. (8,0)   **16.** (0,2)

17. (2,0)   **18.** (0,0)

19. (9,4)   **20.** (8,7)

Write the coordinates for the letter.

21. A   **22.** B   **23.** C   **24.** D

25. E   **26.** F   **27.** H   **28.** J

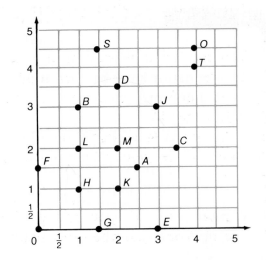

Write the word spelled by the points on the grid.

29. $(3\frac{1}{2},2)$ $(2\frac{1}{2},1\frac{1}{2})$ $(1,3)$

30. $(0,1\frac{1}{2})$ $(2\frac{1}{2},1\frac{1}{2})$ $(1,3)$ $(1,2)$ $(3,0)$

31. $(3\frac{1}{2},2)$ $(2\frac{1}{2},1\frac{1}{2})$ $(2,2)$ $(3,0)$ $(1,2)$

32. $(3,3)$ $(4,4\frac{1}{2})$ $(2,1)$ $(3,0)$

Locate each point on a number grid. Join the points in the given order. Then join the last point to the first. Name the type of quadrilateral that you have drawn.

33. A (2,2)   B (5,2)   **34.** E (1,3)   F (8,3)   **35.** I (3,3),   J (6,3)
     C (5,8)   D (2,8)   G (10,7)   H (3,7)   K (9,6),   L (2,6)

PROBLEM SOLVING APPLICATIONS
Choosing a Strategy

Solve.

36. Steve is making frames. He uses $\frac{1}{3}$ of a piece of molding to make each frame. How many frames can he make out of 13 pieces of molding?

37. Jacki is using boards and cement blocks to make shelves for her apartment. Each shelf uses $\frac{1}{2}$ of a board and 2 cement blocks. Jacki has 7 boards and 16 cement blocks. How many shelves can she make?

38. Costumes for a play each require $1\frac{1}{8}$ yd of gold trim. Gold trim costs $4.50 per yard. How much will it cost to buy trim for 15 costumes?

39. If $\frac{3}{4}$ yd of silver trim is needed for each costume, how many costumes can you make with $5\frac{3}{8}$ yd?

PROBLEM SOLVING
Strategy: Using Equations

One equation may be used to solve problems that seem very different.

Lisa earned $8 mowing lawns. She earned $13 total mowing lawns and delivering papers. How much did she earn delivering papers?

Clark is driving 13 km to town. He knows that there are still 8 km ahead of him. How far did he already drive?

paper earnings		lawn earnings		total earnings
x	+	8	=	13

distance driven		distance to go		total distance
x	+	8	=	13

The same equation, $x + 8 = 13$, can be used to solve both problems.

$$x + 8 = 13$$
$$x + 8 - 8 = 13 - 8$$
$$x = 5$$

Check: $x + 8 = 13$
$5 + 8 = 13$ True

Lisa earned $5 delivering papers. Clark already drove 5 km.

CLASS EXERCISES

Match the problem in the first column with an equation in the second column. Each equation will be used more than once.

1. A number a decreased by 3 is 24.

2. Three times the number a is 24.

3. One third of the number a is 24.

4. Three more than the number a is 24.

5. The product of a number a and 3 is 24.

6. The total of a number a and 3 is 24.

7. The sum of a number a and 3 is 24.

8. A number a shared equally by 3 is 24.

A. $a + 3 = 24$

B. $a - 3 = 24$

C. $3a = 24$

D. $\frac{a}{3} = 24$

PRACTICE

The problems in Exercises 9–14 can be solved using one of these equations: $n + 4 = 20$, $4n = 20$, $n - 4 = 20$, $\frac{n}{4} = 20$. Choose and solve the correct equation for each problem. Then answer the question.

9. Nan has to buy 20 tulip bulbs for the garden. If each package contains 4 bulbs, how many packages does she have to buy?

10. The chorus is arranged in 4 rows. There are 20 students in each row. How many students are in the chorus?

11. This year there are 20 students in the Explorers' Club. This is four fewer students than last year. How many were there last year?

12. Ken has saved $4. If he and his sister put their savings together, they will have $20. What is the amount of his sister's savings?

13. Sue has agreed to pay back a loan in four equal payments. If each payment is $20, what was the amount of the loan?

14. Each of 4 friends will pay the same amount to buy a book. If the book costs $20, how much will each pay?

Write a problem that can be solved using the equation. Then solve the equation and answer the question.

15. $x + 5 = 12$ 16. $c - 9 = 14$ 17. $2n = 18$ 18. $\frac{t}{6} = 3$

CHECKPOINT 2

Solve. *(pages 230–233)*

1. $a + 7 > 15$ 2. $x - 1 > 10$

3. $12 + y < 15$ 4. $b - 5 > 9$

Complete the ordered pair of solutions of $5x = y$. *(pages 234–235)*

5. $(0, \blacksquare)$ 6. $(\blacksquare, 5)$

7. $(7, \blacksquare)$ 8. $(\blacksquare, 45)$

Write the ordered pair for the letter. *(pages 236–237)*

9. A   10. B

11. C   12. D

Solve. *(pages 238–239)*

13. Jo bought 10 more postcards than souvenirs. She bought 14 items in all. Write an equation and solve the problem.

Extra Practice on page 446

CHAPTER 8 TEST

Write as a mathematical expression. *(pages 216–217)*

1. n minus five

2. b multiplied by sixteen

Evaluate the expression. Use $y = 10$ and $z = 32$. *(pages 218–219)*

3. $\frac{z}{8}$

4. $y + z$

Write the equation and solve. *(pages 220–227)*

5. What number times 8 is 104?

6. One-fourth of what number is 23?

Solve. Use trial and error. *(pages 228–229)*

7. The sum of three consecutive numbers is 78. What are the numbers?

8. The perimeter of a rectangular patio is 44 ft. The area is 120 ft^2. What are the patio's dimensions?

Write an inequality for the word sentence. *(pages 230–231)*

9. Three is less than x.

10. t is less than x and greater than y.

Solve. *(pages 232–233)*

11. $16 + a < 47$

12. $b - 51 > 63$

Locate each point on a number grid. *(pages 236–237)*

13. A (3,3) B (7,6) C (0,8) D (5,10)

Choose and solve the correct equation for each problem. Then answer the question. *(pages 238–239)*

$$7 + b = 21 \quad b - 7 = 21 \quad 7b = 21 \quad \frac{b}{7} = 21$$

14. Tickets sell for $7 each. Heather sold $21 worth of tickets. How many tickets did Heather sell?

15. Andy biked 21 km on Tuesday. This is 7 km less than he biked on Monday. How many kilometers did he bike on Monday?

Extra Practice on page 447

MATHEMATICS and GEOGRAPHY

Ordered pairs are used to locate points on a map. In each ordered pair, the first number represents a line of latitude while the second number represents a line of longitude.

Santa Cruz is located on the map at 37°N 122°W. You would read this as *37 degrees north latitude, 122 degrees west longitude.*

West of Greenwich

1. What lake is located at 39°N 120°W?

2. In which state would you be if you were standing at 38°N 115°W?

CAN YOU GET THERE FROM HERE?

3. A national monument named after a tree is located at 34°N 116°W. What is the name of the tree?

★ 4. *North latitude* means north of the equator. *West longitude* means west of Greenwich, England. Find out why Greenwich was chosen as the starting point for longitude.

Enrichment

In Chapter 5 you wrote terminating decimals as fractions. Repeating decimals can also be written as fractions. For example, to write 0.6363 . . . as a fraction in lowest terms, use the method shown below.

1. First let n represent the fraction you want to find.

$$n = 0.6363 \ldots$$

2. Since there are two digits that repeat, multiply both sides of the equation by 100.

$$100 \times n = 0.6363 \ldots \times 100$$
$$100n = 63.6363 \ldots$$

3. Subtract the original equation from the new equation.

$$\begin{array}{r} 100n = 63.6363 \ldots \\ - \quad n = 0.6363 \ldots \\ \hline 99n = 63 \end{array}$$

4. Divide both sides of the equation by 99 to solve for n.

$$\frac{99n}{99} = \frac{63}{99}$$
$$n = \frac{63}{99} = \frac{7}{11}$$

Check: Divide 7 by 11.

$$\begin{array}{r} 0.63 \ldots \\ 11\overline{)7.00} \\ -6\,6 \\ \hline 40 \\ -33 \\ \hline 7 \end{array}$$

REPEATING DECIMALS AS FRACTIONS

Write each repeating decimal as a fraction or mixed number in lowest terms.

1. $0.\overline{3}$ 2. $0.\overline{6}$ 3. $1.\overline{2}$

4. $3.\overline{4}$ 5. $2.\overline{35}$ 6. $7.\overline{27}$

7. $5.\overline{81}$ 8. $8.\overline{09}$ ★9. $2.\overline{351}$

★10. $4.\overline{729}$

242

Sometimes when changing a repeating decimal to a fraction, you may have to multiply the fraction before you can write it in lowest terms. For example, to write $0.145454\ldots$ as a fraction in lowest terms follow the method shown on the preceding page.

1. $$n = 0.145454\ldots$$

2. $$100n = 14.5454\ldots$$

3. $$\begin{array}{r} 100n = 14.5454\ldots \\ -\quad n = 0.1454\ldots \\ \hline 99n = 14.4 \end{array}$$

4. $$\frac{99n}{99} = \frac{14.4}{99}$$
$$n = \frac{14.4}{99}$$

To simplify the fraction, first write the numerator as a whole number by multiplying the numerator and denominator by a power of ten.

$$n = \frac{14.4}{99} \times \frac{10}{10} = \frac{144}{990} = \frac{8}{55}$$

Think: Why do we multiply by $\frac{10}{10}$ and not just by 10?

Write each repeating decimal as a fraction or mixed number in lowest terms.

11. $0.5\overline{36}$ **12.** $0.4\overline{81}$ **13.** $0.2\overline{54}$ **14.** $0.1\overline{27}$ **15.** $0.2\overline{18}$

16. $0.0\overline{45}$ **17.** $0.3\overline{15}$ **18.** $7.3\overline{21}$ ★**19.** $4.0\overline{142}$ ★**20.** $8.4\overline{189}$

 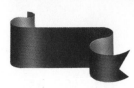

CUMULATIVE REVIEW

Choose the best answer. Write *a, b, c,* or *d.*

Choose the correct answer.

1. the numbers
divisible by 3
   a. 2, 4, 6, 8
   b. 3, 12, 21, 66
   c. 3, 12, 28, 34
   d. None of these

2. the GCF of
16 and 36
   a. 4
   b. 9
   c. 12
   d. None of these

3. the numbers
that are prime
   a. 3, 9, 15, 19
   b. 7, 11, 17, 29
   c. 9, 19, 29, 39
   d. None of these

Order the fractions from greatest to least.

4. $\frac{9}{11}$ $\frac{7}{11}$ $\frac{13}{11}$
   a. $\frac{7}{11}$ $\frac{13}{11}$ $\frac{9}{11}$
   b. $\frac{13}{11}$ $\frac{7}{11}$ $\frac{9}{11}$
   c. $\frac{13}{11}$ $\frac{9}{11}$ $\frac{7}{11}$
   d. None of these

5. $\frac{5}{6}$ $\frac{7}{12}$ $\frac{3}{4}$
   a. $\frac{5}{6}$ $\frac{7}{12}$ $\frac{3}{4}$
   b. $\frac{7}{12}$ $\frac{3}{4}$ $\frac{5}{6}$
   c. $\frac{3}{4}$ $\frac{5}{6}$ $\frac{7}{12}$
   d. None of these

6. $\frac{7}{10}$ $\frac{7}{8}$ $\frac{7}{9}$
   a. $\frac{7}{9}$ $\frac{7}{10}$ $\frac{7}{8}$
   b. $\frac{7}{8}$ $\frac{7}{9}$ $\frac{7}{10}$
   c. $\frac{7}{10}$ $\frac{7}{9}$ $\frac{7}{8}$
   d. None of these

Find the answer.

7. $\frac{3}{4} - \frac{3}{8}$
   a. $\frac{3}{4}$ **b.** $\frac{3}{8}$ **c.** $\frac{1}{12}$
   d. None of these

8. $\frac{3}{10} + \frac{1}{5} + \frac{7}{20}$
   a. $\frac{11}{10}$ **b.** $\frac{17}{20}$ **c.** $\frac{3}{5}$
   d. None of these

9. $\frac{5}{7} - \frac{2}{3}$
   a. $\frac{1}{21}$ **b.** $\frac{7}{10}$ **c.** $\frac{3}{4}$
   d. None of these

Determine if the answer is reasonable. If not, solve.

10. How many orchids at $2.79 each
can you buy with $15?
Answer: 7 orchids

   a. Reasonable answer
   b. 5 orchids
   c. 6 orchids
   d. None of these

11. A baker used $\frac{1}{3}$ of his flour for
rolls and $\frac{1}{4}$ of it for bread. How
much flour is left?
Answer: $\frac{5}{12}$ of the flour

   a. Reasonable answer
   b. $\frac{3}{4}$ of the flour
   c. $\frac{2}{3}$ of the flour
   d. None of these

Find the answer.

12. $2\frac{2}{3} + 5\frac{2}{3}$

   a. $7\frac{1}{3}$

   b. $7\frac{2}{3}$

   c. $8\frac{2}{3}$

   d. None of these

13. $6\frac{7}{9} + 4\frac{5}{6}$

   a. $10\frac{1}{18}$

   b. $11\frac{2}{9}$

   c. $11\frac{11}{18}$

   d. None of these

14. $7\frac{3}{8} - 2\frac{3}{4}$

   a. $4\frac{5}{8}$

   b. $4\frac{1}{8}$

   c. $5\frac{1}{4}$

   d. None of these

Solve.

15. There are 5 coupons in a booklet. Each club member is to get 3 coupons. If there are 42 members, how many booklets will be needed?

   a. 25
   b. 26
   c. 42
   d. None of these

Find the answer.

16. $3\frac{1}{5} \times 4\frac{3}{4}$

   a. $12\frac{3}{20}$

   b. $15\frac{1}{5}$

   c. $7\frac{4}{9}$

   d. None of these

17. $9 \div \frac{3}{4}$

   a. 12

   b. $6\frac{3}{4}$

   c. 27

   d. None of these

18. $3\frac{1}{8} \div 2\frac{1}{2}$

   a. $7\frac{13}{16}$

   b. $1\frac{1}{4}$

   c. $6\frac{1}{16}$

   d. None of these

LANGUAGE and VOCABULARY REVIEW

Write *true* or *false*. If *false*, correct the sentence by replacing the underlined word.

1. In <u>reverse</u> operations one operation undoes the other.

2. <u>Equalities</u> are statements showing that two quantities are not equal.

3. You can locate a point on a <u>grid</u> by naming an ordered pair of numbers.

BINARY CODE

A computer processes information in *Binary Code*. Binary Code uses base two numeration to represent characters, (letters, numbers, symbols, and spaces). The **bi**nary digi**ts**, 0 and 1, are called **bits**.

One standard Binary Code for representing characters uses eight bits for each keyboard character. The eight bits together are called a **byte.**

The computer manufacturer has assigned a decimal number to each character on the keyboard. The number is interpreted by the computer.

LETTER	BINARY CODE
A	01000001
B	01000010
C	01000011
D	01000100
E	01000101
F	01000110
G	01000111
H	01001000
I	01001001
J	01001010
K	01001011
L	01001100
M	01001101
N	01001110
O	01001111
P	01010000
Q	01010001
R	01010010
S	01010011
T	01010100
U	01010101
V	01010110
W	01010111
X	01011000
Y	01011001
Z	01011010

1. Use the binary code to complete the message.

   By the 1990's the government plans to develop a computer that will *01010011 01010000 01000101 01000001 01001011* 3000 *01010111 01001111 01010010 01000100 01010011* and perform one *01010100 01010010 01001001 01001100 01001100 01001001 01001111 01001110* operations per second.

2. Write your name in binary code.

An 8 in. wide fruit bowl appears to be 4 in. wide on the monitor. How wide would a 12 in. bowl appear?

RATIOS AND PROPORTIONS

RATIO

A **ratio** is a quotient of two numbers that is used to compare one quantity to another. The volleyball team won 4 games and lost 10 games this season. You can write the ratio of wins to losses as shown below:

$$4 \text{ to } 10 \qquad 4:10 \qquad \frac{4}{10}$$

All three are read *four to ten*. Since $\frac{4}{10} = \frac{2}{5}$, the ratio of 4 to 10 is the same as 2 to 5, so $4:10 = 2:5$.

We do not usually rewrite ratios as mixed numbers. For example, the ratio of losses to wins is $\frac{10}{4}$, or $\frac{5}{2}$ in lowest terms, but not $2\frac{1}{2}$. Since you cannot divide by zero, you cannot have the ratio of a number to zero.

Think: Is the ratio of 39 to 100 about the same as 4 to 10?

Is the ratio in lowest terms? Write *yes* or *no*.

1. 3 to 9 **2.** 5:3 **3.** $\frac{14}{28}$ **4.** 5:15 **5.** 27 to 18

Use the same expression to write the ratio in lowest terms.

6. 12:15 **7.** $\frac{14}{7}$ **8.** 24 to 9 **9.** $\frac{100}{10}$ **10.** 5 to 15

11. 18:81 **12.** 45:15 **13.** $\frac{17}{51}$ **14.** 80:240 **15.** 3:117

PRACTICE

Write the ratio of responses as a fraction
in lowest terms.

PRODUCT SURVEY CHART	
OPINION	NO. OF RESPONSES
Excellent	550
Good	125
Fair	40
Poor	15

16. excellent to good   **17.** poor to excellent

18. fair to good   **19.** excellent to total

20. good to fair   **21.** poor to total

22. fair to excellent   **23.** poor to fair

Estimate. Is the ratio of the length of $\overline{AB}$ to the length of $\overline{CD}$
stated correctly? Write *yes* or *no*.

ESTIMATE

24. *A   B   C_____ D*

   AB:*CD* is about 1:4.

★ **25.** *A_____ B   C_____ D*

   AB:*CD* is about 2:1.

PROBLEM SOLVING APPLICATIONS
Using Ratios

Solve.

26. A teacher is 152 cm tall and a student is 120 cm tall. Write
the ratio of the teacher's height to the student's height as
a fraction in lowest terms.

27. There are 9 players on a baseball team. Four of these are
infielders and 3 are outfielders. What is the ratio of infielders to outfielders in lowest terms?

28. The marching band spent $275 for new uniforms and $320
for new instruments. Write the ratio for the amount spent
on instruments to uniforms in lowest terms.

29. What is the ratio in lowest terms of the number of prime
numbers between 10 and 25 to the number of whole numbers between 10 and 25?

RATE

A ratio that is used to compare quantities of different kinds is called a **rate**. Rates are usually written in a *per unit* form, that is, as a ratio of a quantity to 1, called the **unit rate**.

Suppose a homing pigeon flies at a rate of 180 mi in 5 h. You can find the unit rate by dividing the number of miles by the number of hours.

$$\frac{\text{distance}}{\text{hours}} = \frac{180}{5} = \frac{36}{1}$$

The unit rate is 36 miles per hour, or 36 mi/h.

M A **unit price** is the cost per unit of a product or a service. A shopper may use mental math to figure that 3 lb of lettuce for 99¢ has a unit price of 33¢ per pound, or 33¢/lb.

CLASS EXERCISES

Complete.

1. $\frac{40}{8} = \frac{\blacksquare}{1}$

2. $\frac{60}{6} = \frac{\blacksquare}{1}$

3. $\frac{25}{5} = \frac{\blacksquare}{1}$

4. $\frac{36}{12} = \frac{\blacksquare}{1}$

5. $\frac{75}{15} = \frac{\blacksquare}{1}$

6. $\frac{810}{90} = \frac{\blacksquare}{1}$

7. $\frac{\$21.90}{3} = \frac{\$\blacksquare}{1}$

8. $\frac{3.5}{14} = \frac{\blacksquare}{1}$

9. 250 ft in 10 min = ▇ ft/min

10. \$360 for 20 lessons = \$▇/lesson

11. 432 pens in 12 cases = ▇ pens/case

12. 75 pages in 15 min = ▇ pages/min

13. 56 bulbs in 7 boxes = ▇ bulbs/box

14. \$1872 for 6 months' rent = \$▇/month

PRACTICE

Write the unit rate.

15. Andrea paid $28.50 for 30 dozen eggs at the market.

16. The Kims drove a total of 1260 mi in 5 days.

17. A printing press prints 30,000 pages in 60 min.

18. A stitcher is paid $54.90 for 366 pockets.

19. A delivery company charges $1730 for 173 packages.

20. The Photo Shop processed 171 rolls of film in 3 days.

21. The Flower Shop made 20 corsages in 5 h.

22. Leslie is paid $46.56 to deliver 582 copies of the Daily News.

23. Furniture Builders Co. charges $259.50 to assemble 30 chairs.

24. The Urban Press sold 1020 copies of the novel in 15 days.

25. Brad sold 208 magazine subscriptions in 16 days.

26. It costs $180 to make 3000 copies of a poster.

27. A typist types 1950 words in 30 min.

★**28.** An accountant completes 3 tax forms in $7\frac{1}{2}$ h.

Use mental math to name the unit price.

29. 4 lb for $1.00

30. 5 h for $15.25

31. 8 pens for $2.00

32. $38.40 for 10 rolls

33. 100 pencils for $5.00

34. 2 cans for $.89

MENTAL MATH

PROBLEM SOLVING APPLICATIONS
Consumer Topics

35. Three pounds of peaches cost $1.68. What is the unit price?

36. A package of fish had this label. Is the price correct?

2.2 KG PACKAGE
PRICE $7.01
UNIT PRICE: $3.19/KG

PROPORTIONS

The hours worked by two computer programmers are shown below.

Becky worked 40 hours in 5 days.

$$\frac{40}{5} = \frac{8}{1}$$

Bryan worked 48 hours in 6 days.

$$\frac{48}{6} = \frac{8}{1}$$

Becky and Bryan both averaged 8 hours per day. The ratios $\frac{40}{5}$ and $\frac{48}{6}$ are equal. An equation which states that two ratios are equal is called a **proportion**. Here are two ways to write a proportion.

$$\frac{40}{5} = \frac{48}{6} \qquad 40:5 = 48:6$$

You read the proportion as

$\qquad$ *40 is to 5 as 48 is to 6.*

$\qquad$ The numbers in a proportion are called the **terms** of the proportion.

Becky Roth

Mon.	7
Tues.	9
Wed.	8
Thurs.	6
Fri.	10

ryan Taylor

Mon.	10
Tues.	9
Wed.	7
Thurs.	10
Fri.	10
Sat.	2

CLASS EXERCISES

Are the ratios equal? Write *yes* or *no*.

1. $\frac{2}{1}$ ■ $\frac{1}{2}$

2. $\frac{7}{7}$ ■ $\frac{3}{3}$

3. $\frac{12}{10}$ ■ $\frac{6}{5}$

4. $\frac{6}{10}$ ■ $\frac{60}{100}$

5. $\frac{15}{20}$ ■ $\frac{30}{100}$

6. $\frac{7}{15}$ ■ $\frac{14}{35}$

7. $\frac{42}{7}$ ■ $\frac{54}{6}$

8. $\frac{9}{81}$ ■ $\frac{5}{25}$

Write as ratios. Are they equal? Write *yes* or *no*.

9. 1 out of 2 votes
5 out of 10 votes

10. 6 out of 7 days
7 out of 8 days

11. 3 absent out of 25
4 absent out of 30

12. 15 out of 21 games
10 out of 14 games

13. 85 out of 100 names
165 out of 200 names

14. 120 sold out of 125
360 sold out of 370

PRACTICE

Match the exercise with an equal ratio.

A. $7:12$ **B.** $3:5$ **C.** $16:4$ **D.** $7:9$ **E.** $\frac{12}{12}$ **F.** $\frac{8}{10}$

G. $\frac{80}{4}$ **H.** $\frac{90}{3}$ **I.** $\frac{100}{2}$ **J.** $\frac{13}{3}$ **K.** $\frac{20}{3}$ **L.** $\frac{12}{1}$

15. 21 to 36 votes **16.** 1 box for a dollar **17.** 30 jobs in 1 hour

18. 20¢ for 1 apple **19.** 4 children per ball **20.** 4 out of 5 trucks

21. 12 out of 20 people **22.** 14 to 18 cups **23.** 26 weeks in 6 months

24. 36 days in 3 years **25.** 300 m in 45 seconds **26.** 50 names in 1 column

Write as many proportions as you can using all four numbers.

27. 2, 3, 10, 15 **28.** 6, 11, 18, 33 **29.** 5, 6, 10, 12

Write the answer.

30. $\begin{array}{r} 612 \\ \times 203 \\ \hline \end{array}$ **31.** $\begin{array}{r} 0.09 \\ \times 8 \\ \hline \end{array}$ **32.** $\begin{array}{r} 5.4 \\ \times 0.72 \\ \hline \end{array}$ **33.** $\begin{array}{r} 2.04 \\ \times 0.89 \\ \hline \end{array}$

MIXED REVIEW

34. $7\overline{)4.34}$ **35.** $26\overline{)9.62}$ **36.** $2.5\overline{)0.72}$ **37.** $0.42\overline{)270.9}$

PROBLEM SOLVING APPLICATIONS
Using Ratios

Solve.

38. Stan went to 15 out of 20 computer programmers' club meetings. Liza went to 12 out of 16 computer graphics club meetings. What is the ratio of meetings attended to total meetings for each person? Are the ratios equal?

39. Bob played Math Maze 30 times and won 8 games. Karen played 32 times and won 6 games. Are their ratios equal? If not, who had the better record?

40. Write a problem that uses the ratio 3 to 4.

PROBLEM SOLVING

Strategy: Consumer Applications and Charts

1. Understand
2. Plan
3. Work
4. Answer/Check

Shoppers can save money by comparing unit prices of the same product.

A supermarket sells a 64 oz bottle of Laundry Bright for $2.99 and a 16 oz bottle for $.99. Which is the better buy?

You need to solve two small problems to answer this question. Divide each selling price by the number of ounces in the bottle. Round answers to the nearest cent.

$$\begin{array}{c} \$ .046 \approx \$.05 \\ 64\overline{)\$2.99} \\ \$.05 \text{ per oz} \end{array} \qquad \begin{array}{c} \$.061 \approx \$.06 \\ 16\overline{)\$.99} \\ \$.06 \text{ per oz} \end{array}$$

The 64 oz bottle costs less per ounce, so it is the better buy.

Think: 64 oz is 4 times as much as 16 oz. How can you tell which is the better buy by rounding and multiplying mentally?

CLASS EXERCISES

Complete the unit price tag. Round missing unit prices to the nearest thousandth. Round missing retail prices to the nearest cent.

1.

Unit Price	Retail Price
?	$2.25
Trash Bags 20 bags	

2.

Unit Price	Retail Price
$.572 per portion	?
Cod 4 fish portions	

3.

Unit Price	Retail Price
?	$1.59
Shampoo 12 fl oz	

4.

Unit Price	Retail Price
$.071 per yard	?
Plastic Wrap 34.8 yd	

5.

Unit Price	Retail Price
?	$3.75
Dog Food 250 g	

6.

Unit Price	Retail Price
$.043 per ounce	?
Soup 10.5 fl oz	

PRACTICE

Which is the better buy? Write *A* or *B*. Round unit prices to the nearest cent. Assume the items you are comparing are the same kind and quality.

ESTIMATE

	ITEM	A AMOUNT	A COST		B AMOUNT	B COST
7.	Water glasses	6	$10.99	or	4	$ 3.99
8.	Yarn	4 oz	$ 1.59	or	2 oz	$ 1.19
9.	Spiral notebook	250 pages	$ 3.97	or	230 pages	$ 2.37
10.	Pencil lead	30 pieces	$ 1.15	or	12 pieces	$ .60
11.	Pencils	1 dozen	$ 1.85	or	12 dozen	$18.00
12.	Paper clips	100	$ 3.90	or	500	$ 6.48
13.	Tape	60 yd	$ 1.79	or	100 yd	$ 1.35

Solve.

14. A store sells three different sizes of the same brand of toothpaste: 3 oz at $1.19, 7 oz at $1.74, and 9 oz at $2.18. Which is the best buy?

15. Which is the better buy, one 800 g bottle of mouthwash for $2.89 or two 520 g bottles for $4.50?

16. Garbage bags are sold in packages of 40 for $3.88 or packages of 50 for $4.50.
    a. Which is the better buy?
    b. How much can you save per bag?

17. Sid saw an ad in the paper for cans of fruit juice at 5 for $1. Another store is advertising the same juice at 3 for $.66.
    a. Which is the better buy?
    b. How much does Sid save on a case of 30 cans?

★ 18. A pint of orange juice costs $.89. A quart costs $1.29.
    a. Which is the better buy?
    b. How much can you save per fluid ounce?

PROPORTIONS AND EQUIVALENT FRACTIONS

If fishing lures cost $3 for a package of two, how much will 8 fishing lures cost? You can use a proportion to solve this problem.

Write n for the number you want to find. **Think:** $3 is to 2 fishing lures as n is to 8 fishing lures.

$$\frac{3}{2} = \frac{n}{8}$$

To solve a proportion, find a value for n so that the ratios are equal. This can be done by finding a fraction that is equivalent to $\frac{3}{2}$ with the denominator 8.

$$\frac{3}{2} = \frac{3 \times 4}{2 \times 4} = \frac{12}{8} \quad \text{So, } n = 12.$$

Eight fishing lures cost $12.

M You can solve a proportion using equivalent fractions or mental math to convert 8 m to centimeters.

Using equivalent fractions:

$$\begin{array}{l} \text{m} \rightarrow \frac{1}{100} = \frac{8}{n} \leftarrow \text{m} \\ \text{cm} \rightarrow \quad\quad\quad\quad \leftarrow \text{cm} \end{array}$$

$$n = 800$$

So, 8 m = 800 cm.

Using mental math:

Think: 1 m = 100 cm

So, 8 m = 800 cm.

CLASS EXERCISES

Complete.

1. $\frac{3}{4} = \frac{3 \times \blacksquare}{4 \times \blacksquare} = \frac{15}{20}$

2. $\frac{5}{7} = \frac{5 \times \blacksquare}{7 \times \blacksquare} = \frac{35}{49}$

3. $\frac{\blacksquare}{\blacksquare} = \frac{\blacksquare \times 3}{\blacksquare \times 3} = \frac{6}{15}$

4. $\frac{7}{8} = \frac{7 \times \blacksquare}{8 \times \blacksquare} = \frac{63}{\blacksquare}$

5. $\frac{6}{7} = \frac{6 \times \blacksquare}{7 \times \blacksquare} = \frac{\blacksquare}{28}$

6. $\frac{9}{5} = \frac{9 \times \blacksquare}{5 \times \blacksquare} = \frac{54}{\blacksquare}$

PRACTICE

Solve the proportion.

7. $\frac{2}{7} = \frac{n}{21}$

8. $\frac{x}{7} = \frac{10}{35}$

9. $\frac{z}{7} = \frac{12}{42}$

10. $\frac{7}{9} = \frac{21}{n}$

11. $\frac{10}{26} = \frac{n}{13}$

12. $\frac{15}{x} = \frac{5}{9}$

13. $\frac{18}{24} = \frac{3}{n}$

14. $\frac{x}{8} = \frac{20}{32}$

15. $\frac{28}{a} = \frac{7}{9}$

16. $\frac{36}{42} = \frac{a}{7}$

17. $\frac{a}{14} = \frac{22}{28}$

18. $\frac{12}{20} = \frac{36}{x}$

19. $\frac{18}{n} = \frac{36}{42}$

20. $\frac{81}{36} = \frac{x}{4}$

21. $\frac{10}{n} = \frac{30}{42}$

22. $\frac{15}{28} = \frac{30}{n}$

Write the proportion. Then solve.

23. 1 is to 3 as 2 is to x

24. 1 is to 6 as h is to 18

25. 4 is to 12 as 20 is to a

26. 2 is to k as 4 is to 9

27. 10 kg is to 15 cm as 2 kg is to b cm

28. b kg is to 3 cm as 20 kg is to 30 cm

29. 5 wins is to 7 games as 10 wins is to x games

30. 3 hits is to 7 times at bat as 9 hits is to b times at bat

★ **31.** If $\frac{x}{5} = \frac{3}{15}$, what is the ratio of x to 3?

★ **32.** If $\frac{21}{m}$ is $\frac{7}{2}$, what is the ratio of m to 21?

Use mental math to complete.

33. 9 m = ▮ cm

34. 7 L = ▮ ml

35. 5000 g = ▮ kg

36. 15 cm = ▮ mm

37. 31 km = ▮ m

38. 900 g = ▮ kg

MENTAL MATH

PROBLEM SOLVING APPLICATIONS
Using Proportions

Use a proportion to solve.

39. Ingrid is paid $15 for 2 h of work. At this rate how much will she earn in 10 h?

★ **40.** A 2.7 kg box of bolts costs $54. At this rate what is the cost of an 800 g box of bolts?

PROPORTIONS AND CROSS MULTIPLICATION

When you cross multiply the terms of a proportion, the cross products are equal.

$$\frac{40}{50} \times \frac{8}{10}$$
$$40 \times 10 = 50 \times 8$$
$$400 = 400$$

You can use cross multiplication to solve proportions.

$$\frac{12}{7} = \frac{60}{n}$$

⇨ Cross multiply.
Solve the equation. ⇨

$$12 \times n = 7 \times 60$$
$$12n = 420$$
$$\frac{12n}{12} = \frac{420}{12}$$
$$n = 35$$

Check your solution by substituting 35 for n in the proportion. Then cross multiply.

$$\frac{12}{7} \times \frac{60}{35}$$
$$12 \times 35 = 7 \times 60$$
$$420 = 420 \checkmark$$

You can use a calculator to solve proportions.

$$\frac{3}{8} = \frac{n}{32}$$
  3 ✕ 32 ÷ 8 🟰 12   Solution: 12

CLASS EXERCISES

Write the cross products. Are the ratios equal? Write *yes* or *no*.

1. $\frac{3}{2}$, $\frac{12}{8}$ 2. $\frac{5}{15}$, $\frac{2}{6}$ 3. $\frac{5}{6}$, $\frac{7}{8}$ 4. $\frac{7}{28}$, $\frac{2}{8}$ 5. $\frac{10}{4}$, $\frac{15}{6}$ 6. $\frac{4}{9}$, $\frac{3}{5}$

PRACTICE

Solve by cross multiplying.

7. $\frac{x}{21} = \frac{2}{6}$ 8. $\frac{14}{a} = \frac{7}{2}$ 9. $\frac{28}{n} = \frac{12}{3}$ 10. $\frac{12}{9} = \frac{x}{6}$

11. $\frac{x}{5} = \frac{10}{2}$

12. $\frac{25}{10} = \frac{15}{a}$

13. $\frac{4}{12} = \frac{n}{30}$

14. $\frac{4}{n} = \frac{14}{35}$

15. $\frac{14}{12} = \frac{175}{x}$

16. $\frac{v}{9} = \frac{143}{117}$

17. $\frac{18}{3} = \frac{n}{4}$

18. $\frac{14}{p} = \frac{7}{3}$

19. $\frac{1.6}{0.8} = \frac{n}{0.6}$

20. $\frac{w}{1.4} = \frac{0.3}{2.1}$

21. $\frac{n}{0.26} = \frac{0.1}{0.65}$

22. $\frac{0.5}{a} = \frac{0.35}{0.07}$

23. $\frac{0.7}{2.8} = \frac{n}{0.8}$

24. $\frac{0.2}{a} = \frac{0.9}{2.7}$

25. $\frac{0.4}{x} = \frac{0.32}{0.08}$

26. $\frac{0.1}{0.15} = \frac{4}{a}$

Solve by cross multiplying. A calculator may be helpful.

27. $\frac{63.9}{n} = \frac{7.1}{13}$

28. $\frac{4.8}{21} = \frac{24}{n}$

29. $\frac{n}{18} = \frac{8.2}{9}$

CALCULATOR

30. $\frac{n}{0.9} = \frac{21}{63}$

31. $\frac{0.45}{0.35} = \frac{n}{0.7}$

32. $\frac{3.6}{5.4} = \frac{n}{0.6}$

33. $\frac{4.2}{n} = \frac{0.7}{0.9}$

34. $\frac{55}{n} = \frac{5}{2}$

35. $\frac{45.9}{n} = \frac{5.1}{10}$

36. Explain how you can use mental math to solve Exercise 29.

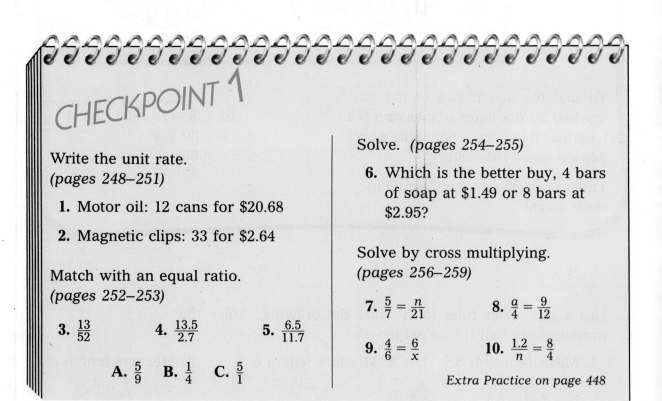

CHECKPOINT 1

Write the unit rate.
(*pages 248–251*)

 1. Motor oil: 12 cans for $20.68

 2. Magnetic clips: 33 for $2.64

Match with an equal ratio.
(*pages 252–253*)

 3. $\frac{13}{52}$ 4. $\frac{13.5}{2.7}$ 5. $\frac{6.5}{11.7}$

  A. $\frac{5}{9}$ B. $\frac{1}{4}$ C. $\frac{5}{1}$

Solve. (*pages 254–255*)

 6. Which is the better buy, 4 bars of soap at $1.49 or 8 bars at $2.95?

Solve by cross multiplying.
(*pages 256–259*)

 7. $\frac{5}{7} = \frac{n}{21}$ 8. $\frac{a}{4} = \frac{9}{12}$

 9. $\frac{4}{6} = \frac{6}{x}$ 10. $\frac{1.2}{n} = \frac{8}{4}$

Extra Practice on page 448

SCALE DRAWING

A **scale drawing** is a representation of a real object. The **scale** gives the ratio of the size in the drawing to the size of the actual object.

Here is a scale drawing of a bicycle.

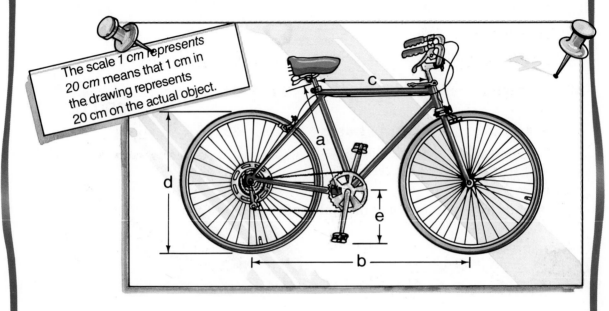

The scale 1 cm represents 20 cm means that 1 cm in the drawing represents 20 cm on the actual object.

To find the actual size of the part marked by the letter a, measure the length a. It is 3 cm. Then write a proportion using the scale.

$$\frac{1}{20} = \frac{3}{n} \leftarrow \text{scale drawing} \atop \leftarrow \text{actual object}$$

$$1 \times n = 20 \times 3$$
$$n = 60$$

The measurement on the actual bicycle is 60 cm.

CLASS EXERCISES

Use a centimeter ruler to measure the drawing. Solve the proportion to find the actual length.

1. Measure length b

$$\frac{1}{20} = \frac{b}{n}$$

2. Measure length c

$$\frac{1}{20} = \frac{c}{n}$$

3. Measure length d

$$\frac{1}{20} = \frac{d}{n}$$

PRACTICE

Draw a line segment to represent the length of each object.
Let 1 cm represent 5 cm.

4. a 5 cm bolt

5. a 10 cm hammer

6. a 15 cm pair of scissors

7. a 90 cm shovel

Let 1 cm represent 1 m.

8. a 6 m length of wire

9. a door 2.1 m high

10. a garage 2.7 m high

11. a ladder 3.9 m long

In the drawing of the bicycle frame, 1 mm represents 16 mm. What is the measurement of each part on the actual frame?

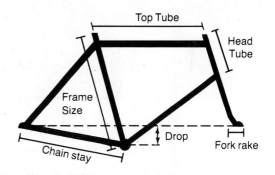

12. top tube

13. head tube

14. frame size

15. chain stay

16. fork rake

17. drop

PROBLEM SOLVING APPLICATIONS
Using Pictures

Solve.

18. In a photograph, a thumbprint is 18 cm wide. If the photograph is 10 times as large as the actual thumbprint, what is the actual width of the thumbprint?

19. Doreen used a scale of 1 cm to 10 cm to make a scale drawing of her bureau. If the height of the bureau is 135 cm, how high should the drawing be?

★20. The paramecium shown is 200 times its actual size. What is the actual length of the paramecium?

READING MAPS

You can look at the map below and estimate that the distance from Chicago to Toledo is about 4 units of the scale or about 400 km. You can check this estimate by copying the scale on a piece of paper and measuring the distance.

If you know that the scale is 6 mm : 100 km, you can use a metric ruler to measure distances on the map instead of copying the scale. If the distance between Montreal and New York measures about 38 mm, you can determine about how far the cities actually are to the nearest kilometer.

$$\begin{array}{c} \text{mm} \longrightarrow \\ \text{km} \longrightarrow \end{array} \quad \frac{6}{100} = \frac{38}{x} \quad \begin{array}{c} \longleftarrow \text{mm} \\ \longleftarrow \text{km} \end{array} \qquad \begin{array}{l} 6x = 3800 \\ x = 633.\overline{3} \end{array}$$

Montreal is about 633 km from New York.

CLASS EXERCISES

What is the actual distance to the nearest kilometer? Use the map above.

	CITIES	MAP SCALE	MAP DISTANCE	ACTUAL DISTANCE
1.	Toronto to Detroit	6 mm: 100 km	24 mm	?
2.	Cleveland to Philadelphia	6 mm: 100 km	39 mm	?
3.	Boston to New York	6 mm: 100 km	?	?

PRACTICE

ESTIMATE

Refer to the map on page 262 for Exercises 4–11. Estimate the actual distance in kilometers. Check your estimate.

4. Chicago to Detroit

5. Buffalo to New York

6. Toronto to Hamilton

7. Grand Rapids to Albany

8. Montreal to Cleveland

9. Chicago to Boston

10. Toronto to New York

11. Albany to Cleveland

Estimate the actual distance in kilometers. Check your estimate.

12. Los Angeles to Blythe

13. Tucson to Yuma

14. Flagstaff to Needles through Williams

15. Barstow to San Diego through Los Angeles

16. Tucson to Flagstaff through Phoenix

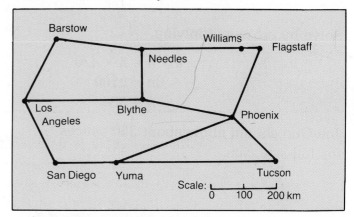

PROBLEM SOLVING APPLICATIONS
Using Maps

Solve using the map above.

17. How many kilometers will a group travel from San Diego to Blythe if they travel through Los Angeles? How many kilometers will they travel if they go through Yuma and Phoenix?

18. Joan's car uses about one liter of gasoline for a distance of 14 km on the highway. About how many liters of gasoline will this car use on a trip from Los Angeles to Phoenix through Blythe?

★ **19.** A family leaves Los Angeles and travels about 2000 km before returning home. What cities on the map might they have visited?

PROBLEM SOLVING
Strategy: Using Proportions

Joe Ono estimates that 5 out of every 6 cars that come into a parking lot are full size. If he wants to accommodate 420 cars in his lot, about how many spaces should he make to accommodate full-size cars?

Let n represent the number of spaces needed for full-size cars and write a proportion.

$$\frac{5}{6} = \frac{n}{420}$$

Solve by cross multiplying.

$$6 \times n = 5 \times 420$$
$$6n = 2100$$
$$n = 350$$

Joe Ono should allow about 350 spaces for full-size cars.

CLASS EXERCISES

Write the proportion for solving the problem. Use n for the unknown number. Then solve.

1. In a typing class, Steve typed 75 words in 2 min. At this rate, how many words can he type in 12 min?

2. The students in room A-402 are making fruit punch for the end-of-term party. The fruit punch contains 5 parts of apple juice to 2 parts of cranberry juice. If 12 L of apple juice are used, about how much cranberry juice should be used?

3. A train has traveled 650 km in 10 h. How far would it travel in 20 h on a non-stop trip?

Solve.

4. The student-teacher ratio at the Beechwood Junior High School is 53:2. There are 18 teachers. How many students are there?

5. The ratio of headphones in the language lab to the number of students who are taking a foreign language is 1:4. If there are 36 headphones in the language lab, how many students are taking a foreign language?

6. Of the 200 students who took part in a survey, 40 said they got their part-time jobs through the school placement office. There are 1750 students with part-time jobs. How many would you expect had gotten their jobs through the placement office?

7. The recipe Jill is reading serves 12. It calls for 6 eggs. If she decreases it to serve 8 people, how many eggs will she need?

8. Andy paid $2.45 for $3\frac{1}{2}$ lb of peaches. Joe bought 5 lb for $3.50. Compare the two purchases. Did Joe pay more per pound than Andy?

9. In the school cafeteria, the cook uses 6.75 kg of meat to serve 60 people. How many people can be served with 24.3 kg of meat?

★ **10.** The Tennis Club bought a dozen cans of tennis balls at $2.50 each. They also bought 3 tennis rackets. If the ratio of the price of one can of balls to the price of one racket is 1:14, what was the total cost?

★ **11.** The ratio of adults to children at the concert is 2:1. If the total attendance is 249, how many adults are present?

★ **12.** The ratio of boys to girls is 4:3 in one class. If there are 3 more boys than girls, how many boys and girls are in the class?

SIMILAR TRIANGLES

Similar triangles have the same shape but not always the same size. In similar triangles the corresponding angles are congruent and the corresponding sides are in proportion.

Triangle *JKL* is similar to triangle *PQR*. This statement can be written $\triangle JKL \sim \triangle PQR$.

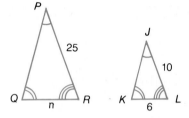

Corresponding angles are congruent.

$$\angle J \cong \angle P \quad \angle K \cong \angle Q \quad \angle L \cong \angle R$$

Corresponding sides are in proportion.

$$\frac{JK}{PQ} = \frac{JL}{PR} = \frac{KL}{QR}$$

Notice that corresponding angles are marked alike.

To find the length of $\overline{QR}$, write a proportion using corresponding sides.

$$\frac{JL}{PR} = \frac{KL}{QR} \quad \Rightarrow \quad \frac{10}{25} = \frac{6}{n}$$
$$10 \times n = 25 \times 6$$
$$10n = 150$$
$$\frac{10n}{10} = \frac{150}{10}$$
$$n = 15$$

The length of $\overline{QR}$ is 15 units.

CLASS EXERCISES

For Exercises 1–3 refer to the diagram at the right.
$\triangle ABC \sim \triangle XYZ$.

1. Name the corresponding angles.

2. Name the corresponding sides.

3. Complete:
$$\frac{AB}{XY} = \frac{AC}{\blacksquare} = \frac{BC}{\blacksquare}$$

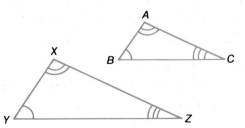

PRACTICE

For the pair of similar triangles, find n.

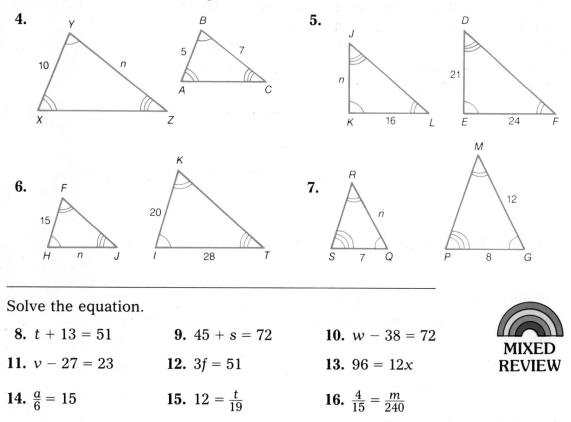

4.

5.

6.

7.

Solve the equation.

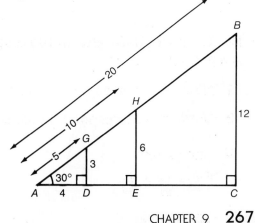

MIXED REVIEW

8. $t + 13 = 51$

9. $45 + s = 72$

10. $w - 38 = 72$

11. $v - 27 = 23$

12. $3f = 51$

13. $96 = 12x$

14. $\frac{a}{6} = 15$

15. $12 = \frac{t}{19}$

16. $\frac{4}{15} = \frac{m}{240}$

PROBLEM SOLVING APPLICATIONS
Logical Thinking

Exercises 17 and 18 refer to the diagram at the right.

17. What is the measure of $\angle AGD$, $\angle AHE$, and $\angle ABC$? Explain how you know this.

18. Are triangles ABC, AGD, and AHE similar? Explain your answer.

USING SIMILAR TRIANGLES

You can use similar triangles and a proportion to find the height of an object without actually measuring it. In the diagram shown below, triangles *ABC* and *DEF* are similar, so you can write and solve a proportion to find the height of the pole. The pole casts a shadow that is 6 m long. The lamppost is 7 m high and casts a shadow that is 2 m long.

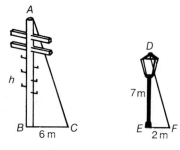

Think: Which sides in the two triangles are in proportion?

$$\frac{h}{7} = \frac{6}{2}$$
$$2 \times h = 7 \times 6$$
$$2h = 42$$
$$h = 21$$

The height of the pole is 21 m.

Think: How can you estimate the height of the Washington Monument using shadows?

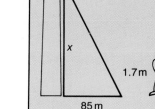

CLASS EXERCISES

The two triangles are similar. Complete the proportion.

1. $\frac{h}{15} = \frac{\blacksquare}{6}$

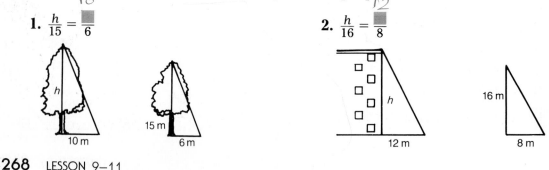

2. $\frac{h}{16} = \frac{\blacksquare}{8}$

PRACTICE

The two triangles are similar. Find h.

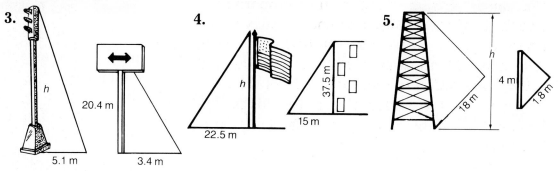

3. h 20.4 m   5.1 m   3.4 m

4. h 22.5 m   37.5 m   15 m

5. h 18 m   4 m   1.8 m

PROBLEM SOLVING APPLICATIONS
Using Proportions

Solve.

6. Triangles *APB* and *CDB* are similar. What is the distance across the river?

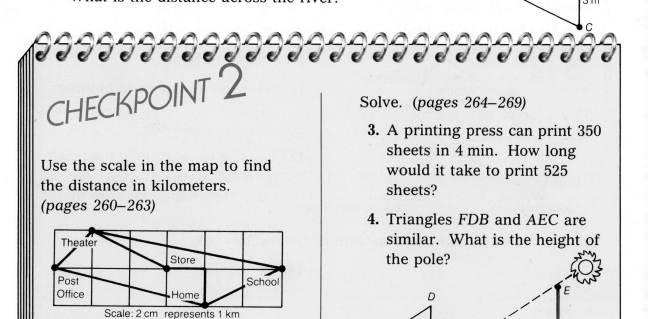

CHECKPOINT 2

Use the scale in the map to find the distance in kilometers.
(*pages 260–263*)

Scale: 2 cm represents 1 km

Theater   Store   Post Office   Home   School

1. theater to school

2. home to post office to theater

Solve. (*pages 264–269*)

3. A printing press can print 350 sheets in 4 min. How long would it take to print 525 sheets?

4. Triangles *FDB* and *AEC* are similar. What is the height of the pole?

D   1.7 m   E   F   2.4 m   B   A   7.2 m   C

Extra Practice on page 448

Write the unit rate. *(pages 250–251)*

1. 360 for $6120

2. $25.95 for 30

Write as many proportions as you can using all four numbers. *(pages 252–253)*

3. 4, 7, 12, 21   **4.** 1, 3, 5, 15

Solve. *(pages 254–255)*

5. Which is the better buy: a 10 oz can of tomatoes for $.89 or a 32 oz can for $2.34?

Solve by cross multiplying. *(pages 256–259)*

6. $\frac{a}{7} = \frac{10}{2}$ **7.** $\frac{b}{18} = \frac{4}{6}$ **8.** $\frac{25}{c} = \frac{75}{90}$ **9.** $\frac{0.8}{0.4} = \frac{1.2}{d}$

Use a proportion to find the actual distance. *(pages 260–263)*

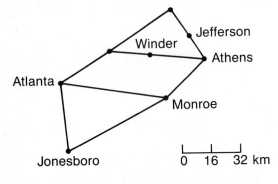
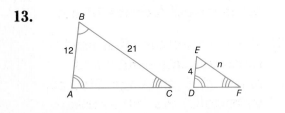

10. Atlanta to Monroe

11. Jefferson to Athens to Monroe

Solve. *(pages 264–65)*

12. The dog to cat ratio in the neighborhood is 7:3. There are 24 cats. How many dogs are there?

For the pair of similar triangles, find *n*. *(pages 266–269)*

13.

14.

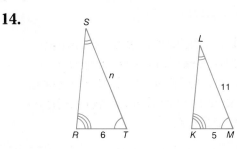

Extra Practice on page 449

MATHEMATICS and MUSIC

When you strike a note on a piano, a string in the instrument vibrates and makes a musical sound. The number of vibrations per second is the note's *frequency*.

An octave on a musical scale is a distance of 8 notes, say from C to C. Any note has twice the frequency of the note an octave below it. Middle A on the piano has a frequency of 440.

D E F G A B C D E F G A B C D E F G A B C D E F

WHAT'S THE NUMBER OF THE NOTE?

1. What is the ratio of the frequency of any note and the note one octave above it?

2. What is the frequency of the A, 2 octaves below middle A? What is the ratio of their frequencies?

3. The lowest note on a piano has a frequency of about 30. How many octaves below middle A is the lowest A on the piano?

4. The highest sound a human can hear has a frequency of about 20,000. Could a person hear a sound 6 octaves above middle A?

★ 5. The Pythagoreans first used ratios to relate numbers to music 2500 years ago. Find out more about the Pythagoreans and what they discovered.

Enrichment

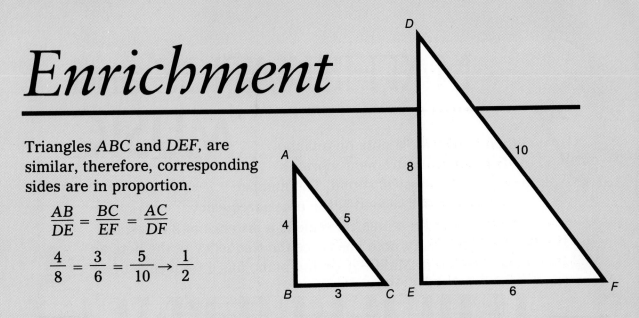

Triangles *ABC* and *DEF*, are similar, therefore, corresponding sides are in proportion.

$$\frac{AB}{DE} = \frac{BC}{EF} = \frac{AC}{DF}$$

$$\frac{4}{8} = \frac{3}{6} = \frac{5}{10} \rightarrow \frac{1}{2}$$

The ratio that compares the sides of similar polygons is called the scale factor. In this case the scale factor is $\frac{1}{2}$. Each side of $\triangle ABC$ is $\frac{1}{2}$ the length of the corresponding side of $\triangle DEF$.

Find a figure similar to the one named.

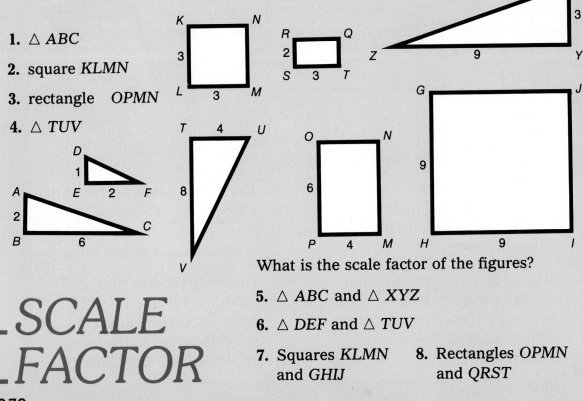

1. $\triangle ABC$

2. square *KLMN*

3. rectangle *OPMN*

4. $\triangle TUV$

What is the scale factor of the figures?

5. $\triangle ABC$ and $\triangle XYZ$

6. $\triangle DEF$ and $\triangle TUV$

7. Squares *KLMN* and *GHIJ*

8. Rectangles *OPMN* and *QRST*

SCALE FACTOR

You can use the scale factor to draw similar figures on a grid. In triangles *DEF* and *ABC*, notice the length of $\overline{DE}$ is 8 units and the length of $\overline{AB}$ is 4 units. Also the length of $\overline{EF}$ is 6 units and the length of $\overline{BC}$ is 3 units. If you measure $\overline{DF}$ you will find it to be exactly 2 times the length of $\overline{AC}$.

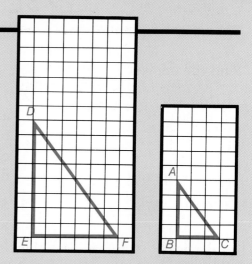

$DE = 2 \times AB$
$EF = 2 \times BC$ The scale factor is $\frac{2}{1}$
$DF = 2 \times AC$

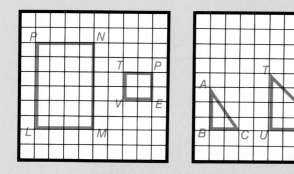

Use graph paper and the scale factor given to draw a similar figure.

9. Rectangle *PLMN*
   Scale factor $\frac{2}{1}$

10. Square *TVEP*
    Scale factor $\frac{2}{3}$

11. Triangle *ABC*
    Scale factor $\frac{2}{3}$

12. Triangle *TUV*
    Scale factor $\frac{4}{3}$

Use graph paper and a scale factor of $\frac{3}{2}$ to enlarge the figure shown at right. How many units long is the segment in the enlarged figure?

13. $\overline{BC}$ 14. $\overline{AP}$ 15. $\overline{LK}$

16. $\overline{JH}$ 17. $\overline{JK}$ 18. $\overline{MN}$

19. $\overline{DC}$ 20. $\overline{FE}$

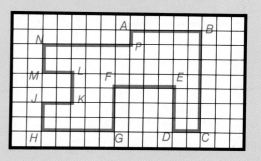

CUMULATIVE REVIEW

Choose the correct answer. Write *a*, *b*, *c*, or *d*.

Find the answer.

1. 849 + 64
  a. 903
  b. 913
  c. 905
  d. None of these

2. 71.6 + 9.84
  a. 17.00
  b. 81.44
  c. 80.44
  d. None of these

3. $14.55 + $83.27
  a. $98.72
  b. $97.82
  c. $97.72
  d. None of these

4. 7010 − 876
  a. 6234
  b. 6144
  c. 6134
  d. None of these

5. $5.81 − $1.06
  a. $4.87
  b. $4.85
  c. $4.75
  d. None of these

6. 26.3 − 13.596
  a. 12.704
  b. 12.714
  c. 13.814
  d. None of these

Find the answer.

7. 372 × 68
  a. 24,296
  b. 25,196
  c. 25,296
  d. None of these

8. 4.06 × 1.3
  a. 5.278
  b. 5.378
  c. 5.268
  d. None of these

9. 0.015 × 4.4
  a. 0.660
  b. 0.0660
  c. 6.60
  d. None of these

10. 8.3 × 10
  a. 83
  b. 0.83
  c. 0.083
  d. None of these

11. 75.2 × 100
  a. 75.20
  b. 7.52
  c. 0.752
  d. None of these

12. 0.925 × 0.25
  a. 23.125
  b. 2.3125
  c. 0.23125
  d. None of these

Find the answer.

13. $27\overline{)4510}$
  a. 166 R28
  b. 167 R1
  c. 157 R1
  d. None of these

14. $72\overline{)1.872}$
  a. 0.016
  b. 0.26
  c. 0.026
  d. None of these

15. $31\overline{)130.2}$
  a. 40.2
  b. 4.2
  c. 42
  d. None of these

Choose the number with the matching value.

16. $3\frac{3}{7}$

   a. $\frac{17}{7}$

   b. $2\frac{1}{7}$

   c. $\frac{13}{7}$

   d. None of these

17. $\frac{11}{5}$

   a. $1\frac{4}{5}$

   b. $2\frac{1}{5}$

   c. $2\frac{2}{5}$

   d. None of these

18. $\frac{3}{5}$

   a. 0.6

   b. 6.0

   c. 0.06

   d. None of these

Solve.

19. Maggie bought $3\frac{3}{4}$ lb of plums and $3\frac{1}{8}$ lb of peaches. How much fruit did Maggie buy altogether?

   a. $6\frac{3}{8}$ lb

   b. $6\frac{5}{8}$ lb

   c. $6\frac{7}{8}$ lb

   d. None of these

20. Bill jogged $\frac{3}{10}$ mi. Sally jogged $\frac{2}{3}$ mi. How much further did Sally jog than Bill?

   a. $\frac{7}{10}$ mi

   b. $\frac{11}{30}$ mi

   c. $\frac{1}{3}$ mi

   d. None of these

LANGUAGE and VOCABULARY REVIEW

Copy the words on your paper. Write the letter of the matching definition next to each word.

1. ratio

2. perimeter

3. variable

4. proportion

5. unit price

6. scale drawing

A. the distance around a polygon

B. cost per unit of a product

C. a representation of a real object

D. a quotient that compares one quantity to another

E. an equation which states that two ratios are equal

F. a letter used to represent a number

PROGRAMS WITH PRINT AND LET

COMPUTER LITERACY

BASIC (Beginners All-purpose Symbolic Instruction Code) is a programming language. In BASIC, **line numbers** tell the computer the order in which to process instructions. **Statements** are instructions that use line numbers. **Commands** tell the computer to do something with a program.

Computers process arithmetic data according to the following order of operations:

1. Do all work inside parentheses.

2. Do all work with exponents ($3 \uparrow 2$ means 3^2).

3. Do all multiplications ($*$) and divisions ($/$), from left to right.

4. Do all additions ($+$) and subtractions ($-$), from left to right.

LET statement assigns a value to a variable.	`10 LET A=10`
	`20 LET B=A-7`
PRINT statement shows what is in quotes, or an output.	`30 PRINT "A STANDS FOR 10"`
	`40 PRINT "(A-B)*3↑2 IS "`
	`50 PRINT (A-B)*3↑2`
	`60 END`
END statement signals the program's end.	`RUN`
RUN is a command.	`A STANDS FOR 10`
	`(A-B)*3↑2 IS`
	`63`

Write the output.

```
1. 10 PRINT "PERIMETER"
   20 LET B=9
   30 LET H=5
   40 PRINT (2*B)+(2*H)
   50 END
```

```
2. 10 PRINT "ANSWER:"
   20 LET M=42
   30 LET T=10
   40 PRINT (M-T)/2*4↑2
   50 END
```

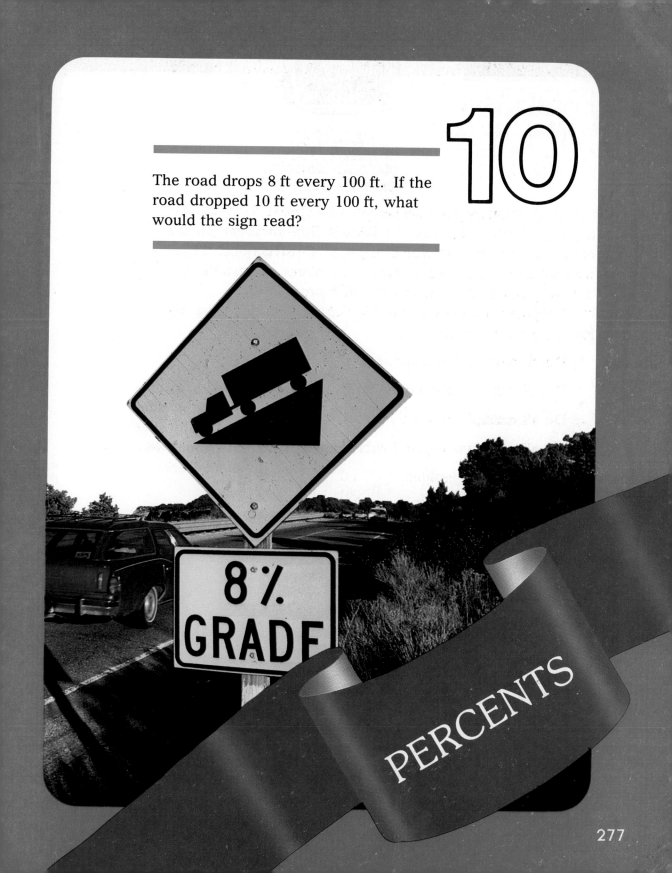

The road drops 8 ft every 100 ft. If the road dropped 10 ft every 100 ft, what would the sign read?

10

8% GRADE

PERCENTS

277

PERCENTS

A **percent** compares a number to 100. The symbol % means *per hundred.* You can think of a percent as the ratio of a number to 100. For example, 50% is the ratio of 50 to 100.

There are 100 squares on the grid. The shaded square represents $\frac{1}{100}$, or 1%, of the grid. The ratio $\frac{100}{100}$ represents the entire grid.

$$\frac{100}{100} = 100\%$$

The part of the grid that is not shaded is

$$100\% - 1\% = 99\%.$$

The ratio $\frac{99}{100}$ represents the not shaded part.

$$\frac{99}{100} = 99\%$$

You can estimate the shaded area as a percent of the whole grid. Count the completely shaded squares and mentally piece together partially shaded squares to make complete squares. About 48 of the 100 squares are shaded. The shaded area covers about 48% of the grid.

CLASS EXERCISES

Write the percent for the shaded part.

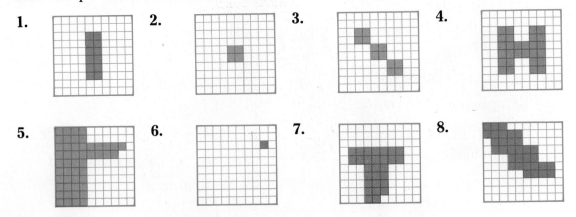

1.   2.   3.   4.

5.   6.   7.   8.

PRACTICE

Write as a percent.

9. $\frac{99}{100}$ **10.** $\frac{57}{100}$ **11.** $\frac{9}{100}$ **12.** $\frac{49}{100}$ **13.** $\frac{27}{100}$ **14.** $\frac{7}{100}$

15. 85 out of 100   **16.** 8 out of 100   **17.** 42 per 100   **18.** 5 out of 100

19. 16 per 100   **20.** 56 hundredths   **21.** 98 per 100   **22.** 13 hundredths

23. 3¢ tax per 100¢   **24.** $11 interest per $100   **25.** 9 rows plowed out of 100

26. 8¢ out of 100¢   **27.** $15 per $100   **28.** 5 out of 100 students

Estimate the shaded area as a percent of the whole grid.
Estimate the unshaded area as a percent of the whole grid.

ESTIMATE

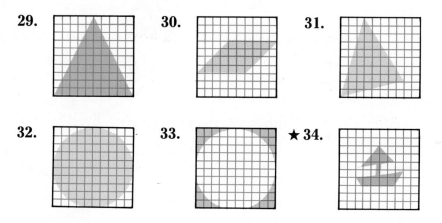

29.   **30.**   **31.**

32.   **33.**   ★ **34.**

PROBLEM SOLVING APPLICATIONS
Using Mental Math

Use mental math to solve.

35. A total of 75% of the campers did not eat their lima beans. What percent ate their lima beans?

36. A total of 90% of the people fishing used worms for bait. What percent did not use worms for bait?

37. A total of $33\frac{1}{3}$% of the hikers got blisters. What percent did not get blisters?

DECIMALS AND PERCENTS

Decimals can be written as percents, and percents can be written as decimals. Study these examples.

Writing a Percent

$0.45 = \frac{45}{100} = 45\%$

$0.07 = \frac{7}{100} = 7\%$

You need a denominator of 100.

$0.725 = \frac{725}{1000}$

$= \frac{725 \div 10}{1000 \div 10}$

$= \frac{72.5}{100} = 72.5\%$

Writing a Decimal

$6\% = \frac{6}{100} = 0.06$

$78\% = \frac{78}{100} = 0.78$

You want a whole number in the numerator.

$5.4\% = \frac{5.4}{100}$

$= \frac{5.4 \times 10}{100 \times 10}$

$= \frac{54}{1000} = 0.054$

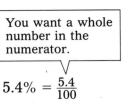

To change a decimal to a percent, move the decimal point two places to the right and write the percent symbol.

$1.25 = 125\%$ $0.03 = 3\%$ $0.005 = 0.5\%$

To change a percent to a decimal, move the decimal point two places to the left and drop the percent symbol.

$125\% = 1.25$ $3\% = 0.03$ $0.5\% = 0.005$

CLASS EXERCISES

Complete.

1. $0.09 = \frac{\blacksquare}{100} = \blacksquare\%$

2. $0.71 = \frac{\blacksquare}{100} = \blacksquare\%$

3. $0.125 = \frac{\blacksquare}{1000} = \frac{\blacksquare}{100} = \blacksquare\%$

4. $84\% = \frac{\blacksquare}{100} = 0.\blacksquare\blacksquare$

5. $6\% = \frac{\blacksquare}{100} = 0.\blacksquare\blacksquare$

6. $20.0\% = \frac{\blacksquare}{100} = \blacksquare$

PRACTICE

Write as a percent.

7. 0.37 **8.** 0.01 **9.** 0.81 **10.** 0.85 **11.** 0.40

12. 0.3 **13.** 0.7 **14.** 0.01 **15.** 0.21 **16.** 0.84

17. 0.52 **18.** 0.33 **19.** 0.74 **20.** 0.05 **21.** 0.12

22. 0.20 **23.** 0.06 **24.** 0.66 **25.** 0.91 **26.** 0.47

Write as a decimal.

27. 25% **28.** 44% **29.** 63% **30.** 8% **31.** 150%

32. 1% **33.** 33.3% **34.** 500% **35.** 20% **36.** 0.6%

37. 80% **38.** 66.7% **39.** 1.5% **40.** 95% **41.** 5%

Use mental math to write the decimal as a percent or the percent as a decimal.

42. 0.072 **43.** 15.8% **44.** 2.5 **45.** 43.3%

46. 0.4 **47.** 75.56% **48.** 0.8980 **49.** 0.2%

MENTAL MATH

PROBLEM SOLVING APPLICATIONS
Using Percents

Solve.

50. A credit card company charges 1.5% per month for customers who do not pay their entire bill. Write the percent as a decimal.

51. More than 0.75 of the money deposited in the Midwest Bank are in checks. Write the decimal as a percent.

52. At the Wild West Bank, 29% of the customers make deposits with electronic tellers, 62% make deposits with human tellers, and the remainder make deposits by mail. What percent make deposits by mail?

★ **53.** At the Midwest Bank 0.689 of all savings accounts have balances under $10,000. What percent of the savings accounts at the bank have balances over $10,000?

PERCENTS AND FRACTIONS

To satisfy the building code, an architect is planning the window space in a building to be 18% of the floor space.

To write a percent as a fraction, just write the percent as a ratio of a number to 100. Then, if possible, rewrite the fraction in lowest terms.

$$18\% = \frac{18}{100} = \frac{9}{50}$$

$$37.5\% = \frac{37.5}{100} = \frac{37.5 \times 10}{100 \times 10} = \frac{375}{1000} = \frac{3}{8}$$

Think: Why were the numerator and denominator each multiplied by 10?

Sometimes percents are mixed numbers or fractions.

$$33\frac{1}{3}\% = \frac{33\frac{1}{3}}{100} = 33\frac{1}{3} \div 100 = \frac{\overset{1}{\cancel{100}}}{3} \times \frac{1}{\underset{1}{\cancel{100}}} = \frac{1}{3}$$

$$\frac{1}{4}\% = \frac{\frac{1}{4}}{100} = \frac{1}{4} \div 100 = \frac{1}{4} \times \frac{1}{100} = \frac{1}{400}$$

$$125\frac{1}{2}\% = \frac{125\frac{1}{2}}{100} = 125\frac{1}{2} \div 100 = \frac{251}{2} \times \frac{1}{100} = \frac{251}{200} = 1\frac{51}{200}$$

To change a percent such as $37\frac{1}{2}\%$ to a fraction or to a decimal, you can write it first as 37.5% and then rewrite it as the fraction $\frac{3}{8}$ as shown at the top of this page, or as the decimal 0.375.

CLASS EXERCISES

Complete. Write the fraction in lowest terms.

1. $35\% = \frac{35}{100} = $ ■

2. $5\% = \frac{5}{100} = $ ■

3. $85\% = \frac{85}{100} = $ ■

4. $8.3\% = \frac{8.3}{100} = \frac{■}{1000}$

5. $98.9\% = \frac{98.9}{100} = \frac{■}{1000}$

6. $27.9\% = \frac{27.9}{100} = \frac{■}{1000}$

7. To write $2\frac{1}{2}\%$ as a fraction, what will your first step be?

PRACTICE

Write as a fraction or mixed number in lowest terms.

8. 22%   **9.** 13%   **10.** 38%   **11.** 27%   **12.** 6%   **13.** 291%

14. 3%   **15.** 82%   **16.** 11%   **17.** 98%   **18.** 150%   **19.** $\frac{3}{4}$%

20. 18.2%   **21.** $110\frac{1}{2}$%   **22.** 116.8%   **23.** 13.9%   **24.** 3.7%   **25.** $99\frac{44}{100}$%

Write as a decimal and a fraction in lowest terms.

26. $16\frac{1}{2}$%   **27.** $8\frac{1}{2}$%   **28.** $\frac{1}{2}$%   **29.** $20\frac{1}{4}$%   **30.** $\frac{3}{4}$%   **31.** $6\frac{1}{4}$%

Write the answer.

32. $13.85
    ×0.05

33. $77.06
    12.29
    + 5.65

34.   165.27
    − 30.59

**MIXED
REVIEW**

35. 1.58 × $285.00   **36.** 15)$182.55   **37.** 49)1421

PROBLEM SOLVING APPLICATIONS
Interpreting Information

Solve. Write fractional answers in lowest terms.

38. A contractor agreed to accept payment in equal installments of 25% of the total cost. What fraction will each payment be? How many equal payments will there be?

39. Ed Martinez estimates that 85% of the houses he builds have wall-to-wall carpeting. What fraction of the houses do not have wall-to-wall carpeting?

★**40.** Susanna is writing a computer game. In the game players can score either three points or seven points. What scores will be impossible for the players to get?

FRACTIONS AND PERCENTS

Gulliver's Travel Service requires a deposit that is $\frac{2}{5}$ of the cost of a trip at the time you make a reservation. What percent of the cost is the deposit?

To write a fraction as a percent you can sometimes write an equivalent fraction with a denominator of 100. Then write the percent for the fraction.

$$\frac{2}{5} = \frac{?}{100} \quad \Rightarrow \quad \frac{2}{5} = \frac{2 \times 20}{5 \times 20} = \frac{40}{100} = 40\%$$

Gulliver's Travel Service requires a 40% deposit when you make a reservation.

Sometimes you may want to write a fraction as a decimal before writing it as a percent.

$$\frac{1}{8} \ \Rightarrow \ 8\overline{)1.000}^{\,0.125} \ \Rightarrow \ 12.5\% \qquad \frac{2}{3} \ \Rightarrow \ 3\overline{)2.00}^{\,0.66\frac{2}{3}} \ \Rightarrow \ 66\frac{2}{3}\%$$

A calculator can simplify the job of changing a fraction to a decimal.

$$\frac{2}{7} \ \Rightarrow \ 2 \div 7 = 0.2857142$$

You frequently round percents to the nearest whole percent or to the nearest tenth of a percent.

$$0.2857142 \ \Rightarrow \ 29\% \ \text{or} \ 28.6\%$$

CLASS EXERCISES

Complete.

1. $\frac{3}{4} = \frac{\blacksquare}{100} = \blacksquare\%$

2. $\frac{1}{5} = \frac{\blacksquare}{100} = \blacksquare\%$

3. $\frac{4}{5} = \frac{\blacksquare}{100} = \blacksquare\%$

4. $\frac{5}{8} \ \Rightarrow \ 8\overline{)5.000}^{\,0.\blacksquare\blacksquare\blacksquare} \ \Rightarrow \ \blacksquare\%$

5. $\frac{7}{16} \ \Rightarrow \ 16\overline{)7.0000}^{\,0.\blacksquare\blacksquare\blacksquare\blacksquare} \ \Rightarrow \ \blacksquare\%$

6. $\frac{1}{7} \ \Rightarrow \ 7\overline{)1.00}^{\,0.\blacksquare\blacksquare\frac{2}{7}} \ \Rightarrow \ \blacksquare\%$

7. $\frac{2}{9} \ \Rightarrow \ 9\overline{)2.00}^{\,0.\blacksquare\blacksquare\frac{2}{9}} \ \Rightarrow \ \blacksquare\%$

PRACTICE

Write as percents.

8. $\frac{1}{2}, \frac{2}{2}$ **9.** $\frac{1}{3}, \frac{2}{3}, \frac{3}{3}$ **10.** $\frac{1}{4}, \frac{2}{4}, \frac{3}{4}, \frac{4}{4}$ **11.** $\frac{1}{5}, \frac{2}{5}, \frac{3}{5}, \frac{4}{5}, \frac{5}{5}$ **12.** $\frac{1}{8}, \frac{3}{8}, \frac{5}{8}, \frac{7}{8}, \frac{8}{8}$

13. $\frac{1}{12}, \frac{5}{12}, \frac{7}{12}, \frac{11}{12}, \frac{12}{12}$ **14.** $\frac{1}{25}, \frac{2}{25}, \frac{3}{25}, \frac{4}{25}, \frac{9}{25}$ **★15.** $\frac{1}{6}, \frac{5}{6}, \frac{7}{6}, \frac{10}{6}$

★16. $\frac{9}{8}, \frac{15}{8}, \frac{24}{8}$ **★17.** $\frac{5}{4}, \frac{7}{4}, \frac{9}{4}$ **★18.** $2\frac{1}{4}, 2\frac{2}{4}, 2\frac{3}{4}$ **★19.** $1\frac{1}{3}, 3\frac{1}{3}, 4\frac{2}{3}$

Write the fraction as a percent. Round answers to the nearest tenth of a percent. A calculator may be helpful.

CALCULATOR

20. $\frac{3}{11}$ **21.** $\frac{11}{15}$ **22.** $\frac{13}{35}$ **23.** $\frac{49}{51}$

24. $\frac{87}{110}$ **25.** $\frac{55}{158}$ **26.** $\frac{225}{739}$ **27.** $\frac{35}{44}$

28. Explain how you could use mental math to quickly give the percents for decimals shown on your calculator display.

PROBLEM SOLVING APPLICATIONS
Using a Chart

Copy and complete the chart to show the percent of customers using each type of service. Use the information below. Round to the nearest thousandth.

Total number of customers: 161

Cruises:	12
Flights:	140
Hotels:	88
Mystery Weekend:	15
Car rentals:	55
Ski trips:	40
Safaris:	33

	Service	Fraction	Decimal	Percent
29.	Cruises	?	?	?
30.	Flights	?	?	?
31.	Hotels	?	?	?
32.	Mystery Weekend	?	?	?
33.	Car rentals	?	?	?
34.	Ski trips	?	?	?
35.	Safaris	?	?	?

PROBLEM SOLVING
Strategy: Consumer Applications and Tables and Graphs

1. Understand
2. Plan
3. Work
4. Answer/Check

A marketing research firm questioned 1962 students about the things they like to buy. Each student was asked to choose only one item he or she would buy if given $100. The results are shown in the table.

You can write a percent to describe the number of people choosing each type of purchase. Survey results are frequently reported as whole percents.

$\dfrac{\text{clothing choice}}{\text{total questioned}}\ \dfrac{530}{1962} = 0.270 = 27\%$

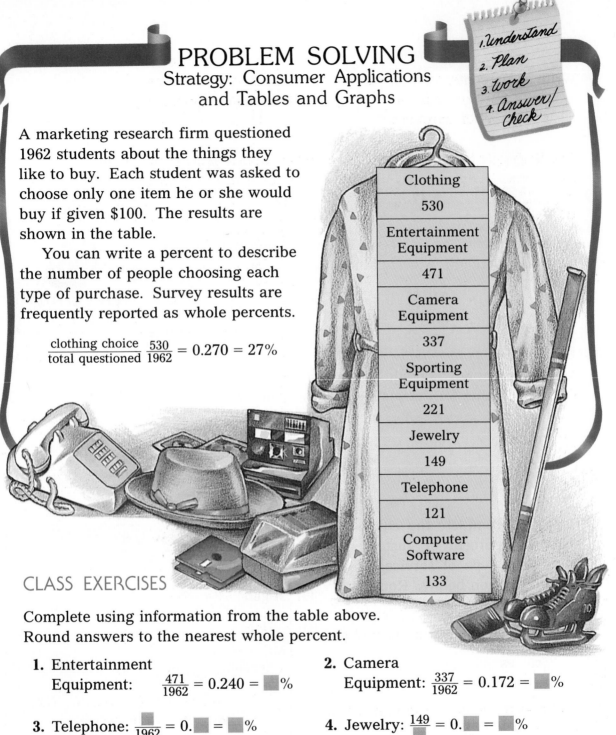

Clothing
530
Entertainment Equipment
471
Camera Equipment
337
Sporting Equipment
221
Jewelry
149
Telephone
121
Computer Software
133

CLASS EXERCISES

Complete using information from the table above. Round answers to the nearest whole percent.

1. Entertainment Equipment: $\dfrac{471}{1962} = 0.240 = \blacksquare\%$

2. Camera Equipment: $\dfrac{337}{1962} = 0.172 = \blacksquare\%$

3. Telephone: $\dfrac{\blacksquare}{1962} = 0.\blacksquare = \blacksquare\%$

4. Jewelry: $\dfrac{149}{\blacksquare} = 0.\blacksquare = \blacksquare\%$

5. Sporting Equipment: $\dfrac{\blacksquare}{1962} = 0.\blacksquare = \blacksquare\%$

6. Computer Software: $\dfrac{133}{\blacksquare} = 0.\blacksquare = \blacksquare\%$

PRACTICE

7. Make a bar graph of the results of the survey on page 286. Let each bar show the percent of people choosing each type of purchase.

The Scramble Soup Company asked 800 people to taste their new soups. The results of the test are shown in the graph.

8. Which soup had a 75% favorable rating?

9. Which soup had less than a 35% favorable rating?

10. What percent favorable rating did Chicken Noodle soup get?

11. Suppose soups with less than a 50% favorable rating are rejected. Which soups will be rejected?

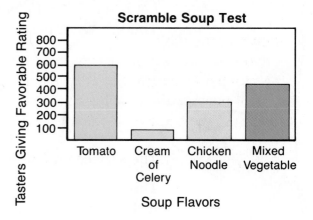

Scramble Soup Test

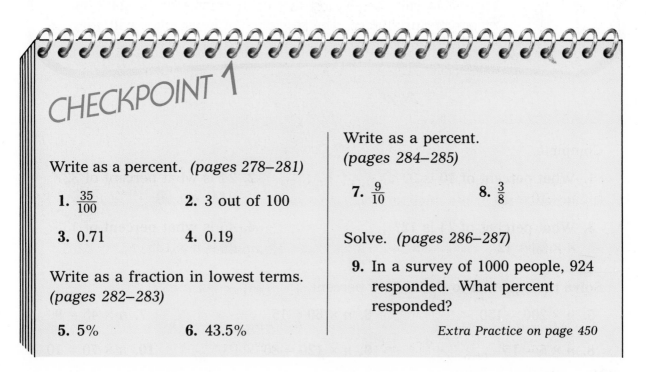

CHECKPOINT 1

Write as a percent. *(pages 278–281)*

1. $\frac{35}{100}$

2. 3 out of 100

3. 0.71

4. 0.19

Write as a fraction in lowest terms. *(pages 282–283)*

5. 5%

6. 43.5%

Write as a percent. *(pages 284–285)*

7. $\frac{9}{10}$

8. $\frac{3}{8}$

Solve. *(pages 286–287)*

9. In a survey of 1000 people, 924 responded. What percent responded?

Extra Practice on page 450

FINDING A PERCENT

Tickets to see the Grant Slim Band cost $7.50 each. The South St. Ticket Agency charges an additional $1.35 per ticket for service. What percent of the cost is the service charge?

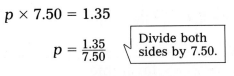

To find the percent, write and solve an equation. Let p stand for the percent in decimal form.

Think: What percent of $7.50 is $1.35?

$$p \times 7.50 = 1.35$$

$$p = \frac{1.35}{7.50}$$ | Divide both sides by 7.50.

$$p = 0.18 = 18\%$$

The service charge is 18% of the ticket price.

Think: Would the amount of the service charge be the same if the price of the tickets were different?

You can use the % key on a calculator to solve many percent problems. The sequence of keystrokes will vary.

CLASS EXERCISES

Complete.

1. What percent of 10 is 9?
$n \times 10 = \blacksquare$

2. 24 is what percent of 32?
$24 = n \times \blacksquare$

3. What percent of 24 is 12?
$n \times \blacksquare = 12$

4. 45 is what percent of 135?
$\blacksquare = n \times 135$

Solve the equation to find n as a percent.

5. $n \times 200 = 150$

6. $n \times 60 = 15$

7. $n \times 45 = 9$

8. $n \times 5 = 15$

9. $n \times 120 = 80$

10. $n \times 70 = 10$

PRACTICE

Find the percent.

11. What percent of 18 is 9?

12. What percent of 28 is 21?

13. What percent of 10 is 8?

14. What percent of 5 is 10?

15. What percent of 55 is 11?

16. What percent of 48 is 12?

17. 4 is what percent of 800?

18. 16 is what percent of 25?

19. 5 is what percent of 20?

20. 13 is what percent of 65?

21. 36 is what percent of 180?

22. 260 is what percent of 650?

Find the percent to the nearest tenth of a percent.
A calculator may be helpful.

CALCULATOR

23. 53 is what percent of 127?

24. 486 is what percent of 777?

25. 6 is what percent of 598?

26. 99 is what percent of 500?

27. Think: If you don't have a ▨ key on your calculator, how can you use the calculator to find a percent?

PROBLEM SOLVING APPLICATIONS
Using Percents

Solve.

28. There are 40 students in the Glee Club. Of those, 8 are in Room 218. What percent of the Glee Club is in Room 218?

29. Of 400 tickets sold to a tennis match, 144 were sold to senior citizens. What percent of the tickets were sold to senior citizens?

★ **30.** Aram bought ten movie passes for $25.00. Those movie tickets normally cost $4.00 apiece. What is the rate of saving on the passes?

FINDING A PERCENT OF A NUMBER

An advertisement claims that 75% of the people questioned preferred riding trains to buses. If 120 people were questioned, how many preferred trains?

To answer this question, you can write and solve an equation. Let n be the number of people who preferred trains.

Think: What number is 75% of 120?

$$n = 75\% \times 120$$

To solve the equation, you may first write 75% as a decimal or a fraction.

Using a decimal	or	Using a fraction
$n = 75\% \times 120$		$n = 75\% \times 120$
$n = 0.75 \times 120$		$n = \frac{3}{4} \times 120$
$n = 90$		$n = 90$

Out of 120 people questioned, 90 preferred trains.

You can estimate a percent of a number by rounding.

$$55\% \text{ of } 168 \approx 60\% \text{ of } 200 = 120$$

CLASS EXERCISES

Complete.

1. a is 10% of 60

   $a = 0.1 \times \blacksquare$

   $a = \blacksquare$

2. b is 50% of 100

   $b = 0.5 \times \blacksquare$

   $b = \blacksquare$

3. c is 25% of 200

   $c = 0.\blacksquare\blacksquare \times \blacksquare$

   $c = \blacksquare$

4. d is 25% of 80

   $d = \frac{1}{4} \times \blacksquare$

   $d = \blacksquare$

5. e is 50% of 150

   $e = \frac{1}{\blacksquare} \times \blacksquare$

   $e = \blacksquare$

6. f is 7% of 400

   $f = \frac{\blacksquare}{\blacksquare} \times 400$

   $f = \blacksquare$

PRACTICE

Write the answer. Use a decimal for the percent.

7. 2% of 90

8. 10% of 40

9. 30% of 75

10. 63% of 70

11. 50% of 84

12. 25% of 96

Write the answer. Use a fraction for the percent.

13. 50% of 40

14. 20% of 120

15. 75% of 52

16. 40% of 60

17. 95% of 60

18. 8% of 50

Solve.

19. 70% of 60 is y

20. 40% of 70 is z

21. 100% of 90 is a

22. 4% of 78 is b

23. $33\frac{1}{3}$% of 100 is c

24. 7% of 63 is d

25. $\frac{1}{2}$% of 200 is y

26. 2.5% of 600 is x

27. 9.25% of 1200 is q

Estimate the answer.

28. 48% of 1156

29. 32% of 87

30. $16\frac{1}{2}$% of 430

31. $9\frac{1}{4}$% of 78

32. 31% of 2292

33. $5\frac{1}{8}$% of 20

ESTIMATE

PROBLEM SOLVING APPLICATIONS
Using Percents

Solve.

34. About 68% of the riders on the 5:20 train use commuter passes. On Tuesday, there were 388 riders on the 5:20. How many riders would you expect to be using passes?

35. A month's worth of round-trip train tickets costs $50. If you buy a monthly train pass you will save 15% of the regular ticket price. How much is a monthly train pass?

★ **36.** The Rapid Express claims to be on schedule 97.5% of the time. If they run eight trains a day, seven days a week, how many trains would you expect to be late?

FINDING THE ORIGINAL NUMBER

Suppose you can save 35% on a health club membership by joining before April 15. This represents a saving of $157.50. How much is the regular membership?

Let p stand for the regular membership.

Think: 35% of what number is $157.50?

$$35\% \times p = \$157.50$$

$$0.35p = 157.50$$

Divide both sides by 0.35. $\longrightarrow$ $p = \dfrac{157.50}{0.35}$

$$p = \$450.00$$

The regular membership is $450.00.

Monday
April
1991

15

Join
Health
Club today.

save
35 %!

CLASS EXERCISES

Complete to write the equation.

1. 50% of n is 14
$0.50 \times \blacksquare = 14$

2. 60% of what number is 20?
$0.60 \times n = \blacksquare$

3. 36 is 25% of what number?
$36 = \blacksquare \times n$

4. 50 is 5% of n
$50 = \blacksquare \times n$

Choose the correct equation. Write a, b, or c.

5. 10% of n is 25

  a. $0.10 \times n = 25$
  b. $0.10 = n \times 25$
  c. $n = 0.10 \times 25$

6. 40% of what number is 30?

  a. $0.40 = n \times 30$
  b. $30 = 0.40 \times n$
  c. $n = 40 \times 30$

PRACTICE

Solve.

7. 20% of f is 6

8. 20% of g is 8

9. 50% of c is 17

10. 60% of p is 21

11. 40% of q is 10

12. 25% of d is 12

13. 80% of n is 52

14. 70% of a is 16.8

15. 50% of t is 12.5

16. 10% of what amount is \$3.20?

17. 8% of what number is 518?

18. What percent of 1000 is 50?

19. What percent of 300 is 96?

20. 62% of what number is 341?

21. What percent of 25 is 24?

22. Find 80% of 425.

23. Find 17% of 1200.

Complete the chart.

MIXED REVIEW

24. $a + 2 = b$

a	b	(a, b)
0	?	(0, ?)
1	?	(1, ?)
?	4	(?, ?)

25. $x = 4y$

x	y	(x, y)
4	?	(4, ?)
8	?	(8, ?)
?	5	(?, ?)

26. $n - 5 = m$

n	m	(n, m)
10	?	(10, ?)
11	?	(11, ?)
?	7	(?, ?)

PROBLEM SOLVING APPLICATIONS
Using Percents

Solve.

27. Bear Trail is 65% as long as Chief Trail. If Chief Trail is 8.6 km long, how long is Bear Trail?

28. The Bear Mountain Club has 120 members. A recent hike attracted 75% of the members. How many members went hiking?

29. The chair lift travels over the Winding River for 0.2 km of its 0.6 km trip. What percent of the chair lift's trip is over the Winding River?

★ **30.** After climbing 1080 m the explorer was 60% of the way to the mountain top. How far was the explorer from the mountain top?

PROBLEM SOLVING
Strategy: Simplifying Problems

Sometimes you can make a problem simpler by rewording it. You can use easier words, supply information you know, and omit anything that is not really necessary to solve the problem.

Station KHWX-TV shows cartoons for 3 h each Saturday morning. This is 40% of the time used for children's shows during a week. How much time does KHWX devote to shows for children during one week?

Write the problem in a simpler form.

> 40% of the time used for children's shows is 3 h. How much time is used for children's shows?

Let n be the number. Write and solve the equation.

$$40\% \times n = 3$$
$$0.40 \times n = 3$$
$$n = \frac{3}{0.40}$$
$$n = 7.5$$

Station KHWX-TV devotes 7.5 h to children's shows in one week.

CLASS EXERCISES

Write a simpler problem and solve.

1. In a survey of 240 viewers, 150 people said they watch *Star Ships* each week. What percent of the viewers questioned watch *Star Ships* each week?

2. KHWX broadcasts commercials for 20% of each hour of prime time. How many minutes of each hour are used for commercials during prime time?

Solve.

3. About 76 million households in the United States have at least one TV set. About 38 million households have more than one set. Of the households that have TVs, about what percent have more than one set?

4. The number of TV stations in California is equal to the sum of all the TV stations in New York and Ohio. If there are 54 TV stations in California, and 30 in New York, how many TV stations are there in Ohio?

Recently there were 12 TV stations in Colorado, and 25% more in Louisiana than in Colorado.

5. How many more TV stations were there in Louisiana than in Colorado?

6. How many TV stations were there in Louisiana in all?

★ 7. What percent of the number of stations in Colorado were the number of stations in Louisiana?

CHECKPOINT 2

Solve. *(pages 288–293)*

1. What percent of 30 is 6?

2. 18 is what percent of 25?

3. 50% of 74 = n

4. $33\frac{1}{3}$% of 54 = x

5. 30% of r is 24.6

6. 75% of n is $25.50

7. 60% of m is 18

8. 85% of p is 68

Solve. *(pages 294–295)*

9. Recently, there were 40 radio stations in Wyoming. If 75% of these stations were AM or AM-FM stations, how many were FM stations only?

Extra Practice on page 450

CHAPTER 10 TEST

Write as a percent. *(pages 278–281)*

1. $\frac{9}{100}$

2. $\frac{7}{25}$

3. 0.03

4. 0.569

Write as a decimal.
(pages 280–281)

Write as a fraction in lowest terms.
(pages 282–283)

5. 62.5%

6. 5%

7. 15%

8. 16.4%

Solve. *(pages 284–287)*

9. A market research firm surveyed 1000 consumers of different brands of laundry soaps. Consumer choices were:

Sudso: 425 Brite: 156 Kleen: 114 Goodwash: 305

Write a percent to describe the number of people choosing each brand.

Write an equation and solve. *(pages 288–293)*

10. 7 is what percent of 35?

11. What percent of 85 is 34?

12. 80% of 60 is a

13. $33\frac{1}{3}$% of 312 is r

14. 7% of 200 is d

15. 60% of q is 27

16. 50% of e is 18.5

17. 4% of f is 5

18. 10% of 55 is t

19. 19 is what percent of 20?

20. 10% of n is 55

Solve. *(pages 294–295)*

21. In a recent survey of 360 magazine readers, 144 said they read Sporty Sports. What percent of those questioned read Sporty Sports?

22. The November issue of Sporty Sports had 216 pages. A total of 25% of the pages were advertisements. How many pages were advertisements?

Extra Practice on page 451

MATHEMATICS and SCIENCE

A meteor is a streak of light in the sky. It's caused by an object from space burning brightly as it travels through Earth's atmo-sphere. A meteorite is an object from space that hits Earth without having completely burned up.

Different meteorites contain different kinds and amounts of material. The charts compare the percent of elements in a meteorite with the elements in Earth's crust.

WHAT'S A SHOOTING STAR?

METEORITE		EARTH'S CRUST	
ELEMENT	PERCENT (APPROX.)	ELEMENT	PERCENT (APPROX.)
Oxygen	36%	Oxygen	49%
Iron	26%	Iron	5%
Silicon	18%	Silicon	26%
Magnesium	14%	Magnesium	2%
Aluminum	2%	Aluminum	8%
Nickel	1%	Calcium	3%
Calcium	1%	Sodium	3%
Other	2%	Other	4%
Total	100%	Total	100%

1. Which element shows the greatest difference in percent between the two charts?

2. Which elements do not appear on both lists?

3. If the chart shows the composition of a 230 kg meteorite, how many kilograms of iron, silicon, and magnesium would it contain?

4. The Barringer Meteorite Crater in Winslow, Arizona is about 1.6 km in diameter. Approximately how long a hike would it be to circle the crater on its rim?

Enrichment

Twenty-five percent of the 120 runners, which is 30 runners, will run in the 100 yard dash.

Some people find it helpful to think of percent facts as proportions. For example, here is how to write *25% of 120 is 30* as a proportion.

- Write 25% as the ratio of 25 to 100.

$$25\% = \frac{25}{100}$$

This is sometimes called the *rate*.

- Write a ratio to compare 30 to 120.

$$\frac{30}{120}$$

The number 120 is called the *base* because it is used as the basis of comparison. The number 30 is compared to the base and is called the *percentage*.

- Now write a proportion to state that these two ratios are equal.

$$\text{rate} \rightarrow \frac{25}{100} = \frac{30}{120} \begin{array}{l} \leftarrow \text{percentage} \\ \leftarrow \quad \text{base} \end{array}$$

Complete the proportion. Then name the rate, the base, and the percentage.

1. 10% of 200 is 20

$$\frac{\blacksquare}{100} = \frac{\blacksquare}{200}$$

2. 50% of 160 is 80

$$\frac{50}{\blacksquare} = \frac{80}{\blacksquare}$$

3. 15% of 60 is 9

$$\frac{15}{100} = \frac{\blacksquare}{\blacksquare}$$

4. 120 is 60% of 200 $\quad \dfrac{\blacksquare}{100} = \dfrac{\blacksquare}{200}$

5. 70 is 20% of 350 $\quad \dfrac{20}{\blacksquare} = \dfrac{70}{\blacksquare}$

6. 18 is 25% of 72

$$\frac{25}{100} = \frac{\blacksquare}{\blacksquare}$$

PERCENTS AND PROPORTIONS

Write as a proportion.

7. 50% of 10 is 5   **8.** 20% of 35 is 7   **9.** 11 is 44% of 25

You can use proportions to solve percent problems.

50% of 112 is a
rate = 50%
base = 112
percentage = a

$$\frac{50}{100} = \frac{a}{112}$$
$$50 \times 112 = 100a$$
$$5600 = 100a$$
$$56 = a$$

b% of 150 is 60
rate = b%
base = 150
percentage = 60

$$\frac{b}{100} = \frac{60}{150}$$
$$150b = 100 \times 60$$
$$150b = 6000$$
$$b = 40$$
$$b\% = 40\%$$

75% of c is 135
rate = 75%
base = c
percentage = 135

$$\frac{75}{100} = \frac{135}{c}$$
$$75c = 100 \times 135$$
$$75c = 13{,}500$$
$$c = 180$$

Complete the proportion. Then solve.

10. $x = 20\%$ of 75
$$\frac{\blacksquare}{100} = \frac{\blacksquare}{75}$$

11. 35 is y% of 700
$$\frac{\blacksquare}{100} = \frac{\blacksquare}{700}$$

12. 3 is 12% of z
$$\frac{12}{100} = \frac{\blacksquare}{\blacksquare}$$

Write and solve a proportion to answer the question.

13. What is 25% of 60?

14. 90% of what number is 36?

15. What percent of 350 is 105?

16. 76% of the 400 runners finished the marathon. How many finished?

17. There are 36 women entered in the road race. This is 45% of all the runners in the race. How many runners are in the race?

CUMULATIVE REVIEW

Choose the correct answer. Write *a*, *b*, *c*, or *d*.

Choose the matching mathematical expression.

1. *a* increased by 11
  a. $a - 11$
  b. $11 < a$
  c. $a + 11$
  d. None of these

2. 8 less than *y*
  a. $8 - y$
  b. $8 \div y$
  c. $y \times 8$
  d. None of these

3. the product of *b* and 7
  a. $7b$
  b. $7 + b$
  c. $b = 7$
  d. None of these

Evaluate the expression. Use $a = 4$, $b = 16$, and $c = 20$.

4. $\frac{c}{5}$
  a. 20 **b.** 4 **c.** 16
  d. None of these

5. $a + b + c$
  a. 40 **b.** 36 **c.** 30
  d. None of these

6. $9a - 2b$
  a. 36 **b.** 20 **c.** 4
  d. None of these

Solve for *x*.

7. $x + 15 = 37$
  a. 12 **b.** 22 **c.** 52
  d. None of these

8. $x - 12 = 26$
  a. 38 **b.** 48 **c.** 26
  d. None of these

9. $x - 54 = 35$
  a. 19 **b.** 29 **c.** 79
  d. None of these

10. $12x = 192$
  a. 204
  b. 180
  c. 16
  d. None of these

11. $\frac{x}{7} = 15$
  a. 7
  b. 105
  c. 150
  d. None of these

12. $3x = 84$
  a. 28
  b. 87
  c. 252
  d. None of these

Choose the matching mathematical expression.

13. *d* is less than the sum of eighteen and five.
  a. $d < 18 + 5$
  b. $d > 18 + 5$
  c. $18 + 5 < d$
  d. None of these

14. *e* is less than thirty and greater than twelve.
  a. $12 > e > 30$
  b. $e < 12 > 30$
  c. $12 < e < 30$
  d. None of these

Solve.

15. $16 + g < 41$
solutions are all numbers
that are:
a. greater than 25
b. less than 25
c. equal to 25
d. None of these

16. $h - 22 > 76$
solutions are all numbers
that are:
a. equal to 98
b. less than 98
c. greater than 98
d. None of these

Choose the correct equation and solution for each problem.

17. Paul earned $12 babysitting. He
earned a total of $28 babysitting
and washing cars. How much did
he earn washing cars?
a. $n + 12 = 28$; $16
b. $n + 12 = 28$; $40
c. $n - 12 = 28$; $40
d. None of these

18. Norma Sue drove 135 km in 3 h.
How far did she drive each hour?

a. $m + 3 = 135$; 132 km
b. $m = 3 \times 135$; 405 km
c. $3m = 135$; 45 km
d. None of these

19. Mildred wants to buy 30 buttons.
If buttons come in packages of 6,
how many packages should she
buy?
a. $30 + n = 6$; 36
b. $6 \times 30 = n$; 180
c. $30 - 6 = n$; 24
d. None of these

20. There are 56 students in the
chorus this year. This is 8 more
than last year. How many students were in last year's chorus?
a. $56 \times n = 8$; $\frac{1}{7}$
b. $n + 8 = 56$; 48
c. $56 + 8 = n$; 64
d. None of these

LANGUAGE and VOCABULARY
REVIEW

Use the words below to complete each sentence.

formula   simplify   percent   decimal   solve

1. A __?__ point separates the ones' place from the tenths' place.

2. A __?__ is a set of symbols expressing a mathematical rule.

3. To __?__ an equation is to replace a variable with a correct solution.

PROGRAMS WITH STRING VARIABLES

COMPUTER LITERACY

A **string** is a series of letters, words, numbers, or symbols, which may be within quotation marks. When a variable stands for a string it is called a **string variable.**

You use the following two signals to tell the computer when you are storing a string variable.
1. The variable name is followed by the symbol for dollar ($).
2. The entire string is enclosed in quotation marks.

Here are some examples.

```
LET AGE$ = "12"
LET A$ = "A STITCH IN TIME"
LET 3$ = "SAVES NINE"
```

READ and DATA statements are a way to store information. READ is followed by one or more variables. The READ statement can contain numeric, string, or a combination of the two variables. The value for the variable is found in the DATA statement.

The program below will display names and ages in columns.

```
10   PRINT "CLASS LIST"
20   PRINT "NAME", "AGE"
30   READ N$, A
40   PRINT N$, A
50   DATA "RAOUL", 13, "SUE", 14
60   DATA "SAM", 12, "KIM", 13
70   GOTO 30
80   END
```

> PRINT with a comma displays data in columns.

> The GOTO statement tells the computer to return to line 30. When all the data have been read, the computer will print either OUT OF DATA ERROR or OUT OF DATA IN LINE 30.

Use the program above to answer the question.

1. In line 30, what do the variables N$ and A stand for?

2. Why are there quotation marks around the names but not the numbers in lines 50 and 60?

3. Which program lines include string variables?

4. Write the program's output.

The cost of transporting a car appears in its price. If 3.3% of the cost of an $8800 car is transportation, how much did it cost to transport the car?

11

PERCENTS AND CONSUMER APPLICATIONS

PERCENT EQUATIONS

You can use this list of information about the brass section of an orchestra to answer the questions below.

1. How many members play the horn?

2. What percent of the brass section play the trombone?

3. How many members are in the whole orchestra?

> **BRASS SECTION**
>
> 15 members
> 40% play the horn
> 3 play the trombone
> brass section makes up 12% of orchestra

First, rewrite the question using the information from the list. Then write an equation, solve it, and answer the questions.

What number is 40% of 15?	What percent of 15 is 3?	12% of what number is 15?
$n = 40\% \times 15$	$n \times 15 = 3$	12% of $n = 15$
$n = 0.40 \times 15$	$n = \frac{3}{15}$	$0.12 \times n = 15$
$n = 6$	$n = 0.20$	$n = \frac{15}{0.12}$
	$n = 20\%$	$n = 125$
6 members play the horn.	20% play the trombone.	There are 125 members.

A calculator is helpful in solving equations that include decimals. To solve the equation $0.12 \times n = 15$ above, enter: $15 \boxed{\div} .12 \boxed{=}$. The calculator will display the value of n, 125.

CLASS EXERCISES

Write an equation to solve the problem.

1. What number is 75% of 200?

2. 10% of 325 is what number?

3. 9 is what percent of 90?

4. 4 is what percent of 50?

5. 4% of what number is 2?

6. 50% of what number is 86?

PRACTICE

Write an equation. Then solve.

7. What percent of 65 is 13?

8. 20% of what number is 420?

9. What number is 20% of 415?

10. What percent of 20 is 2?

11. 5% of 100 is what number?

12. What number is 2.5% of $430?

13. 90% of what number is 72?

14. 30 is what percent of 250?

15. $4.32 is what percent of $36?

16. 16% of 140 is what number?

17. 15% of what number is 96?

18. 5.35 is what percent of 214?

19. What number is 175% of 268?

20. What percent of 45 is 72?

★ 21. $10\frac{1}{4}$% of what number is 2.05?

★ 22. $33\frac{1}{3}$% of $39.93 is what amount?

Solve. A calculator may be helpful.

23. $25\% \times 800,000 = n$

24. $85\% \times 1.2$ million $= n$

25. $65\% \times n = 2,275,000$

26. $\$577,500 = 3.5\% \times n$

CALCULATOR

27. Choose one of Exercises 23–26 to do using mental math and explain how you can do it mentally.

PROBLEM SOLVING APPLICATIONS
Simplifying the Problem

Solve.

28. The percussion section of an orchestra has 8 drum players. This number represents 40% of the section. How many players are in the percussion section?

29. A total of 2500 people attended the end-of-season performance of the local orchestra. Of this total, 750 people sat in the first balcony. What percent of the people sat in the first balcony?

★ 30. Write a word problem about the woodwind section of an orchestra using the equation $12.5\% \times n = 6$.

INTEREST

If you deposit money in the bank, the bank pays you **interest** for the use of your money. The money deposited is called the **principal.** The number of years the money is left in the bank is the **time.** The interest earned in that time is determined by the yearly **rate.** To find simple interest, use the formula below.

$$\text{Interest} = \text{principal} \times \text{rate} \times \text{time}$$
$$I \quad = \quad p \quad \times \quad r \quad \times \quad t$$

Suppose you deposit $500 into a savings account for 6 months. The interest rate per year is 8%. How much interest will your money earn?

$I = p \times r \times t$

$\quad = \$500 \times 8\% \times \frac{1}{2}$ ⟨ **Think:** 6 months $= \frac{6}{12}$ year $= \frac{1}{2}$ year

$\quad = \$20$

This formula can also be used to find the interest you pay when you borrow money.

Ⓜ You can use mental math to compute interest by thinking of the rate as dollars per $100. For example, think of 5% as $5 for every $100 of principal. The yearly interest on $800 of principal is $8 \times \$5$, or $40.

CLASS EXERCISES

Name the principal, the rate, the time, and the interest.

1. Shelley borrowed $650 for 1 year. The rate of interest was 20%. She paid $130 to borrow this money.

2. Steven deposited $1000 in a money market certificate for 1 year at 12.5%. His money earned $125.

3. Sumi borrowed $1960 for 2 years at 13.5%. She paid $529.20 to borrow this money.

PRACTICE

Find the interest. Round to the nearest cent.

4. principal: $200
    rate: $5\frac{1}{2}\%$
    time: 1 year

5. principal: $200
    rate: 13%
    time: 1 year

6. principal: $1000
    rate: 18%
    time: 1 year

7. principal: $750
    rate: $6\frac{1}{4}\%$
    time: $\frac{1}{4}$ year

8. principal: $2300
    rate: $12\frac{1}{4}\%$
    time: $\frac{1}{2}$ year

9. principal: $450
    rate: 10%
    time: $\frac{1}{4}$ year

10. principal: $20,000
    rate: 16%
    time: 1 year

11. principal: $15,000
    rate: $12\frac{1}{2}\%$
    time: $\frac{1}{2}$ year

12. principal: $7500
    rate: 13.5%
    time: 2 years

13. principal: $592
    rate: $12\frac{1}{4}\%$
    time: 3 months

14. principal: $450.67
    rate: $9\frac{3}{4}\%$
    time: 6 months

★ **15.** principal: $851.34
    rate: 12.3%
    time: 13 weeks

Use mental math to find the interest.

16. $900 at 7% for 1 year

17. $1000 at 5% for 1 year

18. $250 at 10% for 2 years

★ **19.** $2500 at 4% for 3 years

MENTAL MATH

PROBLEM SOLVING APPLICATIONS
Using Formulas

Solve.

20. Rita deposits $400 in a savings account. The interest rate is $5\frac{3}{4}\%$. How much interest will $400 earn in 3 months?

21. Carl obtains an educational loan of $3000. The interest rate is 7%. What will the interest be after 6 months?

22. Kim borrows $1600 at 9% for 1 year to pay for a course. She will repay the principal plus interest at the end of the year. How much will she have to pay in all?

PROBLEM SOLVING
Strategy: Organizing Information

1. Understand
2. Plan
3. Work
4. Answer/Check

Eastern Bank offers a NOW account with an interest rate of 7.2%, a service charge of $2.25, a check charge of $.10 per check, and a minimum balance of $500. National Bank offers a NOW account with a service charge of $2.00, an interest rate of 7.2%, a minimum balance of $500, and a check charge of $.15 per check. Which bank offers the more economical plan if you write about 20 checks per month?

You can make a chart to compare the plans.

BANK	INTEREST RATE	SERVICE CHARGE	MINIMUM BALANCE	CHECK CHARGE
Eastern	7.2%	$2.25	$500	$.10 per check
National	7.2%	$2.00	$500	$.15 per check

The interest rates and minimum balances are the same. You need to compare the check charges and service charge.

	Checks		Check Charge		Service Charge		Total Cost
Eastern	20	×	$.10	+	$2.25	=	$4.25
National	20	×	$.15	+	$2.00	=	$5.00

Eastern Bank is more economical.

CLASS EXERCISE

You want to borrow $2000 for 2 years. At State Bank you can repay the loan in 24 payments of $111.66 each. Citizen's Bank charges an annual interest rate of 16.2% and a $7 application fee. State Bank charges a $5 application fee.

1. Make a chart to compare the interest paid, application fee, and total cost at both banks. Which bank is more economical?

PRACTICE

For Exercises 2–6 make a chart to organize the information. Then answer the question.

2. A math teacher gave a quiz containing 15 questions. She figured each student's grade by multiplying the number of correct answers by 6 and adding 10. What are all the possible grades? (Assume that everyone got at least 1 question correct.)

3. The fare to ride the train is $.60. A monthly pass is $15.00. If you ride the train 22 times in a month, is the pass cheaper? At least how many times do you need to ride the train to break even?

4. A computer store bills its charge customers monthly at the following rate: $1\frac{1}{2}$% for the first $300 and 1% for the amounts over $300. What is the interest charge and total charge for the customers owing the following amounts: Gary Murphy — $327.15; Sharon Nichols — $527.82; Bill Marshall — $450.25; Kathy Lee — $265.84?

5. Rent-a-Car offers three plans for renting a compact size car:
   Plan A: $15.95 a day with no mileage charge
   Plan B: $10.95 a day with 23¢ for each mile
   Plan C: $99.00 a week with no mileage charge
   If you plan to have the car for 6 days and drive 250 mi, which is the most economical plan?

6. The seventh grade wants to charter a bus to the Science Expo. It will take about 3 h to get there by bus. They plan to stay at the Expo about 4 h. The Red Line charges a minimum of $155 for the first 5 h and $35 for each additional hour. The Green Line charges a minimum of $170 for the first 4 h and $25 for each additional hour. The Blue Line charges a minimum of $160 for the first 3 h and $30 for each additional hour. Which bus line will be the most economical to charter for a round trip?

PERCENT OF CHANGE

When a quantity increases or decreases, the change can be written as a percent of the original amount, or as a **percent of change.** To find the percent of change use the formula below.

$$\text{Percent of Change} = \frac{\text{amount of change}}{\text{original amount}}$$

Jim's starting salary at the theater was $3.50 per hour. His present salary is $3.92 per hour. What is the percent of increase?

First find the amount of change.

$$\$3.92 - \$3.50 = \$.42$$

Then use the formula to find the percent of increase.

$$\frac{\$.42}{\$3.50} = 0.12 = 12\%$$

The percent of increase is 12%.

Jade's pulse rate dropped from 95 beats per minute to 76 beats per minute after a race. What is the percent of decrease?

First find the amount of change.

$$95 - 76 = 19$$

Then use the formula to find the percent of decrease.

$$\frac{19}{95} = 0.2 = 20\%$$

The percent of decrease is 20%.

Think: Can a percent of increase be greater than 100%?

CLASS EXERCISES

Complete.

1. Original amount: 20
   New amount: 40

   $$\frac{\text{amount of change}}{\text{original amount}} = \frac{\blacksquare}{\blacksquare} = \blacksquare\%$$

2. Original amount: 100
   New amount: 95

   $$\frac{\text{amount of change}}{\text{original amount}} = \frac{\blacksquare}{\blacksquare} = \blacksquare\%$$

3. Original amount: 18.5
   New amount: 14.8

   $$\frac{\text{amount of change}}{\text{original amount}} = \frac{\blacksquare}{\blacksquare} = \blacksquare\%$$

4. Original amount: 75
   New amount: 100

   $$\frac{\text{amount of change}}{\text{original amount}} = \frac{\blacksquare}{\blacksquare} = \blacksquare\%$$

PRACTICE

Find the percent of increase or decrease.

5. 30 to 45   **6.** 46 to 92   **7.** 80 to 40   **8.** 100 to 90

9. 30 to 15   **10.** 40 to 90   **11.** 50 to 47   **12.** 10 to 8.9

13. 80 to 96   **14.** 3.4 to 1.7   **15.** 75 to 27   **16.** 84 to 105

17. 9.6 to 10.8   **18.** 120 to 84   **19.** 88 to 121   **20.** 212 to 53

21. 121 to 242   **22.** 250 to 175   **23.** 66 to 72.6   **24.** 9000 to 7200

25. 360 to 720   **26.** 100 to 250   **27.** $200 to $234   **28.** $7,000 to $8,050

Write as a decimal.

29. 3%   **30.** 15%   **31.** 10%   **32.** 105%

33. 9.2%   **34.** 25.5%   **35.** $18\frac{1}{2}$%   **36.** $12\frac{3}{4}$%

MIXED REVIEW

PROBLEM SOLVING APPLICATIONS
Choosing Mental Math, Calculator, or Pencil and Paper

Tell whether you would choose mental math, pencil and paper, or a calculator to solve. Write *M*, *C*, or *P*. Then solve.

37. Gregg is selling calendars to earn money. Last week he sold 20 calendars. This week he sold 15. What is the percent of change?

38. Last year's sales of arcade games was $670,520. This year's sales were $1,005,780. What is the percent of change?

39. The population of Forest County in 1925 was 135,000. This year it is 81,000. What is the percent of decrease?

★ **40.** After a drop of 20% in depth of water in the Appleton Reservoir, the depth gauge read 56 m. What was the original depth?

TAX RATES

Todd Mulhern bought a camera with a selling price of $139.89. He paid a 6% **sales tax.** A **sales tax rate** of 6% means that 6¢ is added to every dollar of the selling price. So, the sales tax rate on Todd's camera was 6% of $139.89.

You can write an equation to find the sales tax.

$$\text{Sales Tax} = \text{sales tax rate} \times \text{selling price}$$
$$= 6\% \times \$139.89$$
$$= 0.06 \times \$139.89 = \$8.3934$$

Rounded to the nearest cent the sales tax was $8.39.

You can also write an equation to find the total cost.

$$\text{Total Cost} = \text{selling price} + \text{sales tax}$$
$$= \$139.89 + \$8.39 = \$148.28$$

Todd paid a total cost of $148.28 for his camera.

You can use a calculator to compute the sales tax and total cost of an item with a percent key. For example, to find the total cost of film priced at $3.89, which is 100% of the selling price, with a sales tax rate of 6%, you would enter:

3.89 ⊠ 106 ▣ ⊟ 4.1234

The total cost of the film is $4.12 rounded to the nearest cent.

CLASS EXERCISES

Solve. Round to the nearest cent if necessary.

1. 3% of $31.05

2. 8% of $12.82

3. 5.5% of $70

4. 4.25% of $80

5. 4% of $14.50

6. 8% of $33.85

7. 9% of $22.75

8. 7% of $20.36

9. 5% of $19.95

PRACTICE

Find the sales tax. Round to the nearest cent.

10. selling price: $20.25
sales tax rate: 6%

11. selling price: $13.75
sales tax rate: 7.5%

Find the total cost. Round to the nearest cent.

12. selling price: $18.30
sales tax rate: 6%

13. selling price: $24.60
sales tax rate: 8%

14. selling price: $31.20
sales tax rate: 9%

15. selling price: $16.65
sales tax rate: 3%

16. selling price: $27.45
sales tax rate: $7\frac{1}{2}\%$

17. selling price: $250.70
sales tax rate: 6.75%

Find the total cost. A calculator may be helpful.

CALCULATOR

18. selling price: $20,851.25
sales tax rate: 5.5%

19. selling price: $19,900.15
sales tax rate: $6\frac{1}{4}\%$

PROBLEM SOLVING APPLICATIONS
Too Much Information

Use the tax table to solve.

20. What is the total cost of a pen priced at $.99 plus tax?

21. Jane buys a notebook for $2.19, a clipboard for $3.29, and a dictionary for $2.95. What is the total cost plus tax?

5% SALES TAX TABLE			
AMOUNT OF SALE	TAX	AMOUNT OF SALE	TAX
$.10–$.29	$.01	$7.70–$7.89	$.39
.30– .49	.02	7.90– 8.09	.40
.50– .69	.03	8.10– 8.29	.41
.70– .89	.04	8.30– 8.49	.42
.90–1.09	.05	8.50– 8.69	.43

Solve.

★ **22.** A guitar is priced at $69.95. With tax, the price is $75.55. What is the sales tax rate to the nearest percent?

PROBLEM SOLVING
Strategy: Consumer Applications and Graphs

1. Understand
2. Plan
3. Work
4. Answer/Check

Graphs can give you information you need and help you make comparisons. This graph compares gasoline mileage for several vehicles.

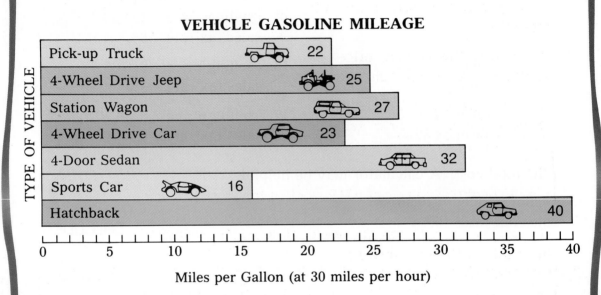

VEHICLE GASOLINE MILEAGE

TYPE OF VEHICLE

Pick-up Truck	22
4-Wheel Drive Jeep	25
Station Wagon	27
4-Wheel Drive Car	23
4-Door Sedan	32
Sports Car	16
Hatchback	40

0   5   10   15   20   25   30   35   40

Miles per Gallon (at 30 miles per hour)

Think: What is the gasoline mileage for the sports car?

To read the gasoline mileage for the sports car, read the number on the scale at the bottom of the graph that marks the end of the bar labelled Sports Car.

Since the space between two tick marks on the scale represents 1 mi/gal, the mileage for the sports car is 16 mi/gal.

CLASS EXERCISES

Use the graph above to answer.

1. How many different vehicles are being compared?

2. At what speed were the mileage ratings determined?

3. Which vehicle has the highest miles per gallon rating?

PRACTICE

The graph at the right shows the closing price per share of AMP stock.

Refer to the graph to answer.

4. What was the lowest closing price per share during the 14 weeks?

5. When was the closing price of AMP stock at $26\frac{1}{4}$ per share?

6. Debbie bought 15 shares of AMP stock at the closing price for the eighth week. How much did she pay?

CLOSING PRICE PER SHARE OF AMP STOCK

7. Blake bought 87 shares of AMP stock at the closing price for the fourth week. He sold these same shares at the closing price for the twelfth week. How much profit did he make on this transaction?

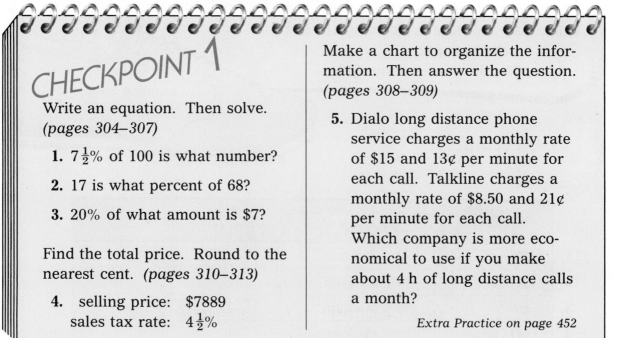

CHECKPOINT 1

Write an equation. Then solve. *(pages 304–307)*

1. $7\frac{1}{2}\%$ of 100 is what number?

2. 17 is what percent of 68?

3. 20% of what amount is $7?

Find the total price. Round to the nearest cent. *(pages 310–313)*

4. selling price: $7889
    sales tax rate: $4\frac{1}{2}\%$

Make a chart to organize the information. Then answer the question. *(pages 308–309)*

5. Dialo long distance phone service charges a monthly rate of $15 and 13¢ per minute for each call. Talkline charges a monthly rate of $8.50 and 21¢ per minute for each call. Which company is more economical to use if you make about 4 h of long distance calls a month?

Extra Practice on page 452

DISCOUNTS AND MARKUPS

A **discount** is a decrease in the price of an item. A discount rate is a percent of the original price. Suppose the regular price of a pair of skis is $90. You buy them at a 40% discount. The amount of discount is 40% of $90.

$$\text{Discount} = 40\% \text{ of } \$90$$
$$= 0.40 \times \$90 = \$36$$

You subtract the discount from the regular price to find the sale price.

$$\text{Sale Price} = \text{reg. price} - \text{discount}$$
$$= \$90 - \$36$$
$$= \$54$$

The sale price is $54.

A **markup** is an increase in the price of an item. The markup rate is a percent of the original price. Suppose the original price, or cost to the store, for a tennis racket is $20. The markup rate is 25%. The amount of markup is 25% of $20.

$$\text{Markup} = 25\% \text{ of } \$20$$
$$= 0.25 \times \$20 = \$5$$

You add the markup to the original price to find the selling price.

$$\text{Selling Price} = \text{orig. price} + \text{markup}$$
$$= \$20 + \$5$$
$$= \$25$$

The selling price is $25.

E To estimate a discount you can use compatible numbers that are easy to work with. Find 30% of a $36 item.

Think: 30% is close to $33\frac{1}{3}\%$, which is $\frac{1}{3}$.
$\frac{1}{3}$ of $36 is $12.
The discount is about $12.

SALE
Running Shoes
Original Price: $35.95
30% off

CLASS EXERCISES

Complete.

	ORIGINAL PRICE	PERCENT OF CHANGE	AMOUNT OF CHANGE	NEW PRICE
1.	$75	20% discount	?	?
2.	$24.80	10% discount	?	?
3.	$55	40% markup	?	?
4.	$115.60	55% markup	?	?

PRACTICE

Find the new price. Round to the nearest cent.

5. original price: $205
   discount rate: 15%

6. original price: $29.90
   discount rate: 10%

7. original price: $90
   discount rate: 30%

8. original price: $99
   discount rate: $33\frac{1}{4}\%$

9. original price: $8.95
   markup rate: 43%

10. original price: $280.73
    markup rate: 49%

11. original price: $52.74
    markup rate: 25%

12. original price: $96
    markup rate: $8\frac{1}{3}\%$

Which store has the lower sale price on the same item?

13. The Attic   original price: $50
                   discount rate: 20%
    Front Porch   original price: $45
                   discount rate: 30%

14. Shoe Lane   original price: $63
                 discount rate: $33\frac{1}{3}\%$
    Hat World   original price: $59
                 discount rate: 30%

Estimate the discount or markup.

15. original price: $59.75
    discount rate: 35%

16. original price: $32
    markup rate: 65%

ESTIMATE

PROBLEM SOLVING APPLICATIONS
Consumer Topics

Solve.

17. Sleeping bags are on sale at a 20% discount. What is the sale price of a bag originally priced at $28.95?

18. All tents are now 50% off. What is the sale price of a tent that was originally priced at $39.95?

★ 19. Hiking shoes originally marked $22.50 are on sale for $15.75. What is the rate of discount?

★ 20. When Alice bought a parka for $14.40, she saved 20% of the original price. What was the original price?

COMMISSION

A **commission** is the amount of money you earn for selling a product or providing a service. Many salespeople receive a percent of their total sales as commission.

For example, a real estate broker earns a 10% commission. If the broker sells a piece of land worth $6000, the commission will be 10% of $6000, or $600. In this case, the commission rate is 10%.

During May, Janice Jones sold $776.50 worth of office supplies. She received as her commission 25% of the amount of sales. What was her commission?

$$\text{Amount of Commission} = \text{commission rate} \times \text{sales}$$
$$= 0.25 \times \$776.50$$
$$= \$194.125$$

To the nearest dollar, Janice's commission was $194.

In addition to the commission, Janice received a monthly salary of $1238 in May. To find her total salary, add her monthly salary and commission.

$$\$1238 + \$194 = \$1432$$

You can do this mentally by thinking of $194 as $200 − $6.

$$\$1238 + \$200 − \$6 = \$1438 − \$6 = \$1432$$

CLASS EXERCISES

Complete.

	1.	2.	3.	4.	5.	6.
Commission Rate	5%	35%	20%	8%	$\frac{1}{2}$%	$12\frac{1}{2}$%
Total Sales	$20,000	$5000	$12,000	$37,000	$18,000	$64,000
Commission	?	?	?	?	?	?

PRACTICE

Find the commission. Round to the nearest cent.

7. total sales: $360
commission rate: 3.5%

8. total sales: $650
commission rate: 5.5%

9. total sales: $420.65
commission rate: 15%

10. total sales: $530.70
commission rate: 20%

11. total sales: $804.75
commission rate: 30%

12. total sales: $1014.10
commission rate: 40%

Find the amount of sales.

13. commission: $350
commission rate: 10%

14. commission: $180
commission rate: 3%

Find the commission rate to the nearest percent.

★ **15.** total sales: $400
commission: $175

★ **16.** total sales: $6000
commission: $862

Find the total earnings.

17. monthly salary: $1076
commission: $198

18. monthly salary: $965
commission: $489

19. monthly salary: $1099
commission: $362

20. monthly salary: $878
commission: $995

MENTAL MATH

PROBLEM SOLVING APPLICATIONS
Using Formulas

Solve.

21. George Stone earns 8% commission on the furniture he sells. Today he sold a couch for $650, a desk set for $300, and a cabinet for $895. What was his total commission?

22. Pamela Weiss receives 6.5% commission on each new insurance policy she sells. Last month she sold $3528 worth of new policies. Her total pay was $1279.32. What is her regular salary?

PROBLEM SOLVING
Strategy: Using Logic

1. Understand
2. Plan
3. Work
4. Answer/ Check

Using logical reasoning to organize facts can help you solve problems. Tonya's apartment is between Ramon's and Megan's. Their jobs are psychologist, astronaut, and technician but not in that order. The astronaut holds Megan's mail when she is out of town. The psychologist taps on Ramon's wall if his music is loud. Match the occupation with the person.

Use a chart to show all the possibilities. Make an x when you have used a fact to eliminate a possibility. Make a ✓ when there is only one possibility left.

The astronaut holds Megan's mail. So, Megan is not the astronaut (x). The psychologist taps on Ramon's wall. So, Ramon is not the psychologist (x). Megan is not the psychologist (x). She couldn't tap on Ramon's wall.

The first row shows that Tonya is the psychologist (✓). The last column shows that Megan is the technician (✓). So, Ramon is the astronaut.

	Ramon	Tonya	Megan
psychologist	x	✓	x
astronaut			x
technician			✓

CLASS EXERCISES

Each card has one of the numbers 3, 4, or 5 on the back.
Match the fact to its chart. Write A, B, or C.

1. The number on ☆ is prime.

2. The number on △ is less than ○.

3. The number on ○ is not even.

A.

	3	4	5
△			
○		×	
☆			

B.

	3	4	5
△			
○			
☆		×	

C.

	3	4	5
△			×
○	×		
☆			

PRACTICE

Use a chart to organize the facts. Then answer the question.

4. Sam, Sue, and Suni each play a different instrument. The instruments are the drums, the flute, and the trumpet. Sue and the drummer are in the same algebra class. The flute player and the drummer come to Suni's house to practice. Who plays the flute?

	DRUMS	FLUTE	TRUMPET
Sam			
Sue			
Suni			

5. Barb, Joe, and Berry were dressed as a rabbit, a scarecrow, and a knight for a costume party. Joe gave the scarecrow and the knight a ride to the party. Berry helped the knight put on its costume. Who was the knight?

6. Art, Arno, and Alex have lockers next to each other. Arno rides the bus with the person whose locker is at the right. Art's locker is not next to Arno's. Who has the locker at the right?

7. A train conductor is talking to three passengers named Baker, Samgrass, and Burgess. The passengers are a teacher, a musician, and a salesperson. Samgrass and the musician are neighbors. Baker and the teacher have not met before. Both the teacher and Burgess enjoy the musician's albums. Who is the salesperson?

★ **8** Joy, Melissa, Sam, Harvey, and Preston are students. One of them is in college, while the others are freshman, sophomore, junior, and senior in high school, but not in that order. Harvey is in a higher class than Melissa. Joy will major in mathematics in college next year. The college student lives on the same street as Harvey and Sam. Preston was an honor graduate from high school last year. Melissa and the sophomore are both in the choir. Sam is a year behind Joy. Who is the freshman?

CIRCLE GRAPHS

Recent U.S. Population by Age Group

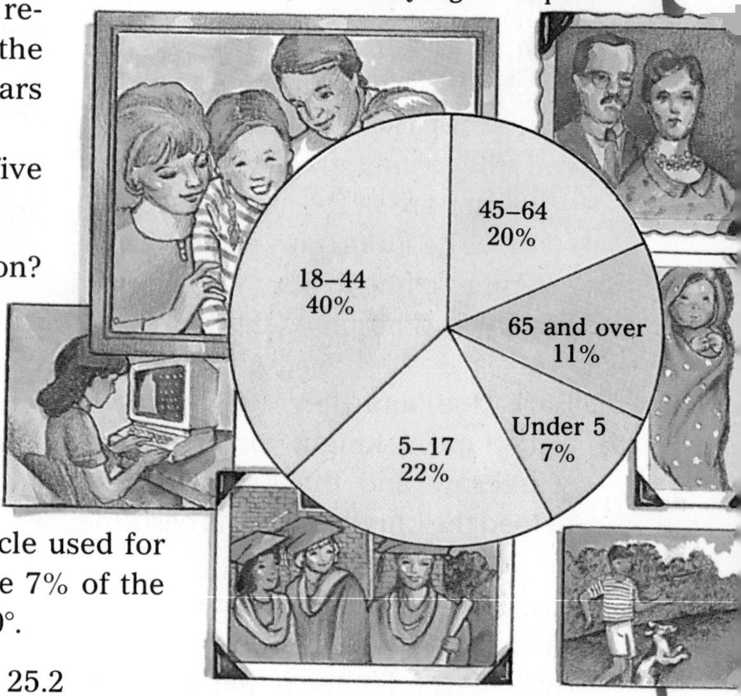

The **circle graph** shows that in a recent year, 7% of the population in the United States was under five years old.

The number of children under five years old is calculated as follows:

What number is 7% of 218 million?

$n = 7\%$ of 218 million
$n = 0.07 \times 218$ million
$n = 15.26$ million

The number of children under five years old is 15.26 million.

To calculate the part of the circle used for the population five and under take 7% of the number of degrees in a circle, 360°.

$$7\% \text{ of } 360 = 25.2$$

In the circle graph an angle of about 25° has been drawn to show that 7% of the population is under 5.

(Circle graph segments: 18–44 40%, 45–64 20%, 65 and over 11%, Under 5 7%, 5–17 22%)

CLASS EXERCISES

Use the graph above for Exercises 1–5.

1. Which age group has the most people?

2. Are there more people in the 5–17 age group or the 45–64 age group?

3. About what fraction of the population is over 45?

4. About how many people are 65 and over?

5. An angle of about how many degrees represents the population between the ages of 18 and 44?

PRACTICE

Use the circle graph at the right to answer Exercises 6–12.

6. How many students play violins?

7. How many students play cellos?

8. How many students play violas?

Find the percent of the orchestra that play the instrument. Round your answer to the nearest tenth of a percent.

9. trumpets: 10 players

11. flutes: 3 players

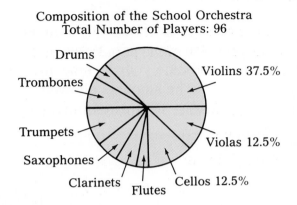

Composition of the School Orchestra
Total Number of Players: 96

Drums

Trombones

Violins 37.5%

Trumpets

Saxophones

Violas 12.5%

Clarinets   Flutes   Cellos 12.5%

10. saxophones: 6 players

12. drums: 4 players

Multiply.

13. 391
      ×12

14. 745
      ×60

15. 1208
       ×35

16. 61,217
        ×303

MIXED REVIEW

17. 0.089 × 1678   **18.** 0.055 × 17,532   **19.** 0.38 × 32,154

PROBLEM SOLVING APPLICATIONS
Making Circle Graphs

Use the table for Exercise 20.

20. Construct a circle graph to show the information in the table.

★ **21.** Sixty students took part in a survey; 45% liked swimming, 15% liked basketball, 25% liked tennis, 10% liked soccer, and 5% liked hiking. Draw a circle graph to picture this information.

**CONTENTS OF
SCHOOL MAGAZINE**

KIND OF MATERIAL	NUMBER OF PAGES
Fiction	32
Essays	8
Sports	16
Puzzles	8
Total	64

BUDGETS

A **budget** is a plan you make to be sure your income will cover your expenses. When you make up a budget you may have to estimate your income and expenses.

The amounts allowed are often shown as a percent of income. One way of showing a budget is with a circle graph.

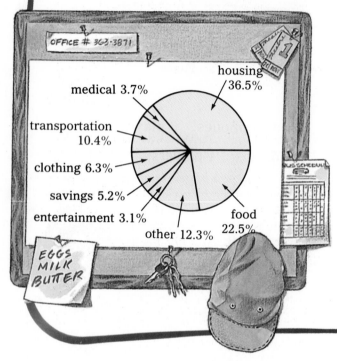

medical 3.7%

transportation 10.4%

clothing 6.3%

savings 5.2%

entertainment 3.1%

other 12.3%

housing 36.5%

food 22.5%

OFFICE # 363-3871

EGGS MILK BUTTER

The graph shows the Hynsons' budget for one year. If their yearly income is $25,000, how much do they plan to spend on transportation?

From the graph you can see that 10.4% of the Hynsons' income is spent on transportation.

What number is 10.4% of $25,000?

$$n = 10.4\% \text{ of } \$25,000$$
$$= 0.104 \times \$25,000 = \$2600$$

The Hynsons expect to spend $2600 on transportation.

Since 10% of $25,000 is $\frac{1}{10}$ of $25,000, or $2500, the answer is reasonable.

CLASS EXERCISES

What percent of the annual income is planned for the expense?
Use the circle graph above.

1. medical

2. food

3. housing

4. entertainment

5. clothing

6. savings

Find the amount budgeted for the expense. Use the circle graph above.

7. housing

8. food

9. entertainment

10. clothing

11. other

12. medical

PRACTICE

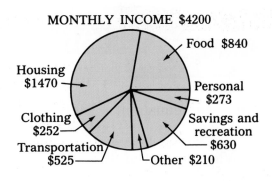

MONTHLY INCOME $4200

Food $840
Housing $1470
Personal $273
Clothing $252
Savings and recreation $630
Transportation $525
Other $210

What percent of the monthly income is budgeted for the expense?

13. housing   **14.** food

15. personal   **16.** transportation

17. clothing   **18.** savings

The Davis family has a monthly income of $1500. The chart at the right shows some of their expenses for May. Use the chart to solve.

ESTIMATE

19. Estimate the amount budgeted for each expense. Is the amount budgeted more or less than the amount spent?

★ **20.** The Lings' groceries bill was $325. They had budgeted $210. Estimate the percent by which they had exceeded the budget.

EXPENSE SUMMARY FOR MAY

EXPENSE	AMOUNT SPENT	PERCENT BUDGETED
Electricity	$48.62	4.0%
Telephone	48.56	2.5%
Gasoline	95.00	6.7%
Miscellaneous	67.50	3.5%

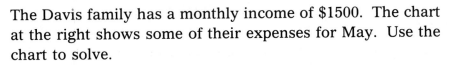

CHECKPOINT 2

Find the new price. *(pages 316–317)*

1. original price: $89.75
   discount rate: 20%

Find the commission.
(pages 318–319)

2. total sales: $725
   commission rate: 15%

Make a chart and solve.
(pages 320–321)

3. P. Cook, M. Tailor, and C. Barber are a cook, a tailor, and a barber. Their jobs do not match their last names. P. Cook is the barber's cousin. Who is the cook?

Use the circle graph above.
(pages 322–325)

4. What percent of the monthly income is budgeted for other?

Extra Practice on page 452

CHAPTER 11 TEST

Write an equation. Then solve. *(pages 304–305)*

1. What percent of 84 is 21?

2. What number is 3.5% of 520?

Find the interest. Round to the nearest cent. *(pages 306–307)*

3. principal: $1700
   rate: $6\frac{1}{2}$%
   time: 3 months

Make a chart to organize the information. Then answer the question. *(pages 308–309)*

4. Pooch's Palace charges $12.95 a day for the first 3 days a dog boards and $11.50 for each day after that. Ken's Kennel charges $15.95 a day for the first 3 days and $8.25 for each day after that. If you need to board your dog for 7 days, which kennel is more economical?

Find the percent of change. *(pages 310–313)*

5. 128 to 70.4 **6.** $6000 to $7920

Find the new price. *(pages 316–319)*

7. original price: $120
   discount rate: 30%

Make a chart to organize the facts. Then answer the question. *(pages 320–321)*

8. Cathy, Carla, and Carol work for an airline. Their jobs are flight attendant, co-pilot, and pilot. Cathy and the co-pilot are neighbors. The pilot and the co-pilot drive to work with Carla. Who is the pilot?

What percent is budgeted for each category? *(pages 322–325)*

9. Housing

10. Clothing

11. Food

12. Savings

Monthly Income: $4800

Clothing, $360
Food, $480
Savings, $720
Housing, $1680
Other, $1560

Extra Practice on page 453

MATHEMATICS and SOCIAL STUDIES

As America has grown and changed, so has the American labor force. Use the graph to help answer questions about American workers.

GROWTH OF U.S. LABOR FORCE 1900–1980

MILLIONS OF WORKERS / YEAR

HOW DOES AMERICA WORK?

1. By about what percent did the labor force grow from 1900 to 1980?

2. During which decade was the percentage increase in the labor force greater, 1930–1940 or 1970–1980?

3. In 1900, women made up 18% of the labor force. In 1980, they made up 42%. How many more women workers were there in 1980 than in 1900?

4. In 1970 there were 140.1 million Americans aged 16 or older. About 80 million of them were in the labor force. To the nearest tenth, what percent was not in the labor force?

5. In 1900, 37.5% of the labor force worked on farms. In 1940, 17% did. Were there more farm workers in 1900 or in 1940?

6. In 1980, schoolteachers made up 2.04% of the labor force. There were 18.7 times as many pupils as teachers in 1980. How many pupils were there?

Enrichment

Some savings accounts earn interest on both the principal and the previously earned interest. This is called **compound interest.** Suppose you deposit $500 in a savings account in which the interest is compounded semiannually at 6%. What will your balance be at the end of one year if no other deposits or withdrawals are made?

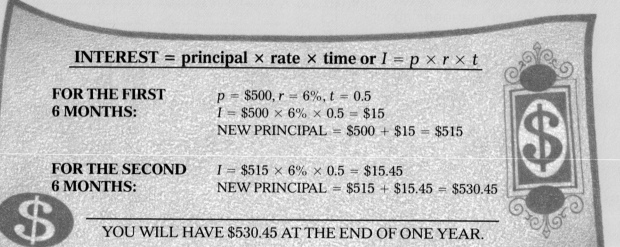

INTEREST = principal × rate × time or $I = p \times r \times t$

FOR THE FIRST 6 MONTHS:
$p = \$500, r = 6\%, t = 0.5$
$I = \$500 \times 6\% \times 0.5 = \$15$
NEW PRINCIPAL $= \$500 + \$15 = \$515$

FOR THE SECOND 6 MONTHS:
$I = \$515 \times 6\% \times 0.5 = \$15.45$
NEW PRINCIPAL $= \$515 + \$15.45 = \$530.45$

YOU WILL HAVE $530.45 AT THE END OF ONE YEAR.

Solve. Round to the nearest cent. A calculator may be helpful.

1. Newtowne Bank pays 5% interest compounded quarterly. If $500 is deposited, what is the balance at the end of one year if no other deposits or withdrawals are made.

2. Sally Barone deposited $1500 in a savings account that earns 8% interest compounded semi-annually. How much will she have at the end of 2 years if she makes no other deposits or withdrawals?

3. Daryl had $2564 in a savings account on April 1. The account earns 6% interest compounded monthly. How much will he have in the account at the end of June if no other deposits or withdrawals are made?

COMPOUND
INTEREST

COMPOUND INTEREST TABLE FOR $1.00

NUMBER OF PERIODS	RATES				
	1.25%	1.5%	2%	2.5%	3%
1	1.0125	1.0150	1.0200	1.0250	1.0300
2	1.0251	1.0302	1.0404	1.0506	1.0609
3	1.0379	1.0456	1.0612	1.0768	1.0927
4	1.0509	1.0613	1.0824	1.1038	1.1255

To compute compound interest quickly, you can use interest tables. Such tables show the interest earned for different rates during different time intervals, or **periods**. Using the table above, you see that $1.00 compounded at 2% interest for 3 periods is $1.0612. Similarly, for $400 the new principal would be $400 × $1.0612 = $424.48

Use the table above to compute the new principal. Round to the nearest cent. A calculator may be helpful.

4. $350 at 2.5% for 4 periods

5. $1000 at 1.25% for 3 periods

6. $625 at 2% for 2 periods

7. $870 at 1.5% for 4 periods

8. $2685 at 1.25% for 1 period

9. $973 at 2.5% for 3 periods

Solve. Round to the nearest cent. A calculator may be helfpul.

10. Use the table above to find the new principal for $100,000 at 3% interest for 4 periods. The simple interest earned at 3% for the same amount is $12,000. How much more is the compound interest earned than the simple interest earned?

11. Which is the more profitable way to invest $6400 for $1\frac{1}{2}$ years: 16% simple interest or 15% compounded semiannually?

12. How long will it take $2560 to grow to $2756.84 at 10% interest compounded quarterly?

Choose the correct answer. Write a, b, c, or d.

Find the unit rate.

1. $448 for 8 days
  a. $448/day
  b. $56/day
  c. $50/day
  d. None of these

2. 322 plants in 14 crates
  a. 20 plants/crate
  b. 14 plants/crate
  c. 23 plants/crate
  d. None of these

Match with the equal ratio that forms a proportion.

3. 10 out of 20 days
  a. $10:20 = 1:2$
  b. $20:10 = 1:2$
  c. $10:20 = 15:25$
  d. None of these

4. 16 lost out of 36
  a. $36:16 = 2:1$
  b. $16:36 = 4:6$
  c. $16:36 = 4:9$
  d. None of these

5. 250 words on a page
  a. $1:250 = 250:500$
  b. $250:1 = 1000:5$
  c. $250:1 = 1000:4$
  d. None of these

Solve.

6. Which is the best buy, a 2 lb bag of carrots for $.72, a 5 lb bag for $1.77, or an 8 lb bag for $2.89?
  a. 2 lb bag for $.72
  b. 5 lb for $1.77
  c. 8 lb bag for $2.89
  d. None of these

7. A store sells cassette tapes at 4 for $12.96. Another store sells the same brand at 5 for $15.95. Which is the better buy?
  a. 4/$12.96
  b. 5/$15.95
  c. Both the same
  d. None of these

Solve.

8. $\frac{a}{78} = \frac{2}{4}$
  a. 34
  b. 36
  c. 44
  d. None of these

9. $\frac{12}{b} = \frac{114}{152}$
  a. 16
  b. 18
  c. 22
  d. None of these

10. $\frac{0.7}{0.42} = \frac{0.6}{c}$
  a. 0.036
  b. 0.36
  c. 3.6
  d. None of these

In a scale drawing of a sailboat, 1 cm represents 20 cm. The length of the boat in the drawing measures 55 cm. The width at the bottom of the sail measures 25 cm. The height of the mast measures 70 cm. What is the measurement of each part of the actual boat?

11. Length of the boat
   a. 110 cm
   b. 1100 cm
   c. 2000 cm
   d. None of these

12. Width of the sail
   a. 500 cm
   b. 250 cm
   c. 100 cm
   d. None of these

13. Height of the mast
   a. 140 cm
   b. 700 cm
   c. 1400 cm
   d. None of these

Each pair of triangles is similar.

14. Find h.

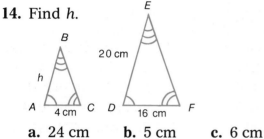

   a. 24 cm   **b.** 5 cm   **c.** 6 cm
   d. None of these

Solve.

15. A total of 6 swim team members won races at the swim meet. This is 12% of the team. How many people are on the swim team?
   a. 18 members
   b. 50 members
   c. 63 members
   d. None of these

LANGUAGE and VOCABULARY REVIEW

Choose the correct word(s) to complete each sentence.

1. When both terms of a fraction are divisible only by 1, the fraction is (a reciprocal, in lowest terms).

2. A sale price is determined by subtracting the (discount, discount rate) from the original price.

3. The amount of money earned for selling a product or providing a service is called a (commission, markup).

4. (Inequalities, Equalities) are statements showing that two quantities are not equal.

5. A (circle graph, budget) is a plan you make to be sure your income will cover your expenses.

SPREADSHEETS

A program called an **electronic spreadsheet** can show a budget of income, expenses, and savings. Each time new amounts are typed in, the computer changes the totals.

The spreadsheet looks like a chart with many boxes. Each box is called a **cell.** To locate each cell, use the column and row name. The spreadsheet below tells about Roger's budget. Cell B4 shows that Roger earned $5.00.

	A	B	C	D	E	F
1		WEEK 1	WEEK 2	WEEK 3	WEEK 4	TOTAL
2	INCOME					
3	ALLOWANCE	$10.00	$10.00	$10.00	$10.00	$40.00
4	JOBS	$ 5.00	$ 0.00	$15.00	$ 5.00	$25.00
5	TOTAL INCOME	?	?	?	?	$65.00
6	EXPENSES					
7	FOOD	$ 4.50	$ 4.50	$ 4.50	$ 4.50	?
8	BUS FARE	$ 4.00	$ 2.00	$ 0.00	$ 7.00	?
9	MOVIES	$ 5.00	$ 3.50	$ 5.00	$ 0.00	?
10	TOTAL EXPENSES	?	?	?	?	?
11	SAVINGS	?	?	?	?	?

The computer will subtract total expenses from total income. Roger saves whatever is left.

1. Complete the spreadsheet above.

A diver dives 12 ft deep, swims up 5 ft, and down another 8 ft. How far beneath the surface is the diver now?

12

PRE-ALGEBRA: INTEGERS

INTEGERS AND ABSOLUTE VALUE

On a cold day, the temperature may drop below zero degrees. Numbers less than zero are **negative numbers.** So far, you have worked mostly with numbers greater than zero. These are called **positive numbers.** Zero is neither positive nor negative. A number line helps you picture these numbers. Negative numbers are shown to the left of zero.

$$\overset{\text{Negative}}{\underset{}{^{-}5 \quad ^{-}4 \quad ^{-}3 \quad ^{-}2 \quad ^{-}1}} \quad \overset{\text{Zero}}{0} \quad \overset{\text{Positive}}{1 \quad 2 \quad 3 \quad 4 \quad 5}$$

Two numbers that are at the same distance from 0 but on opposite sides of 0 are called **opposites.** For example, $^{-}1$ and 1 are opposites. Zero is its own opposite.

The positive numbers 1, 2, 3, . . . and their opposites $^{-}1$, $^{-}2$, $^{-}3$, . . . and zero are called the **integers.**

The **absolute value** of an integer is its distance from zero on the number line. Opposites have the same absolute value.

The absolute value of 0 is 0.   Write $|0| = 0$.

The absolute value of $^{-}5$ is 5.   Write $|^{-}5| = 5$.

The absolute value of 5 is 5.   Write $|5| = 5$.

CLASS EXERCISES

Is the number positive or is it negative? Write *positive* or *negative*.

1. 7   **2.** $^{-}2$ **3.** 12   **4.** 84   **5.** $^{-}72$ **6.** $^{-}100$

Complete.

7. The opposite of 4 is $^{-}4$.
The opposite of $^{-}4$ is ■.
$|4| = |^{-}4| = $ ■

8. The opposite of $^{-}25$ is ■.
The opposite of 25 is ■.
$|^{-}25| = |25| = $ ■

PRACTICE

Write the opposite of the integer.

9. 1   **10.** 7   **11.** 0   **12.** $^-6$ **13.** 8

14. 6   **15.** $^-7$ **16.** $^-8$ **17.** $^-10$ **18.** $^-30$

19. 45   **20.** 72   **21.** $^-17$ **22.** 100   **23.** $^-200$

24. 160   **25.** 240   **26.** 9999   **27.** $^-1000$ **28.** $^-873$

Write the value of n.

29. $n = |65|$ **30.** $n = |^-10|$ **31.** $n = |^-7|$ **32.** $n = |0|$

33. $n = |^-90|$ **34.** $n = |49|$ **35.** $n = |1000|$ **36.** $n = |^-223|$

★ **37.** $n = |^-25| + |47|$ ★ **38.** $n = |7| + |^-15|$ ★ **39.** $n = |^-25| + |25|$

PROBLEM SOLVING APPLICATIONS
Understanding the Problem

Write a positive or negative integer to describe the situation.

40. The shuttle is 6 s into its flight.

41. The temperature is 6° above zero.

42. A diver is 8 m beneath the sea.

43. You owe $5.

44. You live on the 26th floor.

45. The countdown is holding at 15 min before launch.

46. You bought 10 gal of gas.

47. You're 1500 m above sea level.

48. You have $10 in savings.

49. You are $2 short of your goal.

50. The temperature is 3° below zero.

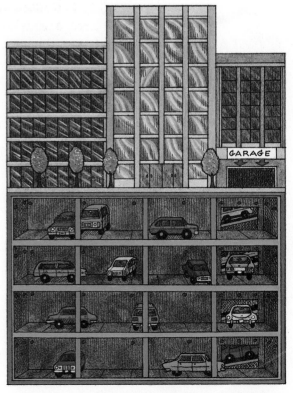

COMPARING AND ORDERING INTEGERS

You can use the number line to compare two integers. The integer to the right on the number line is the greater integer. The integer to the left is the lesser integer.

$$\underset{\begin{array}{ccccccccccccccc} {}^-7 & {}^-6 & {}^-5 & {}^-4 & {}^-3 & {}^-2 & {}^-1 & 0 & 1 & 2 & 3 & 4 & 5 & 6 & 7 \end{array}}{\longleftrightarrow}$$

4 is to the right of $^-2$ $\longrightarrow$ $4 > {}^-2$, or $^-2 < 4$
$^-7$ is to the left of $^-2$ $\longrightarrow$ $^-7 < {}^-2$, or $^-2 > {}^-7$

You can write $^-7 < {}^-2$ and $^-2 < 4$ together as one statement.

$^-7 < {}^-2 < 4$, read $^-2$ *is between* $^-7$ *and 4.*

Ⓜ You can write these numbers in order from least to greatest as $^-7$, $^-2$, 4 by thinking of their order from left to right on the number line.

CLASS EXERCISES

Complete. Write *left* or *right* for the first blank, and < or > for the second blank.

1. $^-1$ is to the ▮ of 0; $^-1$ ▮ 0

2. 0 is to the ▮ of $^-1$; 0 ▮ $^-1$

3. 2 is to the ▮ of $^-1$; 2 ▮ $^-1$

4. $^-1$ is to the ▮ of 2; $^-1$ ▮ 2

5. $^-3$ is to the ▮ of $^-4$; $^-3$ ▮ $^-4$

6. $^-4$ is to the ▮ of 0; $^-4$ ▮ 0

7. 6 is to the ▮ of $^-7$; 6 ▮ $^-7$

8. $^-5$ is to the ▮ of $^-7$; $^-5$ ▮ $^-7$

9. $^-2$ is to the ▮ of 6; $^-2$ ▮ 6

10. 0 is to the ▮ of $^-3$; 0 ▮ $^-3$

PRACTICE

Complete. Write < or >.

11. 0 ▮ 4

12. 0 ▮ $^-4$

13. 4 ▮ 0

14. $^-4$ ▮ 0

15. 2 ▮ 4

16. 4 ▮ 2

17. $^-2$ ▮ 4

18. $^-4$ ▮ $^-2$

19. ⁻2 ▪ ⁻4   **20.** 4 ▪ ⁻2   **21.** ⁻4 ▪ 2   **22.** 0 ▪ ⁻2

23. 3 ▪ ⁻8   **24.** ⁻9 ▪ 0   **25.** ⁻10 ▪ 4   **26.** 10 ▪ ⁻8

27. ⁻6 ▪ ⁻9   **28.** ⁻12 ▪ ⁻5   **29.** ⁻15 ▪ 11   **30.** 16 ▪ ⁻12

31. ⁻19 ▪ ⁻25   **32.** 0 ▪ ⁻34   **33.** ⁻50 ▪ 22   **34.** 99 ▪ ⁻100

Write using two < signs.

35. 2 < 4 and 4 < 6

36. ⁻3 < 0 and 0 < 3

37. ⁻7 < ⁻2 and ⁻2 < 2

38. ⁻6 < ⁻2 and ⁻2 < ⁻1

39. 4 is between 1 and 7

40. 0 is between ⁻5 and 5

41. 3 is between ⁻4 and 4

42. ⁻6 is between ⁻7 and ⁻5

List the integers in order from least to greatest.

43. 5, ⁻4, ⁻7, 0, 3, ⁻1

44. ⁻8, 6, ⁻2, 10, ⁻9, 0

45. ⁻12, 4, 0, ⁻9, ⁻10, 3

46. 0, ⁻1, 6, 2, ⁻15, 12

MENTAL MATH

PROBLEM SOLVING APPLICATIONS
Organizing Data

The elevation of a place is its average height above or below sea level. A positive elevation is above sea level. A negative elevation is below sea level.

List the places in the chart from least to greatest elevation.

47.

LOWEST ELEVATION OF SIX CONTINENTS

CONTINENT	LOWEST ELEVATION IN METERS
Africa	⁻156
Asia	⁻400
Australia	⁻16
Europe	⁻28
North America	⁻86
South America	⁻40

48.

ELEVATION OF SOME CALIFORNIA LOCATIONS

LOCATION	ELEVATION IN METERS
Alameda	9
Brawley	⁻34
Calexico	2
Death Valley	⁻86
El Centro	⁻12
Salton City	⁻70

ADDITION OF INTEGERS

You can show how to add integers by using arrows on a number line. Arrows for adding positive integers point to the right. Arrows for adding negative integers point to the left. Start at 0. The arrow for the first addend is shown in black, the second in color.

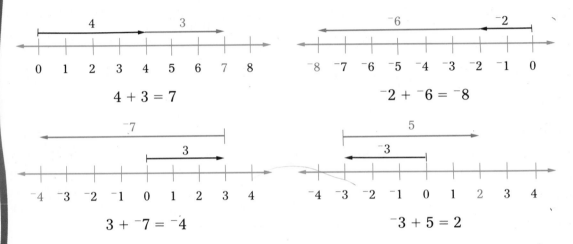

$$4 + 3 = 7$$

$$^-2 + {}^-6 = {}^-8$$

$$3 + {}^-7 = {}^-4$$

$$^-3 + 5 = 2$$

The sum of an integer and its opposite is always zero.

$$4 + {}^-4 = 0 \qquad {}^-7 + 7 = 0 \qquad 0 + 0 = 0$$

- The sum of two positive integers is a positive integer.
- The sum of two negative integers is a negative integer.
- The sum of a positive integer and a negative integer may be a positive integer, a negative integer, or zero.

CLASS EXERCISES

Add. Use a number line if you need help.

1. $1 + 5$
$^-1 + {}^-5$

2. $2 + 5$
$^-2 + {}^-5$

3. $5 + 3$
$^-5 + {}^-3$

4. $2 + 2$
$^-2 + {}^-2$

5. $7 + 1$
$^-7 + {}^-1$

6. $4 + {}^-5$
$^-4 + 5$

7. $^-3 + 7$
$3 + {}^-7$

8. $^-2 + 6$
$2 + {}^-6$

9. $4 + {}^-1$
$^-4 + 1$

10. $9 + {}^-4$
$^-9 + 4$

11. $5 + 9$
$^-5 + {}^-9$

12. $7 + {}^-6$
$^-7 + 6$

13. $8 + 8$
$8 + {}^-8$

14. $6 + 9$
$^-6 + {}^-9$

15. $3 + 3$
$^-3 + 3$

PRACTICE

Add.

16. $^-9 + {}^-9$ **17.** $^-7 + {}^-4$ **18.** $9 + {}^-5$ **19.** $8 + {}^-3$

20. $^-4 + 9$ **21.** $^-8 + {}^-6$ **22.** $3 + {}^-8$ **23.** $^-8 + {}^-5$

24. $6 + {}^-14$ **25.** $^-7 + {}^-16$ **26.** $^-10 + 10$ **27.** $^-14 + {}^-8$

28. $15 + {}^-35$ **29.** $^-14 + 31$ **30.** $^-18 + {}^-45$ **31.** $^-33 + 65$

32. $10 + 2 + 14$ **33.** $^-10 + {}^-7 + {}^-12$ **34.** $^-13 + {}^-11 + {}^-18$

35. $27 + 18 + 35$ **36.** $^-27 + {}^-15 + {}^-34$ **37.** $^-41 + {}^-37 + {}^-13$

Solve the equation.

38. $x + 9 = 23$ **39.** $y - 41 = 50$ **40.** $7z = 49$

41. $w - 12 = 63$ **42.** $4m = 72$ **43.** $\frac{n}{10} = 54$

MIXED REVIEW

PROBLEM SOLVING APPLICATIONS
Simplifying the Problem

Write an integer to represent each number in the problem. Then add the integers and answer the question.

44. You get on an elevator at the 11th floor and go down 7 floors. On what floor are you?

45. You get on an elevator 2 floors below ground level and go up 13 floors. On what floor are you?

★ **46.** You get on an elevator at the 9th floor and go down 10 floors. Then you go up 8 floors. On what floor are you?

★ **47.** You get on an elevator 3 floors below ground level and go up 9 floors. Then you go down 7 floors. On what floor are you?

★ **48.** You get on an elevator at the 12th floor and go down 9 floors. Then you go up 3 floors and down 8 floors. On what floor are you?

SUBTRACTION OF INTEGERS

The temperature was 10°C. Then there was a drop in temperature of 2°C. There are two ways to find the temperature after the drop.

$$10 - 2 = 8 \quad \text{or} \quad 10 + {}^-2 = 8$$

The temperature was 8°C after the drop.

> To subtract an integer, add its opposite.

Here are some other examples.

$$6 - 10 = 6 + {}^-10 = {}^-4 \qquad {}^-6 - 8 = {}^-6 + {}^-8 = {}^-14$$
$$4 - {}^-2 = 4 + 2 = 6 \qquad {}^-7 - {}^-7 = {}^-7 + 7 = 0$$

Scientific calculators have a key that lets you enter a negative number. The ⌐±⌐ or change-sign key will change a number from positive to negative or negative to positive. Here is how to subtract $27 - {}^-65$.

$$27 \; \boxminus \; 65 \; \boxed{±} \; \boxminus \; 92 \qquad \text{The } \boxed{±} \text{ key changes 65 to } {}^-65.$$

CLASS EXERCISES

Complete.

1. $4 - 6 = 4 +$ ▓

2. $4 - {}^-6 = 4 +$ ▓

3. ${}^-8 - 2 = {}^-8 +$ ▓

4. ${}^-8 - {}^-2 = {}^-8 +$ ▓

5. ${}^-2 - 4 = {}^-2 +$ ▓

6. ${}^-8 - {}^-6 = {}^-8 +$ ▓

7. $4 - {}^-4 = 4 +$ ▓

8. $2 - 10 = 2 +$ ▓

9. ${}^-11 - {}^-5 = {}^-11 +$ ▓

Subtract.

10. $8 - 1$
$8 - 0$
$8 - {}^-1$

11. $2 - 2$
$2 - 0$
$2 - {}^-2$

12. ${}^-4 - 1$
${}^-4 - 0$
${}^-4 - {}^-1$

13. ${}^-6 - 2$
${}^-6 - 0$
${}^-6 - {}^-2$

PRACTICE

Subtract.

14. $5 - 9$ 15. $3 - {}^-7$ 16. $14 - {}^-5$ 17. ${}^-17 - 9$

18. ${}^-3 - 8$ 19. ${}^-5 - {}^-8$ 20. ${}^-9 - 12$ 21. ${}^-13 - {}^-4$

22. $0 - 4$ 23. $0 - {}^-7$ 24. $12 - 37$ 25. $42 - {}^-15$

26. ${}^-2 - 0$ 27. ${}^-5 - {}^-5$ 28. $6 - 13$ 29. ${}^-20 - {}^-9$

Add or subtract. Use a calculator with a change-sign key, if possible.

30. $76 + {}^-48$ 31. $56 - {}^-19$ 32. ${}^-34 + 67$

33. ${}^-251 + {}^-666$ 34. ${}^-93 - {}^-115$ 35. ${}^-204 - 188$

CALCULATOR

PROBLEM SOLVING APPLICATIONS
Using Integers

Write the problem as the difference between two integers. Then subtract the integers and answer the question.

36. The greatest recorded drop in temperature is from 7°C to ⁻49°C in a single day at Browning, Montana. What is the difference between these temperatures?

37. The least recorded range of temperatures is from 31°C to 20°C on the island of Saipan. What is the difference between these temperatures?

38. The greatest recorded range of temperatures is from 37°C to ⁻70°C at Verkhoyansk, USSR. What is the difference between these temperatures?

MULTIPLICATION OF INTEGERS

You multiply positive integers just as you multiply whole numbers. For example, $5 \times 2 = 10$.

To multiply a positive and a negative integer, a number line may help. Think of multiplication as repeated addition.

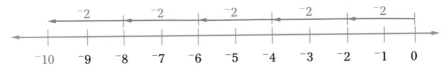

$$5 \times {}^-2 = {}^-10$$

You can use the commutative property with integers.

$$2 \times {}^-5 = {}^-10 \qquad \text{so} \qquad {}^-5 \times 2 = {}^-10$$

To see how to multiply
two negative integers,
look at the pattern of the
products in the series
of multiplications.

$$
\begin{aligned}
{}^-5 \times 2 &= {}^-10 \\
{}^-5 \times 1 &= {}^-5 \\
{}^-5 \times 0 &= 0 \\
{}^-5 \times {}^-1 &= 5 \\
{}^-5 \times {}^-2 &= 10
\end{aligned}
$$

To continue the pattern, these products must be positive.

- The product of two positive or two negative integers is positive.
- The product of a positive integer and a negative integer is negative.
- The product of an integer and zero is zero.

You can estimate a product of integers by rounding. For example, $^-96 \times 23$ is about $^-100 \times 20$, or $^-2000$.

CLASS EXERCISES

Is the product positive or is it negative? Explain how you know.

1. $2 \times {}^-9$ **2.** $^-3 \times 7$ **3.** $^-8 \times {}^-6$ **4.** $^-1 \times {}^-1$

5. $^-4 \times 8$ **6.** $^-9 \times {}^-3$ **7.** $5 \times {}^-6$ **8.** $^-4 \times {}^-10$

PRACTICE

Multiply.

9. $2 \times {}^-1$ **10.** ${}^-6 \times 6$ **11.** ${}^-4 \times {}^-3$ **12.** ${}^-9 \times 0$

13. ${}^-3 \times 8$ **14.** 5×7 **15.** ${}^-8 \times {}^-9$ **16.** $5 \times {}^-9$

17. ${}^-8 \times {}^-5$ **18.** ${}^-1 \times 4$ **19.** 4×0 **20.** $6 \times {}^-2$

21. $10 \times {}^-2$ **22.** ${}^-7 \times {}^-11$ **23.** ${}^-13 \times 2$ **24.** 20×4

25. $2 \times {}^-30$ **26.** ${}^-10 \times {}^-6$ **27.** ${}^-15 \times 3$ **28.** ${}^-6 \times {}^-13$

29. $5 \times {}^-12$ **30.** ${}^-3 \times {}^-17$ **31.** $12 \times {}^-6$ **32.** ${}^-19 \times 0$

Estimate the product.

33. $3 \times {}^-298$ **34.** ${}^-103 \times {}^-76$ **35.** ${}^-224 \times 195$

36. ${}^-43 \times {}^-462$ **37.** $17 \times {}^-391$ **38.** ${}^-1111 \times 567$

ESTIMATE

PROBLEM SOLVING APPLICATIONS
Using a Formula

For each kilometer that you go above the base of Mt. Frosty, the temperature is 3°C colder than at the base of the mountain. Here is a formula for determining the mountain temperature (t) if you know the base temperature (b) and the number of kilometers (n) you are above the base:

$$t = b - (n \times 3)$$

Use the formula to complete the table.

MT. FROSTY TEMPERATURES

	base of mountain	1 km above base	2 km above base	3 km above base	5 km above base
39.	0°C	${}^-3$°C	?	?	?
40.	2°C	${}^-1$°C	?	?	?
41.	${}^-5$°C	?	?	?	?

DIVISION OF INTEGERS

You divide positive integers just as you divide whole numbers. Remember how multiplication and division are related.

$$6 \times 3 = 18 \qquad \text{so} \qquad 18 \div 3 = 6$$

Multiplication and division of integers are related in the same way.

$$6 \times {}^-3 = {}^-18 \qquad \text{so} \qquad {}^-18 \div 3 = {}^-6$$
$${}^-6 \times 3 = {}^-18 \qquad \text{so} \qquad {}^-18 \div {}^-3 = 6$$
$${}^-6 \times {}^-3 = 18 \qquad \text{so} \qquad 18 \div {}^-3 = {}^-6$$

- The quotient of two positive or two negative integers is positive.
- The quotient of a positive integer and a negative integer is negative.

The quotient of zero divided by any other integer is zero.

$$0 \div 8 = 0$$
$$0 \div {}^-5 = 0$$

You cannot divide an integer by zero. You cannot divide 7 by 0, since no number multiplied by zero is 7.

$$7 \div 0 = ? \ \Rightarrow \ ? \times 0 = 7$$

If your calculator does not have a special key for entering negative numbers, divide integers as if they were whole numbers. Then write the quotient as a positive or negative number according to the rules above.

CLASS EXERCISES

Complete.

1. $2 \times 4 = 8$
$8 \div 4 = \blacksquare$

2. $2 \times {}^-4 = {}^-8$
${}^-8 \div {}^-4 = \blacksquare$

3. ${}^-2 \times 4 = {}^-8$
${}^-8 \div 4 = \blacksquare$

4. ${}^-2 \times {}^-4 = 8$
$8 \div {}^-4 = \blacksquare$

Divide.

5. $15 \div 3$
${}^-15 \div 3$

6. $18 \div 9$
$18 \div {}^-9$

7. $21 \div 7$
${}^-21 \div {}^-7$

8. $24 \div 3$
$24 \div {}^-3$

PRACTICE

Divide.

9. ⁻36 ÷ ⁻9	**10.** ⁻48 ÷ 6	**11.** 54 ÷ ⁻9	**12.** ⁻72 ÷ ⁻8
13. ⁻18 ÷ 9	**14.** 16 ÷ ⁻2	**15.** ⁻30 ÷ ⁻5	**16.** 56 ÷ ⁻7
17. ⁻24 ÷ ⁻4	**18.** ⁻64 ÷ 8	**19.** 42 ÷ 6	**20.** 6 ÷ ⁻3
21. 81 ÷ ⁻9	**22.** ⁻7 ÷ 1	**23.** 0 ÷ ⁻9	**24.** ⁻28 ÷ 7
25. ⁻26 ÷ 2	**26.** 84 ÷ ⁻4	**27.** ⁻46 ÷ ⁻2	**28.** ⁻48 ÷ 3

Multiply or divide. Use a calculator with a change-sign key, if possible.

CALCULATOR

29. ⁻768 ÷ 24	**30.** 1440 ÷ ⁻45	**31.** ⁻123 × ⁻206
32. 1653 ÷ ⁻19	**33.** 47 × ⁻513	**34.** ⁻3267 ÷ ⁻99

PROBLEM SOLVING APPLICATIONS
Mental Math, Calculator, or Pencil and Paper

Write an integer to represent the solution to the problem. Use mental math, a calculator, or pencil and paper to solve. Write *M*, *C*, or *P* beside your answer to show the method you chose.

35. A diver went 12 m beneath the surface of the water in 6 min. What was the average change in the diver's position per minute?

36. A woodworking business had a loss of $25 last week and a loss of $17 this week. What is the total loss for both weeks?

37. The temperature dropped ten degrees in 2 h. What was the average change in temperature per hour?

38. A jogger lost an average of 2 lb a month for 1 year. What was the total change in weight?

★ **39.** A business had a loss of $40 in November, a profit of $400 in December, and a loss of $120 in January. What was the average profit or loss per month?

PROBLEM SOLVING
Strategy: Consumer Applications and Tables

1. Understand
2. Plan
3. Work
4. Answer/Check

Many people pay bills by writing checks. Money is deposited into an account and checks are written to show the amount to be withdrawn. The bank sends a regular report, called a *bank statement*, to the customer. Here is how a statement from Ron Scott's bank looked.

CHECKING ACCOUNT SUMMARY				
NEW BALANCE	PREVIOUS BALANCE	DEPOSITS AND CREDITS	RESERVE DEPOSITS	
421.00 =	139.00 +	1000.00 +	0.00	
CHECKS AND DEDUCTIONS	AUTHORIZED PAYMENTS	AUTOMATIC TRANSFERS	SERVICE CHARGES	
− 716.00 −	0.00 +	0.00 −	2.00	

CHECKING TRANSACTIONS				
Date	Checks		Deposits	Balance
2/1	#30	−50.00		89.00
2/8	#31	−25.00		64.00
2/15			700.00	764.00
2/17	#32	−400.00		364.00
2/22			300.00	664.00
2/25	#33	−241.00		423.00
2/26			−2.00 (SERVICE)	421.00

Notice that each check has a number. Also, negative numbers are used to show money taken out of the account. Deposits into the account are shown as positive numbers. This is the way Ron found the total of the checks he had written:

$$\text{Total of checks} = {}^-50.00 + {}^-25.00 + {}^-400 + {}^-241$$
$$= {}^-716.00$$

The total amount withdrawn by check was $716.00.

CLASS EXERCISES

Use the bank statement above. Write an integer to show the withdrawal or deposit.

1. February 17

2. February 25

3. February 1

4. February 8

5. February 15

6. February 22

PRACTICE

Solve.

7. Ron's next check is shown on the right. How will he record it?

8. After check no. 33 Ron's balance was $421. What is Ron's balance after check no. 34?

★**9.** When Jill Scott writes a check she uses a stub like the one on the right to keep a record. What was the previous balance? How much did she deposit? What is her balance after she wrote the check?

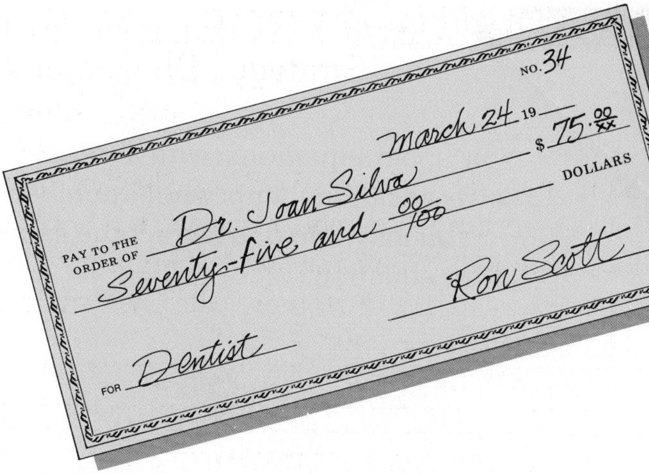

(check image)

NO. 34

march 24 19—— $ 75.⁰⁰ₓₓ

PAY TO THE ORDER OF   Dr. Joan Silva

Seventy-five and ⁰⁰⁄₁₀₀   DOLLARS

                                    Ron Scott

FOR Dentist

	DOLLARS	CENTS
BALANCE BROUGHT FORWARD	150	00
ADD DEPOSITS	87	00
TOTAL		
LESS THIS CHECK	-110	00
BALANCE CARRIED FORWARD		

CHECKPOINT 1

Complete. Write <, >, or =.
(*pages 334–337*)

1. 3 ▓ ⁻4   **2.** ⁻4 ▓ ⁻8

3. ⁻7 ▓ 9   **4.** |⁻10| ▓ |10|

Write the answer. (*pages 338–341*)

5. 3 − 5   **6.** 2 − ⁻10

7. ⁻7 − 6   **8.** ⁻8 − ⁻17

Write the answer. (*pages 342–345*)

9. $3 \times {}^-8$ **10.** ${}^-7 \times {}^-6$

11. ${}^-8 \div 2$ **12.** ${}^-25 \div 5$

Solve. (*pages 346–347*)

13. The balance in an account was $742. Checks for $165 and $280 were written. What is the balance now?

Extra Practice on page 454

SOLVING EQUATIONS
WITH INTEGERS

You solve equations with integers the same way that you solve equations with whole numbers.

You may add or subtract the same integer from both sides of an equation.

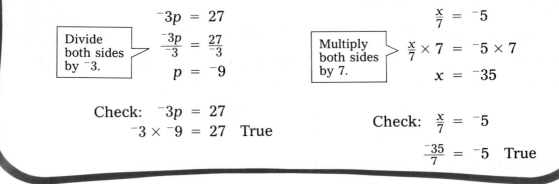

$$a + 5 = {}^-3$$

Subtract 5 from both sides. $\quad a + 5 - 5 = {}^-3 - 5$

$$a = {}^-8$$

Check: $\quad a + 5 = {}^-3$

$\qquad {}^-8 + 5 = {}^-3$ True

$$t - 8 = {}^-2$$

Add 8 to both sides. $\quad t - 8 + 8 = {}^-2 + 8$

$$t = 6$$

Check: $\quad t - 8 = {}^-2$

$\qquad 6 - 8 = {}^-2$ True

You may multiply or divide both sides of an equation by the same integer.

$${}^-3p = 27$$

Divide both sides by ${}^-3$. $\quad \dfrac{{}^-3p}{{}^-3} = \dfrac{27}{{}^-3}$

$$p = {}^-9$$

Check: $\quad {}^-3p = 27$

$\qquad {}^-3 \times {}^-9 = 27$ True

$$\dfrac{x}{7} = {}^-5$$

Multiply both sides by 7. $\quad \dfrac{x}{7} \times 7 = {}^-5 \times 7$

$$x = {}^-35$$

Check: $\quad \dfrac{x}{7} = {}^-5$

$\qquad \dfrac{{}^-35}{7} = {}^-5$ True

CLASS EXERCISES

Complete.

1.
$$y + 8 = 3$$
$$y + 8 - \blacksquare = 3 - \blacksquare$$
$$y = \blacksquare$$

2.
$$c - 3 = {}^-9$$
$$c - 3 + \blacksquare = {}^-9 + \blacksquare$$
$$c = \blacksquare$$

3. $6r = {}^-42$
$$\dfrac{6r}{\blacksquare} = \dfrac{{}^-42}{\blacksquare}$$
$$r = \blacksquare$$

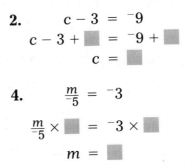

4.
$$\dfrac{m}{{}^-5} = {}^-3$$
$$\dfrac{m}{{}^-5} \times \blacksquare = {}^-3 \times \blacksquare$$
$$m = \blacksquare$$

PRACTICE

Solve the equation.

5. $n + 7 = 3$

6. $x + 9 = {}^-6$

7. $b + 20 = 5$

8. $p - 5 = {}^-4$

9. $z - 7 = {}^-9$

10. $t - 12 = {}^-10$

11. ${}^-4k = 28$

12. $6d = {}^-54$

13. ${}^-8w = {}^-56$

14. $\frac{r}{6} = {}^-3$

15. $\frac{a}{{}^-9} = 7$

16. $\frac{q}{{}^-4} = {}^-8$

17. $b + 38 = {}^-5$

18. $r - 15 = {}^-3$

19. $s + 43 = 0$

20. ${}^-12x = 48$

21. $\frac{y}{12} = {}^-5$

22. ${}^-9t = 9$

23. $\frac{a}{15} = {}^-1$

24. $n - 36 = {}^-17$

25. ${}^-1y = 45$

Write a definition of the term.

26. perpendicular lines

27. parallel lines

28. right triangle

29. congruent figures

**MIXED
REVIEW**

PROBLEM SOLVING APPLICATIONS
Using Equations

Choose an equation to describe the situation. Solve the equation and answer the question.

30. What integer increased by 2 is ${}^-12$?
   a. $n - 2 = {}^-12$ **b.** $n + 2 = {}^-12$ **c.** $2n = {}^-12$

31. What integer divided by 8 is ${}^-16$?
   a. $8n = {}^-16$ **b.** $\frac{n}{{}^-16} = 8$ **c.** $\frac{n}{8} = {}^-16$

32. What integer minus 45 is ${}^-15$?
   a. $n - 45 = {}^-15$ **b.** $n - {}^-15 = 45$ **c.** $\frac{n}{{}^-16} = 45$

33. The product of what integer and ${}^-12$ is 36?
   a. $\frac{n}{{}^-12} = 36$ **b.** ${}^-12n = 36$ **c.** $36n = {}^-12$

GRAPHING ON A COORDINATE PLANE

In the Space Race game, you name the position of your spaceship by an ordered pair of integers on a number grid.

The grid is called the **coordinate plane.** The horizontal number line is the **x-axis.** The vertical number line is the **y-axis.** The point where the axes meet is the **origin.**

Each point in the plane is named by a pair of coordinates. They tell you how far the point is from the origin, and in what direction.

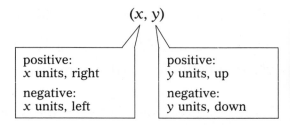

(x, y)

positive:
x units, right

negative:
x units, left

positive:
y units, up

negative:
y units, down

The point $(2, {}^-3)$ is 2 units to the right of the origin and 3 units down.

The point $({}^-2, 3)$ is 2 units to the left of the origin and 3 units up.

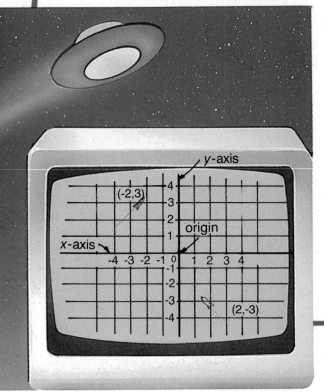

CLASS EXERCISES

Write the coordinates for these directions. Start at the origin.

1. 2 units right and 3 units up

2. 2 units left and 3 units down

3. 4 units right and 2 units down

4. 3 units left and 1 unit up

5. 1 unit right and 0 units up

6. 0 units right and 1 unit down

7. 0 units right and 1 unit up

8. 1 unit left and 0 units up

PRACTICE

Write the letter of the point named by
the coordinates.

9. $(^-3, 7)$ 10. $(3, ^-7)$

11. $(3, 7)$ 12. $(^-3, ^-7)$

13. $(6, ^-2)$ 14. $(^-8, 8)$

15. $(^-5, 0)$ 16. $(0, ^-3)$

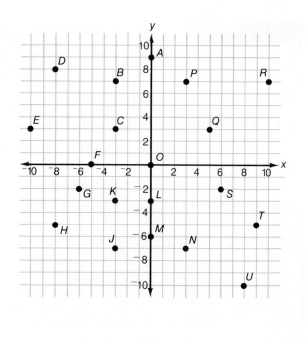

Write the coordinates of the point.

17. Q 18. T 19. A

20. U 21. C 22. M

23. E 24. O 25. G

26. R 27. H 28. K

What is the distance between the points?

29. F, O 30. K, L 31. G, S 32. H, T 33. E, C 34. P, R

35. A, O 36. A, M 37. D, H 38. B, C 39. C, K 40. P, N

PROBLEM SOLVING APPLICATIONS
Classifying Triangles

Graph the set of points on a coordinate plane. Connect the
points in each set. Match the triangle with its description.

41. $(2, 0) (6, 0) (2, 2)$ **A.** acute isosceles

42. $(3, 1) (2, 3) (4, 3)$ **B.** acute scalene

43. $(0, 0) (3, ^-7) (4, 0)$ **C.** right scalene

44. $(^-3, ^-3) (^-1, ^-3) (2, 0)$ **D.** obtuse scalene

45. $(1, 2) (6, 2) (^-3, 7)$

46. $(^-2, 2) (2, ^-1) (2, 7)$

47. $(^-7, ^-2) (^-1, ^-2) (^-4, 6)$

GRAPHING EQUATIONS WITH TWO VARIABLES

When an equation has two variables, you can use a chart to show some of its solutions.

$$x + y = 5$$

x	0	1	2	3	4	5	6	7
y	5	4	3	2	1	0	$^-1$	$^-2$

Ⓜ What patterns do you notice in the chart?

If you write these solutions as ordered pairs, you can show them as points on the coordinate plane.

(0, 5)	(1, 4)	(2, 3)	(3, 2)
(4, 1)	(5, 0)	(6, $^-$1)	(7, $^-$2)

Notice that the points lie on a straight line. You draw the line connecting them to show that the list of solutions is endless. This line is the **graph of the equation.** The equation is called a **linear equation** because its graph is a straight line.

CLASS EXERCISES

Write the solutions as ordered pairs. Then draw the graph of the equation.

1. $x + y = 4$

x	0	1	2	3	4	5	6
y	4	3	2	1	0	$^-1$	$^-2$

2. $x - y = 3$

x	0	1	2	3	4	5	6
y	$^-3$	$^-2$	$^-1$	0	1	2	3

3. $x + 2 = y$

x	0	1	2	3	4	5	6
y	2	3	4	5	6	7	8

4. $x - 5 = y$

x	0	1	2	3	4	5	6
y	$^-5$	$^-4$	$^-3$	$^-2$	$^-1$	0	1

PRACTICE

Copy and complete the chart for the equation. Then draw the graph of the equation.

5. $x + y = 4$

x	0	1	2	3	4	5	6
y	4	3	2	?	?	?	?

6. $x - y = 3$

x	0	1	2	3	4	5	6
y	⁻3	⁻2	?	?	?	?	?

7. $x + 2 = y$

x	0	1	2	3	4	5	6
y	2	3	?	?	?	?	?

8. $x - 5 = y$

x	0	1	2	3	4	5	6
y	⁻5	⁻4	⁻3	?	?	?	?

Use mental math to decide how the *y* values are different from the *x* values in the chart above.

9. Exercise 7

10. Exercise 8

MENTAL MATH

PROBLEM SOLVING APPLICATIONS
Using an Equation

The castle is 150 years older than the fountain. The equation $x - 150 = y$ gives the relationship between their ages. Use this information to solve.

11. Which variable represents the age of the fountain? of the castle?

12. How old was the fountain when the castle was 167 years old?

13. How old was the castle when the fountain was 50 years old?

14. If $x = 100$, $y = ⁻50$. How do you explain the solution $(100, ⁻50)$ in the situation of the castle and the fountain?

★ **15.** Draw the graph of the equation. Mark in color the part of the line with coordinates that represent the ages of the castle and the fountain.

GRAPHING SYSTEMS OF EQUATIONS

Two equations that have the same two variables can be called a **system** of equations. An ordered pair that is a solution of *both* equations is called a **solution of the system.**

If you draw the graphs of two linear equations on the same grid, sometimes the lines intersect. The coordinates of the point of intersection are the solution of the system.

The ordered pair $(4, {}^-2)$ is the solution of the system shown. You can check by substituting 4 for x and ${}^-2$ for y.

Check:
$$x + y = 2 \qquad\qquad x - y = 6$$
$$4 + {}^-2 = 2 \quad \text{True} \qquad 4 - {}^-2 = 6 \quad \text{True}$$

If the coordinates of the intersection of the lines are not integers, you can estimate to the nearest integer.

Sometimes the graphs of two equations are parallel lines. Then there is no point of intersection and the system has no solution.

CLASS EXERCISES

Is the ordered pair a solution of the system of equations? Write *yes* or *no*.

1. $(8, 0)$
$x + y = 8$
$x - y = 8$

2. $(7, {}^-4)$
$x - y = 11$
$x + y = 3$

3. $(4, {}^-2)$
$x - 4 = y$
$x + 2 = y$

4. $(7, 3)$
$x - 8 = y$
$x - 2 = y$

5. $(6, 3)$
$x - y = 3$
$x + y = 9$

6. $(3, 2)$
$x - y = 5$
$x + y = 12$

7. $(11, {}^-3)$
$x - y = 15$
$x + y = 7$

8. $(5, 2)$
$x + y = 10$
$x - y = 2$

PRACTICE

Solve by graphing. Write *no solution* when this is so.

9. $x - y = 9$
$x + y = 3$

10. $x + 3 = y$
$x + 13 = y$

11. $x - 9 = y$
$x + 21 = y$

12. $x + 17 = y$
$x - 9 = y$

13. $x + 25 = y$
$x - y = 5$

14. $x + y = 6$
$x + 2 = y$

15. $x - y = 8$
$x + y = {}^-6$

16. $x + y = 2$
$x - y = 0$

17. $x - y = 4$
$x + y = 6$

★ **18.** $x + 2y = 6$
$x + y = 3$

★ **19.** $2x + y = 12$
$2x - y = 4$

★ **20.** $3x - 3y = 11$
$3x - 3y = 13$

Solve by graphing. Estimate the coordinates to the nearest integer.

21. $x - y = 13$
$x + y = 8$

22. $x - y = 5$
$x + y = 8$

23. $x + y = 2$
$x - y = 5$

PROBLEM SOLVING APPLICATIONS
Using Equations and Graphs

Write two equations with two variables to describe the situation. Then solve the system by graphing.

24. The sum of two integers is 16. Their difference is 8. Name the integers.

25. The sum of two integers is 7. Their difference is 3. Name the integers.

26. One integer is 4 more than another. The sum is 12. Name the integers.

★ **27.** Three times the sum of two integers is 36. Their difference is 10. Name the integers.

★ **28.** The difference of two integers divided by 4 is 2. Their sum is 14. Name the integers.

★ **29.** One fifth times the sum of two integers is 6. Their difference is 8. Name the integers.

GEOMETRIC TRANSFORMATIONS

Some **geometric transformations** change only the position of a figure. The size and shape remain the same.

Triangle A will fit on triangle B if you *slide* it along $\overleftrightarrow{XY}$. This is called a **translation** of triangle A.

Triangle A will fit on triangle B if you *flip* it over $\overleftrightarrow{RS}$. This is a **reflection** of triangle A about line RS.

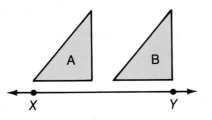 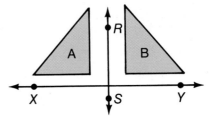

Figure R will fit on figure S if you *turn* it one 90° turn clockwise, on figure T if you turn it two 90° turns clockwise, and on figure U if you turn it three 90° turns clockwise. In each case you will need to use a slide after the turn. These turns are called **rotations** of the figure.

CLASS EXERCISES

Is the motion from A to B a slide, a flip, or a turn?

1.

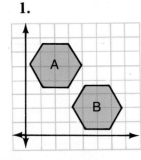

2.

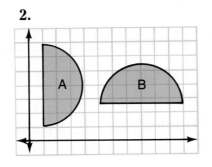

3.

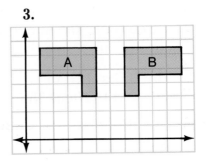

PRACTICE

Can you slide figure A along $\overleftrightarrow{XY}$ to fit on figure B? Write *yes* or *no*.

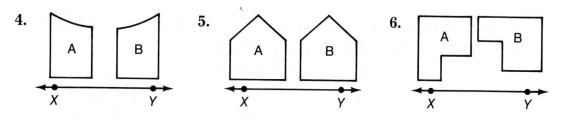

4.   5.   6.

Draw the figure as it will look if you flip it over $\overleftrightarrow{XY}$.

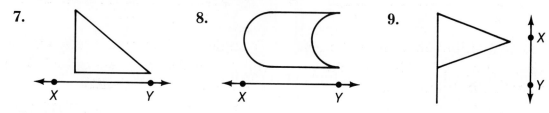

7.   8.   9.

Draw the figure as it will look after one 90° clockwise turn.

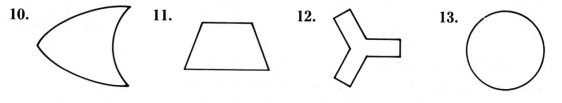

10.   11.   12.   13.

PROBLEM SOLVING APPLICATIONS
Using Transformations

The coordinates of triangle *ABC* are (1, 2), (5, 5), (1, 5). Name its coordinates after the transformation.

14. A slide 2 units to the right.

15. A slide 2 units to the left.

16. A flip over the y-axis.

17. A flip over the x-axis.

★ 18. A 180° turn clockwise around point *A*.

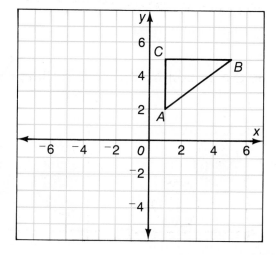

PROBLEM SOLVING
Strategy: Logical Thinking

1. Understand
2. Plan
3. Work
4. Answer/Check

When you find a pattern in a series of numbers, geometric shapes, or events and then decide what will follow next in that pattern, you are using logical thinking. For example, you use logic to predict that this traffic light will turn green next.

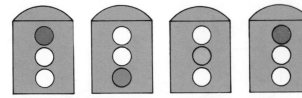

Look for a pattern of slides, flips, or turns in this series of diagrams to predict what will come next.

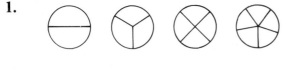

The figure is rotating clockwise in a series of 45° turns. The next shape in the pattern will point directly to the left.

CLASS EXERCISES

Which comes next? Write a or b.

1.   a. b.

2. 1, 9, 25, 49, 81 a. 100 b. 121

3.  a. b.

4. 123, 132, 213, 231, 312 a. 323 b. 321

Draw what comes next in the pattern.

5.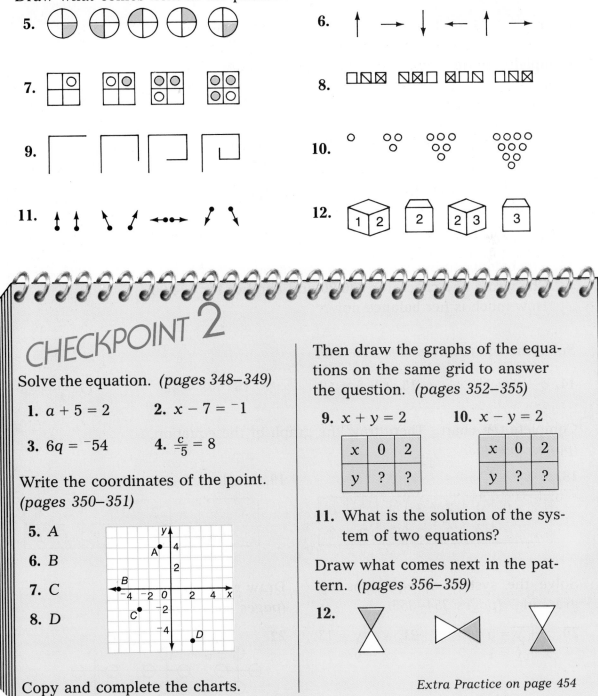

6.

7.

8.

9.

10.

11.

12.

CHECKPOINT 2

Solve the equation. *(pages 348–349)*

1. $a + 5 = 2$ **2.** $x - 7 = {}^-1$

3. $6q = {}^-54$ **4.** $\frac{c}{-5} = 8$

Write the coordinates of the point.
(pages 350–351)

5. A

6. B

7. C

8. D

Copy and complete the charts.

Then draw the graphs of the equations on the same grid to answer the question. *(pages 352–355)*

9. $x + y = 2$ **10.** $x - y = 2$

x	0	2
y	?	?

x	0	2
y	?	?

11. What is the solution of the system of two equations?

Draw what comes next in the pattern. *(pages 356–359)*

12.

Extra Practice on page 454

Complete. Write <, or >, or =. *(pages 334–337)*

1. 5 ▨ $^-$2 **2.** $^-$3 ▨ 1 **3.** $^-$6 ▨ $^-$9 **4.** $|^-3|$ ▨ $|3|$

Write the answer. *(pages 338–345)*

5. $^-5 + ^-3$ **6.** $2 - ^-9$ **7.** $^-5 - 4$ **8.** $^-14 + 6$

9. $5 \times ^-3$ **10.** $^-7 \times ^-4$ **11.** $^-36 \div 9$ **12.** $^-64 \div ^-8$

Solve. *(pages 346–347)*

13. The balance in Secunda's checking account was $378.00. She wrote one check for $36.00 and another for $74.00. How much is her balance now?

Solve the equation. *(pages 348–349)*

14. $q + 4 = 1$ **15.** $r - 5 = ^-2$ **16.** $^-7s = 42$ **17.** $\frac{m}{4} = ^-3$

Complete the chart. Then draw the graph of the equation. *(pages 350–353)*

18. $x + y = 3$

x	0	1	2	3	4	5	6
y	?	?	?	?	?	?	?

19. $x - 4 = y$

x	0	1	2	3	4	5	6
y	?	?	?	?	?	?	?

Solve the system of equations by graphing. *(pages 354–355)*

20. $x + y = 5$
$x - y = 1$

21. $x + y = 13$
$x - y = 7$

Draw what comes next. *(pages 356–359)*

22.

Extra Practice on page 455

MATHEMATICS and
SCIENCE

Scientists sometimes measure temperatures using the Kelvin scale, symbol K. The Kelvin scale uses Celsius degrees, but it starts at a point called *absolute zero,* which is ⁻273.15°C. No temperature can be lower than 0 K. Note that the degree symbol (°) is not used with Kelvin temperature readings.

   To convert Kelvin temperatures to Celsius, subtract 273.15. To convert from Celsius to Kelvin, add 273.15.

The lowest temperature on the surface of Earth was ⁻88°C, recorded in Antarctica. On Mars, the temperature always drops to about 170 K at night.

A MATTER
OF DEGREE

1. Which is colder, a Martian night or the record Antarctic temperature?

2. Earth's record surface temperatures have a range of 146°C. What is Earth's highest recorded temperature?

A mercury thermometer can record temperatures as low as ⁻38.87°C, at which point the mercury freezes. Alcohol freezes at ⁻114.56°C.

3. What is the difference between mercury's freezing point and alcohol's freezing point?

4. Could an alcohol thermometer record the temperature of a Martian night?

Enrichment

When you add, subtract, or multiply two integers, the answer is an integer. But the quotient of two integers is not always an integer.

$$5 + {}^-14 = {}^-9 \qquad {}^-7 - {}^-25 = 18 \qquad {}^-3 \times 17 = {}^-51 \qquad {}^-1 \div 4 = \,?$$

To write the quotient $^-1 \div 4$, you need a different kind of number. A **rational number** is any number that can be written as the quotient of two integers. Remember that 0 can never be used as a divisor. All the following are rational numbers.

$$\frac{^-1}{4} \qquad \frac{10}{7} \qquad {}^-2\frac{1}{2}, \text{ or } \frac{^-5}{2} \qquad 3, \text{ or } \frac{3}{1} \qquad {}^-1.57, \text{ or } \frac{^-157}{100} \qquad 0.\overline{1}, \text{ or } \frac{1}{9}$$

Any repeating decimal represents a rational number. To show a repeating decimal as the quotient of two integers, you can use the facts that $0.\overline{1} = \frac{1}{9}$ and $0.\overline{01} = \frac{1}{99}$.

Numbers such as $\sqrt{2}$, $\sqrt{3}$, and π cannot be written as the quotient of two integers. These are called **irrational numbers**.

$$^-0.\overline{5} = {}^-5 \times 0.\overline{1} = {}^-5 \times \frac{1}{9} = \frac{^-5}{9}$$

$$0.\overline{45} = 45 \times 0.\overline{01} = 45 \times \frac{1}{99} = \frac{45}{99} = \frac{5}{11}$$

RATIONAL NUMBERS

Show that the number is rational by writing it as the quotient of two integers.

1. $4\frac{1}{3}$ 2. $^-7\frac{3}{5}$ 3. 6

4. $^-1$ 5. 0 6. $^-0.7$

7. 0.25 8. $^-1.9$ 9. $0.\overline{2}$

10. $^-0.\overline{3}$ 11. $^-0.\overline{17}$ 12. $0.\overline{06}$

You can add, subtract, multiply, or divide with rational numbers. You decide if the answer is positive or negative the same way that you decide when performing the operations with integers. Here are some examples.

$$\frac{^-7}{9} + \frac{1}{9} = \frac{^-7+1}{9} = \frac{^-6}{9} = \frac{^-2}{3} \qquad\qquad \frac{^-1}{7} - \frac{^-5}{7} = \frac{^-1}{7} + \frac{5}{7} = \frac{4}{7}$$

$$\frac{^-2}{5} \times \frac{^-1}{4} = \frac{2}{20} = \frac{1}{10} \qquad\qquad \frac{^-1}{5} \div \frac{3}{4} = \frac{^-1}{5} \times \frac{4}{3} = \frac{^-4}{15}$$

Add, subtract, multiply, or divide. Write the answer in lowest terms.

13. $\frac{1}{5} + \frac{^-4}{5}$ **14.** $\frac{3}{5} + \frac{^-1}{5}$ **15.** $\frac{^-2}{9} + \frac{5}{9}$ **16.** $\frac{2}{9} - \frac{7}{9}$

17. $\frac{^-1}{4} - \frac{3}{4}$ **18.** $\frac{^-1}{8} - \frac{^-3}{8}$ **19.** $\frac{2}{3} \times \frac{^-1}{3}$ **20.** $\frac{^-1}{2} \times \frac{^-3}{5}$

21. $\frac{^-1}{2} \times \frac{2}{7}$ **22.** $\frac{^-1}{5} \div \frac{^-2}{3}$ **23.** $\frac{1}{2} \div \frac{^-3}{4}$ **24.** $\frac{^-1}{6} \div \frac{1}{2}$

25. $\frac{^-1}{10} \div \frac{^-2}{5}$ **26.** $\frac{^-1}{2} + \frac{^-1}{4} + \frac{^-1}{8}$ **27.** $\frac{^-1}{3} + \frac{^-1}{3} + \frac{^-1}{9}$ **28.** $\frac{^-2}{5} + \frac{^-1}{5} + \frac{4}{5}$

Write *true* or *false*.

29. Every integer is a rational number.

30. The sum of two rational numbers is always a rational number.

31. The difference between two rational numbers is always a rational number.

32. The product of two rational numbers is always a rational number.

33. The quotient of two rational numbers is *not* always a rational number.

Choose the correct answer. Write *a*, *b*, *c*, or *d*.

Find the matching value.

1. 0.03
   a. 30%   **b.** 3%   **c.** 0.3%
   d. None of these

2. $\frac{5}{8}$
   a. 58%   **b.** 625%   **c.** $62\frac{1}{2}$%
   d. None of these

Solve.

3. 1062 people registered to vote. 354 actually voted. What percent voted?
   a. 40%   **b.** $33\frac{1}{3}$%   **c.** 30%   **d.** None of these

Find the answer.

4. What percent of 160 is 8?
   a. 50%   **b.** 5%   **c.** 0.5%
   d. None of these

5. What is 8% of 40?
   a. 32   **b.** 5   **c.** 3.2
   d. None of these

Match the problem to its equation and solution.

6. What number is 125% of 364?
   a. 125 = 364% of *n*; 34.34
   b. 125% of *n* = 365; 292
   c. 125% of 364 = *n*; 455
   d. None of these

7. 60 is what percent of 750?
   a. 60 = *n*% of 750; 8%
   b. 60 of 750 = *n*%; 45,000
   c. 750 − *n*% of 60; 12.5
   d. None of these

Find the interest.

8. principal: $1400
         rate: 12.5%
         time: 1 year
   a. $116.67
   b. $175
   c. $17.50
   d. None of these

9. principal: $500
         rate: 18%
         time: $\frac{1}{2}$ year
   a. $45
   b. $54
   c. $4.50
   d. None of these

10. principal: $15,000
          rate: $12\frac{1}{4}$%
          time: 2 years
   a. $1837
   b. $150.12
   c. $3675
   d. None of these

Make a chart to help you solve the problem.

11. Rent-a-Bus offers three rental plans. Plan 1: $150 for the first 3 h, and $40 per additional hour. Plan 2: $165 for the first 5 h, and $25 per additional hour. Plan 3: $99 for the first 3 h, and $65 per additional hour. Which plan is the most economical for a 10-hour rental?

   a. Plan 1   **b.** Plan 2   **c.** Plan 3   **d.** None of these

Find the percent of change.

12. from 4.8 to 4.5
   a. 0.3%
   b. $4\frac{4}{5}$%
   c. 6.25%
   d. None of these

Find the total cost.

13. marked price: $25.50
    sales tax rate: 6%
   a. $31.50
   b. $25.56
   c. $27.03
   d. None of these

Find the new price.

14. original price: $12.99
    discount rate: $33\frac{1}{3}$%
   a. $8.63
   b. $9.33
   c. $8.66
   d. None of these

Find the commission.

15. total sales: $15,000
    commission rate: 6.5%
   a. $231
   b. $433.33
   c. $975
   d. None of these

LANGUAGE and VOCABULARY REVIEW

Choose the correct word to complete.

prime   integers   negative   equivalent   complementary

1. Numbers less than zero are ___?___ numbers.

2. If the sum of the measures of two angles is 90°, the angles are ___?___.

3. A number having exactly two factors, itself and 1, is ___?___.

4. Fractions that name the same number are ___?___.

COMPUTER
LITERACY

INPUT,
FUNCTIONS

Another BASIC statement is **INPUT.** When you use INPUT, followed by a variable, the computer stops to wait for data to be typed in. A question mark may appear on the screen.

A **function** calls up a formula that is already programmed into the computer. Here are some examples.

> 1. The **ABS** function finds the absolute value of a number.
> 2. The **SQR** function finds the square root of a number.
> 3. The **RND** function displays a random number.
> 4. The **INT** function finds the greatest integer *less than or equal* to a number.

$$INT(3)=3 \quad INT(2.4)=2 \quad INT(-4.5)=-5$$

You can use the INT function to round a decimal to the nearest whole number. To do this, you add 0.5 to the decimal.

$$INT(X + 0.5) \longrightarrow INT(2.1 + 0.5)=INT(2.6) = 2$$
$$INT(3.7 + 0.5)=INT(4.2) = 4$$

Write the output.

1.
```
10 PRINT "WHAT IS YOUR NAME?"
20 INPUT N$          ⟨ Use your name.
30 LET R=INT(5.2)
40 PRINT N$; "YOUR ANSWER IS "
50 PRINT R*15
60 END
```

2.
```
10 LET A=100
20 LET B=150
30 LET C=INT(B/A)
40 PRINT "INT(1.5) = "C
50 END
```

366

13

The National Aquarium in Baltimore is constructed of geometric shapes. What shapes appear in the building? Do any appear to be the same size and shape?

GEOMETRY, SURFACE AREA, AND VOLUME

IDENTIFYING CONGRUENT FIGURES

Figures that have the same size and shape are **congruent.** This means that if one figure is placed on top of the other, there will be an exact match. For example, patterns made from the same stencil are congruent.

Triangles *ABC* and *DEF* at the right are congruent. The symbol △ means *triangle*. You write △*ABC* ≅ △*DEF*.

When referring to congruent polygons, it is customary to list their matching vertexes in the same order. The symbol ⟷ means *corresponds to*.

$$\overline{AB} \longleftrightarrow \overline{DE} \qquad \angle B \longleftrightarrow \angle E$$

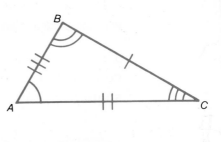
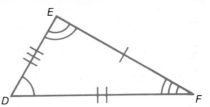

Matching parts of congruent figures are congruent. The marks on the figures at the right are used to indicate corresponding parts, that is, the corresponding sides and the corresponding angles.

$$\overline{AB} \cong \overline{DE} \qquad \angle A \cong \angle D$$
$$\overline{BC} \cong \overline{EF} \qquad \angle B \cong \angle E$$
$$\overline{AC} \cong \overline{DF} \qquad \angle C \cong \angle F$$

CLASS EXERCISES

Complete. △*XYZ* ≅ △*PQR*.

1. ∠X ≅ ▆
2. ∠Z ≅ ▆
3. ∠Y ≅ ▆
4. $\overline{XY}$ ≅ ▆
5. $\overline{YZ}$ ≅ ▆
6. $\overline{XZ}$ ≅ ▆

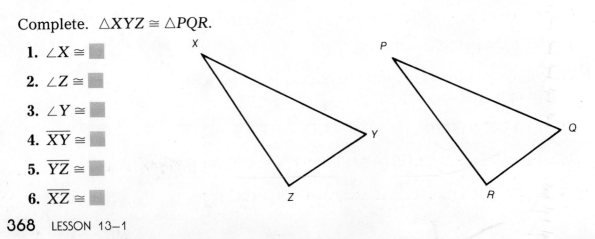

PRACTICE

Complete the statement for each pair of congruent figures.

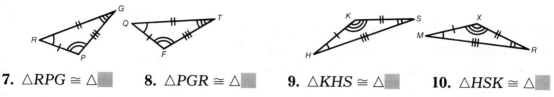

7. $\triangle RPG \cong \triangle$ ▨

8. $\triangle PGR \cong \triangle$ ▨

9. $\triangle KHS \cong \triangle$ ▨

10. $\triangle HSK \cong \triangle$ ▨

Quadrilateral $VRQK \cong$ Quadrilateral $SMHG$.

11. Name the four pairs of corresponding sides.

12. Name the four pairs of corresponding angles.

13. Is it correct to say that $QRVK \cong HMGS$?

14. Is it correct to say that $KQRV \cong GHMS$?

Diagonal $\overline{BD}$ divides parallelogram $ABCD$ into two congruent triangles. $\triangle ABD \cong \triangle CDB$.
Complete the statement.

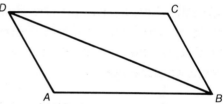

15. $\angle A \cong \angle$ ▨

16. $\overline{AB} \cong$ ▨

17. $\overline{AD} \cong$ ▨

18. $\overline{DB} \cong$ ▨

19. $\angle ADB \cong \angle$ ▨

20. $\angle DBA \cong \angle$ ▨

PROBLEM SOLVING APPLICATIONS
Using Logic

Write *true* or *false*. Give a reason for your answer.

21. All right triangles are congruent.

22. An acute triangle is never congruent to an obtuse triangle.

23. If $\triangle RUN \cong \triangle ACE$, then $\overline{RU} \cong \overline{CE}$.

24. If quadrilateral $BLUE \cong$ quadrilateral $SOCK$, then $\angle B \cong \angle C$.

25. A hexagon is sometimes congruent to a pentagon.

CONSTRUCTING GEOMETRIC FIGURES

A compass and a straightedge are tools used in geometric constructions.

A compass is used to construct a circle or part of a circle, called an **arc.**

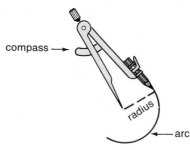

compass →

radius

arc

A straightedge is used to draw a line segment. You may use the edge of a ruler as a straightedge, but do not use the markings.

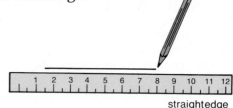

straightedge

You can use a compass to construct a circle with a radius that is congruent to a line segment such as $\overline{AB}$.

First, draw and label Point O.

O

Next, open the compass to the length of $\overline{AB}$.

B
A

Place the point of the compass on O and draw circle O.

O

With a compass and a straightedge you can construct a line segment that is congruent to $\overline{AB}$. First, draw a ray with endpoint Q. Next, open the compass to the length of $\overline{AB}$. Draw an arc that crosses the ray. Label the point of intersection P. $\overline{QP} \cong \overline{AB}$.

$\overline{A\quad B}$

$Q \longrightarrow$

$Q \overset{P}{\longrightarrow}$

CLASS EXERCISES

Use a compass to construct a circle with the radius given.

1. $r = 3$ cm   **2.** $r = 7$ cm   **3.** $r = 2.5$ cm   **4.** $r = 8.6$ cm

PRACTICE

Use a compass and straightedge to construct a line segment congruent to the given line segment.

5. ———————— **6.** ———— **7.** ————————————

Copy the design using a compass and a straightedge.

8. 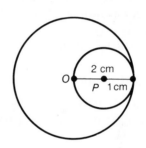 **9.**

Do the construction.

10. Construct a line segment whose length is 2 times the length of $\overline{AB}$.

11. Construct a circle whose radius is congruent to $\overline{AB}$.

12. Construct a circle whose radius is twice as long as $\overline{AB}$.

13. Construct a circle that is congruent to Circle O.

A ——————— B

14. Construct a circle that is congruent to Circle P.

PROBLEM SOLVING APPLICATIONS
Using Geometric Constructions

Geometric constructions are often used in the design of floor tiles.

15. Use a compass and straightedge to copy this design.

16. Use a compass and straightedge to design your own original pattern for floor tiles.

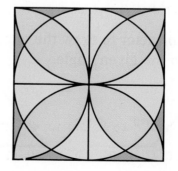

CONSTRUCTING CONGRUENT ANGLES

Geometric constructions are used to draw the finished plans for buildings and machinery. It may be necessary to construct an angle that is congruent to a given angle.

Follow these steps to construct an angle that is congruent to ∠A. First, draw a ray with endpoint O.

Draw an arc with center A. Then with the same radius, draw an arc with center O. Label the intersection P as shown.

Put your compass point at C and open your compass so you can draw an arc through B. Then, with center P and this radius, draw an arc which intersects the other arc at Q. Finally, draw O⃗Q. ∠QOP ≅ ∠A.

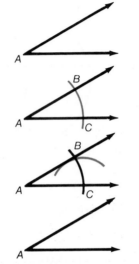
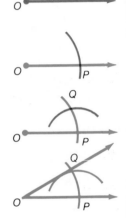

A **straight angle** is an angle with a measure of 180°. The two rays that form a straight angle together form a straight line. You can use this fact to construct the supplement of an angle.

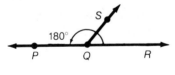

∠PQR is a straight angle.
m∠PQR = 180°.
∠PQS is supplementary to ∠SQR.

CLASS EXERCISES

Use a protractor to draw the angle. Construct an angle congruent to the given angle.

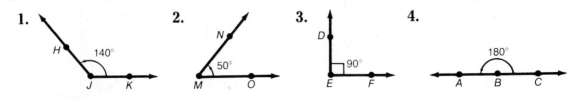

1. *H* 140° *J* *K*

2. *N* 50° *M* *O*

3. *D* 90° *E* *F*

4. 180° *A* *B* *C*

PRACTICE

Use a protractor to draw the angle. Construct an angle that is supplementary to the given angle.

5.

6.

7.

Trace △XYZ. Use your copy of △XYZ to construct an angle with the given measure.

8. $x + y$

9. $2x$

10. $180° - z$

11. $2x - y$

12. $x + y + z$

13. $x + 2z$

Write as a percent.

14. $\frac{6}{10}$

15. $\frac{2}{5}$

16. 0.08

17. $\frac{5}{1000}$

MIXED REVIEW

18. 0.73

19. $\frac{7}{8}$

20. 0.133

21. 3.32

PROBLEM SOLVING APPLICATIONS
Nonroutine Problems

A network is a pattern made up of paths and vertexes. Can the network be drawn without lifting the pencil and without retracing a line segment? Write *yes* or *no*.

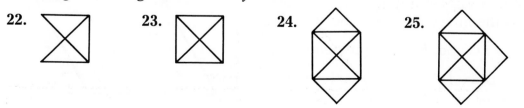

22.

23.

24.

25.

CONSTRUCTING BISECTORS

A **bisector** divides an angle or a line segment into two equal parts.

You can construct an **angle bisector** using a compass and a straightedge.

1. With O as the center, draw an arc that intersects $\overrightarrow{OA}$ at X and $\overrightarrow{OB}$ at Y.

2. Draw an arc with center X and a suitable radius. Draw another arc with Y as center and the same radius that intersects the first arc at C.

3. Draw $\overrightarrow{OC}$. $\overrightarrow{OC}$ bisects $\angle AOB$.
   $\angle AOC \cong \angle COB$.

Think: If you bisect a straight angle, what type of angles are formed?

Here's how you can construct the **perpendicular bisector** of a line segment.

1. Open the compass to a radius that is greater than half the distance from D to E. With D and E as centers, draw arcs that intersect at F and G.

2. Draw $\overline{FG}$. $\overline{FG}$ is the perpendicular bisector of $\overline{DE}$. M is the **midpoint** of $\overline{DE}$. $\overline{DM} \cong \overline{ME}$.

CLASS EXERCISES

Use the figure at the right to complete the statement.

1. E is the midpoint of BD. So $\overline{BE} \cong$ ▨.

2. $\overline{AE} \cong \overline{EC}$. So, E is the midpoint of ▨.

3. $\angle ABD \cong \angle DBC$. So $\overrightarrow{BD}$ is the angle bisector of $\angle$ ▨.

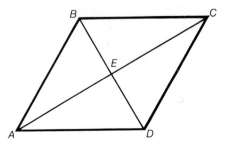

Use a protractor to draw an angle with the given measure. Construct the bisector of the angle.

4. 60°   **5.** 140°   **6.** 42°   **7.** 168°   **8.** 90°

9. 180°   **10.** 30°   **11.** 100°   **12.** 70°   **13.** 48°

Draw the indicated figure. Construct all the angle bisectors.

14. acute triangle   **15.** obtuse triangle   **16.** scalene triangle

17. right triangle   **18.** square   **19.** rectangle

Construct a line segment congruent to the given line segment. Construct the perpendicular bisector of the line segment.

20. _____   **21.** _____   **22.** _____

★**23.** Construct an isosceles right triangle.

★**24.** Construct a right triangle. Construct the perpendicular bisectors of all the sides. What do you notice about the intersection of the bisectors?

PROBLEM SOLVING APPLICATIONS
Nonroutine Problems

Copy the design. Try to color the design using only two colors, and without using the same color on two areas that share a side. Use three or four colors if you can't complete the design with two.

25. 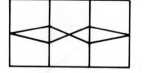   **26.** 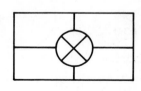   **27.**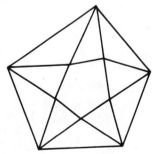

★**28.** Can you draw a design that can't be colored with four colors?

SYMMETRY

If you fold the figure at the right along the dotted line, one side will fit exactly on the other. We say the figure has symmetry with respect to $\overleftrightarrow{AB}$. We refer to $\overleftrightarrow{AB}$ as a **line of symmetry.**

Some figures have more than one line of symmetry. For example:

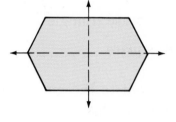

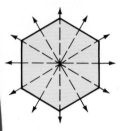

Think: How many lines of symmetry does a circle have?

There is another kind of symmetry, called **point symmetry.** A figure is symmetric with respect to a point if the figure can be turned 180° and match its shape in the original position. In the figure at the right, point O is a point of symmetry. Any segment through O that joins points on the figure will have O as a midpoint.

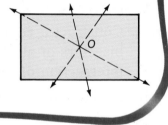

CLASS EXERCISES

Is the dashed line a line of symmetry? Write *yes* or *no*.

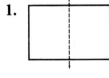

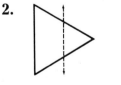

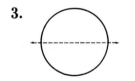

Is the dot a point of symmetry? Write *yes* or *no*.

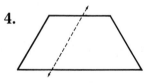

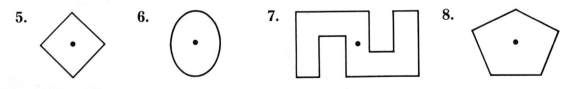

PRACTICE

Does the figure have line symmetry, point symmetry, both, or neither?

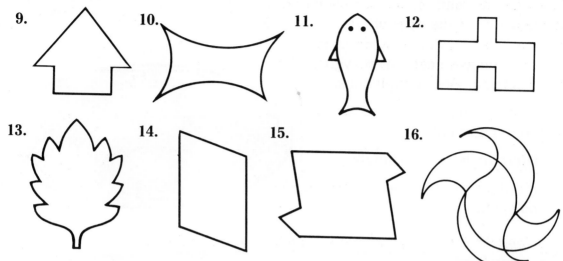

9.

10.

11.

12.

13.

14.

15.

16.

Write *true* or *false*.

MENTAL MATH

17. A regular hexagon has at least six lines of symmetry.

18. An isosceles triangle has two lines of symmetry.

19. A diameter of a circle is in a line of symmetry of that circle.

20. A square has both line and point symmetry.

21. Write seven capital letters of the alphabet that have line symmetry.

PROBLEM SOLVING APPLICATIONS
Using Formulas

Find the area of these symmetric figures.

22.

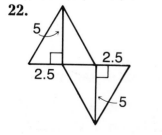

23.

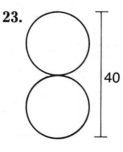

★ 24.

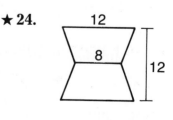

PROBLEM SOLVING
Strategy: Sort and Classify

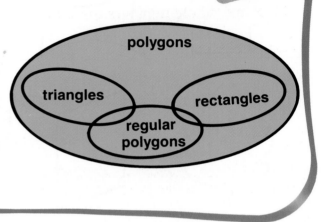

1. Understand
2. Plan
3. Work
4. Answer/Check

You can use Venn diagrams to show many relationships. The diagram at the right shows the following:

1. All triangles, regular polygons, and rectangles are polygons.

2. Some triangles and rectangles are regular polygons.

3. No triangles are rectangles.

4. If a shape is a triangle, then it is a polygon.

CLASS EXERCISES

Tell whether the statement is *true* or *false*, according to the diagram.

1.
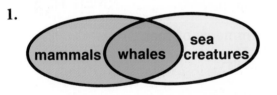

    a. All whales are mammals.
    b. Some sea creatures are mammals.
    c. No whales are sea creatures.

2.
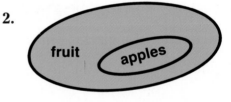

    a. All fruit are apples.
    b. Some apples are fruit.
    c. No fruit are apples.

PRACTICE

Draw a Venn diagram to show the relationship.

3. All hexagons are polygons.

4. No pentagons are hexagons.

5. Some hexagons are regular polygons.

6. If a shape is a regular polygon, then it is a polygon.

Write *true* or *false*.

7. All squares are rhombuses, but not all rhombuses are squares.

8. All odd numbers are less than 75.

9. No odd numbers are divisible by 2.

10. Some whole numbers are both odd and divisible by 10.

Solve. Drawing a diagram will help.

★**11.** There are 23 students. Nine can ski, 8 can skate, and 11 can swim. Two can ski and swim; 3 can ski and skate; none can swim and skate. None can do all three. How many do nothing but skate? nothing but ski? nothing but swim?

CHECKPOINT 1

Write the congruent angle or side.
(pages 368–369)

$ABCD \cong PQRS$

1. $\angle A$ **2.** $\angle S$ **3.** $\overline{BC}$ **4.** $\overline{SR}$

Do the construction.
(pages 370–371)

5. Construct a line segment $\overline{PQ}$.

6. Construct a circle whose radius is congruent to $\overline{PQ}$.

Use a protractor to draw the angle. Then construct a congruent angle and the angle bisector.
(pages 372–375)

7. 140°   **8.** 80°   **9.** 68°   **10.** 90°

Does the figure have line symmetry, point symmetry, or both?
(pages 376–377)

11.   **12.**

Write *true* or *false*.
(pages 378–379)

13. No squares are parallelograms.

14. Some multiples of 5 are also multiples of 4.

Extra Practice on page 456

CLASSIFYING GEOMETRIC SHAPES

Figures that have three dimensions, that is length, width, and height, are called **space figures.** The flat surfaces that form many of these shapes are called **faces.** Two faces intersect at an **edge.** Three or more edges intersect at a vertex.

A **pyramid** is a figure with four or more faces. One face of the pyramid is called a **base.** The base can be any polygon. The other faces of the pyramid are triangles.

A **prism** has two congruent parallel bases. Its bases can be any polygon and its other faces are rectangles.

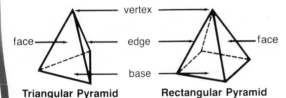

Triangular Pyramid	**Rectangular Pyramid**

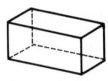

Triangular Prism	**Rectangular Prism**

A **cylinder** has two circular bases; a **cone** has one; a **sphere** has none.

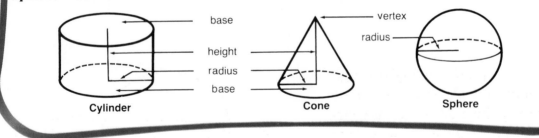

Cylinder	**Cone**	**Sphere**

CLASS EXERCISES

What shape would be formed by folding and taping the pattern together?

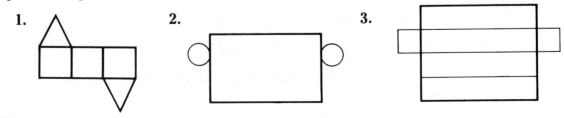

1.

2.

3.

PRACTICE

Write *true* or *false*.

4. A rectangular prism has six faces.

5. The edges of a cube are congruent.

6. A triangular prism has six faces.

7. A cube is a prism.

8. A sphere has no base.

9. All prisms are cubes.

10. A sphere has no edges.

11. All spheres are the same size.

12. A cylinder has no vertex.

13. A cube has six congruent faces.

14. All the faces of a pyramid are triangles.

15. All the faces of a prism are rectangles.

16. A sphere has no faces.

17. A cone has a radius.

18. The bases of a triangular prism are triangles.

19. All the faces of a triangular prism are rectangles.

20. The two bases of a cylinder may be different sizes.

21. A rectangular prism has three pairs of congruent faces.

PROBLEM SOLVING APPLICATIONS
Using a Diagram

Think of a plane slicing through the center of a sphere. The shape formed by the intersection is a circle. The circle is a **cross section** of the sphere.

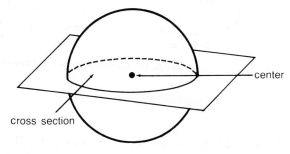

Name the cross section.

22. A cylinder sliced perpendicular to its bases

23. A triangular prism sliced parallel to its bases

24. A square pyramid sliced parallel to the base

25. A triangular pyramid sliced perpendicular to the base and through a vertex

SURFACE AREA:
PRISMS AND PYRAMIDS

The **surface area** of a space figure is the sum of the areas of its faces and its base.

If you cut out a figure like the one shown and fold along the dotted lines, you will have a pyramid with a square base.

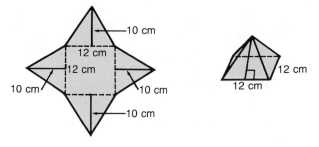

In the pyramid above, the four triangular faces are congruent. So, the surface area is equal to the area of the base plus 4 times the area of one of the triangles.

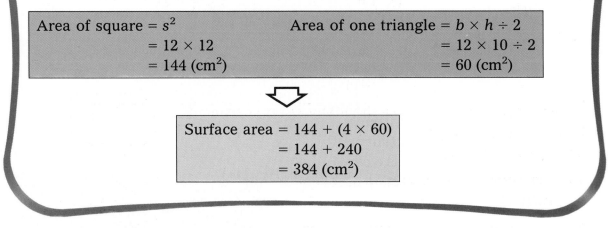

Area of square $= s^2$	Area of one triangle $= b \times h \div 2$
$= 12 \times 12$	$= 12 \times 10 \div 2$
$= 144 \ (cm^2)$	$= 60 \ (cm^2)$

Surface area $= 144 + (4 \times 60)$
$= 144 + 240$
$= 384 \ (cm^2)$

CLASS EXERCISES

What is the total area?

1. Top and bottom

2. Four sides

3. Surface area

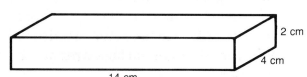

PRACTICE

What is the surface area?

4.
2 cm   2 cm   2 cm   2 cm   2 cm
14 cm

5.
1 m   1 m   1 m   1 m   1 m   1 m

6.
20 cm   20 cm   20 cm   17 cm   17 cm

7.
5 m   10 m   15 m

8.
3 cm   3 cm   3 cm

★9.
5 cm   3 cm   2 cm   8 cm

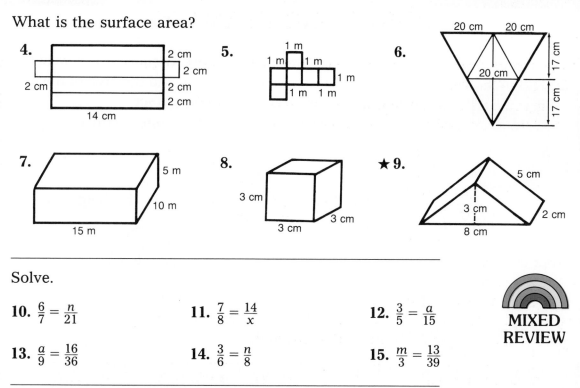

Solve.

10. $\frac{6}{7} = \frac{n}{21}$

11. $\frac{7}{8} = \frac{14}{x}$

12. $\frac{3}{5} = \frac{a}{15}$

13. $\frac{a}{9} = \frac{16}{36}$

14. $\frac{3}{6} = \frac{n}{8}$

15. $\frac{m}{3} = \frac{13}{39}$

MIXED REVIEW

PROBLEM SOLVING APPLICATIONS
Using Formulas

A decorator wishes to make the lobby of an apartment building more attractive. The dimensions of the lobby are given at the right.

5 m   6 m   6 m

16. The floor is to be carpeted. What is the area of the floor?

17. One wall is to get mirrored tiles. What is the area of one wall?

★18. The three walls that are not mirrored and the ceiling are to be painted. About 30% of the three walls is used for an entrance and for windows. What is the total surface area to be painted?

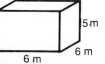

SURFACE AREA: CYLINDERS

The surface area of a cylinder is equal to the sum of the areas of the two circular bases and the area of the rectangle that forms the curved surface.

The base of the rectangle is equal to the circumference of the circular base.

$$base = 2 \times \pi \times r$$

The height of the rectangle is the height of the cylinder.

Area of bases:
$$A = 2 \times (\pi \times r^2)$$
$$\approx 2 \times 3.14 \times 36 = 226.08 \text{ (cm}^2)$$

Area of curved surface:
$$A = (2 \times \pi \times r) \times h$$
$$\approx 2 \times 3.14 \times 6 \times 10 = 376.80 \text{ (cm}^2)$$

Surface Area: 226.08
              +376.80
              _____
               602.88 (cm²)

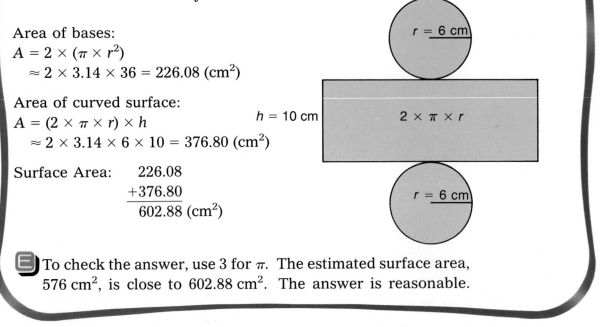

To check the answer, use 3 for π. The estimated surface area, 576 cm², is close to 602.88 cm². The answer is reasonable.

CLASS EXERCISES

Complete.

1. Area of two bases = $2 \times \pi \times \blacksquare^2 = \blacksquare$

2. Circumference = $2 \times \pi \times \blacksquare = \blacksquare$

3. Area of curved surface = circumference $\times \blacksquare = \blacksquare$

4. Surface area = $\blacksquare + \blacksquare = \blacksquare$

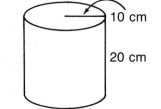

PRACTICE

Find the surface area. Use $\pi \approx 3.14$.

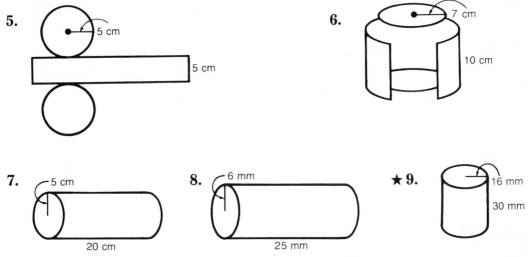

5. 5 cm · 5 cm

6. 7 cm · 10 cm

7. 5 cm · 20 cm

8. 6 mm · 25 mm

★9. 16 mm · 30 mm

Find the surface area of the cylinder. Use $\pi \approx 3.14$. Estimate to check your answer.

10. $r = 7; \quad h = 18$

11. $r = 10.5; \quad h = 4$

★12. $d = 20; \quad h = 11$

★13. $d = 70; \quad h = 20.5$

ESTIMATE

PROBLEM SOLVING APPLICATIONS
Using a Formula

Find the surface area. Use $\pi \approx 3.14$.

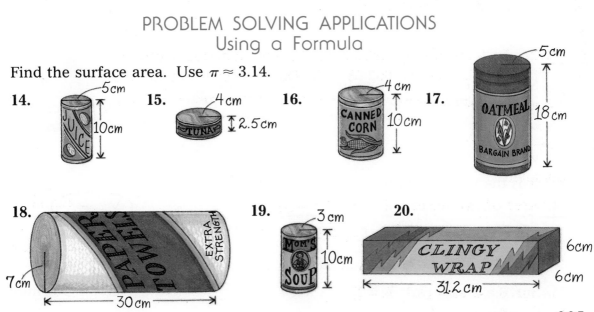

14. JUICE 5 cm · 10 cm

15. TUNA 4 cm · 2.5 cm

16. CANNED CORN 4 cm · 10 cm

17. OATMEAL BARGAIN BRAND 5 cm · 18 cm

18. PAPER TOWELS EXTRA STRENGTH 7 cm · 30 cm

19. MOM'S SOUP 3 cm · 10 cm

20. CLINGY WRAP 6 cm · 6 cm · 31.2 cm

VOLUMES OF PRISMS

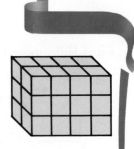

Volume is the amount of space contained in a space figure. Volume is measured in cubic units. Some standard units for measuring volume are cubic meters, m³, cubic centimeters, cm³, and cubic millimeters, mm³.

The volume of the rectangular prism at the right is 24 cubic units. Each layer has 4×2 or 8 cubic units. The volume of any prism equals the area of the base times the height.

Volume (V) = Area of base (B) × height (h)

$$
\begin{aligned}
V &= B \times h \\
&= l \times w \times h \\
&= 2 \times 4 \times 3 \\
&= 24 \text{ cubic units}
\end{aligned}
$$

Similarly, the volume of a triangular prism can be found.

$$
\begin{aligned}
V &= B \times h \\
&= (4.2 \times 10.9 \div 2) \times (6) \\
&= 137.34 \ (cm^3)
\end{aligned}
$$

You can think of this triangular prism as about half of the rectangular prism shown. To estimate the volume of the triangular prism, multiply to find the volume of the rectangular prism and divide by 2.

$$
\begin{aligned}
6 \times 4 \times 11 &= 264 \ (cm^3) \\
264 \div 2 &= 132 \ (cm^3)
\end{aligned}
$$

Since the estimate is close to 137.34 cm³, your answer is reasonable.

CLASS EXERCISES

What is the volume of the prism?

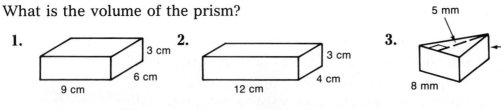

1.
3 cm
6 cm
9 cm

2.
3 cm
4 cm
12 cm

3.
5 mm
6 mm
8 mm

$V = 9 \times 6 \times 3 = $ ▓ cm^3 $V = 12 \times 3 \times 4 = $ ▓ cm^3 $V = (5 \times 8 \div 2) \times 6 = $ ▓ mm^3

PRACTICE

Find the volume of the prism.

4. Area of Base: 26 cm² height: 6 cm

5. Area of Base: 3 m² height: 2 m

6. Area of Base: 20 mm² height: 15 mm

7.
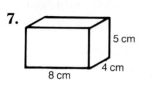

8.
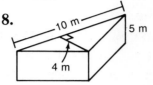

9.
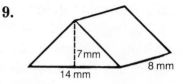

Use estimation to solve.

10. Estimate the overall volume of the figure.

11. Estimate the volume of the portion removed from the figure.

12. Estimate the volume of the figure.

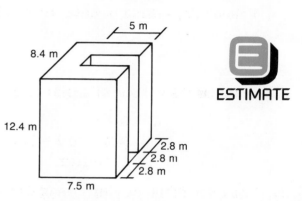

ESTIMATE

PROBLEM SOLVING APPLICATIONS
Pencil and Paper, Calculator, or Estimation

Use pencil and paper, a calculator, or estimation to solve. Write *P*, *C*, or *E* next to your answer to tell which method you used.

13. A prism has a height of 8 m and a volume of 68 m³. What is the area of its base?

14. A rectangular prism has a base that measures 20 cm by 35 cm. The prism's volume is 10,990 cm³. What is its height?

★ **15.** Bill has an aquarium 30 cm long, 10 cm wide and 15 cm deep. How many cubic centimeters of water are needed to fill the aquarium? If Bill buys a new aquarium that is twice as wide, twice as long, and twice as deep, what will the ratio of the new volume be to the old?

VOLUMES OF CYLINDERS

The planter has a base with a radius of 20 cm. It is 35 cm high.
To find how much it will hold, use the volume formula.

Volume = Area of Base × height
$$V = B \times h$$

First find the area of the base.

$$A = \pi \times r^2$$
$$\approx 3.14 \times 20^2$$
$$\approx 3.14 \times 400$$
$$\approx 1256 \ (cm^2)$$

Next, substitute 1256 for B and 35 for h in the formula.

$$V = B \times h$$
$$\approx 1256 \times 35$$
$$\approx 43{,}960 \ (cm^3)$$

The planter holds about 43,960 cm³.

M **Think:** Use mental math to decide what happens to the volume if you use 3 for π in the problem above.

CLASS EXERCISES

Find the area of the base, B, for a cylinder with the given radius. Use $\pi \approx 3.14$.

1. $r = 4$ m

2. $r = 8$ m

3. $r = 11$ cm

4. $r = 22$ cm

5. $r = 7.5$ cm

6. $r = 30$ mm

7. $r = 48.6$ mm

8. $r = 10.5$ m

Complete.

9. $B = 153.86$ cm², $h = 10$ cm
$V = $ ▮ cm³

10. $B = 314$ cm², $h = 15$ cm
$V = $ ▮ cm³

PRACTICE

Find the volume of the cylinder. Use $\pi \approx 3.14$. Round
answers to the nearest hundredth.

11. $B = 75$ cm^2
$h = 10$ cm

12. $B = 100$ cm^2
$h = 24$ cm

13. $r = 8$ m
$h = 40$ m

14. $r = 35$ mm
$h = 120$ mm

★ **15.** $d = 25$ cm
$h = 50$ cm

★ **16.** $d = 1.8$ cm
$h = 3.5$ cm

17.

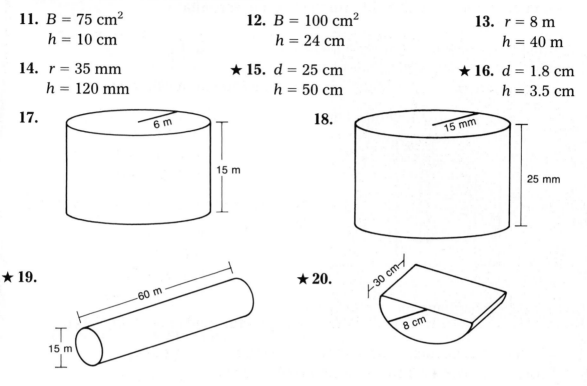

18.

★ **19.**

★ **20.**

21. You know that $\pi \approx 3.14159265$. Without calculating,
write the following approximations for π in the order in
which they would be used to get the most precise answer
for any volume.

MENTAL MATH

$$3\tfrac{1}{7} \qquad 3.14 \qquad 3 \qquad 3.142$$

PROBLEM SOLVING APPLICATIONS
Using Formulas

Solve. Round answers to the nearest hundredth if necessary.

22. A cylindrical gas tank is 1.8 m
long. The base has a radius of
0.6 m. What is the volume of the
gas tank?

★ **23.** A 1000 cm^3 container holds 1 L.
About how many liters will a cylinder hold if it has a radius of 2 m
and a height of 0.5 m?

PROBLEM SOLVING
Strategy: Drawing a Diagram

Sometimes drawing a diagram can help you to see what you need to do to solve a problem.

Suppose you want to make a picture frame that is 12 cm wide by 17 cm long. You plan to use molding that is 5 cm wide. What is the length of the molding that you will need?

Draw a diagram of the picture and frame.

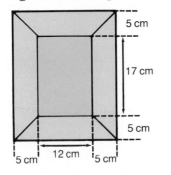

5 cm

17 cm

5 cm

5 cm   12 cm   5 cm

The diagram shows that the frame adds 10 cm to both the length and the width of the picture.

The frame must have these dimensions:

width = 12 + 10 = 22 (cm)
length = 17 + 10 = 27 (cm)

Perimeter = (2 × 22) + (2 × 27)
= 44 + 54
= 98 (cm)

You will need a piece of molding 98 cm long to make the frame.

CLASS EXERCISES

The Jacksons are buying a rug 3 m wide by 4 m long for a room that is 4 m by 5 m.
Copy and complete the diagram to solve.

1. What is the area of the rug?

2. What is the area of the floor?

3. What is the area that will not be covered by the rug?

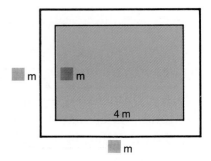

m   m

4 m

m

PRACTICE

Eight basketball teams played in a tournament. Here are the results of the first round of play.

Game 1:	Condors beat the Dragons.
Game 2:	Falcons lost to the Panthers.
Game 3:	Eagles scored two points more than the Jaguars.
Game 4:	Ravens lost to the Bears.

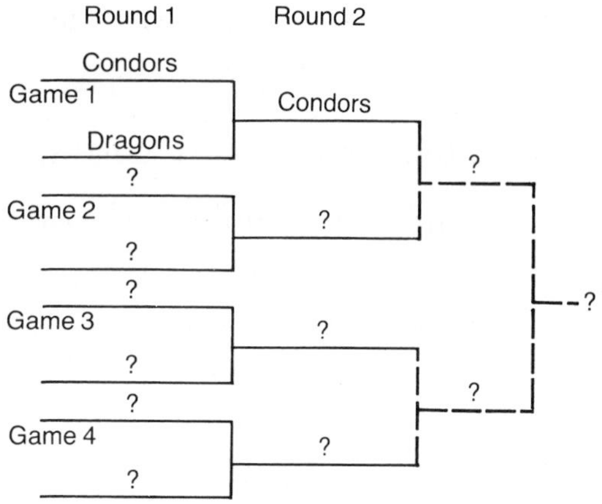

In Round 2 the winner of Game 1 lost to the winner of Game 2. The winner of Game 3 beat the winner of Game 4. The team that beat the Condors in Round 2 won the tournament.

4. Copy and complete the diagram to show who won the tournament.

CHECKPOINT 2

Write *true* or *false*. *(pages 380–381)*

1. A sphere has no faces.

2. A cube has six faces.

What is the surface area? *(pages 382–385)*

3.
25 mm
10 mm

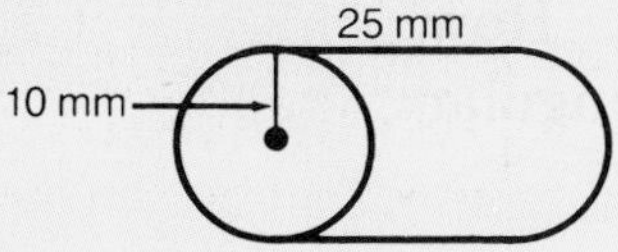

What is the volume? Use $\pi \approx 3.14$. *(pages 386–389)*

4. rectangular prism: $B = 113.04 \text{ m}^2$ $h = 10 \text{ m}$

Use a diagram to solve. *(pages 390–391)*

5. A gallon of paint will cover about 400 ft² of wall. How many gallons will be needed to paint the walls of a rectangular room that is 30 ft by 18 ft and has a 12 ft ceiling?

Extra Practice on page 456

Write the answer. $\triangle BJS \cong \triangle TDW$ *(pages 368–369)*

1. Name the three pairs of corresponding angles.

2. Name the three pairs of corresponding sides.

Draw an angle with the given measure. Construct the angle bisector. *(pages 370–375)*

3. 45°   **4.** 120°

Does the figure have line symmetry, point symmetry, both, or neither? *(pages 376–377)*

5.   **6.**

Write *true* or *false*. *(pages 378–379)*

7. All triangles are isosceles.

8. Some multiples of 2 are multiples of 3.

What is the surface area? Use $\pi \approx 3.14$. *(pages 380–385)*

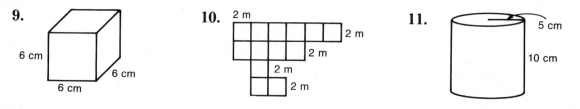

9. 6 cm, 6 cm, 6 cm

10. 2 m, 2 m, 2 m, 2 m, 2 m

11. 5 cm, 10 cm

Find the volume. Use $\pi \approx 3.14$. *(pages 386–389)*

12. rectangular prism:
  $l = 5$ cm; $w = 3$ cm
  $h = 4$ cm

13. triangular prism:
  $B = 48$ m^2
  $h = 7$ m

14. cylinder:
  $B = 144$ mm^2
  $h = 13$ mm

Make a diagram to solve. *(pages 390–391)*

15. One roll of wallpaper will cover 300 ft^2 of wall. How many rolls are needed to paper the walls of a rectangular room that is 23 ft by 17 ft and has a 13 ft ceiling?

Extra Practice on page 457

MATHEMATICS and SHOP

A natural way to describe an object is to draw it. Technical drawings are used to describe objects clearly and precisely.

Special lines are used in technical drawing. The *outline* and visible edges of a figure are shown by solid lines. *Hidden lines* are shown by evenly spread dashes.

They indicate a part of a figure that cannot be seen in the view. *Center lines* are shown by short and long dashes.

Outline —————

Hidden — — — —

Center ———

HOW DO YOU SEE IT?

Match the technical drawing with the figure.

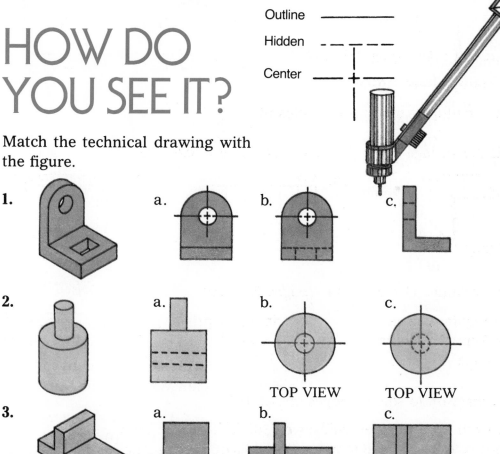

1.   a.   b.   c.

2.   a.   b. TOP VIEW   c. TOP VIEW

3.   a.   b.   c. TOP VIEW

Enrichment

In a right triangle, the side opposite the right angle is called the **hypotenuse**. It is always the longest side. The other two sides are called **legs**.

Over 2500 years ago, a Greek mathematician named Pythagoras proved an important property relating the sides of right triangles. This property is called the **Pythagorean theorem:** In a right triangle, the square of the length of the hypotenuse is equal to the sum of the squares of the lengths of the other two sides. In general, if $\triangle ABC$ is a right triangle with legs a and b and hypotenuse c, then $c^2 = a^2 + b^2$.

If you know the lengths of the sides of a triangle, you can use the Pythagorean theorem to decide if it is a right triangle.

$$c^2 = a^2 + b^2$$
$$13^2 = 5^2 + 12^2$$
$$169 = 25 + 144 \text{ True}$$

The triangle is a right triangle.

THE PYTHAGOREAN THEOREM

Is a triangle with sides of the given lengths a right triangle? Write *Yes* or *No*.

1. 3, 4, 5	**2.** 4, 5, 6
3. 6, 8, 10	**4.** 9, 12, 15
5. 5, 12, 14	**6.** 8, 9, 14
7. 8, 15, 17	**8.** 12, 16, 20
9. 25, 7, 24	**10.** 20, 11, 21

394

If you know the lengths of two sides of a right triangle, you can use the Pythagorean theorem to calculate the length of the third side.

$$c^2 = a^2 + b^2$$
$$c^2 = 12^2 + 16^2$$
$$c^2 = 144 + 256$$
$$c^2 = 400$$
$$c = \sqrt{400} = 20$$

The length of the hypotenuse is 20.

What is the length of the hypotenuse? A calculator may be helpful.

11.   **12.**   **13.**

14. side $a = 7$
side $b = 24$

15. side $a = 18$
side $b = 24$

16. side $a = 16$
side $b = 30$

What is the length of a diagonal of the rectangle?

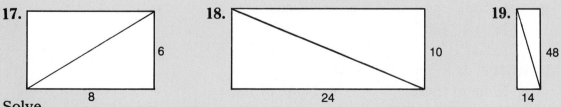

17.   **18.**   **19.**

Solve.

20. Your garden is in the shape of a rectangle that measures 24 m by 32 m. You want to put a diagonal walk from corner to corner across the garden. What will be the length of the walk?

21. A vacant lot is in the shape of a rectangle that measures 20 m by 21 m. How many fewer meters do you walk if you walk diagonally across the lot rather than along two sides of the lot?

CUMULATIVE REVIEW

Choose the correct answer. Write *a*, *b*, *c*, or *d*.

Order the integers from least to greatest.

1. 3, 11, 8, ⁻3, ⁻11, ⁻8
   a. 3, ⁻3, 8, ⁻8, 11, ⁻11
   b. ⁻11, ⁻8, ⁻3, 3, 8, 11
   c. 3, 8, 11, ⁻11, ⁻8, ⁻3
   d. None of these

2. 4, ⁻14, ⁻7, ⁻10, 0, ⁻2
   a. ⁻14, ⁻10, ⁻7, ⁻2, 0, 4
   b. 0, ⁻2, 4, ⁻7, ⁻10, ⁻14
   c. ⁻2, ⁻7, ⁻10, ⁻14, 0, 4
   d. None of these

3. ⁻5, 9, ⁻12, ⁻13, ⁻15, 1
   a. 1, ⁻5, 9, ⁻12, 13, ⁻15
   b ⁻15, ⁻13, ⁻12, ⁻5, 1, 9
   c. ⁻5, ⁻12, ⁻13, ⁻15, ⁻9, 1
   d. None of these

4. 7, ⁻5, 8, ⁻2, 0, 11, ⁻6, 1
   a. ⁻6, ⁻5, ⁻2, 0, 7, 8, 11
   b. 0, ⁻2, ⁻5, ⁻6, 7, 8, 11
   c. 11, 8, 7, 0, ⁻2, ⁻5, ⁻6
   d. None of these

Find the correct expression.

5. ⁻3 < 8 and 9 > 8
   a. ⁻3 > 8 > 9
   b. ⁻3 < 8 < 9
   c. 8 < 9 < ⁻3
   d. None of these

6. 0 > ⁻7 and 7 > 0
   a. 7 < 0 < ⁻7
   b. 0 < ⁻7 < 7
   c. 7 > 0 > ⁻7
   d. None of these

7. ⁻1 > ⁻5 and ⁻1 < 2
   a. ⁻1 < 2 < ⁻5
   b. ⁻1 > 2 > ⁻5
   c. ⁻5 < ⁻1 < 2
   d. None of these

Find the answer.

8. ⁻13 + 46 + ⁻52
   a. 11
   b. ⁻21
   c. ⁻19
   d. None of these

9. ⁻78 − 69
   a. ⁻147
   b. ⁻9
   c. 9
   d. None of these

10. ⁻30 − ⁻67
   a. 37
   b. ⁻97
   c. ⁻27
   d. None of these

Find the answer.

11. ⁻28 × 19
   a. ⁻432
   b. 532
   c. ⁻532
   d. None of these

12. 96 ÷ ⁻6
   a. 16
   b. ⁻16
   c. ⁻19
   d. None of these

13. ⁻84 ÷ ⁻7
   a. ⁻12
   b. 12
   c. ⁻14
   d. None of these

Solve.

14. $^-2 + n = ^-11$

    a. $^-13$

    b. $^-9$

    c. 9

    d. None of these

15. $\frac{r}{16} = ^-4$

    a. $^-64$

    b. 64

    c. $^-4$

    d. None of these

16. $23 + z = ^-5$

    a. 28

    b. $^-18$

    c. $^-28$

    d. None of these

17. $^-3n = 54$

    a. 18

    b. $^-18$

    c. $^-162$

    d. None of these

18. $p - (^-15) = 30$

    a. $^-45$

    b. 15

    c. 30

    d. None of these

19. $\frac{^-87}{n} = 3$

    a. $^-29$

    b. 29

    c. $^-24$

    d. None of these

Name the figure that comes next in the pattern.

20.

    a.

    b.

    c.

    d. None of these

21. A B C

    a.

    b. D

    c.

    d. None of these

LANGUAGE and VOCABULARY REVIEW

Choose a word to complete.

bisector   symmetry   arc   vertex   prism   pyramid   faces

1. A part of a circle is called a(n) _____?_____.

2. A _____?_____ divides a segment or an angle into two equal parts.

3. _____?_____ are the surfaces that form shapes.

4. A(n) _____?_____ has only one base.

5. When a figure is folded along a line of _____?_____, one side will fit exactly on the other.

DEBUGGING

Errors in computer programs are called **bugs.** When you find and correct the errors, you are **debugging** a program. Most program errors are either **syntax errors** or **logic errors.**

Syntax errors are mistakes in the use of a computer language. Here are some examples.

```
10 PRUNT GO FOR IT!
20 LET 23 = A
```

PRINT is misspelled and quotation marks are missing.

LET statements must always have the variable on the left of the equal sign and the value on the right.

Logic errors occur when mistakes are made in the choice or order of statements. They also occur when you fail to correctly use the order of operations. Here are some examples.

```
40 PRINT " PERIMETER IS" P
50 LET P = 2 * L + 2 * W
```

The computer is told to PRINT P before being given a value for P.

Parentheses are needed to compute the perimeter correctly.

When you have a syntax error, a program will not run. You will get a syntax error message followed by the line number. Programs with logic errors will run, but you will not get the output you expect.

Debug the program to get the indicated output.

1.
```
10 LET 10 = A
20 LET B = 15
30 LET C = 20
40 PRINT "THE AVERAGE IS " AVG
50 LET AVG = A + B + C / 3
60 END
```

Output:
THE AVERAGE IS 15

2.
```
10 PRINT " FINDS DISCOUNT RATE
20 LET P = 5
30 LET 3.75 = C
40 LET R = P − C/P
50 PRINT R * 100; "% IS THE RATE"
60 END
```

Output:
25% IS THE RATE

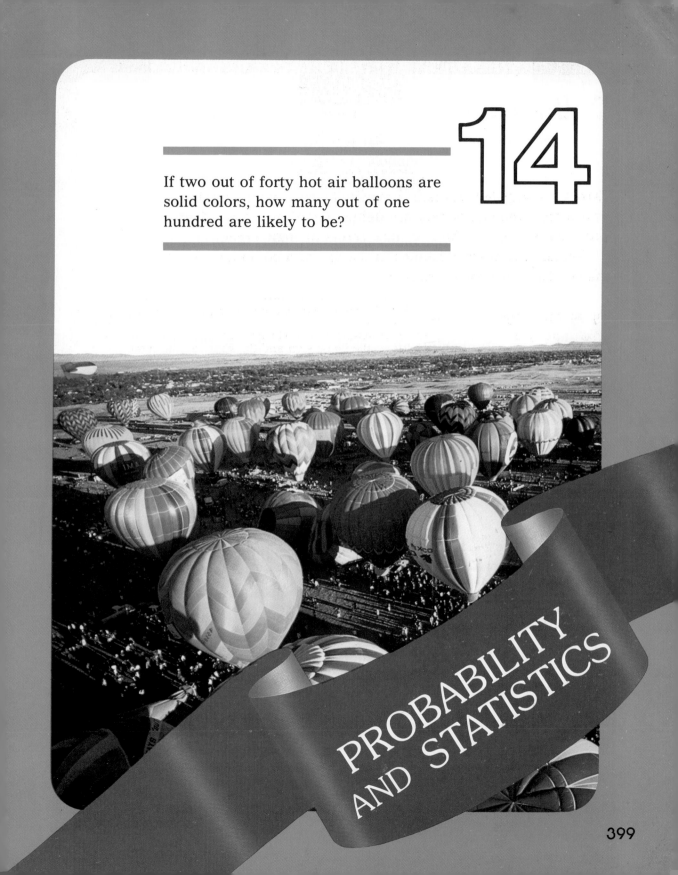

If two out of forty hot air balloons are solid colors, how many out of one hundred are likely to be?

14

PROBABILITY AND STATISTICS

PROBABILITIES AND OUTCOMES

The **probability** of an event is a ratio describing the chance that the event will happen.

Suppose you have a bank containing seven 1980 quarters and four 1985 quarters. You turn the bank upside-down and shake out a coin. There are eleven possible **outcomes,** one for each coin. If all outcomes are equally likely the probability of shaking out a 1980 quarter is 7 out of 11 or $\frac{7}{11}$, written $P(1980) = \frac{7}{11}$.

If all the outcomes are equally likely, you can use a formula to find probabilities.

$$\text{Probability } (P) = \frac{\text{number of favorable outcomes}}{\text{number of possible outcomes}}$$

The probability of shaking out a 1980 quarter *or* a 1985 quarter is written $P(1980 \text{ or } 1985) = \frac{7+4}{11} = 1$. The probability of an event that is certain to happen is 1. It is impossible to shake a nickel out of the bank. The probability of an impossible event is 0, $P(\text{nickel}) = 0$. If an event is neither impossible nor certain, its probability is between 0 and 1.

CLASS EXERCISES

You spin the spinner shown. Complete.

1. There are ▨ outcomes.

2. $P(1) = $ ▨

3. $P(3) = $ ▨

4. $P(6) = $ ▨

5. $P(2 \text{ or } 3) = $ ▨

6. $P(2, 3, \text{ or } 8) = $ ▨

7. $P(\text{even number}) = $ ▨

8. $P(\text{prime number}) = $ ▨

9. $P(\text{a number less than } 10) = $ ▨

10. $P(\text{a number greater than } 3) = $ ▨

PRACTICE

You spin the spinner shown.
Write the given probability.

11. $P(1)$ **12.** $P(2)$ **13.** $P(3)$

14. $P(4)$ **15.** $P(5)$ **16.** $P(1 \text{ or } 2)$

17. $P(\text{not } 4)$ **18.** $P(1, 2, 3, \text{ or } 4)$ **19.** $P(\text{prime number})$

Each letter of the word *excellent* is written on a card. The cards are mixed, and you pick one card without looking. What is the probability?

20. $P(h)$ **21.** $P(t)$ **22.** $P(x)$ **23.** $P(l \text{ or } e)$ **24.** $P(l)$ **25.** $P(\text{vowel})$

★**26.** $P(\text{a letter in the word } surprise)$ ★**27.** $P(\text{a letter in the word } talent)$

Write the answer.

28.
$$\begin{array}{r} 47 \\ \times 1.6 \\ \hline \end{array}$$

29. $288 \div 6$

30.
$$\begin{array}{r} 18.6 \\ 2.9 \\ +135.61 \\ \hline \end{array}$$

MIXED REVIEW

31. $3\frac{1}{2} \times 2\frac{2}{3}$

32. $\frac{7}{9} - \frac{1}{2}$

33. $1\frac{1}{5} + 2\frac{1}{7}$

PROBLEM SOLVING APPLICATIONS
Using Probability

Suppose you must close your eyes and pick a slip of paper to get your weekly household assignment.

What is the probability?

34. You do the laundry. **35.** You don't mow the lawn.

36. You get an indoor job. **37.** You get an outdoor job.

★**38.** You go first. You get "wash car." Then your brother chooses. What is the probability that he gets "do laundry"?

★**39.** Your brother goes first. He gets an indoor job. Then you choose. What is the probability that you get an outdoor job?

COUNTING POSSIBLE OUTCOMES

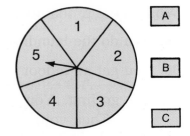

Each player in a game tosses a coin to see whether to move forward (heads) or back (tails). Then a spin of the spinner shows how far to move.

The list below shows all the possible outcomes of tossing the coin and spinning the spinner. We use H for heads on the coin and T for tails.

(H1) (H2) (H3) (H4) (H5) (H6)
(T1) (T2) (T3) (T4) (T5) (T6)

The outcome (T4) means the player moves back 4 places.

To find the total number of outcomes, multiply the 2 possible outcomes for the coin toss by the 6 possible outcomes for the spinner:

$$2 \times 6 = 12$$

The total number of outcomes is 12. When each outcome is equally likely to occur, any outcome is said to be **random.**

The probability of any one outcome of the 12 possible outcomes is $\frac{1}{12}$. For example:

$P(\text{moving back 4 places}) = \frac{1}{12}$

CLASS EXERCISES

The letters A, B, and C are written on cards. You pick a card without looking and spin the spinner. Complete the list of outcomes.

1. (A ▧) (▧2) (▧3) (A ▧) (A ▧)
(B ▧) (B ▧) (▧3) (▧4) (▧5)
(▧1) (C ▧) (C ▧) (▧4) (C ▧)

2. What is the probability of choosing an A card?

PRACTICE

You are going to choose a vegetable and a fruit at random. You have broccoli, corn, turnips, and eggplants. You also have papayas, mangoes, and grapes.

3. List the possible outcomes for choosing one fruit and one vegetable.

4. How many outcomes include turnips or grapes? eggplants or mangoes? eggplants and mangoes?

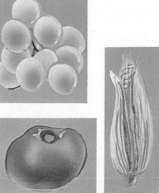

Suppose all the outcomes are equally likely. What is the probability?

5. P(corn or papayas)   6. P(broccoli and mangoes)

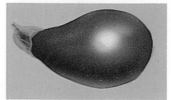

Your class is choosing a class color and a mascot. The color suggestions are blue, maroon, red, and gold. The mascot suggestions are fox, ox, and tiger. Assume the suggestions are written on pieces of paper and drawn randomly from separate containers.

7. List the possible outcomes.

8. What is the probability that gold is the color?

9. What is the probability that ox is the mascot?

10. What is the probability that red and fox are the outcomes?

PROBLEM SOLVING APPLICATIONS
Arrangements

Solve. A calculator may be helpful.

11. How many ways can a president, vice president, secretary, and treasurer be chosen from 30 people? (*Hint:* There are 30 choices for president. Once the president is chosen there are 29 choices for vice president, and so on.)

12. In how many different ways can 8 people be seated in a row?

TREE DIAGRAMS

Three coins are tossed. What are the possible outcomes? What is the probability of getting 3 heads? A **tree diagram** can make this problem clearer.

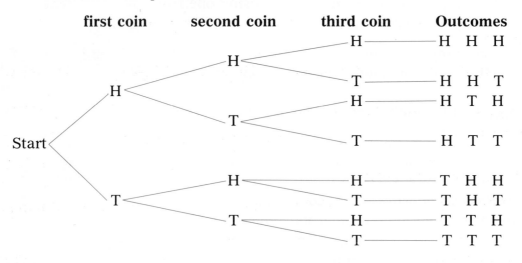

first coin	second coin	third coin	Outcomes

To read the tree diagram, move from start to the first coin column. The first coin can be H or T. If the first coin is H, the second can be H or T, and so on. If the first coin is T, the second coin can still be H or T. You can follow the branch to see the final outcomes.

There are eight possible outcomes. One of the outcomes includes 3 heads, $P(3 \text{ heads}) = \frac{1}{8}$.

Since the probability of 0, 1, 2, or 3 heads is 1,

$$P(not \text{ 3 heads}) = 1 - P(3 \text{ heads}) = 1 - \frac{1}{8} = \frac{7}{8}.$$

CLASS EXERCISES

Use the example and tree diagram above.
What is the probability?

1. $P(1 \text{ tail, 2 heads})$ **2.** $P(3 \text{ tails})$ **3.** $P(not \text{ 3 tails})$

4. $P(\text{neither head nor tail})$ **5.** $P(\text{at most 1 tail})$ **6.** $P(\text{at least 2 heads})$

PRACTICE

You have two bags, each containing one black and one white marble. Without looking you choose a marble from each bag.

7. Make a tree diagram to show the possible outcomes.

What is the probability of choosing the marbles with these colors?

8. both colors   **9.** 2 white   **10.** at least 1 black   **11.** not white

You spin the spinner three times.

12. Make a tree diagram to show the possible outcomes.

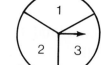

What is the probability?

13. P(3 ones)   **14.** P(3 odd numbers)   **15.** P(no odd numbers)

Find the answer.

16. $87.2 + 6.3$ **17.** 44.55×3.7 **18.** $11\frac{1}{8} - 2\frac{1}{3}$

19. $65\frac{5}{8} + 3\frac{1}{2}$ **20.** $19.7 + 6.21 + 0.68$ **21.** $86.5 - 27.39$

MIXED REVIEW

PROBLEM SOLVING APPLICATIONS
Organizing Data

Two number cubes are numbered from 1 to 6. You toss the cubes and find the sum of the numbers displayed.

22. What are the possible sums?

23. List the ways you could get each sum. For example, a sum of $2 = 1 + 1$.

24. How many outcomes are possible when you toss the two cubes?

What is the probability that the sum is the following?

25. P(3)   **26.** P(12)   **27.** P(15)   ★**28.** P(odd)   ★**29.** P(prime)

INDEPENDENT PROBABILITIES

Four horses are used for riding lessons at Juniper Farm. Each horse, Creamy (C), Sad Sam (S), Gumbo (G), and Turnip Top (T) is equally likely to be chosen.

Sarah takes a lesson. The next day Bill takes a lesson. Horses are chosen for them at random. What is the probability that Sarah rides Creamy and Bill rides Gumbo?

You can list the possible outcomes. The first letter shows Sarah's horse and the second letter shows Bill's.

(CC)	(CS)	(CG)	(CT)
(SC)	(SS)	(SG)	(ST)
(GC)	(GS)	(GG)	(GT)
(TC)	(TS)	(TG)	(TT)

You can see that one out of 16 outcomes includes Creamy and then Gumbo.

$$P(C \text{ and } G) = \frac{1}{16}$$

Since Sarah's choice has no effect on Bill's, the events are **independent**. In general, when two events A and B are independent we use the following formula to find their probability.

$$P(A \text{ and } B) = P(A) \times P(B)$$

$$P(C) = \frac{1}{4} \qquad P(G) = \frac{1}{4}$$

$$P(\text{Sarah on Creamy and Bill on Gumbo}) = \frac{1}{4} \times \frac{1}{4} = \frac{1}{16}$$

CLASS EXERCISES

Use the information in the example above.

1. **a.** How many outcomes include the same horse for both lessons?
   b. What is the probability that the same horse is chosen for both lessons?

2. How many outcomes include Gumbo and Turnip Top in any order?

PRACTICE

In a board game there are 3 bonus (B) cards and 6 chance (C) cards. The cards are shuffled and placed face down on a table. The first player draws a card and replaces it before the next card is drawn. What is the probability?

3. P(B and B)   **4.** P(B and C)   **5.** P(C and B)   **6.** P(C and C)

Suppose you toss a coin, then roll a cube numbered from 1 to 6. What is the probability?

7. P(H and 4)   **8.** P(H and number less than 4)

9. P(T and 8)   **10.** P(T and an even number)

Contestants on a game show choose a money card and trip card without looking. What is the probability?

MONEY	TRIP
$10,000	San Francisco
$100	London
$25,000	Paris
$10	Madrid

11. P($100 and Paris)

12. P($10 and a European city)

13. P(money greater than $100 and London)

14. P(money less than $5000 and U.S. city)

PROBLEM SOLVING APPLICATIONS
Using Probability

When a child is born, the chances are about the same that it will be a girl or a boy. P(girl) $= \frac{1}{2}$ and P(boy) $= \frac{1}{2}$.

A family has 2 children. What is the probability?

15. P(2 boys)   **16.** P(2 girls)

17. P(a boy and a girl)   **18.** P(both boys or both girls)

A family has 3 children. What is the probability?

19. P(3 girls)   **20.** P(3 boys)   **21.** P(neither all boys nor all girls)

DEPENDENT PROBABILITIES

Suppose your gym bag contains 4 white socks and 2 gray socks. You close your eyes and pull out a sock. The probability that the sock is gray is 2 in 6 or 1 in 3.

$$P(G) = \frac{2}{6} = \frac{1}{3}$$

If you do not return the sock and choose a second sock, the probability that it is also gray is 1 in 5.

Since the second choice is affected by the first, the events are **dependent.** In general, the probability of an event B happening given that an event A has occurred is written $P(B/A)$ and is read *the probability of B given A.* The probability of two dependent events is given by the following formula.

$$P(A \text{ and } B) = P(A) \times P(B/A)$$

The probability that two gray socks are chosen is found by multiplying their probabilities.

$$P(G \text{ and } G) = P(G) \times P(G/G)$$
$$= \frac{1}{3} \times \frac{1}{5} = \frac{1}{15}$$

Think: Are you more likely to have a matched pair of gray socks or white socks?

CLASS EXERCISES

Use the experiment above. What is the probability?

1. $P(W \text{ and } W)$

2. $P(G \text{ and } W)$

3. $P(W \text{ and } G)$

Assume that A and B are dependent events. Find $P(A \text{ and } B)$.

4. $P(A) = \frac{2}{3}$; $P(B/A) = \frac{1}{2}$

5. $P(A) = \frac{4}{5}$; $P(B/A) = \frac{2}{9}$

PRACTICE

Twenty cards, numbered from 1 to 20, are shuffled and placed face down on a table. Player One chooses a card and keeps it. Then Player Two chooses a card. What is the probability?

6. P(10 and 20)   **7.** P(two even numbers)   **8.** P(two numbers less than 6)

9. P(two factors of 6)   **10.** P(1 and 1)   **11.** P(two numbers less than 22)

12. P(even number and odd number)   ★ **13.** P(two cards whose sum is 13)

★ **14. Think:**   Player One chooses 10. Player Two chooses 20. What is the probability that Player Three chooses a 5?

There are 5 yellow, 4 blue, and 3 red paint brushes drying in a jar. One student chooses a brush. The first brush is not replaced and a second brush is taken. What is the probability?

15. P(Y and B)   **16.** P(B and R)   **17.** P(R and R)   **18.** P(Y and R)

PROBLEM SOLVING APPLICATIONS
Choosing a Strategy

A basketball team, drama group, gymnastics club, and the debating team all want to use the school gym for one hour. Only two one-hour periods are available. To decide which group gets the gym and in what order, the names are written on cards and two are chosen at random.

19. What is the probability that two athletic groups are chosen?

20. What is the probability that one athletic and one non-athletic group is chosen?

★ **21.** What is the probability that the debating team is not chosen?

RANGE AND MEAN

Toptown gives a competency test once a month to people who wish to apply for town jobs. The scores of five recent applicants are shown in the table.

You can describe the numbers, or **data,** in several ways. To find the **range,** you subtract the lowest score from the highest. The range of scores is 17.

$$98 - 81 = 17$$

To find the **mean,** or average, you divide the sum of the scores by the number of scores.

$$\frac{98 + 90 + 90 + 85 + 81}{5} = 88.8$$

A calculator may be helpful when computing means.

$$98 \boxplus 90 \boxplus 90 \boxplus 85 \boxplus 81 \boxminus 444 \boxdiv 5 \boxminus 88.8$$

If you need only an estimate, note that all the numbers are close to 90, so the average is about 90.

Kwan	98
O'Reilly	90
Harris	90
Guercio	85
Mallis	81

CLASS EXERCISES

Complete to find the range and the mean.

1. 10, 12, 13, 15, 19

$$19 - 10 = \blacksquare$$

$$\frac{10 + 12 + 13 + 15 + 19}{5} = \blacksquare$$

2. 28, 32, 47, 51, 52, 40

$$52 - 28 = \blacksquare$$

$$\frac{28 + 34 + 47 + 51 + 52 + 40}{6} = \blacksquare$$

PRACTICE

Find the range and the mean. Round the mean to the nearest whole number.

3. 5, 8, 11, 6, 2, 4

4. 5, 1, 3, 4, 7, 7, 9, 4

5. 54, 28, 54, 57, 54, 76

6. 88, 78, 68, 58, 48, 71

7. 101, 98, 76, 113, 105

8. 56, 98, 108, 85, 123

9. 2483, 2591, 2675

10. 1800, 1738, 1894, 1522

Find the range and the mean. Use estimation to check.

11. 75.7, 86.1, 81.2

12. 2.068, 3.549, 5.183

13. 1756, 2359, 4276

14. 3847, 4081, 4236, 3985

CALCULATOR

PROBLEM SOLVING APPLICATIONS
Using a Table

The table shows ticket sales for City Ballet.

15. What is the range of ticket sales for all the performances?

16. What is the mean number of tickets sold to Trio?

17. What is the mean number of tickets sold on Saturdays?

★ **18.** The mean price of a ticket to the ballet is $15.75. About how much was collected for the four performances of Coppelia?

CITY BALLET TICKET SALES

BALLET	DAY			
	TH	F	SA	SU
Swan Lake	1586	2218	2433	1645
Coppelia	1218	1788	2850	1999
Trio	1430	2481	3121	2001
Rise and Shine	1889	2616	3333	2506

MEDIAN AND MODE

The table shows prices for various word processing programs.

When the data are written in order, the middle number is called the **median**.

59, 99, 99, 149, 220
↑
median

WORD PROCESSING PROGRAMS	
Name	Price
Wordsworth	$ 99
Author, Jr.	$149
Story Stuff	$ 59
Add-a-Word	$220
School Writer	$ 99

[M] When there is an even number of data in an ordered set, the median is the mean of the two middle numbers. Suppose Write-a-Lot is added to the list selling at $119. What is the new median? Use mental math to calculate.
Think: 99 + 119 is 100 + 120 − 2. Then divide by 2.

$$59, 99, 99, 119, 149, 220 \quad \Rightarrow \quad \frac{218}{2} = 109$$

The median price is now $109.

The number or numbers that appear most frequently in a set of data are called the **mode** or **modes.** If no number appears more than once, there is no mode.
The mode of the above prices is $99.

CLASS EXERCISES

Arrange the data in order from least to greatest.

1. 14, 7, 8, 11, 7, 7, 6

2. 33, 19, 25, 21, 27, 33, 19

3. 56, 56, 72, 56, 68, 72, 72

4. 116, 109, 122, 109, 135, 116, 116

PRACTICE

What is the median? What is the mode or modes?

5. 16, 15, 13, 16, 11

6. 12, 11, 9, 8, 13, 9

7. 28, 21, 23, 27, 21

8. 59, 41, 59, 52, 41, 44

9. 62, 48, 43, 53, 48, 52

10. 536, 498, 525, 498, 252, 536

Use the chart for Exercises 11 and 12.

11. What are the median and the modes for the numbers of minutes practiced daily by members of the track team?

12. Find the median and the mode for the heights of members of the track team.

TRACK TEAM	Lisa	Jim	Lopez	Nancy	Jamie	Kathy	Laurie	Ryan	Ellie	Ed
MINUTES OF DAILY PRACTICE	50	65	75	45	70	70	60	55	75	55
HEIGHT IN CENTIMETERS	146	156	159	165	168	146	156	168	146	170

Use mental math to compute the median.

13. 42, 46, 48, 50, 42, 40

14. 150, 120, 140, 130

15. 300, 500, 200, 900

16. 880, 720, 950, 600

MENTAL MATH

PROBLEM SOLVING APPLICATIONS
Using Statistics

The table below gives the elevation in meters above sea level at locations in British Columbia and Nebraska.

AREA	HIGHEST ELEVATION	LOWEST ELEVATION	ELEVATIONS OF THREE PRINCIPAL CITIES		
BRITISH COLUMBIA	4663	0	676	375	39
NEBRASKA	1654	256	1219	854	356

Use the table to answer the question.

17. Which statistic do you use to find which area varies more in its elevations? Can you use the mode?

18. To find the average elevation in British Columbia, why would it be more helpful to know the elevations of ten or twelve places spread around the area, rather than just two places?

PROBLEM SOLVING
Strategy: Sampling and Estimating

Many times, you don't know the probability of an event. Also, all of the outcomes may not be equally likely. When this is true, you can do an experiment. Then you can use the results of the experiment to estimate a probability.

Workers at Gro-Best Seeds test the corn seeds once a week. They use tally marks to record whether or not a seed sprouts.

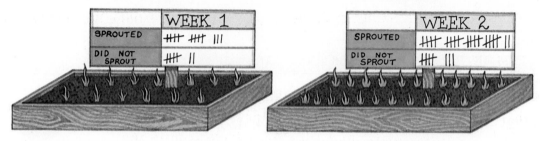

	WEEK 1
SPROUTED	ＨＨ ＨＨ |||
DID NOT SPROUT	ＨＨ ||

	WEEK 2
SPROUTED	ＨＨ ＨＨ ＨＨ ＨＨ ||
DID NOT SPROUT	ＨＨ |||

Using Week 1, what is the probability that a seed will sprout?

$$\text{Probability} = \frac{13}{20}$$

13 seeds sprouted

20 seeds altogether

The probability is $\frac{13}{20}$. This is only an estimate. For a different group of the same type of seeds, the result could be different.

CLASS EXERCISES

Use the information for Week 1 in the chart above.

1. How many seeds did not sprout?   **2.** How many seeds were tested?

3. What is the probability that a seed won't sprout?

Use the information for Week 2.

4. How many seeds sprouted?   **5.** How many seeds did not sprout?

6. How many seeds were tested?   **7.** $P(\text{seed will sprout}) = \blacksquare$

8. $P(\text{seed won't sprout}) = \blacksquare$

PRACTICE

The Student Council members asked several students their opinion on having a school newspaper. The results of the poll are shown in the table.

RESULTS	Grade 7	Grade 8
In Favor	12	13
Not In Favor	15	6
No Opinion	3	1

What is the probability?

9. A seventh grader is in favor.

10. An eighth grader has no opinion.

11. An eighth grader is not in favor.

12. A student from either grade is in favor.

Solve.

★ **13.** Before a town election, 100 voters were asked if they were in favor of building a new library. The results showed: 45 *Yes*, 38 *No*, 17 *No Opinion*. If 5850 people vote in the election, about how many would you expect to vote *Yes*?

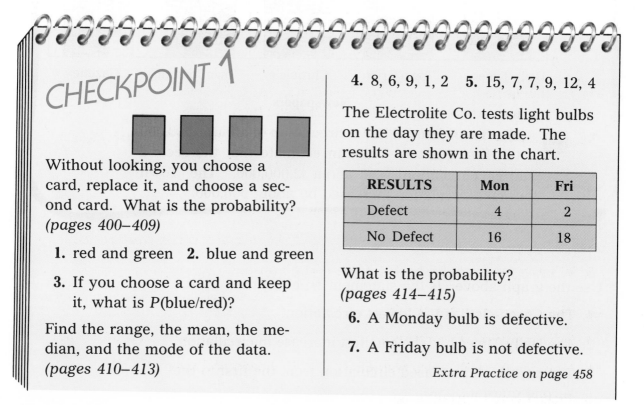

CHECKPOINT 1

Without looking, you choose a card, replace it, and choose a second card. What is the probability? *(pages 400–409)*

1. red and green **2.** blue and green

3. If you choose a card and keep it, what is *P*(blue/red)?

Find the range, the mean, the median, and the mode of the data. *(pages 410–413)*

4. 8, 6, 9, 1, 2 **5.** 15, 7, 7, 9, 12, 4

The Electrolite Co. tests light bulbs on the day they are made. The results are shown in the chart.

RESULTS	Mon	Fri
Defect	4	2
No Defect	16	18

What is the probability? *(pages 414–415)*

6. A Monday bulb is defective.

7. A Friday bulb is not defective.

Extra Practice on page 458

DOUBLE-BAR GRAPHS

A **double-bar graph** compares data. The graph below compares the first and second quarter circulation of five newspapers.

NEWSPAPER CIRCULATION

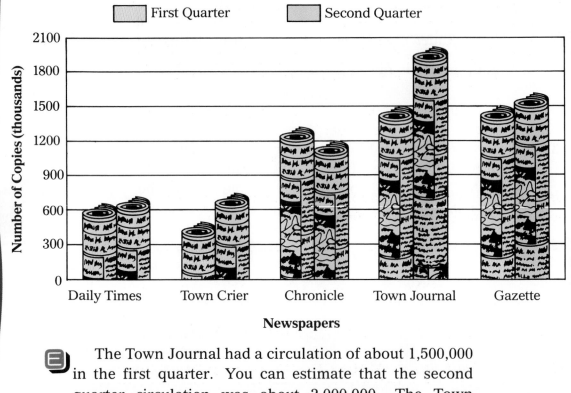

First Quarter   Second Quarter

E The Town Journal had a circulation of about 1,500,000 in the first quarter. You can estimate that the second quarter circulation was about 2,000,000. The Town Journal's circulation increased by about 500,000.

CLASS EXERCISES

Use the graph above. Is the statement *true* or *false*?

1. The Chronicle has the lowest circulation.

2. The Daily Times had the smallest increase in circulation.

3. The papers all increased circulation from the first to the second quarter.

PRACTICE

The double-bar graph below compares the number of books published in various categories in two recent years.

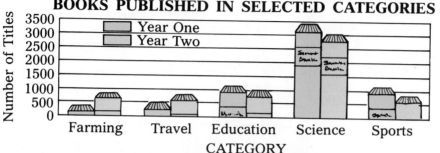

Use the graph above to estimate the number of books published in Year One and then Year Two.

4. farming   **5.** travel   **6.** science   **7.** sports

Use the graph above to estimate the amount of increase or decrease from Year One to Year Two.

8. travel   **9.** education   **10.** science   **11.** sports

PROBLEM SOLVING APPLICATIONS
Making Double-Bar Graphs

Draw a double-bar graph to compare the data in the table.

12.

BOOK SALES THROUGH VARIOUS OUTLETS ($)

YEAR	BOOK CLUBS	MAIL ORDER	SCHOOL DISTRICTS
YEAR ONE	570,000,000	650,000,000	990,000,000
YEAR TWO	590,000,000	604,000,000	1,100,500,000

★ **13.**

ENROLLMENT IN COMPUTER COURSES

YEAR	BASIC	LOGO	COMPUTER SCIENCE	USING SOFTWARE
YEAR ONE	130	40	10	20
YEAR TWO	260	110	30	90

DOUBLE-LINE GRAPHS

Double-line graphs are used to compare the changes over time in two sets of data.

The graph at the right shows the change in average wages for two groups of workers from 1940 through 1980. You can estimate that the difference in average wages in 1940 was about $1000.

Think: Can you tell exactly how much a government worker earned in a given year by reading the graph?

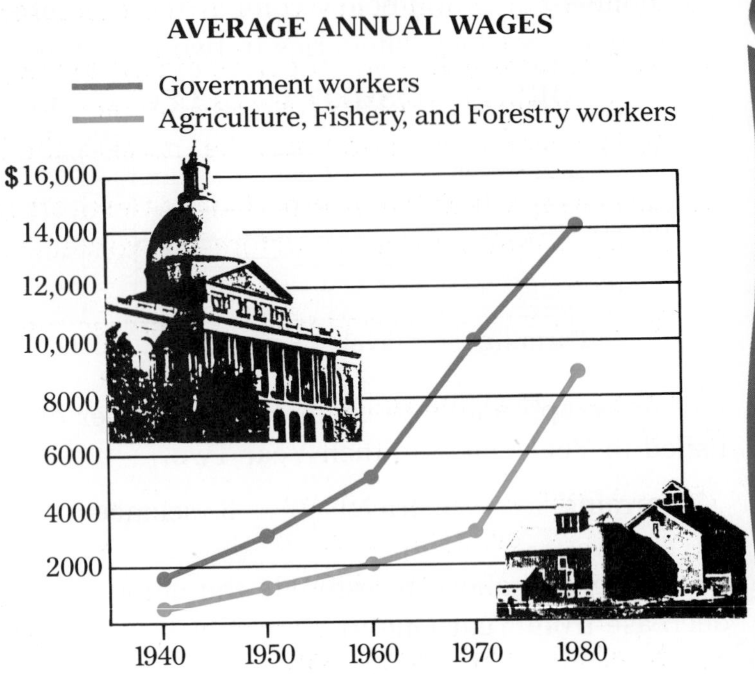

AVERAGE ANNUAL WAGES

—— Government workers
—— Agriculture, Fishery, and Forestry workers

CLASS EXERCISES

Use the graph above for Exercises 1–10.
Estimate the average wages of government workers in each year.

1. 1940   **2.** 1950   **3.** 1960   **4.** 1970   **5.** 1980

Estimate the average wages of agricultural, fishery, and forestry workers in each year.

6. 1940   **7.** 1950   **8.** 1960   **9.** 1970   **10.** 1980

PRACTICE

Use the graph above for Exercises 11–14.

11. By about how much did the wages of government workers increase from 1960 to 1970? from 1960 to 1980?

12. a. Which group of workers had the greater increase in average wages from 1970 to 1980?

b. About how much greater was the increase?

13. a. During which ten-year period did the average wages of government workers increase the most?

b. During which period was the increase the least?

14. a. During which ten-year period did the average wages of agricultural, fishery, and forestry workers increase the most?

b. During which period was the increase the least?

Use the graph at the right.
Estimate.

15. a. About how many canoes does Beasley expect to sell in the six months shown?

b. About how many sailboats?

16. a. In which months does Beasley expect to sell more sailboats than canoes?

b. About how many more?

ESTIMATE

Beasley Boat Company
Six Month Sales Projections

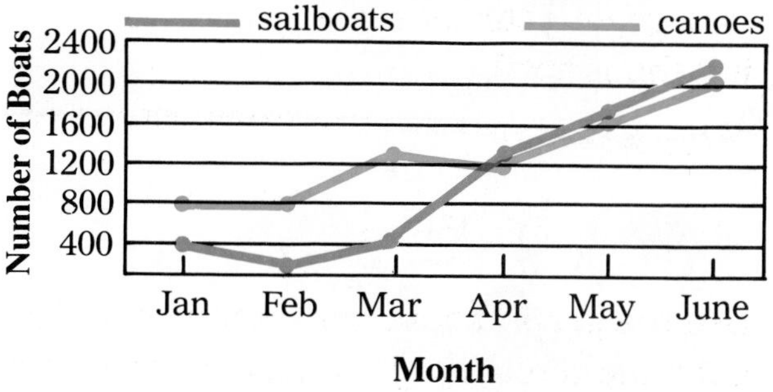

PROBLEM SOLVING APPLICATIONS
Making Graphs

Use the data in the table to make a double-line graph.

17.

BRIGHTON CAR SALES

MONTH	JAN	FEB	MAR	APR	MAY	JUNE
NEW	105	218	189	220	308	414
USED	75	27	90	86	72	63

FREQUENCY TABLES

People who collect data must think of ways to organize the data so that it makes sense to them and to others.

These numbers represent the ages of 20 teenagers leaving a movie theater.

| 17, 13, 15, 15, 14, 16, 15, 13, 18, 15 |
| 19, 13, 14, 15, 16, 15, 18, 17, 15, 17 |

You can use a tally count to see how often each age appears.

TALLY COUNT

AGE	13	14	15	16	17	18	19
TALLY	|||	||	~~||||~~ ||	||	|||	||		

You can see from the tally count that the number 15 appears 7 times. We say 15 has a **frequency** of 7. You can make up a frequency table based on the tally count.

FREQUENCY TABLE

AGE	13	14	15	16	17	18	19
FREQUENCY	3	2	7	2	3	2	1

Total frequency = 20

The ratio of the frequency of each age to the total frequency is called the **relative frequency.** The relative frequency of 15 is $\frac{7}{20}$.

CLASS EXERCISES

Write *true* or *false*. Use the frequency table above.

1. The frequency of 19 is 1.

2. The frequency of 14 is 3.

3. 17 has the lowest frequency.

4. 16 has a frequency of 4.

5. 15 has the highest frequency.

6. The frequency of 13 is 2.

PRACTICE

Write the frequency of the letter.

ALABAMA

	LETTER	FREQUENCY
7.	A	▓
8.	B	▓
9.	L	▓
10.	M	▓

MISSISSIPPI

	LETTER	FREQUENCY
11.	I	▓
12.	M	▓
13.	P	▓
14.	S	▓

Make up the tally count and the frequency table.

15. 9, 7, 10, 5, 7, 9, 9, 7, 6

16. 12, 14, 10, 14, 14, 12, 9, 14, 10

17. 0, 6, 12, 12, 4, 15, 12, 6, 12

18. 18, 5, 18, 6, 5, 0, 18, 18, 17

Find the relative frequency of the number in the frequency table on page 420.

19. 17   **20.** 14   **21.** 19   **22.** 13   **23.** 18

24. In the word ALABAMA, find the relative frequency of *A*.

25. What is the relative frequency of *I* in MISSISSIPPI?

26. Is the relative frequency of *M* in ALABAMA greater than the relative frequency of *M* in MISSISSIPPI?

PROBLEM SOLVING APPLICATIONS
Organizing Information

The data at right give the ages of ten employees in a certain department.

> 33, 33, 32, 35, 31,
> 32, 33, 33, 36, 30

27. Make up a frequency table for the data.

28. Find the relative frequency of each number.

29. Which number has the highest relative frequency?

30. How many numbers have a relative frequency of $\frac{1}{10}$?

PROBLEM SOLVING
Strategy: Surveys and Estimating

1. Understand
2. Plan
3. Work
4. Answer/Check

A department store buyer is planning to order 4000 beach chairs for a sale. To decide how many of each color to order, she randomly surveyed 100 people.

She thinks of the 100 people as a sample of all the people who might order the beach chairs at a later time.

BEACH CHAIR SURVEY

COLOR	NUMBER
Red	38
Blue	9
Yellow	22
Green	23
Purple	8

E She thinks, "If $\frac{38}{100}$ of the sample wants red, then I estimate that $\frac{38}{100}$ of all customers will want red." The buyer will order about

$\frac{38}{100} \times 4000$, or 1520 red chairs.

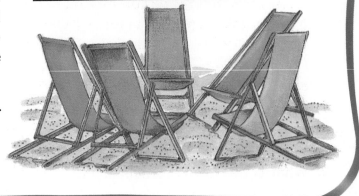

CLASS EXERCISES

Use the information from the survey above to estimate the number of each color the buyer would purchase.

1. blue **2.** yellow **3.** green **4.** purple

5. If the chairs are shipped in lots of 100, would the buyer round up or round down to buy each color? Write *up* or *down*.

    a. red   **b.** blue   **c.** yellow   **d.** green   **e.** purple

6. Using the information from the survey and shipping lots would the buyer order all five colors?

7.

DIGITIME WATCH SURVEY

COLOR	NUMBER
Red	25
Blue	38
Silver	12
Black	25
Total	100

The Digitime Watch Company plans to produce digital watches in five different colors. They can produce 5000 watches a month. Use the results of the survey to decide how many watches should be produced in each color.

RADIO SURVEY

TYPE OF SHOW	NUMBER
Sports	280
Talk	130
Music	420
News	170
Total	1000

8. A radio station wants to plan a new afternoon format. The station estimates that the possible audience is about 3,000,000 people. Use the results of the survey to estimate how large the afternoon audience would be for each type of program.

CHECKPOINT 2

MARCH WATCH PRODUCTION

Use the graph to answer the question. *(pages 416–421)*

1. In which color were fewer analog than digital watches produced? how many fewer?

Solve. *(pages 422–423)*

2. About 8000 people are expected to vote in the election. Use the survey results to predict the number of votes for each candidate.

VOTER SURVEY

CANDIDATE	VOTES
Boyd	24
Carulli	27
Ashcroft	49
Total	100

Extra Practice on page 458

CHAPTER 14 TEST

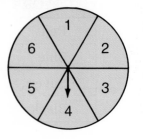

You spin the spinner twice.
What is the probability? *(pages 400–409)*

1. P(1 and 5)   **2.** P(3 and 6)   **3.** P(4 and 5)

What are the range, the mean, the median, and
the mode? *(pages 410–413)*

4. 7, 9, 5, 3, 6, 6

5. 42, 71, 38, 25, 65, 71

6. 105, 80, 97, 111, 101, 105, 94

7. 71.6, 83.4, 69.8, 57.4, 83.4

Quality control inspectors at the QT car tire factory test tires.
The results are shown in the table. What is the probability?
(pages 414–415)

8. A Monday tire is defective.

9. A Wednesday tire is not defective.

10. A Monday tire is not defective.

RESULTS	Mon	Wed
Defect	7	2
No Defect	43	48

11. Use the graph below to estimate the total profits for XYZ
Co. for the four months. *(pages 416–421)*

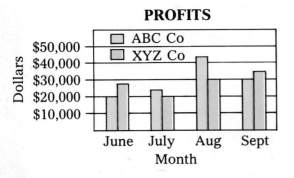

Solve. *(pages 422–423)*

12. Hark, Inc. produces 5 different
models of radios. In March, 650
Model A radios were sold out of
total sales of 8500 radios. Hark
plans to produce 10,000 radios in
April. How many Model A radios
should they produce?

Extra Practice on page 459

MATHEMATICS and HEALTH

The chart below shows the average heights and weights for boys and girls at five different ages.

	AGE	2	10	14	18	ADULT
GIRLS	Height	2 ft 10 in.	4 ft 5 in.	5 ft 2 in.	5 ft 4 in.	5 ft 4 in.
	Weight	25 lb	68 lb	109 lb	125 lb	128 lb
BOYS	Height	2 ft 10 in.	4 ft 6 in.	5 ft 3 in.	5 ft 8 in.	5 ft 9 in.
	Weight	27 lb	70 lb	108 lb	143 lb	155 lb

WAY TO GROW!

1. Make a double-line graph of the boys' heights and weights.

2. Make a double-bar graph of the girls' heights and weights.

3. Has the average boy reached over 15% of his adult weight at the age of two?

4. A girl is 5 ft 3 in. tall. She is one inch above average for her age. How old is she?

5. People grow at different rates. Find out about the different factors which affect growth.

Enrichment

The data in a frequency table can be pictured in a bar graph called a **histogram**. There are no spaces between the bars in a histogram.

Below is a record of the number of books read by the students in English I. The histogram pictures the same information as a graph.

FREQUENCY TABLE

Number of books	3	4	5	6	8	9
Number of students	5	3	6	8	1	1

Solve.

1. How many students read 7 books? 3 books? 5 books? fewer than 5 books?

2. What was the least number of books read by a student? the greatest number?

3. How many students were in the class?

4. How many books were read by all the students?

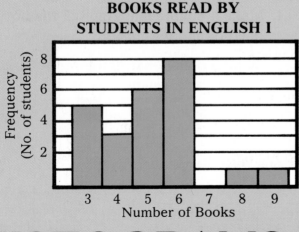

BOOKS READ BY STUDENTS IN ENGLISH I

Frequency (No. of students) vs. Number of Books

HISTOGRAMS

The histogram below shows the Brookview Bears' final scores during last year's baseball season.

BROOKVIEW BEARS' FINAL SCORES

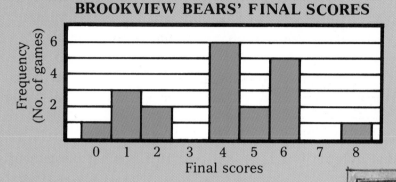

Use the histogram to solve.

5. In how many games were no runs scored?

6. What was the highest score of the season?

7. How many games had a score of 5?

8. What was the most frequent final score?

9. Does the histogram tell you
  a. how many games the team played?
  b. how many players participated?
  c. how many games the team won?
  d. how many runs the team scored altogether?

*10. What does "frequency" represent on the histogram?

*11. Make a frequency table and histogram from this tally count.

Sporting Events Watched per Week	0	1	2	3	4	5
Tally	/ / / /	++++	/ / /		/ / /	/

427

CUMULATIVE REVIEW

Choose the correct answer. Write *a*, *b*, *c*, or *d*.

Find the answer.

1. 32 is what
percent of 50?
  a. 15.62%
  b. 64%
  c. 40%
  d. None of these

2. 2.5% of 300
is what number?
  a. 7.5
  b. 75
  c. 7500
  d. None of these

3. 96% of what
number is 48?
  a. 52
  b. 50
  c. 54
  d. None of these

Find the matching equation and solution.

4. $20\frac{1}{2}\%$ of what number is 4.1?
  a. $20\frac{1}{2}\%$ of $4.1 = r$; $r = 0.84$

  b. $20\frac{1}{2}\% = r$ of 4.1; $r = 0.05$

  c. $4.1 = 20\frac{1}{2}\%$ of r; $r = 20$

  d. None of these

5. 10.7 is what percent of 428?
  a. c of $10.7 = 428$; $c = 40\%$

  b. c of $428 = 10.7$; $c = 2.5\%$

  c. $c = 428$ of 10.7; $c = 4579.6\%$

  d. None of these

Find the percent of change.

6. from $1.75
to $1.96
  a. 12%
  b. 21%
  c. 10.7%
  d. None of these

7. from 4500
to 3600
  a. 25%
  b. 80%
  c. 20%
  d. None of these

Find the sales tax.

8. selling price: $149.98
sales tax rate: 5%
  a. $8.50
  b. $8.99
  c. $7.50
  d. None of these

Find the new price.

9. original price: $156
discount rate: $8\frac{1}{3}\%$
  a. $143
  b. $169
  c. $148
  d. None of these

10. original price: $63.54
markup rate: 34%
  a. $85.14
  b. $41.94
  c. $21.60
  d. None of these

Use the graph to solve the problem.

Recreation Choices of 120 Students

11. How many students in the survey chose visiting friends?
  a. 35
  b. 40
  c. 42
  d. None of these

Find the surface area. Use $\pi \approx 3.14$.

12. rectangular prism:
  length = 12 cm
  width = 5 cm
  height = 6 cm
  a. 275 cm^2
  b. 225 cm^2
  c. 324 cm^2
  d. None of these

13. pyramid:
  square base = 15 m
  height of
    triangular face = 8 m
  a. 240 m^2
  b. 465 m^2
  c. 300 m^2
  d. None of these

14. cylinder:
  height = 10 mm
  radius = 4 mm
  a. 251.2 mm^2
  b. 351.68 mm^2
  c. 100.48 mm^2
  d. None of these

Find the volume. Use $\pi \approx 3.14$.

15. prism:
  area of base = 2.4 cm^2
  height = 16 cm
  a. 284 cm^3
  b. 392 cm^3
  c. 38.4 cm^3
  d. None of these

16. cylinder:
  area of Base = 85 cm^2
  height = 15 cm
  a. 1250 cm^3
  b. 1275 cm^3
  c. 100 cm^3
  d. None of these

17. cylinder:
  radius = 3 cm
  height = 15 cm
  a. 423.9 cm^3
  b. 28.26 cm^3
  c. 45 cm^3
  d. None of these

LANGUAGE and VOCABULARY REVIEW

Choose the correct term to complete each sentence.

1. The (probability, tree diagram) of an event is a number describing the chance that the event will happen.

2. If the choice of a second event is affected by the first choice, the events are said to be (independent, dependent).

3. To find the (median, mean) divide the sum of the scores by the number of scores.

COMPUTER
LITERACY

an imitation of a real-life situation. Experi-
be too expensive, dangerous, or time-con-
e to do, can be simulated by a computer pro-
ulations use a model. The model is easily
ions can be made about the result.

Suppose a landscape architect
is using a computer to design a garden around a greenhouse. He can
move the figure on the monitor
without redrawing it. Any compu-
tations for finding perimeter or
area can also be done by changing
the input.

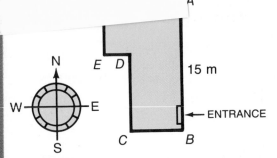

Solve to simulate the architect's plans. Use graph paper.

1. The entrance to the building must face south. Trace
   and label the figure above. Rotate 90° to position it
   correctly.

2. A circular path must be placed around the greenhouse. Draw
   the outer edge of the path by constructing a circle using point A
   as center and side AB as the radius. Label the circle ab. Draw
   the inner edge of the path by constructing another circle using
   point A as center and side AF as radius. Label the circle af. (Do
   not draw through the greenhouse).

3. Grass must be planted inside af. Notice that the figure is not a
   whole circle. Use the formula $A = \frac{3}{4}\pi r^2$ to find the area to be
   covered with grass.

TABLE OF MEASURES

Time

60 seconds (s) = 1 minute (min)
60 minutes (min) = 1 hour (h)
24 hours = 1 day (d)
7 days = 1 week

$\left.\begin{array}{l}\text{365 days} \\ \text{52 weeks} \\ \text{12 months}\end{array}\right\} = 1 \text{ year}$

10 years = 1 decade
100 years = 1 century

Metric

LENGTH

10 millimeters (mm) = 1 centimeter (cm)
10 centimeters = 1 decimeter (dm)

$\left.\begin{array}{l}\text{10 decimeters} \\ \text{100 centimeters}\end{array}\right\} = 1 \text{ meter}$

10 meters = 1 dekameter (dam)
10 dekameters = 1 hectometer (hm)

$\left.\begin{array}{l}\text{10 hectometers} \\ \text{1000 meters}\end{array}\right\} = 1 \text{ kilometer (km)}$

AREA

100 square millimeters = 1 square centimeter
(mm²)   (cm²)
10,000 square centimeters = 1 square meter (m²)
10,000 square meters = 1 hectare (ha)

VOLUME

1000 cubic millimeters = 1 cubic centimeter
(mm³)   (cm³)
1,000,000 cubic centimeters = 1 cubic meter (m³)

MASS

1000 milligrams (mg) = 1 gram (g)
1000 grams = 1 kilogram (kg)

CAPACITY

1000 milliliters (mL) = 1 liter (L)

United States Customary

LENGTH

12 inches (in.) = 1 foot (ft)

$\left.\begin{array}{l}\text{3 feet} \\ \text{36 inches}\end{array}\right\} = 1 \text{ yard (yd)}$

$\left.\begin{array}{l}\text{5280 feet} \\ \text{1760 yards}\end{array}\right\} = 1 \text{ mile (mi)}$

AREA

144 square inches (in.²) = 1 square foot (ft²)
9 square feet = 1 square yard (yd²)
4840 square yards = 1 acre (A)

VOLUME

1728 cubic inches = 1 cubic foot (ft³)
27 cubic feet = 1 cubic yard (yd³)

WEIGHT

16 ounces (oz) = 1 pound (lb)
2000 pounds = 1 ton (t)

CAPACITY

8 fluid ounces (fl oz) = 1 cup (c)
2 cups = 1 pint (pt)
2 pints = 1 quart (qt)
4 quarts = 1 gallon (gal)

Write the standard form. *(pages 2–3)*
1. 3 hundred 7   **2.** 33 million, 286   **3.** 200,000 + 9000 + 60 + 5

Write as a decimal. *(pages 4–5)*
4. 9 tenths   **5.** 10 and 7 tenths   **6.** 8 and 7 hundredths   **7.** 291 thousandths

Order from least to greatest. *(pages 6–9)*
8. 2050, 2005, 2400, 2500   **9.** 7.615, 6.715, 7.623, 7.651

Round to the greatest place value. *(pages 10–11)*
10. 681   **11.** 4381   **12.** 3,906,615   **13.** 37.52

Solve. *(pages 12–13)*
14. Mendez finished the race in 4 min 5.6 s. Jackson finished in
4 min 6.5 s. Who won?

FOR USE AFTER CHECKPOINT 2

Choose the best estimate. *(page 14–19)*
15. The mass of a paper clip
  a. 1 kg   **b.** 1 g   **c.** 10 mg

16. The length of a canoe paddle
  a. 1 m   **b.** 10 cm   **c.** 100 mm

17. The capacity of a bucket
  a. 150 mL   **b.** 500 mL   **c.** 15 L

Name the more precise measurement. *(pages 20–21)*
18. 7 cm or 72 mm   **19.** 420 mL or 0.4 L   **20.** 3 kg or 3100 g

Refer to the chart. *(pages 22–23)*

Goat	39.9°C	King Penguin	37.7°C
Polar Bear	37.3°C	Ostrich	39.2°C

21. Which animal has the highest body temperature? the lowest?

Choose the best estimate. *(pages 24–25)*
22. The weight of a kitten
  a. 10 oz   **b.** 10 lb   **c.** 10 t

23. The height of a table
  a. 5 ft   **b.** 1 yd   **c.** 18 in.

24. The capacity of a bathtub
  a. 20 gal   **b.** 20 qt   **c.** 20 pt

Write the standard form. *(pages 2–5)*

1. 4,000,000 + 3000 + 30   **2.** 10 thousand, 9 hundred 12   **3.** 4 and 55 thousandths

Order from greatest to least using two > symbols. *(pages 6–9)*

4. 273, 293, 239   **5.** 3047, 3048, 3074   **6.** 0.23, 0.02, 0.24

7. 1.029, 0.029, 0.229   **8.** 4.6, 4.06, 0.46   **9.** 0.392, 0.4, 4.3

Round to the place underlined. *(pages 10–11)*

10. 7<u>9</u>2   **11.** 6<u>5</u>,231   **12.** <u>5</u>4,999   **13.** 3<u>8</u>26

14. <u>8</u>.392   **15.** 1.<u>1</u>9   **16.** 16.0<u>6</u>44   **17.** 1.1<u>7</u>26

Complete. *(pages 14–19)*

18. 4 m = ▮ cm   **19.** 9000 mm = ▮ m   **20.** 35 km = ▮ m

21. 17 L = ▮ mL   **22.** 32,000 mL = ▮ L   **23.** 9 g = ▮ mg

Name the more precise measurement. *(pages 20–21)*

24. 5 m or 550 cm   **25.** 0.8 kg or 795 g   **26.** 9 cm or 92 mm

Complete. *(pages 24–25)*

27. 16 in. = ▮ ft ▮ in.   **28.** 18 oz = ▮ lb ▮ oz

29. 12 qt = ▮ gal   **30.** 3 yd = ▮ ft

Use facts from the chart to solve. *(pages 12–13, 22–23)*

MOUNTAIN	HEIGHT
Everest	29,002 ft
Kilimanjaro	19,340 ft
McKinley	20,320 ft
Elbrus	18,480 ft

31. Which mountain is highest?

32. Which two mountains listed are higher than 20,000 ft?

33. How high is Elbrus?

34. Is any mountain listed less than 18,000 ft high?

Answer the question. Write *yes* or *no*. *(pages 34–35)*

1. $5 + n = 13$
Is 8 a solution?

2. $17 - c = 9$
Is 9 a solution?

3. $k - 6 = 7$
Is 13 a solution?

4. $8 + n = 17$
Is 7 a solution?

Name the property illustrated. *(pages 36–37)*

5. $9 + 8 = 8 + 9$

6. $4 + 0 = 4$

7. $2 + (9 + 6) = (2 + 9) + 6$

Estimate. Then add. *(pages 38–41)*

8. 392 +419	**9.** 4709 2864 +5132	**10.** 1.03 +5.92	**11.** 35.43 2.6 + 1.29

Solve. If there is not enough information, write *missing data*. *(pages 42–43)*

12. A pet store sold more gerbils than canaries. It sold 22 gerbils. How many canaries did it sell?

Estimate. Then subtract. *(pages 44–47)*

13. 300 −246	**14.** 3560 − 103	**15.** 0.827 −0.655	**16.** $49.65 − 38.95	**17.** 6 −2.631

Add or subtract. *(pages 48–51)*

18. 7 ft 4 in. +8 ft 9 in.	**19.** 2 c 2 oz −1 c 7 oz	**20.** 30 min − 5 min 25 s	**21.** 5 lb 8 oz +4 lb 9 oz

Organize the data into a table. Then solve. *(pages 52–53)*

22. Stephanie ran 2.3 mi on Monday, 3.4 mi on Tuesday, and 1.1 mi on Wednesday. She rested Thursday, and ran 3.8 mi Friday. How many miles did Stephanie run altogether?

FOR USE AFTER THE CHAPTER TEST

Answer the question. Write *yes* or *no*. (*pages 34–37*)

1. $9 + c = 15$ Is 6 a solution?
2. $13 - b = 4$ Is 8 a solution?
3. $d - 8 = 7$ Is 15 a solution?
4. $f + 8 = 16$ Is 6 a solution?

Estimate. Then write the exact answer. (*pages 38–41*)

5. $329 + 658$
6. $506 + 3956 + 5010$
7. $4.32 + 1.94$
8. $10.60 + 2.05$
9. $3.061 + 1.202$
10. $\$56.02 + \$19.06$

Estimate. Then write the exact answer. (*pages 44–47*)

11. $296 - 181$
12. $3.061 - 1.202$
13. $\$56.02 - 19.06$
14. $13.049 - 4.574$
15. $1060 - 205$
16. $14.09 - 1.049$

Estimate. Then write the exact answer. (*pages 48–51*)

17. $\begin{array}{r} 3\text{ h }25\text{ min} \\ +2\text{ h }41\text{ min} \\ \hline \end{array}$
18. $\begin{array}{r} 17\text{ lb }5\text{ oz} \\ -\ \ 8\text{ lb }3\text{ oz} \\ \hline \end{array}$
19. $\begin{array}{r} 2\text{ pt }1\text{ c} \\ +1\text{ pt }2\text{ c} \\ \hline \end{array}$

20. $\begin{array}{r} 6\text{ ft }8\text{ in.} \\ -2\text{ ft }9\text{ in.} \\ \hline \end{array}$
21. $\begin{array}{r} 15\text{ h }35\text{ min} \\ +\ \ 6\text{ h }42\text{ min} \\ \hline \end{array}$
22. $\begin{array}{r} 8\text{ lb }2\text{ oz} \\ -3\text{ lb }9\text{ oz} \\ \hline \end{array}$

Refer to the table to answer. If there is not enough information write *missing data*. (*pages 42–43, 52–53*)

Visitors to the City Aquarium						
Month	Jan.	Feb.	Mar.	Apr.	May	June
No. of Visitors	3300	3850	2761	2670	2533	2250

23. Which month had the greatest number of visitors?

24. Did more people visit in March or in April?

25. Did more people visit in June than July?

26. Did more than 3900 people ever visit in one month? less than 2200?

Solve the equation. *(pages 62–63)*

1. $3 \times m = 15$ **2.** $g \div 6 = 7$ **3.** $1 \times 9 = n$ **4.** $j \div 9 = 9$

Use a property to solve. Name the property. *(pages 64–65)*

5. $7 \times 2 = 2 \times a$ **6.** $(3 \times 2) \times n = 3 \times (2 \times 4)$ **7.** $1 \times z = 9$

8. $b \times 8 = 0$ **9.** $y \times (1 + 5) = (3 \times 1) + (3 \times 5)$

Write the answer in simplest form. *(pages 66–67)*

10. $(7 - 5) \times 6$ **11.** $(2 + 7) \div 3$ **12.** $20 \div 5 + 3 \times 6$ **13.** $19 - 3 \times 2 + (8 \div 2)$

14. $15 \times (3 + 10) \div 25$ **15.** $26 + 4 \times 3 - 9$ **16.** $(48 \div 8 + 4) \times 9$ **17.** $12 - 6 + 7 - 8$

Estimate. Then write the exact answer. *(pages 68–71)*

18. $\begin{array}{r} 402 \\ \times 39 \\ \hline \end{array}$ **19.** $\begin{array}{r} 0.06 \\ \times 9 \\ \hline \end{array}$ **20.** $\begin{array}{r} 3.4 \\ \times 0.8 \\ \hline \end{array}$ **21.** $\begin{array}{r} 5.43 \\ \times 2.05 \\ \hline \end{array}$

Write the product. *(pages 72–73)*

22. 3^2 **23.** 2^5 **24.** 5^3 **25.** 10^5

FOR USE AFTER CHECKPOINT 2

Solve. *(pages 74–75)*

26. A total of 401 people went to the first showing of a movie, while 332 went to the second. If tickets cost $1.75 each, how much was received by the movie theatre for the two showings?

Multiply or divide. *(pages 76–83)*

27. $55\overline{)236}$ **28.** $8\overline{)7463}$ **29.** $8\overline{)2.4}$ **30.** $7\overline{)82.04}$ **31.** 25.2×100

32. 3.2×10 **33.** $29.52 \div 1000$ **34.** $0.7\overline{)9.1}$ **35.** $0.24\overline{)164.4}$

Estimate the quotient. *(pages 84–85)*

36. $49 \div 22$ **37.** $74,840 \div 4.8$ **38.** $89.8 \div 3.2$ **39.** $37.89 \div 4.32$

40. $68 \div 6$ **41.** $316 \div 15$ **42.** $93.8 \div 21$ **43.** $7.32 \div 0.68$

Estimate the answer. *(pages 86–87)*

44. Elsa mows lawns after school. If she mows a lawn a day Monday through Friday, and charges $8 to $12 a lawn, does she make more or less than $40 a week?

Answer the question. Write *yes* or *no*. (*pages 62–65*)

1. $6 \times n = 18$ Is 3 a solution?   2. $21 \div g = 3$ Is 8 a solution?

3. $(2 \times 5) \times 6 = m \times (5 \times 6)$ Is 2 a solution?

4. $6 \times (f + 9) = (6 \times 5) + (6 \times 9)$ Is 6 a solution?

Estimate. Then write the exact answer. (*pages 66–71*)

5. 745×60 6. 612×203 7. 0.09×8 8. 2.04×0.89

9. 109×27 10. 78.2×53.8 11. 0.29×1.06 12. 487×129

Write the number using exponents. (*pages 72–73*)

13. 7×7 14. $2 \times 2 \times 2 \times 2$ 15. $3 \times 3 \times 3$ 16. $10 \times 10 \times 10 \times 10 \times 10 \times 10$

Write the answer. (*pages 76–83*)

17. $6\overline{)735}$ 18. $12\overline{)6294}$ 19. $39\overline{)24{,}736}$ 20. $7\overline{)4.34}$

21. $26\overline{)9.62}$ 22. $42\overline{)270.9}$ 23. 82.7×100 24. 936.02×10

25. $95.08 \div 1000$ 26. $0.3\overline{)5.22}$ 27. $6.7\overline{)2.412}$ 28. $0.15\overline{)45.6}$

Estimate the answer. (*pages 84–85*)

29. $21{,}493 \div 39$ 30. $679 \div 71$ 31. $69 \div 9$ 32. $9868 \div 49$

33. $417 \div 82$ 34. $985.36 \div 436$ 35. $2906 \div 173$ 36. $5121.6 \div 48$

Solve. (*pages 74–75, 86–87*)

37. A sheet of plywood costs $16.20 and a pound of nails costs $1.09. How much will a total of 5 sheets of plywood and 6 pounds of nails cost?

38. About how many cans of paint at $8.85 each can you buy with $48?

CHAPTER 4   EXTRA PRACTICE
FOR USE AFTER CHECKPOINT 1

Write *true* or *false*. *(pages 96–97)*

1. Vertical angles are formed by parallel lines.

2. A line segment has two endpoints.

3. A plane is a set of points along a line.

4. The endpoint of an angle is called the vertex.

Draw the angle. *(pages 98–101)*

5. m∠SEL = 34°   **6.** an acute angle   **7.** m∠TAN = 172°   **8.** a right angle

Count the number of sides in the polygon. Then name the polygon.
(pages 102–103)

9.   **10.**   **11.**   **12.**

Look for the pattern. Then name the next 3 numbers.
(pages 104–105)

13. 3, 6, 9, . . .   **14.** 1, 2, 4, 8, . . .   **15.** 100, 10, 1, 0.1, . . .   **16.** 1, 1, 2, 3, 5, 8, 13, . . .

Draw the polygon. *(pages 106–109)*

17. trapezoid   **18.** rhombus   **19.** parallelogram   **20.** scalene triangle

FOR USE AFTER CHECKPOINT 2

Find the perimeter or circumference. Use $\pi \approx 3.14$. *(pages 110–113)*

21. square: $s = 13$ in.

22. circle: $d = 12$ ft

23. rectangle: $b = 42$ mm; $h = 30$ mm

24. regular pentagon: $s = 4$ m

Find the area. Use $\pi \approx 3.14$. *(pages 114–119)*

25. rectangle: $b = 12$ cm; $h = 5$ cm

26. circle: $r = 8$ mm

27. square: $s = 16$ in.

28. trapezoid: $b_1 = 5$ m; $b_2 = 7$ m; $h = 3$ m

Use a formula to solve. *(pages 120–121)*

29. What is the perimeter of a rectangular rug that is 11 ft long and 7.5 ft wide?

30. A horse trots around its trainer at the end of a 40 ft tether. How far does the horse travel each time it circles the trainer?

438

FOR USE AFTER CHAPTER TEST

Name the figure using the letters shown. *(pages 96–97)*

1.
   A   B

2.
   C   D

3.
   H
   J

4.
   K
   L   M

Use a protractor to draw the angle. *(pages 98–101)*

5. $m\angle ABC = 33°$

6. an angle complementary to a 50° angle

7. $m\angle DEF = 105°$

8. an angle supplementary to a 120° angle

Name the figure. *(pages 102–103)*

9. a polygon with 8 sides

10. a rectangle with 4 congruent sides

11. a parallelogram with 4 right angles

12. a polygon with 3 sides

Match with the polygons that have the property.
There may be more than one correct answer. *(pages 106–109)*

13. Opposite sides are congruent.

14. At least one pair of sides are parallel.

15. There are four right angles.

A. equilateral triangle

B. rhombus

C. rectangle

Find the perimeter or circumference. Use $\pi \approx 3.14$. *(pages 110–113)*

16. Triangle:
    $s_1 = 6$ cm; $s_2 = 4$ cm; $s_3 = 8$ cm

17. Rectangle:
    $b = 6.5$ m; $h = 7.4$ m

18. Circle:
    $d = 6.3$ cm

19. Square:
    $s = 9.5$ mm

Find the area. Use $\pi \approx 3.14$. *(pages 114–119)*

20. Rectangle:
    $b = 6$ m
    $h = 9$ m

21. Triangle:
    $b = 4.3$ mm
    $h = 6.1$ mm

22. Circle:
    $r = 2.5$ cm

23. Parallelogram:
    $b = 40$ cm
    $h = 15$ cm

Look for the pattern. Then name the next 3 numbers.
(pages 104–105)

24. 1, 2, 4, . . .

25. 128, 64, 32, . . .

26. 2, 5, 3, 6, 4, 7, 5, . . .

27. 1, 3, 9, . . .

Use a formula to solve. *(pages 120–121)*

28. A wall surrounds a square plaza which measures 82 ft on each
    side. How long is the wall?

CHAPTER 5   EXTRA PRACTICE
FOR USE AFTER CHECKPOINT 1

Write the GCF of the numbers. *(pages 130–133)*
1. 4 and 8   2. 3 and 5   3. 6 and 8   4. 28 and 36   5. 10 and 12

Write the prime factorization. *(pages 134–135)*
6. 70   7. 15   8. 50   9. 120   10. 175

Solve. *(pages 136–137)*
11. You pay a 65¢ purchase with a dollar bill. Name 5 combinations of coins, not including pennies, which you could receive in change.

Complete. *(pages 138–143)*
12. $\frac{3}{5} = \frac{\blacksquare}{20}$ 13. $\frac{7}{8} = \frac{21}{\blacksquare}$ 14. $\frac{12}{18} = \frac{2}{\blacksquare}$ 15. $\frac{10}{15} = \frac{2}{\blacksquare}$ 16. $\frac{30}{60} = \frac{\blacksquare}{2}$

Write the LCM of the numbers. *(pages 144–145)*
17. 4 and 6   18. 5 and 8   19. 5 and 7   20. 6 and 10   21. 12 and 16

Write > or < to compare the fractions. *(pages 146–147)*
22. $\frac{5}{12} \blacksquare \frac{7}{12}$ 23. $\frac{2}{3} \blacksquare \frac{5}{18}$ 24. $\frac{4}{5} \blacksquare \frac{3}{7}$ 25. $\frac{5}{7} \blacksquare \frac{6}{8}$ 26. $\frac{1}{4} \blacksquare \frac{1}{6}$

FOR USE AFTER CHECKPOINT 2

Write as a fraction. *(pages 148–149)*
27. $2\frac{4}{9}$ 28. $6\frac{7}{8}$ 29. $3\frac{2}{7}$ 30. $12\frac{1}{4}$ 31. $5\frac{8}{11}$ 32. $4\frac{2}{9}$

Write as a whole number or as a mixed number. *(pages 148–149)*
33. $\frac{13}{8}$ 34. $\frac{15}{5}$ 35. $\frac{9}{7}$ 36. $\frac{16}{15}$ 37. $\frac{28}{7}$ 38. $\frac{15}{2}$

Write as a decimal. Use a bar to show repeating digits. *(pages 150–151)*
39. $\frac{4}{5}$ 40. $\frac{3}{8}$ 41. $\frac{2}{3}$ 42. $\frac{7}{9}$ 43. $\frac{1}{3}$ 44. $\frac{3}{4}$

Write as a fraction in lowest terms. *(pages 152–153)*
45. 0.6   46. 0.225   47. 0.18   48. 0.125   49. 0.68   50. 0.8

Estimate. *(pages 154–155)*
51. Sheila delivers 85 papers after school. About how many papers has she delivered when the job is $\frac{1}{4}$ done?

Write the factors of each number. Then write the GCF of each pair of numbers. *(pages 130–133)*

1. 6 and 15
2. 8 and 12
3. 10 and 15
4. 9 and 27

5. 15 and 45
6. 21 and 35
7. 16 and 40
8. 36 and 45

Is the number prime or composite? Write *prime* or *composite*. *(pages 134–135)*

9. 27
10. 17
11. 49
12. 61

Compare. Write < or >. *(pages 138–147)*

13. $\frac{7}{8}$ ■ $\frac{5}{8}$
14. $\frac{4}{5}$ ■ $\frac{7}{8}$
15. $\frac{2}{7}$ ■ $\frac{1}{4}$
16. $\frac{7}{12}$ ■ $\frac{2}{5}$

Write as a fraction. *(pages 148–149)*

17. $2\frac{4}{5}$
18. $3\frac{1}{4}$
19. $6\frac{2}{3}$
20. $9\frac{1}{9}$

Write as a whole number or as a mixed number. *(pages 148–149)*

21. $\frac{35}{6}$
22. $\frac{21}{4}$
23. $\frac{18}{6}$
24. $\frac{22}{21}$

Write as a decimal. Use a bar to show repeating digits. *(pages 150–151)*

25. $\frac{1}{5}$
26. $\frac{5}{8}$
27. $\frac{5}{6}$
28. $\frac{7}{20}$

Write as a fraction in lowest terms. *(pages 152–153)*

29. 0.31
30. 0.2
31. 0.15
32. 0.75

Solve. *(pages 136–137, 154–155)*

33. Name 5 combinations of coins, not including pennies, with which you could pay for a 45¢ purchase.

34. Ralph had an hour of court time. He played tennis for 43 min. About how much of the hour did he use?

Add or subtract. Write the answer in lowest terms.
(pages 164–169)

1. $\dfrac{1}{5}$
$+\dfrac{3}{5}$

2. $\dfrac{9}{12}$
$-\dfrac{5}{12}$

3. $\dfrac{7}{9}$
$-\dfrac{1}{9}$

4. $\dfrac{2}{3}$
$+\dfrac{5}{6}$

5. $\dfrac{4}{5}$
$+\dfrac{7}{10}$

6. $\dfrac{5}{6}$
$+\dfrac{3}{4}$

7. $\dfrac{1}{3}$
$+\dfrac{1}{5}$

8. $\dfrac{7}{8}$
$-\dfrac{3}{8}$

9. $\dfrac{9}{10}$
$-\dfrac{1}{2}$

10. $\dfrac{11}{12}$
$-\dfrac{3}{4}$

11. $\dfrac{5}{6}$
$-\dfrac{1}{8}$

12. $\dfrac{7}{9}$
$-\dfrac{1}{6}$

13. $\dfrac{4}{7}$
$-\dfrac{1}{8}$

14. $\dfrac{11}{15}$
$+\dfrac{1}{3}$

15. $\dfrac{12}{17}$
$-\dfrac{9}{17}$

16. $\dfrac{16}{21}$
$+\dfrac{3}{7}$

17. $\dfrac{9}{14}$
$+\dfrac{7}{21}$

18. $\dfrac{5}{8}$
$-\dfrac{1}{5}$

Is the answer reasonable? If not, find the correct answer. *(pages 170–171)*

19. Clancy ran $\dfrac{3}{5}$ mi. Edmund ran $\dfrac{7}{10}$ mi. How much farther did Edmund run than Clancy?
Answer: $\dfrac{2}{3}$ mi

Add or subtract. Write the answer in lowest terms. *(pages 172–179)*

20. $2\dfrac{2}{7}$
$+5\dfrac{1}{7}$

21. $6\dfrac{2}{5}$
$+4\dfrac{3}{10}$

22. $3\dfrac{3}{4}$
$+1\dfrac{1}{6}$

23. $4\dfrac{5}{9}$
$+2\dfrac{7}{9}$

24. $2\dfrac{7}{8}$
$+3\dfrac{1}{10}$

25. $12\dfrac{3}{10}$
$-\ 6\dfrac{1}{10}$

26. $13\dfrac{5}{12}$
$-10\dfrac{1}{3}$

27. $9\dfrac{4}{5}$
$-2\dfrac{3}{4}$

28. $8\dfrac{3}{4}$
$-2\dfrac{1}{6}$

29. $12\dfrac{7}{12}$
$-\ 3\dfrac{1}{8}$

30. 7
$-2\dfrac{1}{3}$

31. 17
$-\ 8\dfrac{3}{4}$

32. 15
$-\ 9\dfrac{4}{5}$

33. 4
$-\ \dfrac{5}{6}$

34. $8\dfrac{1}{5}$
$-2\dfrac{3}{5}$

35. $6\dfrac{1}{3}$
$-3\dfrac{5}{6}$

36. $7\dfrac{1}{8}$
$-4\dfrac{2}{3}$

37. $8\dfrac{1}{6}$
$-7\dfrac{3}{4}$

Solve. *(pages 180–181)*

38. 8 students can sit at a table in the cafeteria. How many tables must be set up to seat 70 students?

Write the answer in lowest terms. *(pages 164–169)*

1. $\frac{3}{5} + \frac{7}{10}$ **2.** $\frac{2}{3} + \frac{4}{9}$ **3.** $\frac{3}{4} + \frac{5}{8}$ **4.** $\frac{1}{3} + \frac{9}{10}$

5. $\frac{3}{5} - \frac{1}{10}$ **6.** $\frac{8}{9} - \frac{2}{3}$ **7.** $\frac{3}{4} - \frac{7}{12}$ **8.** $\frac{7}{8} - \frac{1}{3}$

Write the answer in lowest terms. *(pages 172–173)*

9. $6\frac{3}{8} + 4\frac{7}{8}$ **10.** $3\frac{5}{12} + 1\frac{1}{6}$ **11.** $6\frac{5}{8} + 3\frac{5}{6}$ **12.** $7\frac{2}{9} + 4\frac{1}{6}$

13. $9\frac{2}{3} + 3\frac{7}{10}$ **14.** $2\frac{7}{12} + 6\frac{3}{8}$ **15.** $4\frac{1}{2} + 5\frac{8}{11}$ **16.** $2\frac{4}{6} + 3\frac{7}{8}$

Write the answer in lowest terms. *(pages 174–179)*

17. $\begin{array}{r} 4\frac{5}{6} \\ -1\frac{1}{6} \\ \hline \end{array}$ **18.** $\begin{array}{r} 7\frac{3}{4} \\ -2\frac{1}{8} \\ \hline \end{array}$ **19.** $\begin{array}{r} 3\frac{9}{10} \\ -1\frac{5}{6} \\ \hline \end{array}$ **20.** $\begin{array}{r} 7 \\ -\frac{1}{5} \\ \hline \end{array}$

21. $\begin{array}{r} 3 \\ -\frac{6}{7} \\ \hline \end{array}$ **22.** $\begin{array}{r} 5\frac{1}{3} \\ -2\frac{2}{3} \\ \hline \end{array}$ **23.** $\begin{array}{r} 4\frac{1}{6} \\ -2\frac{5}{12} \\ \hline \end{array}$ **24.** $\begin{array}{r} 3\frac{3}{8} \\ -2\frac{5}{6} \\ \hline \end{array}$

25. $\begin{array}{r} 9 \\ -4\frac{5}{8} \\ \hline \end{array}$ **26.** $\begin{array}{r} 7\frac{2}{9} \\ +4\frac{5}{6} \\ \hline \end{array}$ **27.** $\begin{array}{r} 6\frac{1}{5} \\ -2\frac{4}{7} \\ \hline \end{array}$ **28.** $\begin{array}{r} 2\frac{1}{4} \\ -1\frac{2}{3} \\ \hline \end{array}$

Is the answer reasonable or unreasonable? Write *R* or *U*.
If unreasonable, find the correct answer. *(pages 170–171)*

29. Chicken cost $1.80 a pound. Peter spent $5.40 on chicken. How many pounds did he buy? *Answer:* 5 lb

30. A bookshelf is 18 in. wide. How many books, each $1\frac{1}{2}$ in. wide, can fit on the shelf? *Answer:* 12 books

Solve. *(pages 180–181)*

31. The football team is traveling to a game by van. There are 38 team members. If each van can carry 11 people, how many vans will be needed to carry the team?

32. An elevator can carry 1800 lb. How many 160 lb adults can it carry?

FOR USE AFTER CHECKPOINT 1

Multiply. Write the product in lowest terms. *(pages 190–195)*

1. $\frac{2}{3} \times 27$ 2. $14 \times \frac{5}{6}$ 3. $\frac{3}{7} \times 15$ 4. $\frac{3}{5} \times \frac{2}{5}$ 5. $\frac{7}{11} \times \frac{4}{7}$

6. $\frac{3}{7} \times \frac{4}{13}$ 7. $\frac{3}{4} \times \frac{1}{6}$ 8. $\frac{2}{3} \times \frac{9}{10}$ 9. $\frac{6}{7} \times \frac{5}{12}$ 10. $\frac{4}{5} \times \frac{3}{8}$

11. $\frac{9}{15} \times \frac{5}{9}$ 12. $\frac{11}{20} \times \frac{16}{55}$ 13. $\frac{12}{15} \times \frac{9}{15}$ 14. $1\frac{1}{3} \times 2\frac{1}{4}$ 15. $6\frac{3}{5} \times 2\frac{5}{9}$

16. $6\frac{1}{2} \times 8\frac{1}{6}$ 17. $1\frac{5}{7} \times 3\frac{3}{8}$ 18. $3\frac{1}{9} \times 2\frac{5}{6}$ 19. $3\frac{2}{5} \times 1\frac{2}{3}$ 20. $2\frac{7}{8} \times 3\frac{4}{5}$

Solve. *(pages 196–197)*

21. After travelling 24 mi on Saturday, and 21 mi on Sunday, Cynthia's bicycle odometer registered 336 mi. How many miles had she had on her odometer before beginning her weekend trip?

FOR USE AFTER CHECKPOINT 2

Write the reciprocal. *(pages 198–199)*

22. $\frac{3}{4}$ 23. $\frac{7}{8}$ 24. $9\frac{4}{5}$ 25. $3\frac{2}{3}$ 26. $8\frac{7}{11}$ 27. $13\frac{2}{9}$

Divide. Write the quotient in lowest terms. *(pages 200–205)*

28. $10 \div \frac{5}{8}$ 29. $\frac{3}{10} \div 18$ 30. $15 \div \frac{6}{7}$ 31. $\frac{9}{11} \div 24$ 32. $\frac{4}{5} \div 2$

33. $\frac{3}{4} \div \frac{3}{5}$ 34. $\frac{4}{9} \div \frac{8}{27}$ 35. $\frac{7}{8} \div \frac{9}{16}$ 36. $\frac{5}{12} \div \frac{15}{28}$ 37. $\frac{12}{13} \div \frac{2}{3}$

38. $\frac{6}{7} \div \frac{13}{14}$ 39. $\frac{7}{15} \div \frac{3}{2}$ 40. $\frac{4}{15} \div \frac{20}{21}$ 41. $\frac{10}{11} \div \frac{5}{7}$ 42. $\frac{7}{8} \div \frac{8}{9}$

43. $2\frac{1}{3} \div 1\frac{1}{6}$ 44. $6\frac{4}{5} \div \frac{1}{4}$ 45. $7\frac{7}{8} \div 2\frac{3}{4}$ 46. $8\frac{2}{5} \div \frac{3}{10}$ 47. $9\frac{1}{3} \div 5\frac{5}{6}$

48. $6\frac{3}{7} \div 4\frac{1}{2}$ 49. $9\frac{1}{5} \div 2\frac{5}{6}$ 50. $5\frac{3}{10} \div 3$ 51. $10\frac{2}{7} \div 5\frac{1}{4}$ 52. $13\frac{1}{2} \div 2\frac{1}{4}$

Solve. *(pages 206–207)*

53. Steve is planning to bake 3 loaves of bread. Each loaf calls for $5\frac{1}{4}$ cups of flour. He knows he has about 20 cups on hand. Will he have enough flour left for a cake recipe that requires $3\frac{3}{4}$ cups?

Write the answer in lowest terms. *(pages 190–195)*

1. $\frac{3}{4} \times 12$

2. $10 \times \frac{4}{5}$

3. $\frac{1}{3} \times \frac{4}{5}$

4. $\frac{1}{6} \times \frac{5}{8}$

5. $\frac{4}{9} \times \frac{2}{7}$

6. $\frac{3}{5} \times \frac{2}{9}$

7. $\frac{7}{10} \times \frac{20}{21}$

8. $\frac{8}{15} \times \frac{5}{24}$

9. $9 \times 2\frac{1}{3}$

10. $5\frac{1}{5} \times 2\frac{1}{4}$

11. $4\frac{1}{2} \times 2\frac{5}{6}$

12. $3\frac{2}{7} \times 2\frac{2}{3}$

Write the reciprocal. *(pages 198–199)*

13. $\frac{1}{5}$

14. $\frac{13}{15}$

15. 5

16. 8

17. $9\frac{2}{3}$

18. $3\frac{1}{4}$

19. $4\frac{2}{5}$

20. $11\frac{1}{2}$

Write the answer in lowest terms. *(pages 200–205)*

21. $8 \div \frac{4}{5}$

22. $\frac{3}{4} \div 9$

23. $19 \div \frac{6}{7}$

24. $\frac{2}{3} \div \frac{6}{7}$

25. $\frac{3}{8} \div \frac{1}{4}$

26. $\frac{10}{12} \div \frac{5}{9}$

27. $\frac{7}{16} \div \frac{3}{4}$

28. $3\frac{2}{3} \div \frac{1}{6}$

29. $4\frac{1}{5} \div \frac{1}{2}$

30. $8 \div 2\frac{1}{6}$

31. $2\frac{1}{8} \div 1\frac{5}{6}$

32. $4\frac{2}{7} \div 5$

Work backwards to solve. *(pages 196–197)*

33. Jim arrived home from school at 3:35 P.M. If the walk takes 25 min, and he spent 45 min shopping at the supermarket on the way, when did he leave school?

34. Joe lost $\frac{1}{2}$ of his golf balls during his first game of golf. He finished with 6 golf balls. How many did he begin with?

Solve. *(pages 206–207)*

35. A pair of running shoes usually costs $36.90. You buy them on sale for $\frac{1}{3}$ off. How much change will you receive from $30?

36. Edward weighed 145 lb on Sunday. He gained $\frac{1}{2}$ lb on Monday and lost $\frac{3}{4}$ lb on Tuesday. How much did he weigh on Tuesday?

445

FOR USE AFTER CHECKPOINT 1

Write as a mathematical expression. *(pages 216–217)*
1. Six more than a number b **2.** Nine minus four

Evaluate the expression. Use $a = 15$, $b = 3$, $c = 5$. *(pages 218–219)*

3. $a + b$ **4.** $\frac{a}{b}$ **5.** $6b$ **6.** $16 - a$ **7.** $ab - c$

Use a variable to write an equation. Solve. *(pages 220–227)*
8. What number plus 6 is 15?   **9.** What number minus 7 is 11?

10. What number times 35 is 140?   **11.** One half of what number is 18?

Solve. Use trial and error. *(pages 228–229)*
12. The sum of three consecutive numbers is 96. What are the numbers?

FOR USE AFTER CHECKPOINT 2

Write an inequality for the word sentence. *(pages 230–231)*
13. The number x is between eleven and thirty. **14.** Forty is less than a number b.

Solve. *(pages 232–233)*
15. $86 - 17 > y$ **16.** $45 + m > 93$ **17.** $c - 16 < 93$

Complete the ordered pairs of solutions of $x - 6 = y$. *(pages 234–235)*
18. $(8,\blacksquare)$ **19.** $(\blacksquare,0)$ **20.** $(23,\blacksquare)$ **21.** $(\blacksquare,3)$

Write the ordered pair for the letter.
(pages 236–237)
22. A **23.** B **24.** C

25. D **26.** E **27.** F

Choose and solve the correct equation for each
problem. Then answer the question. *(pages 238–239)*

$$c - 9 = 27 \qquad 9 + c = 27 \qquad 9c = 27 \qquad \frac{c}{9} = 27$$

28. Each row contained 9 chairs. There were 27 chairs altogether.
How many rows of chairs were there?

29. A sapling grew 9 in. in one month. It is now 27 in. high. How
tall was it a month ago?

Write as a mathematical expression. *(pages 216–217)*
1. thirteen plus a **2.** c minus fifteen   **3.** six times d **4.** b divided by three

Evaluate the expression. Use $a = 2$ and $c = 6$. *(pages 218–219)*
5. $c - a$ **6.** $7a$ **7.** $\dfrac{c}{a}$ **8.** $4ac$

Solve the equation. *(pages 220–225)*
9. $c + 9 = 31$ **10.** $m - 42 = 18$ **11.** $t + 15 = 83$ **12.** $x - 60 = 8$

13. $4m = 72$ **14.** $\dfrac{t}{8} = 6$ **15.** $7z = 49$ **16.** $\dfrac{x}{15} = 3$

Write the equation and solve. *(pages 226–227)*
17. What number plus 15 is 100?   **18.** What number minus 35 is 75?

19. One tenth of what number is 10?   **20.** Twelve times what number is 108?

Write an inequality for the word sentence. *(pages 230–231)*
21. Six is less than a number x.   **22.** Fifteen is greater than a number z.

23. A number b is between sixteen and nineteen.   **24.** The sum of a number n and 5 is less than thirty.

Solve. *(pages 232–233)*
25. $15 + b < 51$ **26.** $a - 60 > 72$ **27.** $n < 5 + 39$ **28.** $55 - 43 > y$

Locate each point on a number grid. *(pages 236–237)*
29. $A(2, 3)$; $B(0, 5)$; $C(6, 1)$; $D(0, 0)$; $E(4, 6)$; $F(9, 0)$

Solve. Use trial and error. *(pages 228–229)*
30. The product of two consecutive, three-digit numbers is 15,750. Find the numbers.

31. The area of a rectangular rug is 180 ft^2. The perimeter is 56 ft. What are the rug's dimensions?

Choose and solve the correct equation for each problem. Then answer the question. *(pages 238–239)*

$m - 5 = 15$ $5m = 15$ $m + 5 = 15$ $\dfrac{m}{5} = 15$

32. Alice had some apples. She shared 5 with her friends. Now she has 15 apples left. How many apples did she start with?

33. Mike spent 5 h planting each garden. He worked for 15 h altogether. How many gardens did he plant?

Write the ratio in lowest terms. *(pages 248–249)*

1. 3 to 12   **2.** 25 to 5   **3.** 10:15   **4.** $\frac{18}{27}$ **5.** $\frac{32}{30}$

Write the unit rate. *(pages 250–251)*
6. Juice: 3 bottles for $1.56   **7.** Cheese: 3 kg for $8.52   **8.** Soap: 5 bars for $1.85

Match with an equal ratio. *(pages 252–253)*

9. $\frac{2}{3}$ **10.** $\frac{17}{102}$ **11.** $\frac{7}{1}$ **12.** $\frac{9}{11}$ **A.** $\frac{29.4}{4.2}$ **B.** $\frac{42}{63}$ **C.** $\frac{72}{88}$ **D.** $\frac{1}{6}$

Solve. *(pages 254–255)*
13. Which is the better buy, 4 cans of cat food for 88¢ or 5 cans of the same cat food for $1.00?

14. One store sells a 3 gal container of detergent for $4.95. Another sells a 5 gal container for $8.49. Which is the better buy?

Solve the proportion. *(pages 256–259)*

15. $\frac{3}{c} = \frac{2}{4}$ **16.** $\frac{3}{4} = \frac{a}{36}$ **17.** $\frac{9}{13} = \frac{54}{m}$ **18.** $\frac{c}{5} = \frac{21}{35}$ **19.** $\frac{63}{n} = \frac{189}{57}$

FOR USE AFTER CHECKPOINT 2

The scale on a map is 1 cm:2 km. Use proportions to find the actual distance. *(pages 260–263)*
20. 3 cm   **21.** 4.5 cm   **22.** 1.2 cm   **23.** 0.75 cm

Solve. *(pages 264–265)*
24. A car travels 4 mi in 5 min. At that rate, how far would it travel in an hour?

25. The ratio of coaches to players in a league is 3:28. There are 112 players in the league. How many coaches are there?

Triangles *JFK* and *LBP* are similar. *(pages 266–269)*
26. What is the height of the tree?

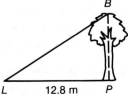

Write the unit rate. *(pages 248–251)*
1. 12 for $1.80   **2.** 48 for $95.04   **3.** 3 for $4.56   **4.** $6.75 for 5

Write as many proportions as you can using all four numbers. *(pages 252–253)*
5. 3, 4, 15, 20   **6.** 1, 3, 6, 18   **7.** 9, 10, 18, 20   **8.** 2, 9, 6, 27

Solve the proportion. *(pages 256–259)*
9. $\frac{2}{3} = \frac{a}{21}$ **10.** $\frac{8}{m} = \frac{10}{5}$ **11.** $\frac{5}{11} = \frac{15}{x}$ **12.** $\frac{6}{5} = \frac{c}{120}$

13. $\frac{8}{4} = \frac{6}{y}$ **14.** $\frac{w}{2.1} = \frac{4}{3}$ **15.** $\frac{6}{d} = \frac{4.8}{8}$ **16.** $\frac{1.2}{8.4} = \frac{e}{0.7}$

The scale on a map is 1 cm: 150 km. Use proportions to find the actual distance. *(pages 260–263)*
17. 3 cm   **18.** 5 cm   **19.** 10 cm   **20.** 4 cm

$\triangle ABC \sim \triangle DEF$. *(pages 266–269)*
21. Find h.

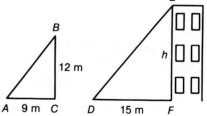

Solve. *(pages 254–255, 264–265)*
22. Which is the better buy, a 200 g box of soap for $1.09, or a 500 g box for $2.69?

23. Which is the best buy, one can of tomato paste for $.34, 3 for $.98, or 12 for $3.89?

24. Yesterday, 8 out of every 20 students who went to the school library checked out a book. If 90 students went to the library, how many checked out books?

25. You know that 2 kg of natural gas can boil 19 L of water. How many kilograms of natural gas does it take to boil 95 L of water?

CHAPTER 10   EXTRA PRACTICE

FOR USE AFTER CHECKPOINT 1

Write as a percent. *(pages 278–279)*

1. $\frac{45}{100}$ **2.** $\frac{16}{100}$ **3.** 18 out of 100   **4.** 43 out of 100

Complete. *(pages 280–281)*

5. $0.72 = \blacksquare\%$ **6.** $0.325 = \blacksquare\%$ **7.** $48\% = 0.\blacksquare$ **8.** $12.5\% = 0.\blacksquare$

Write as a fraction in lowest terms. *(pages 282–283)*

9. 35%   **10.** 90%   **11.** 28%   **12.** 16.5%   **13.** 55.5%

Write as a percent. *(pages 284–285)*

14. $\frac{11}{20}$ **15.** $\frac{4}{5}$ **16.** $\frac{23}{40}$ **17.** $\frac{1}{6}$ **18.** $\frac{1}{80}$

Solve. *(pages 286–287)*

19. In a survey of 440 people, 396 responded. What percent responded?

FOR USE AFTER CHECKPOINT 2

Solve. *(pages 288–293)*

20. What percent of 80 is 32?   **21.** What percent of 60 is 21?

22. 18 is what percent of 75?   **23.** 290 is what percent of 580?

24. What percent of 124 is 93?   **25.** 20 is what percent of 25?

26. 30% of 90 is m.   **27.** 12% of 150 is a.   **28.** 6% of 55 is n.

29. 20% of 120 is q.   **30.** 75% of v is 42.   **31.** 63% of w is 126.

32. 8% of c is 9.6.   **33.** 20% of x is 36.   **34.** 16% of 430 is b.

Solve. *(pages 294–295)*

35. Of 30 radio stations in a city, 60% broadcast 24 h a day. How many do not broadcast 24 h a day?

Write as a percent. *(pages 278–279)*

1. $\frac{19}{100}$ 2. $\frac{19}{20}$ 3. $\frac{3}{4}$ 4. $\frac{5}{8}$ 5. $\frac{19}{40}$

6. 0.09   7. 0.88   8. 0.7   9. 0.48   10. 0.01

Write as a decimal. *(pages 280–281)*

11. 1.8%   12. 46%   13. 95%   14. 6.3%   15. 1%

16. 43.92%   17. 0.15%   18. 0.5%   19. 107.4%   20. 367.2%

Write as a fraction in lowest terms. *(pages 282–285)*

21. 90%   22. 18%   23. 52%   24. 17.5%   25. 0.5%

26. 1.5%   27. 46%   28. 25.25%   29. 0.45%   30. 0.1%

Solve. *(pages 288–293)*

31. What is 62% of 50?

32. 90 is what percent of 150?

33. What percent of 52 is 39?

34. 72% of what number is 61.2?

35. What is 17% of 300?

36. What percent of 40 is 14?

37. 28% of what number is 21?

38. 95% of what number is 76?

Solve. *(pages 286–287, 294–295)*

39. A market research firm asked 500 dog owners which brand of dog food their pets preferred. Responses were:

    Bowser's Best: 35   Fido Feast: 355   Barkers: 110

    Write a percent to describe the number choosing each brand.

40. In a recent year, there were 762 commercial television stations in the U.S. There were about $\frac{1}{3}$ as many educational stations as there were commercial stations. About how many educational stations were there? About how many stations were there altogether?

Write an equation. Then solve. *(pages 304–307)*
1. What percent of 45 is 18?
2. $750 at 10% for 2 years

Make a chart to organize the information. Then answer the question.
(pages 308–309)
3. Lemo Car Rental charges $18 a day and 26¢ a mile. Rusty's Auto Rental charges $14 a day and 30¢ a mile. To rent a car for 2 days and drive it 250 mi, which rental company is more economical?

Solve. Round to the nearest cent. *(pages 310–313)*
4. 1965 population: 7500
    1985 population: 6600
    What is the percent of change?
5. Selling price: $19.95
    Sales tax rate: 5%
    What is the total cost?

Use the chart to answer the questions. *(pages 314–315)*
6. Which was the rainiest day of the week?

7. How much more did it rain on Thursday than Tuesday?

Rainfall (in centimeters)

Sun	Mon	Tues	Wed	Thur	Fri	Sat
0.00	0.15	0.55	0.00	0.95	0.00	1.10

FOR USE AFTER CHECKPOINT 2

Solve for the new price. *(pages 316–319)*
8. original price: $75.00
    discount rate: 20%
    What is the discount price?
9. original price: $4.65
    markup rate: 40%
    What is the new price?

Make a chart and solve. *(pages 320–321)*
10. Jim, Jack, and Joe were the first three to finish in a road race. Joe lives next door to the person who finished third. Jack did not finish behind Joe. Who won the race?

What amount is budgeted for each category?
(pages 322–325)
11. Food

12. Housing

13. Transportation

14. Medical

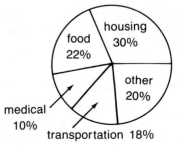

Monthly Income: $1100

Write an equation. Then solve. *(pages 304–305)*
1. What percent of 180 is 27?
2. 45% of what number is 18?
3. 95 is what percent of 250?
4. 8% of 225 is what number?

Find the interest. *(pages 306–307)*
5. principal: $2000
   rate: 5%
   time: 1 year
6. principal: $1750
   rate: 15%
   time: 6 months
7. principal: $7460
   rate: 11.5%
   time: 18 months

Find the percent of change. *(pages 310–313)*
8. 150 to 177
9. 45 to 36
10. $4200 to $6510
11. $3.70 to $4.07

Solve for the new price. *(pages 316–319)*
12. original price: $34.50
    discount rate: 30%
13. original price: $55.80
    markup: 40%

The Ky family has a monthly income of $2200. How much is budgeted for each expense? *(pages 322–325)*
14. housing
15. food
16. transportation
17. medical
18. entertainment
19. other

Monthly Income: $2200

housing 32%, food 20%, medical 10%, transportation 12%, entertainment 10%, other 16%

Make a chart to organize the information. Then answer the question. *(pages 308–309, 314–315, 320–321)*
20. Tom's Taxi charges $1.10 for the first $\frac{1}{5}$ mi, then $.25 for every additional $\frac{1}{5}$ mi. Rorby's Cab charges $.90 for the first $\frac{1}{5}$ mi, then $.30 for each $\frac{1}{5}$ mi after that. If you need to travel $1\frac{1}{5}$ mi, which company is more economical?

21. Steve, Jim, and Will are on the baseball, soccer, and track teams. The soccer player and the baseball player congratulated Will for setting a school record in the mile. Steve and the soccer player eat lunch together. Name each person's sport.

CHAPTER 12   EXTRA PRACTICE
FOR USE AFTER CHECKPOINT 1

Complete. Write <, >, or =. *(pages 334–337)*

1. 5 ▮ $^-$8   **2.** 20 ▮ $^-$21   **3.** $^-$14 ▮ 8   **4.** $^-$36 ▮ 36   **5.** $^-$13 ▮ 12

Write the answer. *(pages 338–341)*

6. $^-$9 + 13   **7.** $^-$16 + $^-$17   **8.** 19 + $^-$26   **9.** $^-$20 + $^-$11   **10.** 50 + $^-$50

11. 7 − 30   **12.** 8 − $^-$15   **13.** $^-$6 − 14   **14.** $^-$17 − $^-$27   **15.** $^-$16 − 60

Write the answer. *(pages 342–345)*

16. 14 × 9   **17.** $^-$12 × $^-$3   **18.** $^-$13 × 2   **19.** $^-$1 × 59   **20.** $^-$3 × $^-$33

21. $^-$14 ÷ 2   **22.** 30 ÷ $^-$3   **23.** 40 ÷ 5   **24.** $^-$42 ÷ $^-$6   **25.** $^-$81 ÷ 9

Solve. *(pages 346–347)*

26. The balance in an account was $846. Checks for $201 and $155 were written and $355 was deposited. What is the balance?

FOR USE AFTER CHECKPOINT 2

Solve the equation. *(pages 348–349)*

27. $a + 6 = 1$ **28.** $x − 9 = 3$ **29.** $5m = {}^-60$ **30.** $\frac{b}{^-5} = 9$ **31.** $\frac{b}{16} = {}^-2$

Write the coordinates of the point. *(pages 350–351)*

32. A

33. B

34. C

35. D

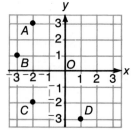

Copy and complete the charts. Then draw the graphs of the equations on the same grid to answer Exercise 38. *(pages 352–355)*

36. $x + y = 5$

x	0	2
y	?	?

37. $x − y = 3$

x	0	2
y	?	?

38. What is the solution of the system of the two equations?

Draw what comes next in the pattern. *(pages 356–359)*

39.   **40.**

454

Complete. Write <, or >, or =. *(pages 334–337)*

1. 3 ▨ 1
2. $^-2$ ▨ $^-3$
3. $^-6$ ▨ 2
4. $^-1$ ▨ $^-1$

5. 6 ▨ 4
6. 0 ▨ $^-3$
7. 4 ▨ $^-5$
8. 2 ▨ $^-2$

Write the answer. *(pages 338–345)*

9. $^-9 + 7$
10. $^-21 - {}^-11$
11. $^-15 + {}^-12$
12. $^-7 - 18$

13. $^-9 \times {}^-4$
14. $^-36 \div 9$
15. $^-12 \times 7$
16. $^-24 \div {}^-8$

Solve the equation. *(pages 348–349)*

17. $14 + q = 4$
18. $m - 7 = {}^-3$
19. $^-3 + n = 5$
20. $6 - s = 9$

21. $^-3n = 27$
22. $\frac{x}{4} = {}^-5$
23. $4f = {}^-36$
24. $\frac{14}{r} = {}^-7$

Complete the chart. Then draw the graph of the equation.
(pages 350–353)

25. $x + y = 4$

x	0	1	2	3	4	5
y	?	?	?	?	?	?

26. $a - b = 2$

a	$^-2$	$^-1$	0	1	2	3
b	?	?	?	?	?	?

Solve the system of equations by graphing. *(pages 354–355)*

27. $x + y = 8$
    $x - y = 0$

28. $x + y = 5$
    $x - y = 1$

29. $y - x = 6$
    $x + y = 4$

Solve. *(pages 346–347)*

30. On Monday, Emily had a balance of $93.55 in her checking account. On Tuesday she wrote two checks for $47.00 each and deposited $93.40. Was her final balance on Tuesday more or less than her Monday balance?

Draw what comes next. *(pages 356–359)*

31.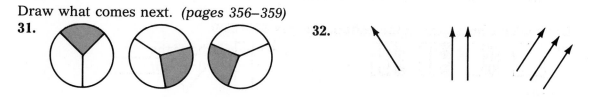

32.

Quadrilateral *MACK* is congruent to quadrilateral *BITE*.
Write the congruent angle or side. *(pages 368–369)*
1. ∠*K*   2. ∠*M*   3. $\overline{MA}$ 4. $\overline{TE}$

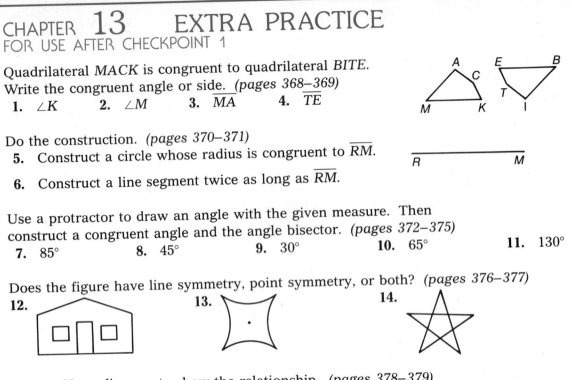

Do the construction. *(pages 370–371)*
5. Construct a circle whose radius is congruent to $\overline{RM}$.
6. Construct a line segment twice as long as $\overline{RM}$.

Use a protractor to draw an angle with the given measure. Then
construct a congruent angle and the angle bisector. *(pages 372–375)*
7. 85°   8. 45°   9. 30°   10. 65°   11. 130°

Does the figure have line symmetry, point symmetry, or both? *(pages 376–377)*
12.   13.   14.

Draw a Venn diagram to show the relationship. *(pages 378–379)*
15. Some houses are brick.   16. All multiples of 10 are also multiples of 5.

FOR USE AFTER CHECKPOINT 2

Write *true* or *false*. *(pages 380–381)*
17. A cylinder has two circular bases.   18. The faces of a pyramid are parallel.

What is the surface area? Use $\pi \approx 3.14$. *(pages 382–385)*
19.   20. 8 cm   21. 5 cm
3 m   3 cm   2 cm
5 m   8 cm
8 m   16 cm

What is the volume? Use $\pi \approx 3.14$. *(pages 386–389)*
22. cube: 23. rectangular prism: 24. cylinder:
  $s = 9$ mm $b = 21$ cm by 3 cm $r = 5$ mm
              $h = 3$ cm $h = 4$ mm

Use a diagram to solve. *(pages 390–391)*
25. A circular rug with a diameter of 4 m covers the middle of the
floor in a 5 m by 6 m room. What is the area of the floor *not*
covered by the rug?

Pentagon *LMNOP* is congruent to pentagon *QRSTV*. Write the congruent side or angle. *(pages 368–369)*

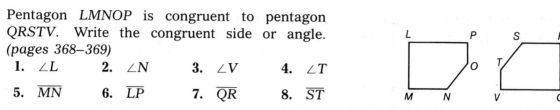

1. ∠L   2. ∠N   3. ∠V   4. ∠T

5. $\overline{MN}$ 6. $\overline{LP}$ 7. $\overline{QR}$ 8. $\overline{ST}$

Draw an acute angle. Label it ∠ABC. Do the construction. *(pages 370–375)*

9. Construct an angle that is congruent to ∠ABC.

10. Construct the bisector of ∠ABC.

Does the figure have line symmetry, point symmetry, both, or neither? *(pages 376–377)*

11.   12.   13.   14.

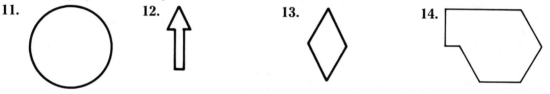

What is the surface area? Use $\pi \approx 3.14$. *(pages 380–385)*

15. cube
side: 6 cm

16. rectangular prism
base: 10 cm by 12 cm
height: 13 cm

17. cylinder
radius: 5 cm
height: 25 cm

18. cylinder
radius: 5 m
height: 8 m

Find the volume. Use $\pi \approx 3.14$. *(pages 386–389)*

19.   20.   21.

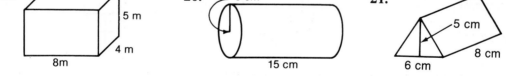

Draw a Venn diagram to show the relationship. *(pages 378–379)*

22. All multiples of 4 are even numbers.   23. Some rectangles are squares.

Use a diagram to solve. *(pages 390–391)*

24. Judy wants to replace the tiles on her kitchen floor. The floor is 480 cm by 600 cm, and the tiles Judy plans to use are 24 cm by 30 cm. How many tiles will she need?

You spin the spinner. Complete. *(pages 400–409)*

1. P(4) = ▧   **2.** P(0) = ▧   **3.** P(3) = ▧

4. P(2) = ▧   **5.** P(5) = ▧   **6.** P(6) = ▧

You spin the spinner at the right, then toss a coin.
7. How many outcomes include a 2?

You spin the spinner at the right twice. What is the probability?
8. P(1,1)   **9.** P(3,3)   **10.** P(1,6)   **11.** P(4,5)   **12.** P(1,4)

Find the range, the mean, the median, and the mode of the data.
(pages 410–413)
13. 3, 6, 6, 7, 9, 11, 14   **14.** 75, 71, 75, 69, 79, 81   **15.** 261, 250, 250, 278, 250, 301, 384

Solve. *(pages 414–415)*
16. At a clock factory, 90 clocks were inspected and 6 were rejected for defects. What is the probability of a defect?

17. Thirty spark plugs were tested on Monday. Six were defective. What is the probability that a spark plug was not defective on Monday?

Use the graph to answer the question. *(pages 416–421)*
18. During which month is there the greatest difference in the mean highest and lowest temperatures?

19. During which month is there the least difference in the mean highest and lowest temperatures?

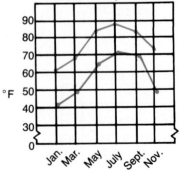

**Mean Highest and
Lowest Temperatures**

°F

CAR-BUYER SURVEY

TYPE OF CAR	NUMBER
Sedan	66
Station wagon	24
Convertible	4
4-wheel drive	6
Total	100

Use the survey at the left to solve.
(pages 422–423)
20. A car dealership expects to sell 1600 cars. Use the survey results to predict the number of different types of cars which will be sold.

You spin the spinner. What is the probability? *(pages 400–409)*
1. P(3)   2. P(4)   3. P(5)   4. P(7)

You spin the spinner and toss a coin.
5. How many outcomes include an H and a 2?

You spin the spinner twice. What is the probability?

6. P(3, 3)   7. P(6, 7)   8. P(2, 6)   9. P(4, 4)

What are the range, the mean, the median, and the mode?
(pages 410–413)
10. 32, 32, 45, 50, 120   11. 80, 85, 85, 85, 90

12. 5, 8, 9, 9, 11, 12   13. 2, 3, 7, 12, 13, 13, 20

Estimate the height of the highest mountain on the continent. *(pages 416–421)*

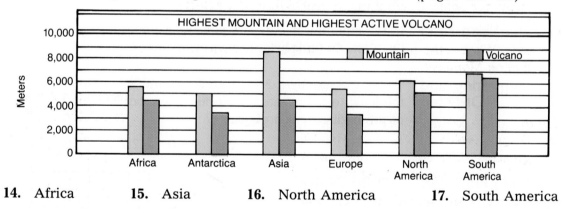

14. Africa   15. Asia   16. North America   17. South America

Solve. *(pages 414–415, 422–423)*
18. At a radio factory, 150 radios were inspected and 12 were rejected for defects. What is the probability of a defect?

19. Before a class election, 50 students were surveyed. A total of 28 said they would vote for Jackson. If there are 550 students, how many may be expected to vote for Jackson?

20. The Lincoln Bird Harbor wants to determine the number of birds nesting in the park. They capture and tag 400 birds, which are then released. One week later they capture 25 birds and find that 5 of them are tagged. About how many birds nest in the park?

USING MENTAL MATH STRATEGIES

Sometimes you can use mental mathematics to solve problems. You may be doubling a recipe in cooking, building a birdhouse, or counting change in a store. You use mental math to find an exact answer without using paper and pencil or a calculator. In this book, strategies for mental math are used that will help you improve your skills. Here are some examples.

Counting On and Back To find the amount of elapsed time from 10:45 A.M. to 12:30 P.M. you can count on as:

10:45 ⟶ 11:00 (15 min), 11:00 ⟶ 12:00 (1 h),
12:00 ⟶ 12:30 (30 min)

The amount of elapsed time is 1 h 45 min.

Using Facts In the equation $n + 4 = 11$, you think about one of these two facts to find the solution for n: $7 + 4 = 11$ or $11 - 4 = 7$.

Comparing and Ordering To list the numbers 2.73, 2.37, 2.337 and 2.3 in order from the least to the greatest, you mentally compare the values of the digits in each place.

2.3   2.337   2.37   2.73

Using Properties The distributive property helps you determine a product such as 6×57 by thinking, $6 \times (50 + 7) = 300 + 42 = 342$.

Using Patterns
$735 \times 1 = 735$
$735 \times 0.1 = 73.5$ This pattern helps you determine that
$735 \times 0.01 = 7.35$ $735 \times 0.001 = 0.735$.

Using Visual Images Picturing a number line in your head helps you see that
$$2 - \tfrac{3}{4} = 1\tfrac{1}{4}.$$

Changing Numbers and Operations When working with a percent such as 120%, you may want to change it to a decimal such as 1.2.

When adding the decimals 2.85 and 3.15, you can think $2 + 3 = 5$ and $0.85 + 0.15 = 1$. The sum is 6.

460

To find $\frac{2}{3}$ of 270, divide 270 by 3 and multiply the quotient by 2 to get 180.

To add 3854 and 2999, you can think of 2999 as $3000 - 1$. Then $3854 + 3000 = 6854$. Adjust by subtracting 1 to get 6853.

USING ESTIMATION STRATEGIES

Sometimes you may not need an exact answer, and an estimate will do. Each person develops a personal style of estimation to use in practical situations such as shopping, figuring the time needed to complete a job, or walking to a friend's house. In this book strategies for estimation are used that should help you in using math in everyday life. Here are some examples.

Rounding An area of 63.725 cm² when rounded to the nearest whole number is 64 cm².

The attendances on Saturday and Sunday were 8097 and 6500. When rounded to the greatest place value, the difference in attendance was about $8000 - 7000$, or 1000.

Front-End Estimating To estimate the total length, you can add the left-hand digits, $7 + 4 + 9 = 20$, and adjust by adding on 2 after observing that the tenths have a sum closer to 2 than to 1. The sum is about 22 m.

$$7.7 \text{ m}$$
$$4.2 \text{ m}$$
$$+9.8 \text{ m}$$

Comparing An estimate for 985×69 is 1000×70, or 70,000. The exact answer is less than 70,000 because 985 and 69 were both rounded up.

To find a range of values for 7.3×8.94, think:

$$7 \times 8 = 56 \qquad 8 \times 9 = 72 \qquad \text{So, } 7.3 \times 8.94 \text{ is between 56 and 72.}$$

Using Compatible Numbers To estimate $8\overline{)54.79}$ you can think $8\overline{)56}$ or 7. You found this estimate by looking for an appropriate whole number fact.

461

Using Clustering When estimating the mean for the scores 92, 89, 91, 88, and 87, observe that all the scores cluster around 90, so the mean is about 90.

Using Measurement

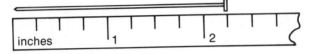

The nail is about $2\frac{1}{4}$ in. to the nearest $\frac{1}{4}$ in.

Of the following choices, the best estimate for the thickness of a piece of cord is 1.2 mm.

1.2 mm   1.2 cm   1.2 dm

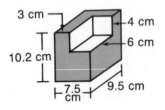

To estimate the volume of the figure, you can think of it as two prisms and subtract their volumes.

$$(10 \times 8 \times 10) - (6 \times 4 \times 5) = 680$$

The volume is about 680 cm^3.

Reading Graphs The height of the line on the graph is about halfway between 50 and 100, so it is about 75.

Sampling and Predicting If about $\frac{3}{4}$ of a good random sample of 400 employees of Brown Corporation are satisfied with the benefits they receive, then you can predict that about $\frac{3}{4}$ of 800, or 600, employees would feel the same way.

USING A CALCULATOR

Every calculator is different. You should read the instructions for your calculator to learn how to use it. Most scientific calculators have the keys (buttons) pictured below but they may be in different places.

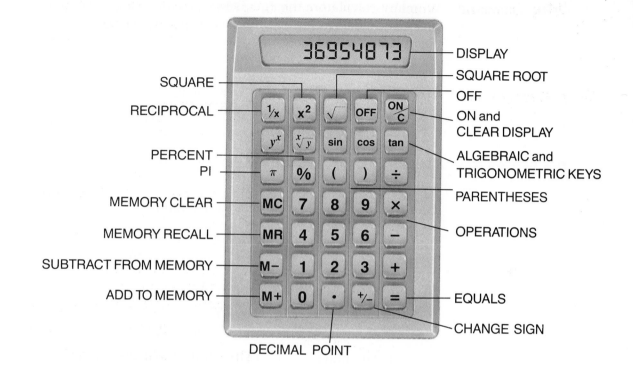

DISPLAY

`36954873`

SQUARE ROOT

OFF

ON and CLEAR DISPLAY

SQUARE

RECIPROCAL

PERCENT

PI

ALGEBRAIC and TRIGONOMETRIC KEYS

MEMORY CLEAR

MEMORY RECALL

SUBTRACT FROM MEMORY

ADD TO MEMORY

PARENTHESES

OPERATIONS

EQUALS

CHANGE SIGN

DECIMAL POINT

The Display A calculator display usually does not show commas. Usually 8 digits are the most the display will show. A display never shows a dollar sign. You must press the decimal point key to show a decimal number. You press the clear key to remove the display.

The Memory Feature You can add the same number to several other numbers by using the memory keys.

Add 36 to each of these numbers: 9, 29, 58.

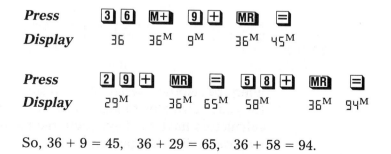

| *Press* | 3 | 6 | M+ | 9 | + | MR | = |
| *Display* | 36 | | 36ᴹ | 9ᴹ | | 36ᴹ | 45ᴹ |

| *Press* | 2 | 9 | + | MR | = | 5 | 8 | + | MR | = |
| *Display* | | 29ᴹ | | 36ᴹ | 65ᴹ | | 58ᴹ | | 36ᴹ | 94ᴹ |

So, $36 + 9 = 45$, $36 + 29 = 65$, $36 + 58 = 94$.

The Constant Feature On many calculators the equals key is also a constant key. This feature lets you press the equals key to perform an operation over and over again with the same number. For example, you can count by twos on the calculator.

Press 2 + = = = The calculator is adding 2 each
Display 2   4   6   8   time you press the equals key.

The Percent Key Many calculators have a percent key. You can use it to solve problems with percents.

Find 50% of 80. On most calculators, enter the base first.

Press 8 0 × 5 0 % =
Display 80   50   40   50% of 80 is 40.

The π Key Some calculators have a π key. You can use this key to calculate with a more exact value of π than 3.14.

Find the circumference of a circle with a diameter of 4 cm. Use the formula $C = \pi d$.

Press   π   × 4   =   The circumference is
Display 3.1415927   4 12.566371 about 12.57 cm.

The Reciprocal Key Some calculators have a reciprocal key. You can find the reciprocal of a number using this key.

Find the reciprocal of 4.

Press 4   1/x   The reciprocal of 4 is 0.25
Display 4   0.25   because $4 \times 0.25 = 1$.

The Change-Sign Key Some calculators have a change-sign key. You can use it to enter a negative number.

Find the sum of ⁻27 and 9.

Press 2 7 +/− + 9 =
Display 27   ⁻27   9 ⁻18 $^-27 + 9 = {}^-18$

464

For each problem, choose the method you think is best: calculator, mental math, or estimation. Write C, M, or E. Then solve the problem using that method.

Chapter 1

1. The length of a board is 709 cm. About how many meters is this?

2. List the numbers in order from the greatest to the least.

   30.69   3.093   6.069   3.6   3.69   36.9   63

3. At dawn, the temperature was ⁻3°C. By noon, it was 9°C. Was the difference in temperature greater or less than 10°C?

4. If the pattern of dots continues, how many dots will be in the fifteenth row? in the twentieth row?

Chapter 2

1. What is the difference between five more than 2.9, and nine less than 11.2?

2. The moving van left San Diego at 6:18 A.M. on Monday, and arrived at its destination on Tuesday at 6:39 P.M. About how many hours was it on the road?

Use the chart to answer Exercises 3 and 4.

3. Name two islands of the United States that have a combined area closest to that of Vancouver.

4. How much larger is the combined area of the Canadian islands than that of the United States islands?

Some Islands of the United States and Canada	
Hawaiian, U.S.	6450*
Aleutian, U.S.	6821
Kodiak, U.S.	6370
Vancouver, Can.	12,079
Cape Breton, Can.	3981
Newfoundland, Can.	42,030

*Measurements are in square miles and are not exact.

465

For each problem, choose the method you think is best: calculator, mental math, or estimation. Write C, M, or E. Then solve the problem using that method.

Chapter 3

1. Write the sum. $12^3 + 7^2 + 11^3 + 9^4$

2. What is the quotient when 6.9 is divided by the product of 1.5 and 2?

3. The moon orbits Earth in about 27 days, 7 hours, and 43.2 minutes. About how many weeks is this?

4. Charon, a satellite of Pluto, orbits Pluto in 6.4 days. About how many times does it orbit Pluto in a year?

Chapter 4

1. What is the area of the shaded figure to the right?

2. Which has the greater perimeter?

   square: $s = 7.29$ cm
   rectangle: $l = 9.9$ cm $w = 4.8$ cm

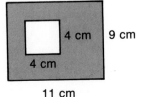

3. Are the areas of these parallelograms the same or different? Explain.

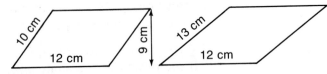

4. Insulation tape is to be put around the edges of this stained glass window. How much tape is needed?

Chapter 5

1. Write the numbers from the least to the greatest.

   $\frac{3}{7}$ $\frac{2}{5}$ $\frac{4}{9}$ 0.42 $\frac{4}{11}$ 0.3

2. What are the first ten multiples of 36?

3. Write these fractions as pairs of equivalent fractions.

   $\frac{32}{12}$ $\frac{12}{21}$ $\frac{7}{11}$ $\frac{8}{3}$ $\frac{4}{7}$ $\frac{21}{33}$

4. This region represents 1. Is the shaded part closer to $\frac{1}{3}$, $\frac{1}{2}$, or $\frac{3}{4}$?

Chapter 6

1. What is the difference between 11 and the sum of $9\frac{3}{4}$ and $\frac{1}{2}$?

2. Which is greater?

$$6\frac{3}{4} + 2.8 + 9\frac{7}{8} \quad \text{or} \quad 3.7 + 7\frac{5}{8} + 2.25 + 6\frac{1}{3}$$

3. Did a share of stock increase or decrease from yesterday to today? by how much?

Yesterday: $36\frac{1}{8}$ Today: $36\frac{3}{4}$

4. The carpenter is building a railing on the house. He needs these lengths of boards. About how much is the total length?

3 boards: $4\frac{1}{2}$ ft   3 boards: $7\frac{3}{4}$ ft   3 boards: $2\frac{1}{3}$ ft

5 boards: $3\frac{1}{2}$ ft   2 boards: $1\frac{1}{4}$ ft

Chapter 7

1. About how much money is one third of $247, decreased by $7.89?

2. Name the reciprocals of each number. $\frac{3}{5}$ 6 $\frac{9}{2}$ $2\frac{1}{2}$

3. Fran bought 20 shares of stock at $34\frac{1}{2}$ dollars a share. How much did she pay for the stock?

4. When making costumes, $6\frac{1}{3}$ yd of fabric are divided into three pieces of the same size. Will each piece be closer to 2 yd or $2\frac{1}{3}$ yd?

Chapter 8

1. Write as a mathematical expression.
   Nine more than the product of 5 and a number.

Use these values to answer Exercises 2 and 3.

$$a = 6.2 \quad b = 8.9 \quad c = 7.6$$

2. Evaluate the expression $5ab + 2c$.

3. Is this expression greater or less than 20? $\dfrac{3(a + b)}{2}$

4. The Sports Club had $18 in its treasury at the end of last year. No money was spent. Each member paid $2 in dues this year. There is $70 in the treasury now. How many members are in the club?

For each problem, choose the method you think is best: calculator, mental math, or estimate. Write C, M, or E. Then solve the problem using that method.

Chapter 9

1. The ratio of swimmers to runners to take part in the event is 22 to 49. Is this ratio closer to $\frac{1}{2}$ or 1?

2. Select the value for a to make a proportion.

   $a = 9.176$
   $a = 6.65$ $\frac{6.2}{12.5} = \frac{a}{18.5}$
   $a = 15.9$

3. Are these triangles similar?

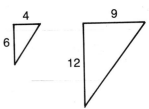

4. A scale on a drawing is 1 cm:2.5 m. How long will you draw an object that is actually 62.75 m?

Chapter 10

1. Which of these percents are less than $\frac{1}{10}$?

   $11\frac{1}{2}\%$ $6\frac{1}{4}\%$ 7.89% 15%

2. Write each percent as a fraction in lowest terms.

   25% 50% 30% 95%

3. In a recent election, Joan received $\frac{1}{4}$ of the 380 votes, while Jack received 35% of them. Who received more votes?

4. Fifteen percent of the students in the school are in the fifth grade. There are 48 students in the fifth grade. How many students are in the school?

Chapter 11

1. How much are 10%, 20%, 30%, 40%, and 50% of $60?

2. Alice paid an $11\frac{1}{4}\%$ annual interest rate on a loan of $1200. Was the interest she paid in a year more or less than $120?

3. When bought on sale, which coat costs less?

25% off $78.95

$\frac{1}{3}$ off $85.50

4. The sales tax rate is changing from 6.25% to 6.75%. How much money can be saved on taxes by buying a car priced at $9875 before the tax rate changes?

Chapter 12

1. Estimate the sum.

start — 6.3 — 6.01 — 5.92 — 6.23 — 6 — stop

2. Let $a = {}^-3.6$, $b = {}^-8.5$, $c = 17.4$. Is $ab - c$ greater or less than 0?

3. In the equation $y = 6x + 1.5$, what is the value of y when $x = 8.5$?

4. Imagine that you have a point located in a coordinate plane that has the ordered pair $({}^-3, 2)$. What point will you get when you move two spaces to the left, then 2 spaces up?

Chapter 13

1. Name a solid figure that has two congruent bases whose shape is a polygon.

2. About how many square centimeters are contained in this figure?

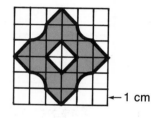

←1 cm

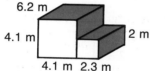

6.2 m

4.1 m

2 m

4.1 m   2.3 m

3. About how much area is painted in red?

4. What is the volume of the figure?

Chapter 14

1. The probability of landing on a blue region in a game is $\frac{1}{5}$. If the spinner spins 1269 times, about how many times would you expect it to land on a blue region?

2. The scores of a math class's tests were recorded. The mode of the scores was 82. Were there more scores of 82 or of 100?

3. Ronald's odometer registers ⟨8 | 7 | 4 | 6 | 2 | 9⟩. He has had the car for 5 years. About how many miles has he traveled in a day?

4. Data collected about rainfall within different counties during a month indicated that the range was $1\frac{1}{4}$ in. If the smallest amount within a county was $\frac{1}{8}$ in., what was the largest amount?

469

TABLE OF NUMBERS

	A	B	C	D	E	F	G	H
1	32	5	278	387	0.8	2	$\frac{1}{10}$	$\frac{2}{5}$
2	16	75	692	962	1.5	6.7	$\frac{1}{3}$	$\frac{2}{3}$
3	8	2	8451	8541	0.2	5	$\frac{3}{4}$	$\frac{1}{2}$
4	95	150	6261	2726	9.5	8.72	$\frac{1}{2}$	$\frac{1}{3}$
5	5	8	4989	5021	2	4	$\frac{2}{3}$	$\frac{3}{4}$
6	89	2	3893	5323	1.5	0.5	$1\frac{1}{5}$	$1\frac{3}{10}$
7	33	50	784	748	4.6	0.25	$4\frac{1}{3}$	$3\frac{2}{3}$
8	67	421	1026	973	1.5	7.3	$8\frac{1}{2}$	$7\frac{3}{4}$
9	55	20	874	647	0.4	8	$2\frac{1}{3}$	5
10	435	4	513	831	3.2	10	$6\frac{3}{4}$	7
11	450	350	250	150	1.6	2	2.4	2.8
12	65	55	45	35	0.8	0.85	0.9	0.95
13	7428	7528	7628	7728	4.2	5.2	6.2	7.2
14	25%	1%	50%	80%	75%	90%	10%	5%

Ideas for using this table for mental math, estimation, and calculator activities are found under *Computation Strategies* on the Cumulative Review pages at the end of each chapter of the Teacher's Edition.

PROBLEM SOLVING ACTIVITIES

CHAPTER 1

Newspapers and magazines often use drawings, charts, or tables to display data.

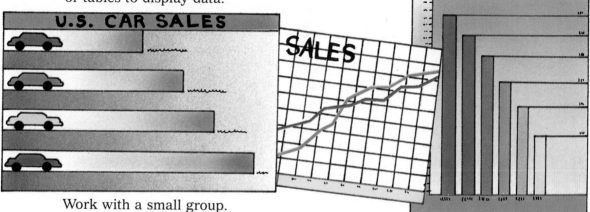

Work with a small group.

- Look in newspapers and magazines to find as many different ways to display data as you can.

- Study the drawings, graphs, and charts you have collected. Discuss each one and write a description of the data shown by it.

- Ask another group to study your drawings, graphs, or charts. See if they can write accurate descriptions of the data. How do their descriptions compare to yours?

CHAPTER 2

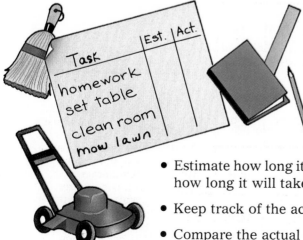

Can you judge how much time a task will take to complete? It's a useful skill to have, especially when you have a lot of things to do in a given amount of time.

Try this experiment. Choose several tasks such as doing homework, cleaning your room, mowing the lawn, cooking dinner, or getting ready for school.

- Estimate how long it will take you to do each task. Then estimate how long it will take to complete all the tasks together.

- Keep track of the actual time it takes you to do your tasks.

- Compare the actual and estimated totals.

CHAPTER 3

You're helping plan a family vacation for this summer. You have thirty days of vacation and are going to travel by car in the United States.

Work with a partner. Decide where you want to travel. Use maps or atlases to help you plan your route.

- Think about where you would like to stop along your route. Which cities and places have you wanted to see? How long will you need to stay in each place? How many miles apart are the places you plan to see?

- Design a chart that shows the plan for your trip. Then ask the members of another group to look at your chart and show your trip using a map in the atlas. If you have designed your chart well, they should be able to do this. Make adjustments to your chart if you need to.

CHAPTER 4

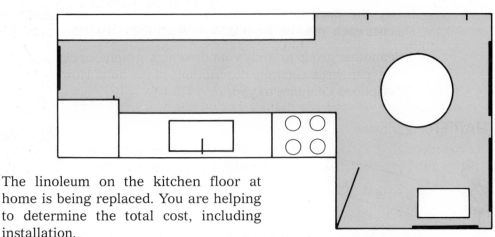

The linoleum on the kitchen floor at home is being replaced. You are helping to determine the total cost, including installation.

Work with a partner.

- Find the price of linoleum in newspaper ads or by visiting a floor covering store. Pick the kind of linoleum you would like to use.

- Find out how much the installation of the linoleum costs. (Some stores may include it in the price per square yard.)

- How much will it cost in all to recover each of your kitchen floors? Discuss what you need to do to find the answer.

CHAPTER 5

You are planning to set up a vegetable stand this summer to sell the potatoes, tomatoes, and corn you have grown. All vegetables will be sold by the pound. You have a calculator and a simple scale marked in pounds and ounces.

Work with a partner.

- Decide on a price per pound for each type of vegetable. Discuss what things you need to think about when considering your selling price.

- How will you use your scale and calculator to determine the price of different amounts of vegetables that people will buy? Give several examples.

- Compare your method and examples with another group. Did you use different methods? Is one better than another? Why?

CHAPTER 6

You want to put a series of posters side by side on two walls of your bedroom. Each poster is $18\frac{1}{2}$ in. wide. You want a space of at least $3\frac{1}{2}$ in. on both sides of each poster. No windows will be covered.

- Choose and measure two walls of your room. Write the measurements down in inches. What should you do if either wall has windows or something on the wall already?

- Determine the number of posters that will fit on the walls. Draw a diagram to show your plan.

CHAPTER 7

Your class is having a dinner to celebrate your teacher's birthday. You are in charge of making some kind of salad.

- Find a recipe that you would like to make. Adjust the ingredient amounts in the recipe to serve the number of people in your class.

SALADS

PASTA SALAD

1 lb pasta
¼ c vegetable oil
2 c chopped tomatoes
2 c sliced green beans

- Write out your recipe so that it reflects amounts needed to serve all the people in your class. Use the largest unit of measure that you can. (For example, convert cups to pints.)

- Compare your recipe with a partner's recipe. Do you have any ingredients that are the same? Do you both use the same amount of that ingredient? Discuss why you may not.

CHAPTER 8

How much money do you spend in a week? Keep track of your expenses for a month and see how your weekly expenses compare.

- Think about the different kinds of expenses you have. Use a table to collect data about your expenses.

- Make a bar graph to display your total weekly expenses for four weeks. What should the two scales on the graph show?

- Pick one of your weekly expense totals. What if it increased by an amount n? Write an equation that shows what your new weekly expenses would be. Suppose n represented $3.25. Solve your equation.

CHAPTER 9

Work with a partner.

- Use an atlas and a map scale to find out how many kilometers your hometown is from: Washington, DC; Mount Rushmore, SD; your state capital; and El Paso, TX.

- Each of you select two other locations and determine their distances from your hometown. Exchange locations and have your partner find the distances. Compare the answers to see if they are the same.

CHAPTER 10

GREENFIELD'S CAFE
MENU

Salad Plate	$4.50
Chef's Salad	$4.00
Turkey Sandwich	$3.50
Chili	$2.75
Soup	$0.95
Juice	$0.95

PRICES INCLUDE TAX

You are treating your friend to lunch at Greenfield's.

- Use the menu to choose what each of you will order for lunch.

- You want to leave a 15% tip. What is the total bill for the lunch, including tip?

- Once you know the total cost of the food, how can you figure the total cost of lunch, with tip, in just one step?

CHAPTER 11

What is your favorite half-hour television program? How much of that time is spent on commercials? Try this experiment.

Keep a record as you watch your favorite program.

- Use a watch to time the number of minutes spent on commercials and the number of minutes spent on the program itself.

- Now work with a group. Compare your findings. Are the results the same for different programs?

CHAPTER 12

Your sister wants to buy a new car. She plans to keep it for six years, and then buy another car.

- Look at the new car ads in the newspapers. Find the price of a car you would like to buy.

- Research information about how a car decreases in value from year to year. You may wish to speak to someone who works at a car dealership.

- How much do you think your car will be worth in six years?

Some items increase in value over the years. Make a list of three items that you think might increase in value. Work in a group and compare lists.

CHAPTER 13

Many homes have hot water heaters that are separate from the boiler or furnace. To help keep in heat and conserve energy, utility companies recommend covering the heater with special insulating material.

- Find out the shape and dimensions of one type of hot water heater from a utility company or appliance store. Draw a diagram of the hot water heater and label the dimensions.

- What would you have to know in order to estimate the amount of insulating material needed to cover the water heater? Describe how you would estimate.

CHAPTER 14

Who gets the most telephone calls at your house? Do this experiment for a two-week period of time.

- Keep track of each week's calls in a table like the one below. Make a tally mark for every phone call received.

TALLY COUNT

	SUN	MON	TUES	WED	THURS	FRI	SAT
(Write the							
names of							
people at							
home here.)							

- Draw a graph to show all the phone calls received by each person listed in the table. Design the graph so that it is easy to compare the numbers for both weeks.

- Show your graph to a partner. Ask them to tell you what statements they can make about the information in your graph. Does your graph show what you wanted it to?

GLOSSARY

A

absolute value (p. 334) The distance of an integer from zero on the number line.

acute angle (p. 100) An angle measuring greater than 0° and less than 90°.

acute triangle (p. 106) A triangle with all angles acute.

angle (p. 96) Two rays that have the same endpoint.

angle bisector (p. 374) A ray that divides an angle into two congruent parts.

arc (p. 370) A part of a circle.

area (p. 114) The measure of a surface inside a closed figure.

Associative Property (pp. 36, 64) Changing the grouping of the numbers does not change the sum or product.

B

base (p. 380) The face of a pyramid or a cone opposite the vertex. One of two congruent parallel faces of a prism or a cylinder.

bisector (p. 374) A line that divides a line segment or an angle into two equal parts.

budget (p. 324) A plan you make to be sure your income will cover your expenses.

C

capacity (p. 16) The amount of fluid a container will hold.

center of a circle (p. 112) The point in a plane from which all the points in a circle are the same distance.

centimeter (cm) (p. 14) A metric unit of length. 1 cm = 10 mm

chord (p. 112) A segment that joins two points on a circle.

circle (p. 112) The set of all points in a plane that are at the same distance from a point in the plane.

circle graph (p. 322) A circle divided into parts to show data.

circumference (p. 112) The distance around a circle.

collinear points (p. 96) Points that lie in the same line.

commission (p. 318) The amount of money you earn for selling a product or providing a service.

common denominator (p. 146) A common multiple of the denominators.

common factor (p. 132) A number which is a factor of two or more numbers.

common multiple (p. 144) A number that is a multiple of two or more numbers.

Commutative Property (pp. 36, 64) A property stating that changing the order of the numbers does not change the sum or product.

compatible numbers (p. 84) Numbers close to given numbers that make estimation easier.

complementary angles (p. 100) Angles the sum of whose measures is 90°.

composite number (p. 134) Any whole number that has more than two factors.

compound interest (p. 328) Interest paid on both the principal and previously earned interest.

cone (p. 380) A space figure with one circular base and one vertex.

congruent angles (p. 98) Angles with equal measures.

congruent figures (p. 368) Figures that have the same size and shape.

congruent line segments (p. 102) Two line segments with the same length.

coordinate plane (p. 350) A grid on a plane with two perpendicular number lines.

coordinates (p. 236) The numbers in an ordered pair associated with a point on a graph.

corresponding angles (p. 266) The angles at matching vertexes of congruent figures.

corresponding sides (p. 266) The matching sides of congruent figures.

cross products (p. 140) Products used to check if two fractions are equivalent.

cross section (p. 381) The figure formed when a space figure is sliced by a plane.

cubic centimeter (p. 16) The amount of space contained in a cube with all edges 1 cm long.

cylinder (p. 380) A space figure with two parallel congruent circular bases.

D

data (p. 410) Numbers that give information.

degree (p. 98) The unit of measure used to measure angles.

degrees Celsius (°C) (p. 22) The metric unit for measuring temperature.

denominator (p. 138) The bottom number in a fraction.

dependent events (p. 408) Two events in which the result of the first affects the result of the second.

diagonal (p. 102) A line segment that joins two vertexes of a polygon and is not a side of the polygon.

diameter (p. 112) A chord through the center of a circle or its measure.

discount (p. 316) A decrease in the price of an item.

discount rate (p. 316) A reduction that is a percent of the original price.

Distributive Property (p. 64) The product of a factor and a sum is equal to the sum of the products.

divisible (p. 130) Capable of being divided evenly without a remainder.

double bar graph (p. 416) A graph that uses bars to compare two sets of data.

double line graph (p. 418) A graph that uses lines to compare the change over time of two sets of data.

E

edge (p. 380) The intersection of two faces or two sides of a space figure.

elapsed time (p. 50) The time that passes between the start and end of an event.

equation (pp. 34, 220) A statement using the equals sign to show that two numbers or quantities are equal.

equilateral triangle (p. 106) A triangle with three congruent sides and three congruent angles.

equivalent decimals (p. 4) Decimals that name the same number.

equivalent fractions (p. 140) Fractions that name the same number.

estimate (p. 38) An answer that is not exact.

evaluate (p. 218) To substitute a number for each variable in an expression and then do the indicated arithmetic.

even numbers (p. 130) Numbers that are divisible by 2.

expanded form (p. 2) The representation of a number as the sum of products of each digit and a power of 10.

exponent (p. 72) The number showing how many times a base is used as a factor.

F

faces (p. 380) The flat surfaces that form space figures.

factor (p. 132) A number that can divide evenly into another number.

formula (p. 110) A short way of stating a rule.

fraction (p. 138) A number in the form $\frac{a}{b}$, where b is not zero, that compares part of an object or a set with the whole.

frequency (p. 420) The number of times a given item appears in a set of data.

front-end estimation (p. 86) An estimation method using the left digits of the numbers involved.

G

geometric transformations (p. 356) Changes in the position of a figure while the size and shape remain the same.

gram (g) (p. 18) A metric unit of mass. 1 g = 1000 mg

graph of an equation (p. 352) The line consisting of all the points whose coordinates satisfy the equation.

graph of a number (p. 6) The point paired with a number on a number line.

greatest common factor (GCF) (p. 132) The greatest of the common factors of two or more numbers.

greatest possible error (GPE) (p. 20) The allowance of half a unit either way in a measurement.

H

histogram (p. 426) A bar graph showing frequency data.

hypotenuse (p. 394) The side opposite the right angle in a right triangle.

I

Identity Property (p. 64) The property stating the product of one and any other number is that number.

integers (p. 334) The positive numbers 1, 2, 3, . . . , the negative numbers $^-$1, $^-$2, $^-$3, . . . , and zero.

independent events (p. 406) Events that have no effect on each other.

interest (p. 306) The money that the bank pays you for use of your money.

interest rate (p. 306) A percent used to calculate the interest, usually for a year.

intersecting lines (p. 96) Lines that cross each other.

inverse operations (p. 222) One operation that "undoes" the other.

irrational number (p. 362) Any number that cannot be written as the quotient of two integers, $\frac{a}{b}$, where b is not zero.

isosceles triangle (p. 106) A triangle with two congruent sides and two congruent angles.

K

kilogram (kg) (p. 18) A metric unit of mass. 1 kg = 1000 g

kilometer (km) (p. 14) A metric unit of length. 1 km = 1000 m

L

least common denominator (LCD) (p. 146) The LCM of two or more denominators.

least common multiple (LCM) (p. 144) The least of the common multiples of two nonzero numbers.

legs of a right triangle (p. 394) The sides of a right triangle that are not the hypotenuse.

line (p. 96) A set of points that extends without end in opposite directions.

linear equation (p. 352) An equation whose graph is a straight line.

line of symmetry (p. 376) A line through a figure so that if the figure were folded on the line, one side would fit exactly on the other.

line segment (p. 96) A part of a line with two endpoints.

liter (L) (p. 16) A metric unit of capacity. 1 L = 1000 mL

lowest terms (p. 142) A fraction is in lowest terms if the GCF of the numerator and the denominator is 1.

M

markup (p. 316) An increase in the price of an item.

mass (p. 18) The amount of matter in an object.

mathematical expression (p. 216) A combination of numbers, variables, and operation symbols.

mean (p. 410) The sum of the data items divided by the number of data items.

median (p. 412) The middle number in a set of data arranged in order.

meter (m) (p. 14) A metric unit of length. 1000 m = 1 km

midpoint (p. 374) The point of a segment that divides it into two congruent parts.

milligram (mg) (p. 18) A metric unit of mass. 1000 mg = 1 g

milliliter (mL) (p. 16) A metric unit of capacity. 1000 mL = 1 L

millimeter (mm) (p. 14) A metric unit of length. 1 mm = 0.1 cm

mixed number (p. 148) A number that has a whole number part and a fractional part.

mode (p. 412) The number or numbers that appear most frequently in a set of data.

multiple (p. 144) The product of a given number and any whole number.

N

negative numbers (p. 334) Numbers less than zero.

number line (p. 6) A line in which numbers have been paired with points.

numerator (p. 138) The top number in a fraction.

O

obtuse angle (p. 100) An angle that has a measure greater than 90° and less than 180°.

obtuse triangle (p. 106) A triangle with one obtuse angle.

odd numbers (p. 130) Numbers that are not divisible by 2.

opposites (p. 334) Two numbers that are the same distance from 0 but on opposite sides of 0.

ordered pair (p. 234) A pair of numbers in which the order shows the location of a point on a grid. (4, 3) is an ordered pair.

origin (p. 350) The point where the x-axis and the y-axis intersect.

outcome (p. 400) The result of a probability experiment.

P

parallel lines (p. 96) Two lines in a plane that do not intersect.

parallelogram (p. 108) A quadrilateral whose opposite sides are parallel.

percent (p. 278) The ratio of a number to 100. The symbol % means per hundred.

percent of change (p. 310) The increase or decrease in a quantity divided by the original quantity.

perimeter (p. 110) The distance around a polygon.

period (p. 328) An interval of time during which a bank pays interest earned on an account.

perpendicular (p. 100) Two lines, line segments, or rays that form a right angle.

perpendicular bisector (p. 374) The bisector of a line segment that is also perpendicular to the line segment.

plane (p. 96) A set of points on a flat surface that extends without end.

point (p. 96) An exact location.

point symmetry (p. 376) A figure is symmetric with respect to a point if the figure can be turned 180° and match its shape in the original position.

polygon (p. 102) A plane figure formed by joining three or more segments at their endpoints.

positive numbers (p. 334) Numbers greater than zero.

precision (p. 20) The precision of a measurement depends on the unit of measure you use. A smaller unit results in a more precise measure.

prime factorization (p. 134) The product of prime numbers that name a given number, such as $2 \times 2 \times 3 \times 5$ to name 60.

prime number (p. 134) A number that has exactly two factors, itself and 1.

principal (p. 306) The money you deposit in the bank.

prism (p. 380) A space figure with two congruent parallel bases. Its base can be any polygon and its other faces are rectangles.

probability (p. 400) A number describing the chance that an event will happen.

proportion (p. 252) An equation which states that two ratios are equal.

pyramid (p. 380) A space figure with four or more faces. The base can be any polygon. The other faces of the pyramid are triangles.

Pythagorean theorem (p. 394) If a triangle is a right triangle, the square of the hypotenuse is equal to the sum of the squares of the other two sides.

R

radius (p. 112) A line segment that joins the center of a circle and a point on the circle.

random outcome (p. 402) When each outcome is equally likely to occur.

range (p. 410) The difference between the greatest number and the least number in a list of data.

rate (p. 250) A ratio that compares quantities of two different kinds. A rate may be expressed as a ratio, a decimal, or a percent.

ratio (p. 248) A quotient of two numbers that is used to compare one quantity to another.

rational number (p. 362) Any number that can be written as the quotient of two integers, $\frac{a}{b}$, where b is not zero.

ray (p. 96) A part of a line with one endpoint.

reciprocals (p. 198) Two numbers whose product is 1.

rectangle (p. 108) A parallelogram with four right angles.

reflection (p. 356) A geometric transformation that changes the position of a figure through the motion of a flip.

regular polygon (p. 102) A polygon in which all sides are congruent and all angles are congruent.

relative frequency (p. 420) The ratio of the frequency of an item to the total of the frequencies.

relatively prime numbers (p. 142) Two numbers whose GCF is 1.

repeating decimal (p. 150) A decimal in which the last digit or block of digits repeats without end.

rhombus (p. 108) A parallelogram with four congruent sides.

right angle (p. 100) An angle with a measure of 90°.

right triangle (p. 106) A triangle with one right angle.

rotation (p. 356) A geometric transformation that changes the position of a figure through the motion of a turn.

S

sales tax rate (p. 312) The rate at which a tax is figured on the price of a purchase. A 6% rate means 6¢ is charged on every 100¢.

scale drawing (p. 260) A sketch of an object with all lengths in proportion to corresponding actual lengths.

scale (p. 260) The ratio of the size of a drawing to the size of the actual object.

scalene triangle (p. 106) A triangle with no congruent sides and no congruent angles.

scientific notation (p. 90) A way of naming numbers in which a given number is expressed as a product of another number between 1 and 10. For example, $43{,}000 = 4.3 \times 10^4$.

similar triangles (p. 266) Triangles that have the same shape but not always the same size.

solution (p. 34) The number that replaces a variable to form a true equation.

solution of a system (p. 354) An ordered pair that is a solution of both equations in a system.

solve (p. 34) Find a number that replaces the variable to form a true equation.

space figures (p. 380) Figures that have three dimensions, that is, length, width, and height.

sphere (p. 380) A space figure, the points of which are the same distance from a point called the center.

square (p. 108) A parallelogram with four congruent sides and four right angles.

square root (p. 124) One of two equal factors of a number.

standard form (p. 2) The usual, short form of a number. 573 is the standard form for 5 hundreds, 7 tens, 3 ones.

straight angle (p. 372) An angle with a measure of 180°.

substitution (p. 220) To replace the variable with numbers.

supplementary angles (p. 100) Two angles whose measures add up to 180°.

surface area (p. 382) The sum of the areas of the faces and base of a space figure.

symmetry (p. 376) A property that a figure has when parts match on opposite sides of a line or about a point.

system of equations (p. 354) Two equations that have the same two variables.

T

terminating decimal (p. 150) A decimal with a limited number of nonzero digits.

terms of a proportion (p. 252) The numbers in a proportion.

time (p. 306) The period during which you leave your money in the bank.

translation (p. 356) A geometric transformation that changes the position of a figure through the motion of a slide.

trapezoid (p. 108) A quadrilateral with only one pair of parallel sides.

tree diagram (p. 404) A picture showing possible outcomes of an activity.

U

unit rate (p. 250) The ratio of a number to 1.

unit price (p. 250) The cost per unit of a product.

V

variable (p. 34) A letter used to represent one or more numbers.

vertex (p. 96, 380) The common endpoint of two rays or two segments. The intersection of three or more edges of a space figure.

vertical angles (p. 96) Opposite angles formed by two intersecting lines.

volume (p. 386) The amount of space contained in a space figure.

W

word form (p. 2) The long, written form for a number in words.

X

x-axis (p. 350) The horizontal number line on a coordinate plane.

Y

y-axis (p. 350) The vertical number line on a coordinate plane.

Z

Zero Property of Addition (p. 36) The property stating that the sum of zero and any other number is that number.

Zero Property of Multiplication (p. 64) The property stating that the product of zero and any other number is zero.

INDEX

A

Absolute value, 334–335
Addition
  addend, 38
  calculator activities, 40–41,
    44–45
  column, 38–39
  decimals, 40–41
  equations, 34–37, 220–227
  estimating with, 38–41,
    48–49, 110–111, 172–173
  fractions, 164–167
  integers, 338–339
  of measurements, 48–49
  mental math with, 34–37,
    164–165
  mixed numbers, 172–173
  properties of, 36–37,
    164–165
  sum, 38
  of units of time, 50–51
  whole number, 38–39
Angle(s)
  acute, 100–101
  bisector, 374–375
  complementary, 100–101
  congruent, 98–99, 372–373
  corresponding, 368–369
  measuring, 98–99
  obtuse, 100–101
  right, 100–101
  straight, 372
  supplementary, 100–101
  vertical, 96–97
Applications, *see* Problem
  solving applications
Arc, 370
Area
  circle, 118–119
  estimating with, 114–115,
    278–279, 384–385
  parallelogram, 116–117
  rectangle, 114–115
  square, 114–115
  trapezoid, 116–117
  triangle, 116–117
Arrangements, 135, 403
Associative property, 36, 64
Average, 410–411

B

Bar graphs, 23, 287, 314,
  416–417
Base eight, 210–211
Base two, 210–211
Bisectors, 374–375
Budgets, 324–325

C

Calculator activites
  addition, 40–41, 44–45
  areas, 118–119
  averages, 410–411
  checking, 40–41, 140–141
  checking mistakes, 68–69
  decimal remainders,
    130–131
  decimals, 150–151, 284–285
  divisibility, 130–131
  division, 112–113, 130–131,
    150–151, 202–203,
    224–225, 258–259, 284–285
  equations, 224–225
  equivalent form, 150–151,
    284–285
  exponents, 72–73
  features
    change-sign key,
      340–341, 344–345
    constant, 72–73
    display, 2–3, 8–9
    exponent key, 72–73
    list of, 462–464
    memory, 168–169
    percent key, 288–289,
      312–313
    pi key, 112–113, 118–119
    square root key, 124–125
  fractions, 140–141, 168–169,
    202–203, 284–285
  integers, 340–341, 344–345
  inverse operations, 44–45
  multiplication, 68–69, 80–81,
    140–141, 224–225, 258–259
  order of operations, 66–67
  patterns, 80–81
  place value, 2–3, 8–9
  proportions, 258–259
  repeating decimals, 150–151
  statistics, 410–411
  subtraction, 44–45, 168–169
  trial and error, 228–229
  when to use, 71, 77, 199, 203,
    311, 345, 387, 465–469
Calendar, 219
Capacity
  metric units of, 16–17
  U.S. Customary units of, 24
Careers, 69, 74–75, 123, 154,
  170, 188, 192, 206, 214, 252,
  282–283, 284, 286–287, 310,
  318–319, 321, 372, 383
Celsius, 22–23, 340–341
Chapter Test, *see* Tests
Checkpoint, *see* Review
Chord, 112
Circle
  arc, 370
  area, 118–119
  chord, 112
  circumference, 112–113
  diameter, 112–113
  radius, 112
Circle graphs, 322–323

Circumference, 112–113
Classifying
   angles, 100–101
   triangles, 106–107
Clock arithmetic, 56–57
Combinations, 404–405
Commission, 318–319
Common denominator,
  146–147
Common factors, 132–133
Common multiples, 144–145
Commutative property, 36–37,
  64–65, 342–343
Comparing
   decimals, 6–9
   fractions, 146–147
   integers, 336–337
   using the number line, 6
   whole numbers, 8–9
Compass, 370–371
Compatible numbers, 84–85,
  316–317
Composite numbers, 134–135
Compound interest, 328–329
Computer literacy
   Arithmetic-Logic Unit, 94
   binary code, 246
   Central Processing Unit, 94,
    128
   Control Unit, 128
   data statement, 302
   debugging, 398
   flowcharts, 128, 188, 214
   function, 366
   history of computers, 32
   input, output, 366
   logic, 162
   memory, 60
   parts, 60
   planning a program, 214
   PRINT, LET statements, 276
   simulation, 430
   spreadsheets, 332
   string variables, 302
Congruence
   of angles, 98–99, 372–373
   of line segments, 102, 370
   of triangles, 368–369
Consumer, 3, 41, 42, 47, 71, 79,
  81, 83, 85, 86–87, 111, 115, 119,
  139, 145, 147, 169, 171, 173,

177, 179, 180–181, 183, 184,
185, 191, 192, 195, 196–197,
203, 205, 207, 223, 228–229,
237, 238–239, 249, 264–265,
281, 283, 284–285, 289, 291,
292, 306–307, 310–311,
314–315, 345, 372, 383,
401, 411
   better buy, 25, 254–255
   budgets, 324–325
   checking accounts, 346–347
   commissions, 318–319
   compound interest, 328–329
   discounts and markups,
    316–317
   food preparation, 193
   interest, 308–309
   interpreting surveys,
    286–287
   overtime, 74–75
   stock prices, 157
   tax rates, 312–313
   unit pricing, 250–251.
    254–255
Coordinate plane, 350–351
Coordinates, 236–237, 350–355
Cross multiplication, 258–259
Cross products, 140–141
Cubic units, 386
Cumulative Review, *see* Review
Customary units, *see* U.S.
  Customary units
Cylinder, 380–381

D
Decimals
   addition, 40–41
   calculator activities,
    150–151, 284–285
   comparing, 6–9
   division, 78–79, 82–85
   estimating with, 10–11,
    40–41, 46–47, 70–71,
    84–85, 111
   expanded form, 4–5
   and fractions, 152–153
   mental math with, 280–281
   and metric measurement,
    14–23
   and mixed numbers,
    152–153

   multiplication, 70–71
   on the number line, 6–7
   ordering, 8–9, 12–13
   and percents, 280–281
   and place value, 4–5
   problem solving with, *see*
    Problem solving
    applications
   repeating, 150–151, 242–243
   rounding, 10–11
   subtraction, 46–47
   terminating, 150–151
Denominator, 138–139
Diagonal of polygon, 102–103
Diameter, 112–113
Discount, 316–317
Distributive property, 64
Divisibility, 130–133
Division
   calculator activities,
    112–113, 130–131, 150–151,
    202–203, 224–225,
    258–259, 284–285
   compatible numbers, 84
   with decimals, 78–79, 82–85
   equations, 62–63, 224–227
   estimating with, 84–85,
    204–205
   with fractions, 202–203
   with fractions and whole
    numbers, 200–201
   with integers, 344–345
   mental math with, 76–77,
    132–133, 250–251
   mixed numbers, 204–205
   powers of ten, 80–81
   rules of divisibility, 130–133
   of whole numbers, 76–77
Double bar graphs, 416–417

E
Elapsed time, 50–51
Enrichment lessons
   base eight, 210–211
   base two, 210–211, 246
   clock arithmetic, 56–57
   compound interest, 328–329
   Egyptian numerals, 28–29
   functions, 184–185
   GCF, LCM, prime factors,
    158–159

histograms, 426–427
percents and proportions,
 298–299
Pythagorean theorem, 394
rational numbers, 362–363
repeating decimals, 150–151,
 242–243
Roman numerals, 28–29
scale factor, 272–273
scientific notation, 90–91
square roots, 124–125
Equations
 addition, 34–37, 220–223,
  226–227
 decimal, 223, 225, 233
 division, 62–63, 224–227
 fraction, 165, 199, 223–227,
  238–239
 graphing, 352–355
 integers, 348–349
 multiplication, 62–65,
  220–221, 224–227
 percent, 290–293, 304–309,
  312–319
 problem solving with, see
  Problem solving strategies
 subtraction, 45, 165, 177,
  220–223
 system of, 354
 two variables, 234–235,
  352–353
 writing and solving,
  226–227
Equivalent fractions, 140–141,
 256–257
Estimating
 area, 114–115, 278–279,
  384–385
 decimals, 10–11, 40–41,
  46–47, 70–71, 84–85, 111
 differences, 44–45, 46–47,
  48–49, 68–69, 178–179
 fractions, 152–153, 154–155,
  172–173, 178–179, 194–195,
  204–205
 integers, 342–343, 354–355
 measures, 10–11, 14–19,
  48–49, 85, 110–111,
  114–115, 205, 254–255,
  262–263, 384–387
 percents, 290–291, 316–317,
  324–325

problem solving and, 11, 83,
 85, 121, 154–155, 199, 205,
 227, 254–255, 263, 297,
 322–325, 383, 385, 387,
 389, 414–417, 422–423
products, 68–69, 70–71,
 194–195, 342–343
quotients, 84–85, 204–205
ratio and proportion,
 248–249, 254–255, 262–265
square roots, 124–125
strategies
 clustering, 172–173,
  410–411
 comparisons, 68–69, 149,
  254–255
 compatible numbers,
  84–85, 316–317
 front-end, 86–87
 list of, 461–462
 range, 195
 reading graphs, 354–355,
  416–417, 418–419
 reasonable answers, 11,
  38–41, 44–45, 48–49,
  68–69, 71, 86–87,
  110–111, 170–171,
  194–195, 204–205,
  226–227, 290–291,
  384–385, 386–387, 411
 rounding, 10–13, 27,
  38–39, 48–49, 152–153,
  284–285, 290–291,
  354–355
 sampling and predicting,
  414–415, 422–423
 using measurement,
  10–11, 14–19, 48–49, 85,
  110–111, 114–115, 205,
  254–255, 262–263,
  384–387
 sums, 38–39, 40–41, 48–49,
  110–111, 172–173
 volume, 386–387
 when to use, 199, 387,
  465–469

Even numbers, 130

Expanded form
 decimals, 4–5
 with exponents, 72–73
 whole numbers. 2–3

Exponents, 72–73
Expressions, 216–219
Extra Practice, 432–459

F
Factor
 common, 132–133
 greatest common (GCF),
  132–133, 142–143
 prime, 134–135
 tree, 134–135
Finite sets, 132–135, 402–405
Flowcharts, 128, 188, 214
Formula(s)
 areas
  of circles, 118
  of parallelograms, 116
  of rectangles, 114
  of squares, 114
  of trapezoids, 116
  of triangles, 116
 circumference, 112
 percent, 306–307, 316–319
 perimeters, 110
 probability, 400–401,
  406–409
 problem solving with, see
  Problem solving strategies
 surface area
  of cylinders, 384–385
  of prisms, 382–383
  of pyramids, 382–383
 volume
  of cylinders, 388–389
  of prisms, 386–387
Fractions
 addition, 164–167
 calculator activities,
  140–141, 168–169, 202–203,
  284–285
 comparing, 146–147
 and decimals, 150–151, 152,
  169
 division of, 200–201,
  202–203
 division and whole
  numbers, 200–201
 equivalent, 140–141,
  256–257
 estimating with, 152–155,
  172–173, 178–179, 194–195,
  204–205

lowest terms, 142–143
meaning of, 138–139
and measurement, 143
mental math with, 148–149,
164–165, 199, 256–257, 279
and mixed numbers,
148–149
multiplication, 192–195
multiplication with whole
numbers, 190–191
on the number line, 140, 146,
152
ordering, 146–147
and percents, 282–285
problem solving with, *see*
Problem solving
applications
rounding, 152–155
subtraction, 164–165,
168–169
Frequency, 420–421
Frequency tables, 420–421
Front-end estimation, 86–87
Functions, 184–185, 218–219,
235, 293, 352–353, 366

G
Geometry
angles, 96–97, 100–101,
368–369, 372–375
area, 114–119, 382–385
bisectors, 374–375
circumference, 112–113
classifying triangles,
106–107
collinear points, 96
congruent angles, 98–99,
372–373
congruent figures, 368–369
constructions, 370–375
cylinder, 380–381
diagonal, 102
diameter,
of circle, 112–113
of sphere, 381
formulas, 110, 112, 114, 116,
118, 382, 384, 386, 388
intersecting lines, 96
line, 96
line segment, 96
parallel lines, 96
perimeter, 110–111

perpendicular lines, 100–101
plane, 96
point, 96
polygons
regular, 102–103
similar, 266–267
problem solving with, *see*
Problem solving
applications
Pythagorean theorem,
394–395
radius, 112
ray, 96
slide, flip, turn, 356–357
surface area, 382–385
symmetry, 376–377
three-dimensional figures,
see Space figures
transformation in, 356–357
translation, rotation,
reflection, 356–357
two-dimensional figures, *see*
Plane figures
vertex, 96, 380
vertical angles, 96
volume, 386–389
Glossary, 477–483
Graphing
coordinates, 236–237
equations, systems of,
354–355
inequalities, 230–231
on a number line, 6–7
ordered pairs, 236–237,
350–351
in two variables, 352–353
Graphs
bar, 23, 287, 314, 416–417
circle, 322–323
coordinate, 236, 350
line, 52–53, 418–419
pictograph, 42–43
Greatest common factor (GCF),
132–133, 142–143, 158–159
Greatest possible error (GPE),
20–21
Grid, 236

H
Hexagon, 102–103
Histogram, 426–427
Hypotenuse, 394–395

I
Identity property, 64
Inequalities
graphing, 6–7, 230–231
problem solving with, *see*
Problem solving
applications
solving, 6–7, 9, 94, 230–233
Infinite sets, 144–145, 230–231,
352–355
Integers
absolute value, 334–335
addition, 338–339
calculator activities,
340–341
comparing, 336–337
division, 344–345
equations, 348–349
estimating with, 342–343,
354–355
graphing ordered pairs,
350–355
mental math with, 336–337
multiplication, 342–343
on the number line, 334, 336
ordering, 336–337
problem solving with, *see*
Problem solving
applications
subtraction, 340–341
Interest, 306–309
Intersecting lines, 96
Inverse operations, 222–227,
232–233
Irrational numbers, 362–363
Isosceles triangle, 106–107

L
Language review, *see* Review
Least common denominator
(LCD), 146–147, 166–167,
168–169, 174–175
Least common multiple (LCM),
144–145, 158–159
Length
metric units of, 14–15
U.S. Customary units of,
24–25
Line, 96
Line graphs, 52–53, 418–419
Line segment, 96, 102, 370
Line of symmetry, 376–377

Logical thinking
  analogies, 248–268, 368–369
  classifying
    geometry, 98, 101, 107,
      109, 335, 351, 356–357,
      369, 376–377, 380–381
    statements, 9, 57, 59, 63,
      94, 131, 245, 363, 369,
      377, 381
    Venn diagrams, 378–379
  closed and open questions,
    3, 5, 13, 53, 65, 67, 136–137,
    196–197, 231, 353
  cues and clues, 133, 320–321
  deductive reasoning
    classifying, 9, 57, 59, 63,
      94, 98, 101, 107, 109, 131,
      245, 335, 351, 356, 363,
      369, 376–379, 380–381
    decoding, 28–29,
      210–211, 246
    divisibility, 130–131
    flow charts, 128, 188, 214
    properties
      geometry, 97–98, 267
      numbers, 36–37,
        64–67, 222–223,
        224–225, 338, 340,
        342, 344
    tree diagrams, 404–405
    Venn diagrams, 378–379
  equalities and inequalities,
    6–7, 9, 35, 41, 45, 56–57,
    62–65, 94, 165, 201,
    216–235, 336–337, 353
  flowcharts, 128, 188, 214
  inductive reasoning
    making generalizations,
      99, 103, 105, 375
    patterns, 39, 81, 103,
      104–105, 107, 210–211,
      358–359, 373
    predictions, 357, 380, 381,
      393, 414–415, 422–423
  logic words, 109, 162, 369,
    378–381
  multiple strategy analysis,
    12, 41, 47, 49, 71, 77, 113,
    115, 133, 135, 139, 141, 173,
    177, 199, 237, 311, 345, 387,
    409

nonroutine problems, 103,
  131, 223, 373, 375, 377, 385,
  387
non-unique solutions, 5, 13,
  53, 65, 67, 136–137, 231
predictions and outcomes,
  400–409, 414–415, 422–423
problem solving with, *see*
  Problem solving strategies
process of elimination, 31,
  93, 127, 131, 137, 145, 161,
  179, 228–229, 301, 351, 365,
  375, 397
reasonable answers, 11,
  38–41, 44–45, 48–49,
  68–69, 71, 86–87, 110–111,
  170–171, 180–181, 194–195,
  204–205, 226–227, 283,
  290–291, 384–387, 411
reasonable choices, 15, 17,
  19, 30–31, 58–59, 63, 92–93,
  115, 126–127, 149, 160–161,
  186–187, 195, 212–213, 216,
  238–239, 244–245,
  274–275, 300–301,
  330–331, 349, 351, 364–365,
  396–397, 428–429
Venn diagrams, 378–379

M

Maps, 241, 262–263
Markups, 316–317
Mass, 18–19
Math across the curriculum
  art, 123, 371, 375
  geography, 8–9, 23, 226–227,
    241, 262–263, 337, 341
  health, 425
  history, 7, 28–29, 32, 113, 152,
    209, 219, 394–395
  home economics, 169, 193,
    194, 264–265
  library, 55
  music, 271, 304–305, 313, 323
  physical education, 2, 218, 248
  science, 11, 22–23, 52–53, 87,
    89, 90–91, 113, 153, 174–175,
    190, 215, 230, 261, 297, 310,
    334–335, 337, 341, 343, 361
  shop, 183, 393

  social studies, 8–9, 10–11,
    27, 157, 166–167, 327,
    418–419
Mathematical expressions,
  216–219
Mean, 410–411
Measurement(s)
  addition, 48–49
  of angles, 98–101
  area, 114–119
  circumference, 112–113
  and decimals, 14–23
  estimating with, 10–11,
    14–19, 48–49, 85, 110–111,
    114–115, 205, 254–255,
    262–263, 384–387
  fractions and, 143
  greatest possible error,
    20–21
  Kelvin scale, 361
  mental math and, 49, 345,
    388–389
  metric system of
    capacity, 16–17
    length, 14–15
    mass, 18–19
    temperature, 21–23
  perimeter, 110–111
  precision in, 20–21
  problem solving with, *see*
    Problem solving
    applications
  protractor, 98–99
  ratios in, 260–261
  ruler, 370
  subtraction, 48–49
  surface area, 382–385
  of time, 5, 7, 12, 50–51, 219
  U.S. Customary system of
    capacity, 24–25
    length, 24–25
    temperature, 235
    weight, 24–25
Measures of central tendency,
  410–411
Median, 412–413
Mental math
  addition, 36–37, 106–107,
    164–165
  decimals, 280–281

division, 76–77, 132–133, 250–251
fractions, 148–149, 164–165, 199, 256–257, 279
geometry, 376–377
integers, 336–337
measurement, 49, 345, 388–389
money, 41, 47, 71
multiplication, 64–65, 134–135, 254–255
percents, 279, 280–281, 306–307
strategies
  changing numbers and operations, 46–47, 148–149, 250–251, 256–257, 259, 279, 306–307, 318–319, 412–413
  comparing and ordering, 6–7, 8–9, 12–13, 146–147, 149, 336–337, 388–389
  counting on, 46–47, 50–51
  facts using, 34–35, 62–63, 132–133, 218–219, 220–221, 232–233
  list of, 460–461
  patterns using, 80–81, 104–105, 136–137, 352–353
  properties using, 36–37, 64–65, 164–165
  visual images using, 6–7, 376–377
subtraction, 46–47, 106–107
time, 50–51
when to use, 41, 47, 49, 71, 77, 199, 279, 311, 345, 465–469
Metric system, see Measurement
Midpoint, 374
Mixed numbers
  addition, 172–173
  and decimals, 150–153
  division, 204–205
  estimation with, 152–155, 172–173, 178–179, 194–195, 204–205

and fractions, 148–149
meaning of, 148–149
multiplication, 194–195
rounding, 172–173, 178–179
subtraction
  with renaming, 178–179
  without renaming, 174–175
  from whole numbers, 176–177
Mixed review, see Review
Mode, 412–413
Multiples, 144–145
Multiplication
  calculator activities, 68–69, 80–81, 140–141, 224–225, 258–259
  cross, 258–259
  decimals, 70–71
  equations, 62–65, 220–221, 224–227, 234–235
  estimating with, 68–69, 70–71, 194–195, 342–343
  of fractions, 192–193
  of fractions and whole numbers, 190–191
  of integers, 342–343
  mental math with, 64–65, 134–135, 254–255
  mixed numbers, 194–195
  by powers of ten, 80–81
  properties of, 64–65
  whole numbers, 68–69

N

Number line
  comparing on, 6–7
  decimals, 6–7
  fractions, 140, 146, 152
  graphing on, 6–7
  integers, 334, 336
  rounding on, 10–11
  whole numbers, 6–7
Number theory
  composite number, 134–135
  divisibility, 130–131
  even numbers, 130–131
  factor, 132
  greatest common factor (GCF), 132–133, 142–143

least common multiple (LCM), 144–145
multiples, 144–145
odd numbers, 130–131
prime factorization, 134–135
prime numbers, 134–135
square numbers, 105
triangular numbers, 105
Numerator, 138–139

O

Obtuse angle, 100–101
Obtuse triangle, 106–107
Octagon, 102–103
Odd numbers, 130
Opposites, 334, 338, 340
Order of operations, 66–67, 276
Ordered pairs, 234–237, 350–351
Ordering
  decimals, 8–9, 12–13
  fractions, 146–147
  integers, 336–337
  whole numbers, 8–9, 12–13, 412–413
Outcomes, 400, 402–403

P

Parallel lines, 96–97
Parallelogram, 108–109, 116–117
Patterns, 39, 81, 103, 104–105, 107, 136, 210–211, 235, 358–359, 373
Pentagon, 102–103
Percent, 278–295
  budget, 324–325
  calculator activities, 288–289, 312–313
  of change, 310–311
  circle graphs, 322–323
  commission, 318–319
  and decimals, 280–281
  discounts, 316–317
  estimating, 278–279, 290–291
  finding the base, 292–293
  finding the percent, 288–289
  and fractions, 282–283

increase or decrease, 310–311
interest, 306–307
markups, 316–317
mental math with, 279, 280–281, 306–307
of a number, 290–291
problem solving with, *see* Problem solving applications
proportion and, 298–299
rounding, 284–285
sales tax, 312–313
Perimeter, 110–111
Perpendicular bisector, 374–375
Perpendicular lines, 100–101
Pi, 112–113
Pictograph, 42–43
Place value
bases other than ten, 210–211
expanded form
decimals, 4–5
whole numbers, 2–3
with exponents, 72–73
standard form
decimals, 4–5
whole numbers, 2–3
word form
decimals, 4–5
whole numbers, 2–3
Plane, 96
Plane figures
circle, 112–113, 118–119, 370–371
hexagon, 102–103
octagon, 102–103
parallelogram, 108–109, 116–117
pentagon, 102–103
polygon, 102–103
quadrilateral, 108–109
rectangle, 108–109
rhombus, 108–109
square, 108–109
trapezoid, 108–109
triangles, 106–107
Point, 96
Point of symmetry, 376–377
Polygon(s), 102–103

Powers of ten, 80–81
Pre-algebra, *see* Equations, Exponents, Formulas, Inequalities, Integers, Percent, Properties, Proportion, Ratio, Rational numbers
Precision in measurement, 20–21
Prime factorization, 134–135
Prime factors, 134–135, 158–159
Prime numbers, 134–135
Principal, 306–307
Prism
rectangular, 380–381
surface area, 382–383
triangular, 380–381
volume, 386–387
Probability
arrangements, 135, 403
combinations, 404–405
complement of an event, 404–405
counting principle, 402–403
dependent events, 408–409
equally likely, 400–401
independent events, 406–407
of one, 400–401
outcome, 400, 402–403
problem solving with, *see* Problem solving applications
sample space, 402–403, 406
tree diagrams, 404–405
using "and," 402–403, 406
using "or," 402–403
of zero, 400–401
Problem solving activities, 471–476

Problem solving applications
consumer, 3, 41, 47, 71, 74–75, 79, 81, 83, 85, 86–87, 111, 115, 119, 139, 145, 147, 157, 165, 169, 171, 173, 177, 179, 180–181, 183, 184–185, 191, 193, 195, 196–197, 203, 205, 207, 223, 228–229, 237, 238–239, 249, 251, 254–255, 264–265, 281, 283, 284–285,

286–287, 289, 291, 306–309, 311, 313, 314–315, 317, 319, 328–329, 346–347, 383, 401
better buy, 25, 254–255
budgets, 324–325
checking accounts, 346–347
commission, 318–319
compound interest, 328–329
discounts and markups, 316–317
food preparation, 193
interest, 308–309
interpreting surveys, 286–287
overtime, 74–75
stock prices, 157
tax rates, 312–313
unit pricing, 251
decimals, 5, 9, 13, 15, 17, 21, 23, 41, 47, 71, 74–75, 79, 81, 83, 85, 86, 151, 153, 170–171, 180, 201, 207, 221, 223, 228–229, 254–255, 281, 285, 286, 289, 291
equations and inequalities, 9, 15, 17, 19, 35, 63, 67, 135, 201, 217, 225, 227, 231, 233, 235, 238–239, 289, 291, 293, 294–295, 305, 312–313, 349, 353, 355
fractions, 139, 141, 143, 147, 149, 151, 153, 155, 157, 165, 167, 169, 170–171, 173, 175, 177, 179, 180, 191, 193, 195, 196–197, 199, 201, 203, 205, 206–207, 217, 219, 223, 237, 249, 283, 285, 286, 289, 291
geometry, 97, 99, 101, 107, 109, 111, 113, 115, 117, 119, 120–121, 195, 267, 269, 357, 369, 371, 377, 379, 381, 383, 385, 387, 389
integers, 23, 335, 337, 339, 341, 343, 345, 346–347, 349, 351, 353, 355, 361
measurement, 5, 13, 15, 17, 21, 23, 25, 37, 49, 51, 52–53, 63, 65, 71, 74–75, 79, 83, 85, 87, 107, 111, 113, 115, 117,

119, 120–121, 137, 149, 155, 165, 173, 175, 177, 191, 193, 195, 196–197, 199, 203, 205, 207, 221, 227, 235, 251, 254–255, 257, 261, 265, 267, 269, 293, 297, 335, 341, 343, 345, 361, 385, 390

percent, 279, 281, 283, 285, 286–287, 289, 291, 293, 294–295, 297, 298–299, 305, 307, 309, 311, 313, 317, 319, 323, 324–325, 327, 328–329

probability, 401, 403, 405, 407, 409, 414–415, 422–423

ratio and proportion, 249, 253, 254–255, 257, 263, 264–265, 267, 269, 271

statistics, 3, 42–43, 53, 287, 314–315, 327, 411, 413, 414–423, 426–427

whole numbers, 3, 5, 7, 9, 11, 15, 21, 35, 37, 39, 42–43, 45, 53, 67, 69, 77, 79, 81, 85, 104–105, 131, 133, 135, 136–137, 145, 217, 219, 221, 223, 227, 231, 233

Problem solving strategies
choosing an operation, 37, 45, 69, 81, 83, 165, 175, 203, 206–207, 217
choosing a strategy, 12, 41, 47, 49, 51, 71, 77, 113, 115, 133, 135, 139, 141, 173, 177, 199, 237, 279, 311, 345, 387, 409
drawing a picture, diagram, and graph, 53, 97, 99, 103, 107, 309, 323, 351, 353, 355, 359, 371, 375, 378–379, 390–391, 417, 419, 425
estimating, 11, 85, 86–87, 154–155, 205, 387, 389, 414–415, 422–423
formulating a problem, 1, 13, 33, 53, 61, 65, 95, 129, 163, 189, 215, 239, 247, 253, 277, 303, 305, 333, 367, 399, 421, 425

four-step method, 12–13, 22–23, 42–43, 52–53, 74–75, 86–87, 104–105, 120–121, 136–137, 154–155, 170–171, 180–181, 196–197, 206–207, 228–229, 238–239, 254–255, 264–265, 283, 286–287, 294–295, 308–309, 320–321, 341, 346–347, 358–359, 378–379, 390–391, 414–415, 422–423
interpreting answers, 141, 180–181
logical thinking, 7, 9, 17, 22, 25, 39, 43, 47, 49, 63, 83, 99, 103, 107, 109, 113, 131, 133, 135, 145, 267, 320–321, 349, 353, 355, 357, 358–359, 369, 373, 375, 401, 403, 405, 413
nonroutine, 63, 103, 131, 223, 349, 355, 373, 375, 377, 385, 387
open-ended, 5, 67, 135, 136–137, 231, 403, 405
reasonable answers, 11, 21, 170–171, 180–181, 205, 283
simplifying the problem, 294–295, 305, 339
sorting and classifying, 149, 351, 378–379
too much or too little information, 42–43, 169, 313
trial and error, 137, 145, 181, 228–229, 373, 375
two- or multi-step problem, 15, 17, 25, 43, 49, 51, 71, 74–75, 77, 79, 86–87, 177, 191, 197, 199, 237, 255, 265, 289, 306–309, 316–317, 319, 327, 328–329
using data on a chart, table, menu, schedule, 3, 5, 7, 15, 17, 19, 39, 52–53, 55, 105, 151, 167, 169, 179, 183, 184–185, 193, 201, 228–229, 235, 251, 254–255, 285, 286, 297, 308, 313, 320–321, 323, 328–329, 337, 343, 346–347, 411, 413, 414–415, 419, 421, 422–423, 425–427

using data on a picture, diagram, graph, map, 7, 22–23, 42–43, 52–53, 99, 101, 105, 107, 109, 117, 137, 143, 153, 154, 241, 261, 263, 267, 287, 314–315, 324–325, 327, 351, 371, 378–379, 381, 391, 414, 417, 419, 426–427

using equations, 35, 63, 67, 135, 201, 217, 225, 227, 231, 233, 235, 238–239, 289, 291, 293, 294–295, 305, 312–313, 349, 353, 355

using formulas, 111, 119, 120–121, 157, 195, 219, 221, 307, 310–311, 317, 319, 328–329, 343, 377, 383, 385, 387, 389

using patterns, 39, 99, 104–105, 107, 136, 235, 358–359

using proportions, 249, 253, 254–255, 257, 261, 263, 264–265, 267, 269, 271

working backwards, 196–197, 225

Properties
associative, 36–37, 64–65
commutative, 36–37, 64–65
distributive, 64–65
identity, 64–65
of zero, 36, 64

Proportion
calculator activities, 258–259
cross multiplying, 258–259
equal ratios, 252–253
equivalent fractions, 256–257
estimating with, 263
mental math and, 256–257
problem solving with, see Problem solving strategies
solving proportions, 256–269

Protractor, 98–99

Pyramid
rectangular, 380–381
surface area of, 382–383
triangular, 380–381

Pythagorean theorem, 394–395

Q

Quadrilaterals, 102–103, 108–109

R

Radius, 112–113
Range, 410–411
Rate, 250–251, 306
Ratio, 248–249, 260–261
  estimating with, 248–249
  mental math and, 250–251
  problem solving with, *see* Problem solving applications
Rational numbers, 362–363
Ray, 96
Reasonable answers, 11, 38–41, 44–45, 48–49, 68–69, 71, 86–87, 110–111, 170–171, 180–181, 194–195, 204–205, 226–227, 283, 290–291, 384–385, 411
Reciprocals, 198–199
Rectangle, 108–109
Rectangular prism, 380–381
Rectangular pyramid, 380–381
Reflections, 356–357
Regular polygon, 102–103
Relative frequency, 420–421
Relatively prime, 142–143
Repeating decimal, 150–151
Review
  Checkpoint, 13, 25, 43, 53, 73, 87, 109, 121, 147, 155, 171, 181, 197, 207, 229, 239, 259, 269, 287, 295, 315, 325, 347, 359, 379, 391, 415, 423
  Cumulative Review, 30–31, 58–59, 92–93, 126–127, 160–161, 186–187, 212–213, 244–245, 274–275, 300–301, 330–331, 364–365, 396–397, 428–429
  Extra Practice, 432–459
  Language and Vocabulary Review, 31, 59, 93, 127, 161, 187, 213, 245, 275, 301, 331, 365, 397, 429
  Mixed Review, 5, 21, 37, 49, 71, 83, 103, 117, 139, 145, 167, 175, 193, 201, 223, 235, 253, 267, 283, 293, 311, 323, 339, 349, 373, 383, 401, 405
Rhombus, 108–109
Right angle, 100–101
Right triangle, 106–107
Roman numerals, 28–29
Rotation, 356–357
Rounding
  decimal quotients, 78
  decimals, 10–13, 40–41
  mixed numbers, 172–173
  whole numbers, 10–13, 44–45, 68–69

S

Sales tax, 312–313
Sampling, 414–415, 422–423
Scale drawings, 260–261
Scale factor, 272
Scalene triangle, 106–107
Scientific notation, 90–91
Sets
  finite, 132–135, 403–405
  infinite, 144–145, 230–231, 352–355
  solution, 230–231, 352–353
Similarity, 266–269
Single line graph, 52–53
Slide, flip, turn, 356–357
Solution sets, 230–231, 352–353
Space figures
  cone, 380
  cross section of, 381
  cube, 381
  cylinder, 380
  rectangular prism, 380
  rectangular pyramid, 380
  sphere, 380
  triangular prism, 380
  triangular pyramid, 380
Sphere, 380
Square, 108–109
Square root, 124–125
Square unit, 114–115
Standard form
  decimals, 2–3
  whole numbers, 4–5
Statistics
  bar graph, 23, 287, 314, 416–417
  calculator activities, 410–411
  circle graph, 322–325
  data sources, 3, 5, 7, 17, 19, 22–23, 39, 42–43, 52–53, 55, 99, 101, 105, 107, 109, 117, 137, 143, 151, 153, 154, 167, 169, 179, 183, 184–185, 193, 201, 228–229, 235, 241, 251, 254–255, 261, 263, 267, 286–287, 297, 308, 313, 314–315, 320–321, 323, 324–325, 327, 328–329, 337, 343, 346–347, 351, 371, 378–379, 381, 391, 411, 413, 414–415, 417, 419, 421–423, 425, 426–427
  frequency table, 420–421
  histogram, 426–427
  line graph, 52–53, 315, 418–419
  mean, 410–411
  median, 412–413
  mode, 412–413
  problem solving with, *see* Problem solving applications
  range, 410–411
  sampling, 414–415
  tally, 420
Subtraction
  calculator activities, 44–45, 168–169
  of decimals, 46–47
  equations, 45, 165, 177, 220–223
  estimating, 44–45, 46–47, 48–49, 178–179
  of fractions, 164–165, 168–169
  of integers, 340–341
  of measurements, 48–49
  mental math with, 46–47, 106–107
  of mixed numbers, 174–179
  of units of time, 50–51
  of whole numbers, 44–45
Supplementary angles, 100–101
Surface area
  cylinders, 384–385
  prisms, 382–383
  pyramids, 382–383

Symbols to show relations, 7–8, 9, 35, 73, 90–91, 94, 124–125, 201, 353, 368–369
Symmetry, 376–377

T

Table of Measures, 431
Tax rates, 312–313
Temperature
  Celsius, 22–23, 340–341
  Fahrenheit, 235
Terminating decimal, 150–152
Tests, Chapter, 26, 54, 88, 122, 156, 182, 208, 240, 270, 296, 326, 360, 392, 424
Three-dimensional figures, *see* Space figures
Translation, 356–357
Trapezoid, 108–109
Tree diagrams, 404–405
Triangle(s), 102, 106–107
  acute, 106, 107
  area of, 116–117
  classifying, 106–107
  congruent, 368–369
  equilateral, 106–107
  isosceles, 106–107
  obtuse, 106–107
  right, 106–107
  scalene, 106–107
  similar, 266–267

Triangular prism, 380–381
Triangular pyramid, 380–381
Two-dimensional figures, *see* Plane figures

U

U.S. Customary units, 24–25, 235
Unit pricing, 250–251, 254–255
Unit rate, 250–251

V

Variables, 34–35, 36–37, 41, 45, 62–63, 64–65, 165, 177, 199, 201, 203, 216–227, 230–235, 238–239, 242–243, 256–267, 288–293, 304–305, 348–349, 352–355, 394–395
  two in an equation, 234–235
Venn diagrams, 378–379
Vertex, 96
  of a polygon, 103
  of a prism, 380
Vocabulary review, *see* Review
Volume
  cylinder, 388–389
  prism, 386–387
  units of, 386–389

W

Whole numbers
  addition, 38–39
  comparing, 6–9
  division, 76–77
  estimating with, 38–39, 44–45, 68–69, 84–85
  expanded form, 2–3
  multiplication, 68–69
  on a number line, 6–7
  ordering, 6–9
  place value, 2–3
  problem solving with, *see* Problem solving applications
  rounding, 10–11
  standard form, 2–3
  subtraction, 44–45

X

x-axis, 350

Y

y-axis, 350

Z

Zero property, 36, 64, 342

CREDITS

Cover concept and photography by Lehman Millet Incorporated.
Title page photography by Lehman Millet Incorporated.
Common Art Elements by Linda Phinney.

ILLUSTRATION

ANCO/Boston   22, 96-102, 105-116, 118,
   119, 186, 188, 225, 236, 237, 266-270,
   278, 279, 287, 314, 315, 320, 323, 325,
   326, 331, 351, 352, 354, 356-359, 368-384,
   386, 387, 389, 390, 392, 416-419, 423,
   424, 429, 430
Lisa Adams   286, 322, 324, 341, 358, 410, 411
Michael Blaser   22, 305, 306, 307, 309, 312,
   317, 318, 350, 402, 403
Barbara Higgins Bond   84
Ray Boultinghouse   158, 159, 210, 211, 327,
   362, 363
Paul Breeden   183
Mindy Brooks   242, 243, 395
Ruth Brunner-Strosser   57
Bradley Clark   394
Bill Colrus   426, 427
Carolyn Croll   124
Bob Eggleton   157, 297
M. C. Escher, *Three Spheres*, © M.C.
   Escher Heirs, % Cordon Art, Baarn,
   Holland 123
Gordon Fiedor   214
Simon Galkin   361
Bonnie Gee   28, 29, 328, 329
Sylvia Giblin   74, 164, 165, 168
Josette Gourley   167, 174, 175
Dierdre Griffin   272, 273
Meryl Henderson   329
Henry Heymann   194
Meg Kelleher   209
David Lindroth   241
Linda Phinney   16, 18, 20, 40, 62, 71, 76,
   79, 151, 172, 180, 304, 471, 474, 476
Terry Presnall   393
Irena Roman   10, 38, 41, 195, 205, 218, 228,
   230, 231, 250, 251, 252, 254, 263, 264

Margaret Sanfilippo   184, 185, 299
Claudia Karabaic Sargent   53, 65, 77, 86,
   113, 114, 116, 117, 119, 120, 136, 137,
   141, 143, 145, 146, 149, 154, 193, 201,
   334, 343, 345, 349, 353, 385, 400, 401,
   406, 408, 409, 414, 473, 475
Michael Smith   316, 320
Gary Torrisi   3, 11, 43, 89, 178, 271, 280,
   288, 290, 294
Joseph Veno   420
Alex Wallach   262
Cheri Wyman   224

PHOTOGRAPHY

ANIMALS, ANIMALS   J. & C. Kroeger
   190: Stouffer Enterprises, Inc.   222
   James Ballard   169, 388
Ed Bishop   138, 170, 176, 177, 283, 412
BLACK STAR   Tom Kennedy 12;   John
   Launois 200;   Andy Levin 152;   Sue
   Ann Miller 256
BRUCE COLEMAN, INC.   Eric Carle
   268;   Dr. E. R. Degginger
   261;   Jonathan T. Wright 27
FOCUS ON SPORTS   248
FOCUS WEST   Robert Brown 78
   (bottom);   Tim Davis 310;
   Brian Drake 85;   Keith Gunnar 293;
   Rick Stewart 132
FOLIO, INC.   Peter Garfield 32 (top
   left);   Richard J. Quataert 282;
   Robert Shafer 104
Robert Gray   298
Don Hammerman   © 247
GRANT HEILMAN PHOTOGRAPHY   44
Michal Heron   48, 66, 110, 191, 192, 204,
   232, 238

TABLE OF NUMBERS

	A	B	C	D	E	F	G	H
1	32	5	278	387	0.8	2	$\frac{1}{10}$	$\frac{2}{5}$
2	16	75	692	962	1.5	6.7	$\frac{1}{3}$	$\frac{2}{3}$
3	8	2	8451	8541	0.2	5	$\frac{3}{4}$	$\frac{1}{2}$
4	95	150	6261	2726	9.5	8.72	$\frac{1}{2}$	$\frac{1}{3}$
5	5	8	4989	5021	2	4	$\frac{2}{3}$	$\frac{3}{4}$
6	89	2	3893	5323	1.5	0.5	$1\frac{1}{5}$	$1\frac{3}{10}$
7	33	50	784	748	4.6	0.25	$4\frac{1}{3}$	$3\frac{2}{3}$
8	67	421	1026	973	1.5	7.3	$8\frac{1}{2}$	$7\frac{3}{4}$
9	55	20	874	647	0.4	8	$2\frac{1}{3}$	5
10	435	4	513	831	3.2	10	$6\frac{3}{4}$	7
11	450	350	250	150	1.6	2	2.4	2.8
12	65	55	45	35	0.8	0.85	0.9	0.95
13	7428	7528	7628	7728	4.2	5.2	6.2	7.2
14	25%	1%	50%	80%	75%	90%	10%	5%

Ideas for using this table for mental math, estimation, and calculator activities are found under *Computation Strategies* on the Cumulative Review pages at the end of each chapter of the Teacher's Edition.